Bloody Living

Reimagining Ireland

Volume 20

Edited by Dr Eamon Maher
Institute of Technology, Tallaght

PETER LANG

Oxford • Bern • Berlin • Bruxelles • Frankfurt am Main • New York • Wien

Rhona Trench

Bloody Living

The Loss of Selfhood
in the Plays of Marina Carr

PETER LANG

Oxford • Bern • Berlin • Bruxelles • Frankfurt am Main • New York • Wien

Bibliographic information published by Die Deutsche Nationalbibliothek.
Die Deutsche Nationalbibliothek lists this publication in the Deutsche
Nationalbibliografie; detailed bibliographic data is available on the Internet at
http://dnb.d-nb.de.

A catalogue record for this book is available from the British Library.

Library of Congress Cataloging-in-Publication Data:

Trench, Rhona
 Bloody living : the loss of selfhood in the plays of Marina Carr /
Rhona Trench.
   p. cm. -- (Reimagining Ireland ; v. 20)
 Includes bibliographical references and index.
 ISBN 978-3-03911-964-6 (alk. paper)
 1. Carr, Marina, 1964---Criticism and interpretation. 2. Self in
literature. 3. Self-destructive behavior in literature. 4. Abjection
in literature. I. Title.
 PR6053.A6944Z92 2010
 822.914--dc22
                         2010002084

ISSN 1662-9094
ISBN 978-3-03911-964-6

Cover image: Olwen Fouéré as Woman in the Irish première of *Woman and
Scarecrow* at the Peacock Theatre, Dublin, in 2007. Photo by Ros Kavanagh.
Courtesy of the Abbey Theatre.

© Peter Lang AG, International Academic Publishers, Bern 2010
Hochfeldstrasse 32, CH-3012 Bern, Switzerland
info@peterlang.com, www.peterlang.com, www.peterlang.net

Printed in Germany

Contents

Acknowledgements

In the course of this work I encountered many people whose support and advice will remain a lasting value: my thanks to David Johnston for his continuous encouragement, guidance and intellectual challenges; to Melissa Sihra, whose capacity to push the boundaries of my argument in a consistent and thorough manner ensured my dedication and commitment throughout; to Eamonn Jordan for his support as both an academic and a friend; to Paul Murphy whose friendship and encouragement will always be appreciated.

Much of this work started while I was a postgraduate student at Queen's University Belfast. Thanks to the staff in the School of Languages, Literatures and Performing Arts at Queen's.

Thanks especially to Anna McMullan and Cathy Leeney for their many helpful comments and suggestions. Thanks to my colleagues in Performing Arts at IT Sligo. Many thanks to Holly Maples, Enrica Cerquoni, Edie Shillue, Emily Morin, Charlie Dillon, Mike Durr, John McDwyer and Marion Jordan, for their encouragement and support. Thanks to Louise Murray and Geraldine Duignan. A special thanks to Noelle Kielty for her input. I owe a great deal of appreciation to Kate Duke, who is copy editor for this book.

To the Navan Traveller's Centre, Co. Meath, particularly Michael McDonagh who provided me with invaluable spoken and written information on Travellers. Thanks to Pavee Point in Dublin who provided me with resources on Travellers; to the Travelling Community in Athlone, Co. Westmeath and to Tom Stokes in Carrick-on-Shannon, Co. Leitrim, for their availability for informal interviews.

I would like to thank the following publishers for their kind permission to quote from plays: Gallery Press for *The Mai, Portia Coughlan, By the Bog of Cats, On Raftery's Hill, Ariel, Woman and Scarecrow, The Cordelia Dream* and *Marble*. Excerpts from *Low in the Dark* copyright © 1990

Marina Carr were originally published in *The Crack in the Emerald – New Irish Plays* (ISBN: 978-1-85459-237) reprinted with permission from Nick Hern Books: www.nickhernbooks.co.uk, Faber and Faber for permission to quote from 'Low in the Dark' in Marina Carr, *Plays 1*, published in 1999. Many thanks to Ros Kavanagh for the cover photo of this book. Thank you to Mairéad Delaney, Abbey Theatre Archivist.

Finally I would like to thank my family: parents Anne and James, Sandra and Daithi, James, Richard and Ethna, Anraoi and Muireann Trench. Love and thanks to Tomás.

Introduction

In 1994, Marina Carr's *The Mai*, first performed at the Peacock Theatre Dublin, won the *Irish Times Award* for Best New Play, and her work became recognised on the international stage. An Offaly woman, whose plays both challenge and perpetuate a century of Irish theatre, Carr gives a universal dimension to the destructive familial concerns, so that *Portia Coughlan* (1996) and *By the Bog of Cats* (1998) not only earn her acclaim in Europe and America but are also regularly produced on the professional and amateur circuits of Ireland.

Carr's plays are concerned with the nature of self-destruction, emerging through various forms of power, corruption, repression and abuse. The strength of her work lies in the ability to fluctuate between the fragility of the past and its place in an equally elusive present. The past oscillates between visibility and invisibility; visibility in the sense that characters' names or place in the world carry a whole range of cultural and social significance and are historically contextualised; invisibility in the sense that the characters find the notion of loss a force to contend with, a loss which stems from the past, and of which they are fully aware but cannot seem to process.

This book, *Bloody Living: The Loss of Selfhood in the Plays of Marina Carr*, explores the nature of self-destruction in Carr's plays. The theme of abjection, as articulated in Julia Kristeva's *Powers of Horror: An Essay on Abjection* is the throughline which links each chapter.

Abjection is the reaction to the threatened breakdown of meaning caused by the loss of the distinction between subject and object. Kristeva discusses the privately embodied subject's relation with its own borders and excess. At the earliest stages of development the narcissistic infant's self is not yet demarcated by an outside world. In the formation of a subjective identity, the child comes to recognise its own subject (I) as separate from mother (object). Narcissism correlates with the emptiness caused as a result of separation and thus identification at this stage is based on wanting for love. The abject as formative of the 'I' sees a subjective disunity in the early experience when separation takes place, which Kristeva refers to as the pre-oedipal or semiotic phase of development and which occurs before the acquisition of language (the post-oedipal or symbolic phase of development). For Kristeva, the early movements and drives of the semiotic child are pre-representational: 'The abject confronts us, on the one hand, and this time within our personal archaeology, with our earliest attempts to release the hold of maternal entity even before existing outside her, thanks to the autonomy of language.'[1]

The rejection of self, which occurs during the process of abjection, is the act which establishes identity through absence. The loss of unity as a result of separation, is for the abject being, the incentive to be drawn back to this stage, confusing the boundaries between the self and the mother's body. The process of sublimation is the individual's way of structuring their sense of self out of the loss accrued by separation in order to restore a degree of value and purpose. Kristeva refers to the movement out of the mother's body, the maternal space that is nourishing and prior to the individual, as the *chora*. The *chora* is where the drives and desires of the semiotic exist, a space which opens a fault in language, showing what lies beyond the limits of the naming function. The *chora* tears apart the symbolic order revealing the illusory description of the homogeneous complete subject. The process of semiosis represents the possibility of the subject's self-reflection, as a subject divided, in the course of becoming. Kristeva's use of the term *jouissance* sums up the excess of pleasure, newness or creativity found in the drives and desires of the semiotic.

The symbolic phase chronologically follows the semiotic phase of development and is one of signification or the 'Law of the Father', a domain of language, position, judgement, law and control. In this phase, 'I' signifies within the field of the Other, that is, within the fields of linguistic, social and cultural practices, always determined by others that have come

---

1   Julia Kristeva, *Powers of Horror: An Essay on Abjection*, trans. Leon S. Roudiez (New York: Columbia University Press, 1982), p. 13.

before. Kristeva outlines the role of the 'maternal metaphor' in signifying with the 'Other' (which can be the father though this does not have to be the case), as aiding the child in pursuit of its place in the symbolic order, during the infant's conflictual dilemma throughout its separation from the maternal:

> [T]he symbolic light that a third party, eventually the father, can contribute, helps the future subject, the more so if it happens to be endowed with a robust supply of drive energy, in pursuing a reluctant struggle against what, having been the mother, will turn into an abject.[2]

The child's identification with the third party helps to further the process of differentiation towards individual selfhood by deflecting the interest of the mother away from the child. It is Kristeva's idea that for personal stability as well as for social unity, an individual needs to assume a more or less comfortable place in the symbolic order, in the realm of language and in relation to others.

What is beyond or other of language, eluding a strictly symbolic interpretation of experience, resembles the interplay between the conscious resistance of the world of Carr's plays and the unconscious instinctual residues that the plays cannot symbolise. Kristeva's theory gives emphasis to Carr's representation of the body, femininity, masculinity, death and dying through issues of marginal subjectivity, self-suffering, repression and images of dissolution in the plays.

Carr's characters strongly react against the social situations in which they find themselves. The plays from 1988 to 2009 are concerned with the infiltration of the past upon the present and they explore the self-sabotaging nature of the characters, the fluid forms of identity, the struggle for

---

2   Kristeva, p. 13. Kristeva's theory is a critique of Jacques Lacan's linguistic interpretation of the unconscious. For Lacan, the 'symbolic light' affords order and regulating articulations necessary for subjectivity; drives which, according to Kristeva, resist all that has been abjected from the maternal. She argues that Lacan's linguistic conceptualisation of unconscious processes restricts access to essential and hidden elements of experience. See Lacan's *Écrits*, trans. Bruce Fink (New York: W.W. Norton & Company, 2002).

communication, the politics of gender and the incompatibility of the sexes. Because many of Carr's plays, especially those of the 1990s, have female protagonists, the idea of woman as paired with its concomitant 'femininity' is a dominant concern, but considerations of masculinity also feature, particularly in her more recent plays.

There is as yet no monograph on Carr's works and there is only one co-edited book of essays, despite the expanding area of 'Carr Studies'. Indeed, there is very little written about Carr's pre-1994 work that holds any serious engagement, apart from essays by Bernadette Sweeney and Melissa Sihra. Sweeney's essay on *Low in the Dark* includes a shorter discussion of *Ullaloo* in relation to its theatrical form and its staging of the body.[3] Sihra discusses the stylistic and performative elements of the early work, and explores themes of gender identity.[4]

Marina Carr is exceptional as a young Irish playwright in that she is the only woman in recent years to have had her plays produced on the main stages of Ireland. Nationally, her work has been staged by the Druid Theatre Company, the Abbey, the Gate and the Project Theatre; internationally, it has been staged in the United States, Britain, Germany, Holland, Estonia and The Czech Republic, among many other countries, and it has been translated into many languages. Academically, her plays continue to be researched, as demonstrated by articles in academic books, journals and magazines.[5] The plays are also studied in third level colleges and universities worldwide.

---

3   See for example Christopher Murray, *Twentieth Century Irish Drama: Mirror to a Nation* (Manchester University Press, 1997), which briefly refers to Carr's earlier works (and excludes *Ullaloo*). See Bernadette Sweeney's *Performing the Body in Irish Theatre* (London: Palgrave Macmillan 2008), Chapter 6 'The Indeterminate Body: Low in the Dark', pp. 168–193.

4   See Melissa Sihra, 'The House of Woman and the Plays of Marina Carr' in Melissa Sihra (ed.), *Women in Irish Drama: A Century of Authorship and Representation* (London: Palgrave Macmillan, 2007), pp. 201–206 specifically.

5   There is one edited collection of essays on her work – *The Theatre of Marina Carr: "before rules was made"*, Cathy Leeney and Anna McMullan (eds) (Dublin: Carysfort Press, 2003). Numerous essays found in journals and magazines include for example *Bullan – An Irish Studies Journal*, Summer /Fall, 2001 VI 1, *Irish University Review*,

In 1994, Carr made a transition from her earlier plays which were styled in non-naturalistic theatre of the absurd, characterised by fragmented plot, non-linear narrative and symbolic characterisation, to more 'mainstream' theatre, featuring recognisable forms of behaviour for her characters, such as causally related plots with observable time frames and identifiable settings. In an interview with Belinda McKeon in 1994, Carr stated that the absurdist style had a negative affect on the plays' structure, which restricted her writing style:

> There was a fashion for devising plays, but writing like that is dicey; I learned that it doesn't work for me. The first four plays I wrote were very stylised, influenced by the Theatre of the Absurd. *The Mai* has elements of the Absurd but it is a more naturalistic work. Its themes are relationships, memory, patterns repeating themselves through generations.[6]

Clare Wallace remarks how Carr's work moves from the absurd style to a more naturalistic mode of expression, yet still retains elements of the absurd, and she describes how 'the "assimilation" process would appear to have occurred quite extensively and indeed has led to the success her drama now enjoys.'[7] However, as Wallace indicates, the 'mainstream' elements of Carr's plays are usually framed by other-worlds of myth, dreams and fantasy and they typically deal with incest, rape, patricide, matricide, filicide and suicide, in multiple and dynamic ways. The plays that followed *The Mai* – *Portia Coughlan* and *By the Bog of Cats* – became known collectively as Carr's 'Midlands Trilogy', now her best known work. *Meat and Salt* (2003), written in the fairy tale genre, is a return to Carr's sense of the theatrical seen in her earlier plays and a move away from the tragic featured in much of her 'mainstream' work. Although aimed at a younger audience, this one-act play retains the elements of resistance to authority

Spring/Summer, 31.2.2001 and *(Per)forming Ireland; Australasian Journal of Drama Studies*, 43/2003.

6   Belinda McKeon, 'Putting Passion on the Stage', *Irish Press*, 2 November 1994.

7   Clare Wallace, 'Tragic Destiny and Abjection in Marina Carr's *The Mai, Portia Coughlan* and *By the Bog of Cats*' in Anthony Roche (ed.), *Irish University Review*, 31:2:2001, p. 433.

and institutions evident in all of Carr's works. The theatrical, non-real form fully emerges once again with *Woman and Scarecrow* (2006) and *The Cordelia Dream* (2008), showing how Carr, as a mature writer, handles the stylised less real form once more. In *Marble* (2009), Carr brings together the real and the non-real theatrical elements, dramatising them within the same plane.

Carr's transition into a more 'mainstream' theatre in 1994, coinciding with her *Irish Times Award* of Best New Play, continued until *Ariel* (2002). In the Programme Note of *Portia Coughlan*, Frank McGuinness observes: 'Marina Carr is a writer haunted by memories that she could not possibly possess, but they seem determined to possess her'; he might have been declaring the choices, efforts and compromises which Carr has had to make in order to be an accomplished contemporary Irish playwright within a male-dominated dramatic tradition.[8] As Anna McMullan writes: 'During the twentieth century the staging of the Irish nation's struggle to define itself was primarily in the hands of male authors from W.B. Yeats to Brian Friel.'[9] Cathy Leeney states: 'Traditionally woman has been the icon, and not the icon maker. When she becomes the creator of representations the woman playwright must negotiate the representational inheritance in relation to which she inevitably works.'[10] Thus, some of the particular dramatic trends and mindsets of Irish theatre which have conditioned audiences over a significant period of time and tended to offer a rather homogeneous vision of Irish theatre, are being renegotiated. Anna Cutler argues that 'women's theatre, so often written differently, is not so

8   Frank McGuinness in 'Masks: An Introduction to Portia Coughlan from Dazzling Dark' in *The Theatre of Marina Carr: "before rules was made"* in Cathy Leeney and Anna McMullan (eds) (Dublin: Carysfort Press 2003), p. 70.

9   Anna McMullan, 'Gender, Authorship and Performance in Contemporary Irish Women Playwrights: Mary Elizabeth Burke-Kennedy, Marie Jones, Marina Carr, Emma Donoghoe', in Eamonn Jordan (ed.), *Theatre Stuff: Critical Essays on Contemporary Irish Theatre* (Dublin: Carysfort, 2000), pp. 34–46, p. 34.

10   Cathy Leeney, 'Ireland's "exiled" women playwrights: Teresa Deevy and Marina Carr' in Shaun Richards (ed.), *The Cambridge Companion to Twentieth Century Irish Drama* (Cambridge University Press, 2004), pp. 150–163, p. 162.

well served by the processes of official documentation, theatre history and memory.'[11] McMullan notes that the lack of women playwrights and the undervalued role of women in theatre are being challenged. Women's work today is increasingly seen in various forms of theatre practice, initiated by women in response to practices of female exclusion. As Sihra writes, 'Since the 1970s immense social and cultural changes have taken place for women in Ireland, North and South. [A] new energy [has] emerged with the next generation of women who began directing, writing and acting in their own theatre companies in the 1980s and 1990s.'[12] While Sihra correctly argues that much has been achieved in terms of women in Irish theatre, she points out that 'Irish women playwrights were and are still the exception.'[13]

With this in mind, the value of Carr's work lies particularly in her ability to shape characteristic traditional Irish theatrical form and content onto the contemporary scene. The collaborative nature of her early work and the form and content of her plays demonstrate the position of marginalisation in the relationship between the individual and the greater world. Her plays demonstrate the complexities involved in gender hierarchies, sexual inequalities within familial and social dynamics and the oppression and repression involved in the painful processes of personal, familial and cultural identity.

Carr expressed her insecurities as a young writer in a talk at the Peacock Theatre in 1997, since her powerful and poetic representations of rural familial life have secured her position as one of Ireland's leading dramatists. In this talk, she spoke of major influences such as Anton Chekhov, Henrik Ibsen, Tennessee Williams, Eugene O'Neill, Oscar Wilde, Samuel Beckett and William Shakespeare, referring to what she regards as 'standards so high [that] you feel like flinging the pen out of the window and retreating

---

11   Anna Cutler in Bernadette Sweeney, *Performing the Body in Irish Theatre* (London: Palgrave Macmillan, 2008), p. 187.
12   Melissa Sihra, 'Interchapter III: 1970–2005' in Melissa Sihra (ed.), *Women in Irish Drama: A Century of Authorship and Representation* (London: Palgrave Macmillan, 2007), pp. 151–159, p. 151.
13   Sihra, *Women in Irish Drama*, p. 158.

into silence. You feel crushed under the weight of Apollo's darlings, for that is what they are.'[14]

Situated over a legacy of internationally acclaimed male authors, her literary anxieties and aspirations have to operate within the predominantly male-authored Irish theatrical canon. Frank McGuinness, Tom Kilroy, Brian Friel, Tom Murphy, John B. Keane, Martin McDonagh, Conall Morrison, Dermot Bolger, Conor McPherson, Sebastian Barry, Vincent Woods and Enda Walsh represent some of the defining Irish contemporary playwrights. Carr enters this theatrical tradition in a culture whose fundamental dramatic definitions are overtly and covertly male but her dramas simultaneously perpetuate and contest dramatic traditions. Carr shares with the older generation, namely John Millington Synge, Seán O'Casey and Samuel Beckett, some dramaturgical conventions such as devices of storytelling, fantasy, the split self, dreams, self-conscious performativity, re-enactments and concerns with identity, place, authority, exclusion and home, but she also demonstrates similarities with the work of her own generation, namely Dermot Bolger, Sebastian Barry and Vincent Woods.[15]

This contemporary work could be defined as a post-modern sensibility, in the sense that it presents the dislocation of the individual from a received and shared sense of community, society and culture in terms of value systems, together with the resonance of a post-colonial consciousness that carries elements of insecurity and mistrust. Carr shares with these writers an unrelenting sense of confrontation with issues, in a world that at best holds a fragile confidence and at worst is sceptical of meaning. Carr's

---

14   Marina Carr, 'Dealing with the Dead', in *Irish University Review: A Journal of Irish Studies*, Anthony Roche (ed.), Spring/Summer 1998, Vol. 28/1, pp. 190–191.

15   See for example Synge's *The Playboy of the Western World* (1907), O'Casey's *Juno and the Paycock* (1924), McGuinness's *Observe the Sons of Ulster* (1985) and Murphy's *Bailegangaire* (1985) for utilising the notion of self-reflexivity and the dramatic devices listed above as paths of possibility and transformation in the works. Bolger's *The Lament for Arthur Cleary* (1989), Barry's *The Steward of Christendom* (1995) and Wood's *At the Black Pig's Dyke* (1993) are dramatisations of absence, loss, death, dying and the use of violence, which graphically demonstrate the internalisation of subjectivity in terms of performance.

complex blend of the post-colonial and post-modern presents a volatile and self-annihilating subjectivity demonstrated within the interior world of the characters.

What distinguishes Carr from other Irish playwrights however is her sense of marginal subjectivity in a contemporary context, with very little scope to unify such a position. Representations and aspects of identity in the plays, whether that of Traveller woman, corrupt politician, traitor or displaced mother figure, present the subject as occupying a peripheral position. This is a condition of Carr's protagonists, where they experience an analogous culpability and exclusion. The world of the plays depicts the confluence of contradictory forces, with characters seeking to belong and yet being bereft of the spiritual and emotional capacity to do so. Often Carr's characters are astutely aware of their own isolation, but it is their journey towards self-destruction that carries with it a peculiar 'self-confidence'.

The 'new' Irish climate of self-confidence, cosmopolitanism and economic wealth, which typically marked the rhetoric of the 1990s Celtic Tiger, sought to promote mind-sets that served the needs of the market. Such a focus defined a way to sever the present from the past, failing to acknowledge the forces of the past that had shaped Ireland's coming of age. As Peader Kirby et al. note: 'Ireland's contemporary culture is seen as an eloquent expression of new-found confidence where the liberalisation of internal markets is matched by the celebration of individual rights and liberties,' with muted attention given to social and cultural changes.[16] Kirby comments on how recent literature on the economy 'assumes that economic growth has beneficial outcomes; it does not examine whether this is in fact the case.'[17] The speed at which Ireland has changed suggests a cultural ambivalence over how to process some of these changes and bears the implication that camouflages have been placed over the cracks that

---

16   Peadar Kirby, Luke Gibbons and Michael Cronin in 'Introduction: The Reinvention of Ireland: A Critical Perspective' in Peadar Kirby, Luke Gibbons and Michael Cronin (eds), *Reinventing Ireland: Culture, Society and the Global Economy* (London: Pluto Press, 2002), p. 7.

17   Kirby et al. in *Reinventing Ireland*, p. 28.

must accompany such rapid social and cultural developments. Eamonn Jordan suggests that Ireland's tendency to leave its old culture behind and to embrace the new should be viewed cautiously and he highlights the paradoxes and, by implication, the ambivalences of the Celtic Tiger:

> Effectively, the confusions and confidences delivered by a period of social liberalism, the collapse of political difference with the demise of left-wing alternatives, the apparent confluence of political thinking and the influence of politically correct ideology have ensured that difference has been submerged and the impact of oppositional energies diluted.[18]

Read against this background, Carr's plays depict many of the problems that lie beneath the camouflages of the 'Celtic Tiger', locating them in the contexts of repressed identities and cultural disillusionment and placing them centre stage. The influences of genealogy, memory, history, absence and loss all converge in worlds of short-term hope undercut by despair.

For Carr, processes of identity are ingrained in the past, but their impact is always present and significantly powerful. The cyclical nature of the dramas depicts how issues and concerns in the work are, literally and metaphorically, repeatedly drawn from history and memory. As she states in an interview with Melissa Sihra:

> I have never believed that time is linear. If you don't believe that time is linear, then it's all up for grabs really, isn't it? I believe so much in the ways in which my parents and grandparents have shaped me. I can almost see what my great-grandparents were like because of my grandparents.[19]

Carr's dramas command a consideration of difficult issues such as suicide, murder, incest and rape in the climate of the 'Celtic Tiger'. They suggest a scepticism and anxiety about the 'Tiger', with a sense of optimism at best only part of the picture. As Kiberd points out '[C]hange is not growth. Growth is a synthesis of change and continuity ... The past still

---

18   Eamonn Jordan, *Theatre Stuff*, p. xiv.
19   Lillian Chambers, Ger Fitzgibbon and Eamonn Jordan (eds), *Theatre Talk: Voices of Irish Theatre Practitioners* (Dublin: Carysfort Press, 2001), pp. 59–60, p. 62.

holds untapped energies and unused potentials, which may be released in the present.'[20] He observes the thin veil that cloaked modernity and thus convinced 'the outside world that we were more addicted to the past than was really the case.'[21] While tradition and the past are explored in Carr's plays of the 1990s, her narratives demonstrate that we are not merely passive prisoners of our past, but rather that the past is the fruit of power and self-knowledge, and its analysis is always necessary.

Significant aspects of Carr's childhood echo throughout her plays with connections to the sense of loss that pervades the works. Lakes, bogs, animals, nature and wildlife are important signifiers that reflect issues of loss, marginalisation, oppressions and repression, revealed through painful processes of personal, familial and cultural identity. The bogscape where she grew up, known as Gortnamona, is literally called 'turf-field', from the Gaelic and is close to Pallas Lake, which was located near the family house. The setting of *By the Bog of Cats* is a boggy landscape which literally and metaphorically reflects the unstable ground on which the characters tread. The presentation of the protagonist Hester at her home on the bog is central to the story. Owl Lake and Cuura Lake, in *The Mai* and *Ariel* respectively are sites which draw upon issues of suicide and murder, signifying Carr's concern with destructive pasts that continue to haunt the present in harmful ways. The Belmont River in *Portia Coughlan* is the place where the eponymous Portia escapes regularly from her home and where the ghost of her dead twin who drowned now 'resides'. It is also the river where Portia commits suicide.

The loss of Carr's mother at the age of seventeen had a big effect on her and she recalls the death as a terrible time for the family. Such a dramatic separation from her mother reconfigures throughout much of the spectrum of her plays and this kind of separation frames much of the theoretical argument in this book surrounding loss. Notably too, Carr remembers the swans coming back to Pallas Lake beside her house when her mother died:

20   Declan Kiberd, *The Irish Writer and the World* (Cambridge University Press, 2005), p. 280.
21   Kiberd, *The Irish Writer and the World*, p. 280.

When my mother died all the swans returned, which was quite extraordinary. It was that cold, cold January, the winter of 1981, a terrible winter, the roads were impassable, but all the swans returned as she was being removed from our house – and they were just there. She always loved swans, so I think they came to say goodbye.[22]

The swan in *By the Bog of Cats* holds a resonance with Hester's surname, Swane, and is the signifier of death in the play. In *Woman and Scarecrow*, the 'crow' is strongly implied to be 'The Thing in the Wardrobe', which Scarecrow spends much time physically resisting and which symbolises the onslaught of Woman's death. At the beginning of Act 2, Woman is seen lying in her bed, blood dripping from her lips and chin, clutching a bunch of black feathers in her hands, indicating that her death is near. In an interview with Mike Murphy, Carr described the lifestyle of the Midlands as quaint, carefree and picturesque, with little disturbance from the outside world:

My first seven or eight summers were spent running around the fields, eating grass, chasing tractors, picking mushrooms, blackberries, all that stuff. It was quite idyllic for a child.[23]

At one with nature as a child, Carr turns that very landscape into spaces of both menace and solace, with bogs, lakes and hills featuring significantly in her dramatic works from 1994 to 2002. Landscape in Carr's work takes on an almost human presence, which in turn plays a role in shaping the characters' subjectivity. Landscape, together with genealogy, offers notions of subjectivity in the context of self-destruction and displacement.

This book engages with the body of Carr's work that, from her first play onwards, explores this kind of destructive subjectivity. Self-destruction and displacement involve the loss of what one might call 'being', the ability to

---

22   Marina Carr, 'Marina Carr in Conversation with Mike Murphy' in Cliodhna Ní Anluain (ed.), *Reading the Future: Irish Writers in Conversations with Mike Murphy* (Dublin: Lilliput Press, 2000), p. 51.

23   Marina Carr, *Reading the Future: Irish Writers in Conversations with Mike Murphy*, p. 45.

exist and to be content with oneself as a result of the early separation caused at birth. Kristeva describes the loss as a collapse from the (m)other:

> Through that experience, which is nevertheless managed by the Other, 'subject' and 'object' push away from each other, confront each other, collapse, and start again – inseparable, contaminated, condemned, on the boundary of what is assimable, thinkable, abject.[24]

This existential void can be considered as the breakdown in connection between the self and I. All Carr's plays employ, to varying degrees, notions of family and home, which provide both literal and metaphorical borders and boundaries that define the space between self and other. As with other contemporary playwrights, family and home, with their pitfalls, dangers and challenges, act as a catalyst which can allow the self to undergo a kind of process of self-formation. Frank McGuinness's works, for example, demonstrate a dramatisation of the present, haunted by a moral crisis in the past, in an effort to consider different forms of sexual, political and cultural identity. The world of Martin McDonagh's plays, with family and home as sites of never ending physical and emotional feuds, is cruel and violent, but softened by vicious comedy. Sebastian Barry's protagonists regularly confront their pasts, enabling them to move towards some kind of personal acceptance. With Carr, such crises are fraught with a greater degree of viciousness with little room for a sense of hope.

Carr's dramas of family and home fundamentally challenge the notion that metaphorical boundaries exist, that define the space between self and other. The suspension of security and intimacy, the hallmarks of family and home, point to the fragility and instability of subjectivity in a largely hostile environment. Family, which is inextricably linked to home, is what Silva and Smart refer to as 'a heterosexual conjugal unit based on marriage and co-residence.'[25] The paradigm of family and home in Carr's plays is used

---

24 Julia Kristeva, *Powers of Horror, An Essay on Abjection*, trans. Leon S. Roudiez (New York, Columbia University Press, 1982), p. 18.

25 Elizabeth B. Silva & Carol Smart (eds), *The New Family* (London: Sage, 1999), pp. 1–12, p. 1.

to relate to the experience of self-estrangement, the precarious boundaries between self and other and the heterogeneity of subjectivity.

This book will examine the repressed identities inherent in Carr's work, propelling the protagonists in 'bloody living', mapped by a conflictual continuum of personal and social paranoia and phobia. This living reflects not only the journey of the protagonists' individual disposition, their personal anxieties, concerns and fears, but also their relationship to the familial and social world, which tries to protect its boundaries through mechanisms of exclusion. The central self-destructive protagonists of these dramas are not members of family and home in the conservative Irish sense; they are challenging and subversive familial figures trapped in a partly self-constructed and socially constructed labyrinth, where all movement is prohibitive and self-defeating. Driven by the longing to belong, Carr's characters stray through territories where their longing is misplaced and is evidence of their otherness.

The title *Bloody Living: The Loss of Selfhood in the Plays of Marina Carr* frames the work, connoting the pathway towards destruction and the sense of lethargy accrued along the way. 'Blood' calls to mind issues of lineage, birth, life, death, relationship and kinship, as well as feelings of sensuality, passion, temper and anger. 'Bloody' suggests injury, loss and damage, but it also expresses the sense of frustration found in Carr's plays, from Tilly's sense of irritation about living in *Ullaloo*, to Sorrel's rape in *On Raftery's Hill*, to Woman's inquiry into what life has been all about in *Woman and Scarecrow* and to Woman's exasperation in convincing Man that they won't survive one another in *The Cordelia Dream*. Blood is literally and metaphorically the vein of identity that makes up our very being.

Yet significantly, another factor that influences subjectivity comes from outside of blood – that is nurture. The complex nature/nurture debate and the extent to which either can be measured in the processes of identity are an ongoing force to be contended with. The physical and behavioural characteristics in human growth and development are determined by genetics (nature), and personal experience, shaped by the environment (nurture). However, the interplay between both nature and nurture argues that most aspects of human growth and development are a product of both.[26] Thus the nature/nurture aspect of development, echoed in the significance of ancestry and genealogy in Carr's plays, is explored through issues of violence, retribution, punishment, sacrifice, familial relationships, female sexuality and reproduction, and are some of the associations triggered by this idea of blood.

While the theoretical cornerstone of this study draws upon Kristeva's notion of abjection, it will also make use of Freudian psychoanalysis as well as post-colonial theories to explore the ontological and psychological displacement articulated in Carr's plays. Selfhood is presented as tenuous, through central concerns of incest, rape, patricide, matricide, filicide and suicide, as subjectivity is either threatened or in fear of being threatened by a power that denies a discrete identity for the characters.

The plays articulate the experience of self-displacement – abjection – from the contemporary (Irish) viewpoint, expressive also of a peripheralised female subjectivity in practices of Irish theatre and culture. The works depict the conditions of the protagonists' subjectivity, which takes place during the early stages of individual identity, where borders and boundaries of identities are formed. These borders constitute how the characters see themselves in the world, which come to reveal a disruption to the margins of their identity, a disruption that places subjectivity continuously on the verge of collapse. Thus Carr's Portia, Hester, The Mai, Sorrel, Dinah, Woman (*Woman and Scarecrow*), Little Daughter, Woman (*The Cordelia Dream*) negotiate the kinds of limited representations of woman which have preceded them. Leeney believes that such representations stem from exile, 'exile from self-expression, from self-determination. Only the crossing of a boundary makes that boundary visible.'[27] The plays offer grounds as to why the characters are alienated from themselves – parental abandon-

---

26   See Cynthia García Coll, Elaine L. Bearer & Richard M. Lerner (eds), *Nature and Nurture, The Complex Interplay of Genetic and Environmental Influences on Human Behavior and Development* (Mahwah, NJ: Lawrence Erlbaum Associates, 2004), pp. xvii–xxiv and Michael Rutter, *Genes and Behavior: Nature Nurture Interplay Explained* (Oxford: Blackwell Publishing, 2006), pp. 40–63.

27   Leeney, *The Cambridge Companion to Twentieth Century Irish Drama*, p. 150.

ment, familial abuse or entrapment within the confines of social roles of motherhood. They reveal the reaction to the breakdown of such borders through, for example, murder, violence, self-harm or the blurring of received notions of gender and sexual boundaries, thereby drawing attention to the vulnerability of individual, familial and social 'laws', and indeed to the fragility of life itself. In some of the plays, the reactions are responses to abject corporeal materials such as corpses, overgrown toenails, filth, breast milk or the acrid smell of rotting carcasses. The confrontation of such materiality re-charges what is essentially a nascent response to the state before the existence of a separate self, and a return to the time when individual abject identity was first created. The plays reveal that the characters are, metaphorically speaking, repeatedly drawn to this earlier state, despite the self-destruction and harm accrued in doing so. The return to the nascent phase of individual identity, which is always a looming presence for the individual, recurs throughout the work, confronting the characters in various abject ways. The sphere of abjection is the in-between, the ambiguous, that which does not respect borders, rules on systems. Abjection is the reverse side of assimilation.

Prevalent in Carr's works is the role of parents, particularly the mother, in the archaeology of subjectivity. The 'boundaries' between the self and (m)other, inside and outside, proper and improper, clean and unclean, are tenuous, without secure borders before the subject speaks. Kristeva refers to this space before the subject speaks as the *chora*, describing it as 'a self-contemplative, conservative, self-sufficient haven', shared by mother and child and preceding Lacan's 'mirror stage', where the child learns that she is a separate individual to the (m)other.[28] The plays are fundamentally concerned with Irish notions of motherhood and fatherhood, with a focus on their relationship to subjectivity. Traditional representations of motherhood, presented as domestic and carer, are challenged and subverted in

28   Julia Kristeva, *Powers of Horror: An Essay on Abjection*, trans. Leon S. Roudiez (New York: Columbia University Press, 1982), p. 1. For more on 'The Mirror Stage' see Jacques Lacan's *Écrits*, trans. Bruce Fink (New York: W.W. Norton & Company, 2002). The child in Jacques Lacan's 'Mirror Stage' of development understands that the world is a representational place of subjects and objects, pp. 3–10.

various ways in the works. Absent mothers, or mothers who are present but who cannot function as traditional maternal figures, the rejection of mothers or mothers who simply refuse to play the roles expected of them, feature strongly. Kristeva notes the maternal regulation for the infant as the primary caregiver – the first monitor of the child's psychic growth as well as the first arbiter of social dictates: 'Toward the mother there is convergence not only of survival needs but of the first mimetic yearnings. She is the other subject, and abject that guarantees my being as subject.'[29] While the maternal function is commonly associated with 'mother', 'feminine' and 'woman', Carr's plays suggest that this does not necessarily have to be the case, and where it is, offers difficulties and conflicts. The plays reveal the maternal, seen in terms of nature only, as reductive and confining. Carr presents gender roles as fluid and interchangeable, particularly in the theatrical non-real works.

The traditional role of fatherhood, observed in terms of financial provider and lawmaker, is either fundamentally perpetuated and problematic or resisted in the works. Fatherhood and its concomitant association with 'masculine' and 'man', is therefore also linked to the maternal. The father is typically the 'maternal metaphor' in Carr's plays.

Carr's portraits predominantly demonstrate identifiable states of abjection for the individuals within the family unit, regularly manifested by the offspring of families in the plays persistently harking back to a childhood which offers them distress and pain. The return to childhood is observed largely through personal memory or the desire for family members to learn about this crucial stage in the development of their subjectivity. Carr's protagonists regularly interrogate their family or any individuals in the community who may hold knowledge about their genealogy, bringing them closer to when their identity was first formed.

29   Kristeva, p. 32.

Chapter Overview

The book is written in such a way that each chapter can be read as a single study.

Chapter 1: 'Unnatural Blood' considers Carr's first two plays, *Ullaloo* and *Low in the Dark*, and her later play *Woman and Scarecrow*, because they are all experimental in style, having much in common with plays in the non-naturalistic approach which Martin Esslin describes in *The Theatre of the Absurd*, as well as sharing similarities with the work of Samuel Beckett.[30] The chapter considers the foundations of abjection and the loss of selfhood within the early works, demonstrating Carr's return to the theatrical and the non-real founded on abjection in *Woman and Scarecrow*. *Ullaloo* and *Low in the Dark* thematically deal with issues considered more universal that are explored in *Woman and Scarecrow*. These are inflated in an Irish cultural context in Carr's plays from 1994. Existential issues of the human condition in the context of abjection will be examined in the plays through themes of alienation, the struggle for communication and the politics of gender.

Ullaloo portrays two characters struggling to make sense of their existence. They are hopelessly caught up in a world of ideals and unattainable desires. Often their dialogue is speculative and what they say and do does not connect. Their individual ambitions are fruitless and the tragic quality of the play is linked to the title, which is an old Gaelic word for keening or mourning, emphasising the endless repetitions, and creating claustrophobia in the drama. The play is framed by the notion of loss, emphasised by the continuous recurrence of dialogue and gesture.

Low in the Dark presents characters whose genders are continuously interchangeable. The stage is split between 'the sexes' where on one side, the bathroom-like space is presented as 'female', and on the other, the building space, is presented as 'male'. Both genders can have offspring, where age

---

30   See Martin Esslin, *The Theatre of the Absurd* (Harmondsworth, UK: Pelican Books, 1980).

is of no consequence to fertility and foetal growth does not concur with the biological nine months necessary for a neonate's full development. Chapter 1 explores how the play draws upon its own performativity, calling for the characters to role-play, particularly for the male characters to play 'female' roles, in an effort to expose ideological assumptions and essentialisations about cultural constructions of male and female subjectivities. It is in this play that Carr lays the foundation for exploring female identity that becomes so significant in her later plays. In *Low in the Dark*, physical abuse (here in the form of beatings), 'females' refusing to fit into the definition categorised by a patriarchal culture, specifically regarding power relations and the policing of women's bodies, are central aspects which become a major concern in her later works. The discussion examines how Carr queries what it means to be 'male' and 'female'. The character Curtains, whose body is never seen throughout, is the central narrator in the play and is referred to as female. She is the storyteller who interrupts the action and behaviour of the other characters, with her tale of the man from the north and the woman from the south, which comments ironically on the central characters in the drama.

Woman as abject other is central to the discussion of *Woman and Scarecrow*. The structures of family and home are revealed and relate to female representation and displacement. The play succeeds in demonstrating abjection as concomitant to the world of the play as well as to the characters, presenting the world as a frightening web of entrapment, with the protagonist in a permanent dislocation. Similar to *Ullaloo* and *Low in the Dark*, the play reveals the feasibility and (in)compatibility of both sexes living together. The circularity of self-savagery in the work will be illuminated to reveal the play's return to images of death, mythological spaces, darkness, bravery, (with the influence of Beckett) and the unrelenting journey of pain and to show how the protagonist's death relinquishes all previous efforts against marginalisation, thereby forsaking any kind of hope in the drama.

Chapter 2: 'Coagulated Blood, Congealed Blood and Mixed Blood' considers Carr's trilogy, *The Mai, Portia Coughlan* and *By the Bog of Cats* and the conditions of abjection within these works. Aspects of Brian Friel's *Dancing at Lughnasa* (1990), John Millington Synge's *The Playboy of the*

Western World (1907) and Lady Gregory's *Spreading the News* (1904) and *The Rising of the Moon* (1907) are noted, specifically because of the metatheatrical device of the narrator in *Lughnasa* and Synge's and Lady Gregory's use of local dialect.[31] In all three plays, female subjectivity is central, and all three protagonists commit suicide. However, the displaced mother figure struggles against patriarchal hegemony, in spite of her suicide. Parenthood and its relationship to subjectivity are explored. As Carla J. McDonagh notes: 'Marina Carr uses[s] drama to reclaim matrilineal histories and explore women's lives and thus goes against the grain of traditional Irish theatre.'[32]

This trilogy both embodies and subverts traditional elements of Irish theatre and culture, such as troubled familial relationships, sexual repression and the Catholic Church. The chapter discusses how Carr permits her females a sense of authority and agency before ending their lives, but also how the significance of their actions, though self-destructive, demonstrates a challenge to traditions of Irish drama. Brian Singleton identifies the conflict that contemporary Irish dramatists negotiate,

> with the texts of great writers for the stage sharply contrasting with the standard representational practices of their interpreters. Postmodern attempts to shift emphasis to the performative, few but significant in the 1990s, have battled with insecurity and critical opinion.[33]

The gap Singleton refers to challenges a century of Irish theatrical traditions. In terms of Carr's female protagonists, Anna McMullan observes how 'their critique of the lack of accommodation of difference in small town or rural Ireland is powerfully articulated.'[34] Certainly, Carr's work

---

31 See Lady Gregory, *Selected Writings* (London: Penguin, 1995).
32 Carla J. McDonagh, '"I've Never Been Just Me": Rethinking Women's Position in the Plays of Christina Reid', in *A Century of Irish Theatre*, Stephen Watt, Eileen Morgan and Shakir Mustafa (eds) (Tuscaloosca and London: Indiana University Press, 2000), p. 182.
33 Brian Singleton, 'Challenging Myth and Tradition: National/Cultural Identity and the Irish Theatrical Canon,' in *Modern Drama* Vol. XLIII 2 Summer 2000, p. 267.
34 McMullan, *Theatre Stuff*, p. 41.

can be located within the traditions and genealogies of Irish Theatre, operating from within in order to challenge representations of confinement, marginality and exclusion.

The discussion of *The Mai*, a memory-play, looks at the ways in which the strategy of the narrator operates theatrically in terms of representing the loss of selfhood. The play shows the Bhabhian notion of how historical agency is transformed through the signifying process of memory.[35] The house on Owl Lake embodies a metaphor of familial memory, which contains issues of absence, violence and death. This chapter concentrates on Carr's concern with the influence of genealogy and its relationship to repeating self-destructive actions. *The Mai* shows the house on Owl Lake as the primal scene of lost and found childhood memories, the site as a memorial to the suicide of the eponymous character in the drama, and the *mise en scène* as the portrayal of the eroticism of the protagonist's loss throughout. *The Mai* retells past familial relationships and their complex dynamics, in order to project a contemporary drama of women's history.

The exploration of *Portia Coughlan* considers the protagonist's abject identity in relation to her dead twin brother, the twin motif in the play acting as a device to consider the ways in which matriarchy and patriarchy are in crisis. Cultural and symbolic representations of motherhood and fatherhood are contested in the drama. According to Helen Gilbert and Joanne Tompkins: 'the perceived binary categories of male/female ... are never merely biologically determined, but are also historically and ideologically conditioned.'[36] Judith Butler's theory of subjectivity also seeks to deconstruct and challenge fixed or naturalised identities of masculine and feminine in an effort to show how the process is socially and culturally regulated, in order to open up other possibilities of identity. Butler writes of 'the necessary limits of identity politics as boundaries that can qualify intended and unintended significance.'[37] Her critique is used to

---

35 Homi Bhabha, *The Location of Culture* (London: Routledge, 1994).

36 Helen Gilbert and Joanne Tompkins, *Post Colonial Drama Theory, Practice, Politics* (London: Routledge, 1996), p. 205.

37 Judith Butler, *Gender Trouble: Feminism and the Subversion of Identity* (London: Routledge, 1999), pp. 7–8.

reveal Carr's portrayal of male and female subjectivities in *Portia Coughlan*, and the ways in which Carr subverts traditional assumptions and essentialisations (fixed notions) of gender. In examining aspects of femininity in 'the specific context of Irish cultural history', Margaret Llwellyn-Jones writes how the 'symbolic identification of women has been intensified both by the influence of Catholicism and by association with images of Nationalism.'[38] In considering the inextricable binary relationship between male and female identities in Ireland, Carr's drama exposes the difficulties of female confrontation with patriarchy, what Clare Wallace describes as 'questions concerning desire, subjectivity and the traumatic unstable space of subjectivity.'[39] *Portia Coughlan* reveals how Carr fractures the perpetration and perpetuation of traditional stereotypical representations of male and female identities. In doing so, dislocation of subjectivities in the play demonstrates Homi Bhabha's notion of

> the social articulation of difference ... as an on-going negotiation ... The borderline engagements of cultural difference may as often be consensual as conflictual; they may confound our definitions of tradition and modernity; realign the customary boundaries between the private and the public, high and low; and challenge normative expectations of development and progress.[40]

Bhabha's approach in relation to *Portia Coughlan* implies that female subjectivity can have other possibilities that negotiate beyond the typically perceived roles of mother and wife.

The discussion of *By the Bog of Cats* explores the abject protagonist, Hester Swane, and her relationship to the community in the drama. The play examines social difference in Ireland, specifically in relation to cultural minorities. The complexities involved in the recognition of Hester, as

---

38   Margaret Llwellyn-Jones, *Contemporary Irish Drama And Cultural Identity* (Bristol, UK: Intellect, 2002), p. 67.

39   Clare Wallace, 'Tragic Destiny and Abjection in Marina Carr's *The Mai, Portia Coughlan* and *By the Bog of Cats* ...', in Anthony Roche (ed.), *Irish University Review*, Vol. 31 2 2001, pp. 435–436.

40   Homi K. Bhabha, 'Introduction: Locations of culture' in *The Location of Culture* (London: Routledge, 1994), p. 2.

female and as Traveller, are investigated using Edward Said's colonial and post colonial theory, as articulated in *Orientalism* (1978), to identify how the dominant Settled Community gains its identity and power by setting itself with its 'psychologically fixed' attitude to home, against its surrogate 'other', the Travelling Community, as 'psychologically nomadic'.[41] Said states in his Introduction to *Orientalism*: 'the Orient is not an inert fact of nature. It is not merely *there*, just as the Occident itself is not just *there* either.'[42] He also observes that 'both geographical and cultural entities – to say nothing of historical entities – such locales, regions, geographical sectors of "Orient" and "Occident" are man made.'[43] That the Orient is a construction by the West is central to the argument in *Orientalism*, but significantly the political, economic and cultural interdependence between the two cultures emerges, where the West is 'superior' to the Orient. Such a system to an extent parallels the relationship between the 'settled' and the 'travelling' cultures in Ireland in the production of different levels of power and domination.

The dislocation of existing between cultures and the ways in which the dominant culture seeks to place its perceived minority 'other' are complex. Said describes the devices at work in the production of Orientalism which strongly parallel the Settled community's 'production' of the Travelling community. One of the devices of Orientalism is the principle of 'binomial' opposition, a mode of categorical comparison that stems from 'the culturally sanctioned habit of deploying large generalizations by which "reality" is divided into various collectives: languages, races, types, colors, mentalities, each category being not so much a neutral designation as an evaluative interpretation.'[44] Said argues that 'theirs' is dependent on and therefore inferior to 'ours'. The relationship between the two cultures demonstrates how the dominant community is dependent on yet also superior

41   I have coined the terms 'psychologically nomadic' and 'psychologically fixed' to refer to the differences between Travellers and Settled people's notion of home respectively.

42   Edward W. Said, *Orientalism* (London: Penguin, 1978), p. 4.

43   Said, *Orientalism*, p. 5.

44   Said, *Orientalism*, p. 227.

to its other. In showing this, the play reveals the assumptions and essentialisations associated with Travellers.

This chapter examines Hester's sense of place, which lies both between and outside of the settled and the travelling communities. Hester's liminal position between the two cultures, which is also abject, means that she does not fully belong to either, yet she is part of both (due to her mixed parentage). Her position emerges largely from the settled community's perspective and its response to her as a member of the travelling community. Despite Hester's origin of mixed blood, the one-sided settled perspective given by the other characters in the play is presented as a lack of acknowledgement and understanding of the travelling heritage. It manifests as suspicion and anxiety and a threat to the dominant settled community. Hester's right to be perceived as a member of the settled community is never a consideration. Hester wants security, a home, a voice and a place free of an oppressive dominant culture. Coming from the minority culture, her acts of resistance are reactions. What Carr does in *By the Bog of Cats* is to dramatise Irish cultural anxiety and resistance to difference.

Chapter 3: 'The One Blood' examines the conditions and nature of individual and cultural boundaries in terms of abjection in *On Raftery's Hill* (2000) and *Meat and Salt* (2003), exploring Leeney's statement: 'Only the crossing of a boundary makes that boundary visible.'[45] The chapter shows the processes of abusive power relationships, built around individually appropriated value systems, revealing abjection in both plays to be destructive and most explicit in *On Raftery's Hill*.

On Raftery's Hill, set in the rural Midlands of Ireland, is a plot-propelled drama, secured well within the 'reach of reality'[46] while *Meat and Salt* is written in the fairy tale genre; both are family dramas whose narrative is driven by male actions. Abjection is discussed in relation to the close familial bonds of self-destruction and with *Meat and Salt*, abjection

45 Leeney, *The Cambridge Companion to Twentieth Century Irish Drama*, pp. 150–163, p. 150.

46 Mulrooney, Deirdre, in 'Marina Carr Climbs Up Raftery's Hill', www.deir.ie/onrafteryshill, accessed 6 May 2004.

is considered symbolically in the context of Carr's other plays. The fact that no one dies in either play offers different meanings in terms of form and content. In *On Raftery's Hill*, incest and abuse are perpetuated by patriarchal power while *Meat and Salt* dramatises patriarchal power, apprehended and reformed by the successfully resistant female protagonist.

On Raftery's Hill makes a distinct shift from both the form and content of the earlier plays. Carr offers no release from the immediate savagery that is presented in the drama. Hypocrisy, abuse, silence and deceit are continuous throughout. This reveals a contrast with the1990s dramas, as well as with the plays since 2002, where features of the imagination such as fantasy, myth, story telling, dreams and memory allow escapist shadow worlds for the protagonists.

On Raftery's Hill marks a significant move away from the thematic concerns dramatised in the previous trilogy.[47] The content of *On Raftery's Hill* resonates with plot, structure, symbols and tropes which are present in many of the male-authored Irish plays of the twentieth century. Characteristics such as a kitchen setting, land ownership, oppressive parent(s), sexual commodification and repression create thematic echoes of specifically, Keane's *The Field* (1965) and *Sive* (1959) as well as Friel's *Philadelphia, Here I Come!* (1964). These plays, which centre on the alienating and reductive conditions that can emerge in the relationship between a parent and child, strongly resonate in *On Raftery's Hill*, a play 'inhabited ... by a long chain of parasitical presences, echoes, allusions, guests, ghosts of previous texts.'[48] While the inter-play of past and present shapes the dramatic content and form, the narrative moves between realism and the grotesque.

'Home' as a spatial boundary is specifically examined in *On Raftery's Hill*. The fact that an act of rape between father and daughter takes place in the kitchen demonstrates how, for Carr, 'family' becomes the site in which

---

47   The thematic concerns in the trilogy are the main focus of Melissa Sihra's PhD dissertation.

48   Miller, J. Hillis, 'The Limits of Pluralism, III: The Critic as Host', *Critical Inquiry* (Spring 1977), 188–196 cited in Robyn R. Warhol and Diane Price Hernell (eds), *Feminisms – An Anthology of Literary Theory and Criticism* (Basingstoke, UK: Macmillan, 1997), p. 22.

to examine and interrogate the presumptive cohesion in Irish life as defined by the 1937 Irish Constitution. The play challenges the assumptions made in the Constitution in defining 'family' together with the unequivocal characteristic sense of 'authority' and 'social order'. The idea of family and home being synonymous with one another is also questioned. Home, as the domestic sphere of 'goodness' (and the Constitution's implication that it is a safe place), is a crucible of fear in *On Raftery's Hill*. The playwright subverts the ideologies of gender defined by the State, and represents the ostensible domestic Eden in the play as a site of servitude, submission and suffering.

Meat and Salt dramatises 'inside the kingdom'/'outside the kingdom' in the fairy tale genre which is linked with Kristeva's symbolic and semiotic modes of unconscious development, revealing the problems surrounding the unstructured drives and energies of the semiotic phase prohibited by the signifying system of the symbolic phase. *Meat and Salt*, reconfiguring the fairy tale blueprint, and read against the symbolic lens of abjection, portrays new ways of considering stable femalehood, which does not involve or need her suffering and death.

Chapter 4: 'Sacrificial Blood' examines abjection in *Ariel* and *The Cordelia Dream* and the implications of a destructive selfhood both within and outside of the family. *Ariel* is loosely based on Euripides's *Iphigenia at Aulis* and *The Cordelia Dream* draws references to the final moments of Shakespeare's *King Lear*, when Lear carries on stage his dead daughter just before his own death, the moment which infiltrates *The Cordelia Dream*. Both *Ariel* and *The Cordelia Dream* explore father/daughter relationships and centre upon issues of power, corruption, infidelity, murder and death. In both plays, the return to the mythic and the framework of the Classical provide a way of processing the pain that Carr's characters carry. Like *On Raftery's Hill*, *Ariel* does not offer any positive resolutions, 'just the unstoppable blood pah a the soul', and similarly in *The Cordelia Dream*, the mythic-like world allows a search for the reconnection with a deep-seated injurious past in the present, in spite of the incidences of murder, death and retribution in the work.[49] As Sihra states in the Programme Note of *Ariel*:

> For Carr, death in the theatre is not the end, it is a poetic drive to excavate what it means to live. Her plays perform the exorcisms and exhumations necessary to the progression of our souls.[50]

This chapter incorporates aspects of all of Carr's previous dramatic and thematic concerns which are brought together in *Ariel*. In *The Cordelia Dream*, Man and Woman successfully obliterate one another at their own expense. Once again, the play deals with the social positioning of men, women and children, the dead, memory, history, and the importance of being able to imagine as a form of escape and absolution. The force of each play's action is in the hands of the male protagonist, Fermoy Fitzgerald in *Ariel*, Man in *The Cordelia Dream*, and the narratives demonstrate how, through a sudden, constructed system of belief, one becomes the leader of Ireland and the other a genius composer. From the male perspective, *Ariel* dramatises the process of displacement outside of the family home and into the public domain, while *The Cordelia Dream* dramatises destruction within the containment of family.

Chapter 5: 'New Blood' is designated solely to *Marble* (2009) because of the change in the dramaturgy of this play. The work identifies a shift away from abjection towards a different form of loss, in a despondency shown by the characters that involves the melancholic sensibility. Like the characters in *On Raftery's Hill* and *Meat and Salt*, no one dies in *Marble*, but significantly, the play ends with characters confronting and taking action as a result of their loss. While *Marble* dramatises dreams as realms of escape, they are first and foremost considered in Sigmund Freud's *Interpretation of Dreams* as insights into the workings of the unconscious mind.[51] Freud

---

49   Marina Carr, *Ariel* (Oldcastle, Co. Meath: Gallery Press, 2002), pp. 17–18.
50   Melissa Sihra, Abbey Theatre Programme Note of *Ariel*, 2002, p. 3.
51   See Sigmund Freud's 'The Interpretation of Dreams' Vols 4–5 in *The Standard Edition of the Complete Psychological Works of Sigmund Freud*, trans. James Strachey (London: Hogarth Press, 1959).

makes a distinction between 'manifest', or conscious, 'dream content', which can be described by the dreamer upon waking, and the 'latent', or unconscious, 'dream thoughts', which are only revealed upon analysis. For Freud, the urge to express a desire and the effort to censor the expression of that desire are two psychical forces, which together act in the formation of the dream. One of these forces works to express the wish, while the other imposes a censorship on it. The tension between these forces can be seen in *Marble*, dramatising the meaning of dreams as a fulfilment of a repressed/suppressed wish.

This book shows how Kristeva's observation of the paradoxical lure of the symptomatic dissolution of subjectivity, threatened by the abject, relates crucially to Carr's theatre. Not only do helplessness, impotence and inactivity periodically characterise the behaviour of Carr's protagonists, but the foregrounding of parents in the process of abjection in *Powers of Horror* provides a means of reading the 'abject' sense of self which punctuates the plays. This book aims to locate and explore the marginal refuge of the self. The terms 'self', 'subject', 'abject' and 'identity' regularly emerge, but they strain their way towards expressing something that cannot ever be fully expressed and is always in a process of reconfiguration.

There are some unavoidable omissions. The plays not included are Carr's third play, *The Deer's Surrender*, performed at The Project Theatre in 1990, which is not available, her fourth play *This Love Thing*, produced by Tinderbox Theatre Company and performed in Belfast and Dublin in 1991 and *The Giant Blue Hand*, which was produced at The Ark Theatre, Dublin from 10 February to 14 March 2009. Carr withholds publication and production rights for *The Deer's Surrender* and *This Love Thing*, while *The Giant Blue Hand*, directed by Selina Cartmell and aimed at children, is not published and is too far removed from the thrust of the argument in this book.

Unnatural Blood

Marina Carr's early phase goes back to the late 1980s, when *Ullaloo* was performed in the Peacock Theatre in 1991. Carr acknowledges the influence of Beckett in her early works; his theatre was to be the subject of her Master's degree in 1988 but she abandoned the Master's in exchange for writing for theatre. *Ullaloo* (1988) and *Low in the Dark* (1989) are imbued with what is central to the Beckettian vision of theatre – the poetic and dramatic notion of failure. In the early plays, Carr consciously resists theatrical traditions of Irish theatre such as the rural, the land, the Catholic Church and the cottage kitchen. Yet the 'Irish-ness' in *Ullaloo* and *Low in the Dark* functions as Judith Roof says of Beckett's theatre 'as structure in a dramatic practice that depends upon exteriorization, distance, removal and alienation.'[1] These features have particular resonance across the spectrum of Carr's work, specifically expressed in the loss of selfhood. Anthony Roche notes Beckett's rejection of 'the then predominant mode of Irishness, the Celtic Twilight of the Irish Literary Revival,'[2] but also the influence of his Irish predecessors on the work and reception of Beckett's theatre. Roche notes:

> [I]n embracing a Yeatsian theatre Beckett was (s)electing a theatre of failure, one which would of necessity have a limited audience and which would tackle failure as one of its themes and conditions of creation.[3]

1   Judith Roof, 'Playing Outside with Samuel Beckett' in Stephen Watt, Eileen Morgan, and Shakir Mustafa (eds), *A Century of Irish Drama: Widening the Stage* (Bloomington: Indiana University Press, 2000), p. 147.
2   Anthony Roche, *Contemporary Irish Drama: From Beckett to McGuinness* (Dublin: Gill & Macmillan, 1994), p. 5.
3   Roche, *Contemporary Irish Drama*, p. 5.

However, what becomes apparent in Carr's plays from 1994 is the tension between a theatre that founds itself on Irish theatrical traditions and a subject matter and form that is outside of it.

The experimental, non-naturalistic theatrical style with which Carr begins her career puts the audience into those uncertain places in which her characters find themselves. *Ullaloo* and *Low in the Dark* are open to critical questioning about the certainty of the meanings that emerge from their form and content. These early plays, although non-naturalistic in style, can be explored to reveal Carr's concerns with the Catholic Church and with issues of sexuality, reproduction, fatherhood, motherhood, child-hood, violence, gender and death, which are more fully explored in the later plays. Thus *Woman and Scarecrow* (2006) is included in this chapter as an example of a later play, because it strongly echoes images from *Ullaloo* with the dying woman in bed and it demonstrates the thematic issues of death, life and dying to which Carr persistently returns. As Melissa Sihra states: '*Woman and Scarecrow* is a deeply-wrought thematic and aesthetic distillation of Marina Carr's entire body of work over the last twenty years.'[4]

This chapter considers *Ullaloo*, *Low in the Dark* and *Woman and Scarecrow* and the ways in which Carr explores the theme of self-destruction, read in Julia Kristeva's climate of abjection. The sense of loss is constructed through the lyricism of the language, its rhythms and emotional tonalities, the role of repetition and of gesture, the sounds spoken or in the heads of the characters. Examined in the Kristevan context, boundaries, laws, and rules of existence are manipulated to the point where meaning is undermined or collapses altogether. More than emphasising the notion that identity is plural, the plays strive to comment on what is expected to happen but doesn't, on where characters would like to be but are not, on what people purport to be but are not, and on what is not said but is meant. *Ullaloo*, *Low in the Dark* and *Woman and Scarecrow* demonstrate how the characters direct attention to the words and actions in themselves,

4   Melissa Sihra, 'The Unbearable Darkness of Being: Marina Carr's Woman and Scarecrow' in *Irish Theatre International* (Dublin: Carysfort Press, 2008) Vol. 1 No. 1 April, pp. 22–37, p. 22.

rather than to the forces underlying them. The absences of the plot, such as resistances towards living (breathing, seeing and speaking depicted in *Ullaloo* and *Woman and Scarecrow*), and narrow definitions of gender and language as pointing towards referential meaning, are the presences dramatised in the works.

Kristeva's vocabulary offers a useful way of exploring the internal dynamics of Carr's subjects and their relation to language and society. The semiotic phase of development, characterised by the subject's experiences of the non-representational drives and desires which typify the emerging relationships between the (non)subject and (non)objects, is fitting with the anti-literary mode, symbolic characterisation and fragmented narrative presented in Carr's non-natural theatrical style. The pre-symbolic drives and rejections of the semiotic continue to exist in the symbolic linguistic subject as silences, murmurings, repetitions and intonation, among other non-symbolic yet meaningful attributes of communication and language, which are dominant features of Carr's plays. The works dramatise the co-existence of elements of the social order alongside other elements that it seeks to define and exclude (silences, murmurings and so on) through oppression and repression.

Ullaloo, *Low in the Dark* and *Woman and Scarecrow* underscore the limits of social discourse and attest to what it represses. They subvert the idea that everyday behaviour provides signifiers of information that enable a concrete sense of identity in the form of the signified. In line with Kristeva's theory of abjection, Carr's plays suggest that a gap occurs in this process. Her work presents the idea that everyday behaviour is a work in progress, a performance continuously developing and never stable. This gap is the hidden drive within Carr's protagonists, and is the source of their crisis.

In *Ullaloo*, the two characters, Tomred and Tilly, come from nowhere, are going nowhere, and are sustained only by a hope that is shown to be, at best, an illusion. In *Low in the Dark*, the five characters present adaptable and interchangeable representations of performative notions of behaviour, specifically male and female behaviour. Their preoccupations are framed by Curtains' ironic narrative, which charts the progressively static behaviour of the man from the north and the woman from the south. The result produces endless possibilities beyond the allocated orders of conventional behaviour. Dying and death in *Woman and Scarecrow* is presented as the means through which to explore woman and the maternal. The long process of dying and death in the play and its relation to origins of identity produces a destabilised and ambivalent subjectivity.

The reasons for Carr's characters' unstable existence lie in how they manage to displace the *tour de force* of filling the space, both temporal and physical, which is assigned to them. How they represent their experiences in the dramas is tentative, and produces a non-committed image of existence in terms of other possibilities, manifested in transformative and transcendent moments in the plays. Performativity in this context questions any notion of naturalised behaviour as stable, exploding received and prescribed forms of personal and social existence in the works.

A close exploration of *Ullaloo*, *Low in the Dark* and *Woman and Scarecrow* demonstrates the ways in which the plays liberate themselves from the constraints of the Irish literary theatre, which is heavily word based, to become more aligned with the style described by Martin Esslin in the *Theatre of the Absurd*:

> In the 'literary' theatre, language remains the predominant component. In the anti-literary theatre of circus or the music hall, language is reduced to a very subordinate role ... By putting the language of a scene in contrast to the action, by reducing it to meaningless patter, or by abandoning discursive logic for the poetic logic of association or assonance, the Theatre of the Absurd has opened up a new dimension of the stage.[5]

Carr's deployment of symbolic characterisation in terms of theme, the fruitless search for certainty, the fragmentation of the conventional narrative form and content and her calling on the plays' own theatricality, marks a shift in contemporary Irish theatre practice. In 'Refiguring Linearity' Susan Kozel writes:

---

5   Martin Esslin, *The Theatre of the Absurd* (Harmondsworth, UK: Pelican Books, 1980), p. 406.

> Linearity and clear narrative structures have been associated with conventional or
> 'mainstream' theatre ... The Performance invited by linearity is one of 'following the
> line', whether this be dictated by tradition, a political party or a playwright.[6]

Examined in the Kristevan context, *Ullaloo*, *Low in the Dark* and *Woman and Scarecrow* unequivocally portray meaning as ambiguous, multilayered and not easily accessible. The characters take on multiple forms and functions, their singularity dissolving into the narrative frame. The plays give contrast and emphasis to the *avant garde* non-natural theatrical style's distrust of stable, singular meaning and signification. In his programme note for Carr's fifth play, *The Mai*, Tom MacIntyre identified the development of her earlier works:

> Marina Carr's *Low in the Dark* gave evidence of an original voice – zany, enquiring, free-wheeling as regards structure, the focus on love and the sensual. In *Ullaloo* (1989) – three plays later [*sic*] – you could see her testing, with a kind of proper hesitancy, the languages available, testing especially the relationship between word and image.[7]

Sarahjane Scaife recalls the collaborative nature of Carr's early devised style of script writing together with Crooked Sixpence Theatre Company's production of *Low in the Dark*: 'a different approach to the purely literary based work that had dominated [the Abbey] up until then, but this scenario was still, by mainstream standards, whacky.'[8] Specifically Scaife recollects the rehearsal process:

6   Susan Kozel in 'Refiguring Linearity' in Lizbeth Goodman and Jane de Gay (eds), *The Routledge Reader in Politics and Performance* (London: Routledge, 2000), p. 258.
7   Tom MacIntyre in 'Where Your Treasure Is: The Mai' in Cathy Leeney and Anna McMullan (eds), *The Theatre of Marina Carr: "before rules was made"* (Dublin: Carysfort Press, 2002), p. 75.
8   Sarahjane Scaife in 'Mutual Beginnings: Marina Carr's Low in the Dark' in Cathy Leeney and Anna McMullan (eds), *The Theatre of Marina Carr: "before rules was made"* (Dublin: Carysfort Press, 2002), pp. 5–6.

[A]t times for the performer it could be a particular character you were playing,
maybe many different characters, but they each had a sense of logic to them. At
other times, there could be many different stories being told at the same time with
no reference to each other ... We would all have our individual lines which had no
relation to the other actors' lines. Each one's lines had a logical throughline of their
own but not to anyone else's.[9]

Edward Gordon Craig's approach to the conception of theatre as a
whole, identified by three central dramatic categories – Action, Scene and
Voice – opens up the shaping devices that Carr utilises in *Ullaloo, Low in the
Dark* and *Woman and Scarecrow*. In his essay *The Art of the Theatre* (1905),
Craig outlined the practical elements of theatre as the central components of
the entire theatrical process. He sees a written play as unfinished 'because it
is incomplete without its action, its colour, its line and its rhythm in movement and in scene.'[10] The dexterous use of these factors allows the theatre as
an art form to be seen as equivalent to music or poetry.[11] Craig emphasises
the difference between words written to be read and words written to be
spoken: 'When I say voice, I mean the spoken word or the word which is
sung, in contradiction to the word which is read, for the word written to be
spoken and the word written to be read are two entirely different things.'[12]
Considering *Ullaloo, Low in the Dark* and *Woman and Scarecrow*, in Craig's
way, supported by Kristevan theory, exploits the totality of the theatrical
experience incorporated into their form and content.

Carr explores the existential meaning of being and identity through
linguistic, gestural and thematic repetition. The structure of these three
plays explores variable elements of repetition and recurring leitmotifs.
Each character takes refuge in replicating behaviours and events as ways of
resisting self-awareness, which would lead to the confrontation of abjection. 'Habit' noted Beckett

9   Scaife in *The Theatre of Marina Carr*, p. 14.
10   E. Gordon Craig in 'The Art of the Theatre' in Eric Bentley (ed.), *The Theory of the
     Modern Stage: An Introduction to Modern Theatre and Drama* (London: Penguin,
     1992), p. 117.
11   See Gordon Craig, p. 115.
12   Gordon Craig, p. 137.

is a compromise effected between the individual and his environment, or between the individual and his organic eccentricities, the guarantee of a dull inviolability ... Habit is the ballast that chains the dog to his vomit. Breathing is habit. Life is habit ... Or rather life is a succession of habits, since the individual is a succession of individuals; the world being a projection of the individual consciousness.[13]

The dominant shape imposed on the drama, as in Beckettian theatre, is that of repetition, or circularity. Repetition emphasises sameness, and the monotonous quality of the plays is an important part of their effect. Repetition devices, of behaviour, action, word and gesture, signify, as Kristeva observes, 'a desire for meaning, which make [the subject] ceaselessly and infinitely homologous to it.'[14] As Scaife asks: 'Do we just, as seems an overriding theme in Marina's work, keep repeating the appalling patterns of human behaviour despite our attempts to the contrary?'[15] The act of repeating inevitably introduces difference. It is in this difference that identity can be conceived, since difference is an identity that is comparable to something else, as Richard Schechner has pointed out:

Performances are made from bits of restored behaviour, but every performance is different from every other. First, fixed bits of behaviour can be combined in endless variations. Second, no event can exactly copy another event. Not only the behaviour itself – the mood, tone of voice, body language, and so on, but also the specific occasion and context make each instance unique. [...] In other words, the uniqueness of an event is not in its materiality but in its interactivity.[16]

According to Schechner, performance also invokes ritual:

Performances ... consist of ritualized gestures and sounds ... Rituals are a way people remember. Rituals are memories in action, encoded into actions. Rituals also help people deal with difficult transitions, ambivalent relationships, hierarchies, and desires that trouble, exceed, or violate the norms of daily life.[17]

13   Samuel Beckett, *Proust* (London: Chatto and Windus, 1931), pp. 7–8.
14   Kristeva, *Powers of Horror*, p. 2.
15   Scaife in *The Theatre of Marina Carr*, p. 13.
16   Schechner, p. 23.
17   Schechner, p. 45.

For the subject, caught up in the desire for meaning and continuously threatened by a fear of falling back to the state of having no identity, forms of repetition and ritual become signifiers for Kristeva's condition of abjection.

In *Ullaloo*, the role of time, the cycle of human existence, the notion of performativity and the idea of heteronormativity is predominantly filtered through abjection. The play consists of two acts, the second repeating much of the outline of the first: a couple, Tilly and Tomred, regret their existence and are caught up in achieving their personal aims of doing nothing and growing the world's longest toenails. The two versions of *Ullaloo* will be referred to: the play script written in 1988, available in the National Library of Ireland, Dublin, and the production of the play at the Peacock Theatre in 1991, available to view on video cassette in the Abbey Theatre's Archive, with Olwen Fouéré as Tilly and Mark Lambert as Tomred. Differences between the two will be outlined by drawing attention to either the play text or the production and general discussion will be made when both dialogue versions are the same.

The abject exists on the border between the conscious and the unconscious and is elaborated in the world of the play as well as through the characters. It is the process which enables the subject to assert its own individuality by differentiating its *self* from the unity of an Other. Tilly and Tomred are each other's Other and their relationship demonstrates their struggle to establish their individual sense of being.

> It seems to be the first authentic feeling of a subject in the process of constituting itself as such, as it emerges out of its jail and goes to meet what will become, but only later, objects. Abjection of self: the first approach to a self that would otherwise be walled in. Abjection of others, of the other ('I feel like vomiting the mother'), of the analyst, the only violent link to the world.[18]

Tilly's and Tomred's ambitions are abject and their self-conscious verbal and physical routines create a temporary avoidance of regret. Their behaviours are momentary deceptions which alleviate the fear of emptiness characteristic of the abject selfhood. The lapsing into the ritual of their respective

18   Kristeva, *Powers of Horror*, p. 47.

ambition that is their daily event, shows Tomred and Tilly experiencing regret and demonstrates them beholding 'the breaking down of a world that has erased its borders.'[19] The abject does not respect borders in the same way as the semiotic order cancels out the borders between the subject and the (m)other. The abject is continually challenging the subject with its presence and thus threatening it with annihilation. Tilly's recurrent desire to stop all bodily functions and Tomred's growing of his toenails signify transgressions of the borders of their bodies.

Tilly's and Tomred's world exists in the non-coherent signifiers of the semiotic. Their attempt to connect with the signified fails in their struggle to articulate and comprehend words and gestures. The affiliation between words and actions is directly relational in *Ullaloo* in that the words that occur onstage are directly related to the actions on stage. The way that Carr shapes the dialogue in *Ullaloo* never lets us forget that these are words to be performed. The performative element incorporated into Carr's use of language points to what Kristeva describes as an emptiness that exists within the spoken word, which constantly strives to be filled: 'Through the mouth that I fill with words instead of my mother whom I miss from now on more than ever, I elaborate that want, and the aggressivity that accompanies it, by *saying*.'[20] Tilly and Tomred's talk is centred on the immediate concerns of their individual ambition. The contradictions on their journey towards their goal is spoken by Tilly, when she says to Tomred, referring to his shorter nail:

> You see little one, we're all just phenomena in time, that's all, so why the rebellion? The little rebellion? We are the sacrificial matter of the universe and no rebellion great or small can alter that.[21]

Their repetitive dialogue becomes more intense as their inner emptiness increases, manifested in their growing eagerness for their unattainable goals. Yet toenails are no means of measuring immortality, and to define

19   Kristeva, *Powers of Horror*, p. 4.
20   Kristeva, *Powers of Horror*, p. 41. [Emphasis in the original]
21   Carr, *Ullaloo*, National Library, Dublin, p. 25.

'nothingness' can be read as already self-defeating. The discussion modulates towards moments in their relationship that signify its complexity. The hammock that hangs across and up-stage in the production of the play represents a shared space between them, where their ambitions dissolve in their actions towards intimacy:

> TOMRED: Tilly?
> TILLY: Hmm.
> TOMRED: Will you?
> TILLY: No.
> TOMRED: Please Tilly.
> TILLY: What?
> TOMRED: Come into the hammock.
> TILLY: No. I'll waste everything, besides I haven't my face on.
> TOMRED: The hammock, the leg, come on.
> TILLY: Really, but the waste! No face on. Will I? Really?
> TOMRED: Yes really! Come on!
>   (*He reaches over and pushes the hammock towards her, it swings back to him, he pushes it again, she tries to catch it but with minimal movement*)
> TOMRED: Stretch just a little more.
>   (*She does, gets into hammock slowly and neurotically, i.e. saving eyes, ears and head. Gasping for breath she eventually rolls into it like a sack of potatoes. Hammock swings in Tomred's direction, he catches hold of her green leg, gazes at it, caresses it, kisses it, Tilly is working furiously to conserve the wasted organs. She ends up with hair over her face, one eye is visible through the hair, and the other eye is covered by the hair and also a hand. The other hand is dividing its time between the nostril and the ear. She examines the leg with free eye, a close inspection*)
> TILLY: It's greener, the waste!
> TOMRED: (*still kissing it*) It's lovely.
> TILLY: Go easy on it ... spare it, it is a nice colour isn't it.[22]

The play gives more emphasis to emotions than to plot in the conventional sense. Plot is compressed and characters are presented as symbolic. Tomred, especially, cannot speak without being sure that he has Tilly to rely on as his audience. His elaborate formula for self-preening and self-enhancement contrasts with Tilly's preserving behaviours, significantly

---

22   Carr, *Ullaloo*, pp. 36–37.

described as doing 'nothing'. Their speeches modulate between the toenail aspirations of reaching immortality and the preserving of faculties in order to achieve the abstract state of bodily nothingness. If the notion of 'nothing' is examined in Martin Heidegger's terms, as a mood of anxiety along the lines of an indeterminate object, then it is close to Carr's representation of Tilly and Tomred's struggle with encountering the place where meaning disintegrates. Heidegger states: 'Anxiety is indeed the anxiety in the face of ... but not in the face of this or that thing.'[23] With anxiety comes an emptiness of being, an uneasy sense of loss of being: 'In this slipping away of beings only this "no hold on things" comes over us and remains.'[24]

Tomred and Tilly's relentless questions and 'answers' form a cycle of interrogations throughout the drama that produce conversations which remain continuously parallel. In their conjugal bickering, Tilly challenges Tomred about having no awareness of her needs or ambition. Tomred, somewhat offended, attempts to respond but Tilly shows few scruples toward him in a reply that undermines his confidence: 'Nothing will matter! That's my ambition, Thicko.'[25] Their language varies from the respectful to the antagonistic throughout. In some cases it employs Irish colloquialisms such as 'yis' 'thicko', 'eejit'and 'slainte'.[26] Each character's speech follows an individual through-line, but not necessarily in dialogue with one another. Esslin notes:

> The Theatre of the Absurd ... tends towards a radical devaluation of language, toward a poetry that is to emerge from the concrete and objectified images of the stage itself. The element of language still plays an important part in this conception, but what *happens* on the stage transcends, and often contradicts, the words *spoken* by the characters.[27]

23 Martin Heidegger, What is metaphysics? in *Martin Heidegger: Basic Writings* (New York: Harper and Row, 1977), pp. 102–103.
24 Heidegger, p. 103.
25 Carr, *Ullaloo*, p. 33.
26 Carr, *Ullaloo*, Act 1 sc. 1, 3, 4 and Act 2 sc. 2 respectively.
27 Esslin, *The Theatre of the Absurd*, p. 26.

Language cannot 'reveal the anguish of original want' and therefore 'the non-spoken' is called upon 'in order to get at the meaning of such a strongly barricaded discourse.'[28] Meaning is pushed out of context or exceeds its context into the situation where words fail to deliver meaning. The representation of the abject as absences and silences in the play reinforces its status as belonging to the non-verbal state of the semiotic order. The abject escapes the codes and definitions of the symbolic order, while its presence draws attention to the absence of the Other and the lack of a coherent self underlying the symbolic order.

Carr's non-naturalistic style of theatre, where the play's content dramatises the characters' struggle for individual achievements is continually inter-penetrated and undercut by patterns of structural repetition. Bert O. States, referring to the structure of Beckett's plays, considers their intelligibility to be based on the 'presence of a massive duplicity which is at once the source of its peculiar openness and its resistance to interpretation.'[29] Applying this notion to *Ullaloo* draws upon the shape of the drama. The vocal delivery in which we hear this 'co-operation of text and metatext',[30] where something other than the text is inferred, is evident in *Ullaloo*, in devices such as the incantation Tilly repeats in the production: 'How are you? I'm fine. How are you? I'm fine and how are you? Fine. Fine, I'm not fine!'[31] Tilly depicts its significance on a number of levels. The ritual of asking after someone's well being draws our attention to the human behavioural habits and makes us consider whether it is a genuine enquiry. The reply 'I'm fine' carries with it a sense of expectation in the response and the subversive reply by Tilly, 'I'm not fine', highlights the performative aspect of such a ritual. By calling attention to it, Tilly enhances the performative nature of human interaction that challenges received notions about com-

28   Kristeva, *Powers of Horror*, p. 41.
29   Bert O. States, *The Shape of Paradox: An Essay on Waiting for Godot* (Berkeley: University of California Press, 1978), p. 7.
30   See Bert O. States, *Great Reckonings in Little Rooms, On the Phenomenology of Theater* (Berkeley: University of California, 1987), p. 82.
31   *Ullaloo* by Marina Carr, Dir. David Byrne, Perf. Peacock Theatre, Dublin (1991), Videocassette Abbey Archive, 23 August 2004.

munication. In the production of *Ullaloo*, she repeats another variation of it in the form of a dialogic monologue:

> TILLY: (*smiles insanely*) Okay! Alright! Tilly Behan, how are you? I'm fine, how are you? Fine, how are you? Fine, and you? Oh! Fine, and how are you?
> TOMRED: (*puts down leg*) Stop it! You're driving me crazy!
> TILLY: (*continues as if she hasn't heard him*) And how are you? Oh, fine really, how are you? Fine, how are you? Fine, and you? Fine ... No! I'm not fine! If you'd just shut up for a minute I'd tell you how I am! HOW I AM! (*Pounds chest*) How I am! In here ... (*Pounds heart*) ... in here and out there are not the same ... never were! Never will be! Never can be.[32]

Carr incorporates comic moments, song and caricature in order to heighten contrasts between the characters and to suggest the inconsequential spontaneity of everyday speech. The scene enacts Marvin Carlson's notion of performance:

> [T]he recognition that our lives are structured according to repeated and socially sanctioned modes of behaviour raises the possibility that all human activity could potentially be considered as 'performance', or at least all activity carried out with a consciousness of itself.[33]

The play demonstrates the ways in which abstract and symbolic characterisation destabilise external social codes and practices and turn theatrical conventions in on themselves to reveal their inner contradictions.

Where conversations in *Ullaloo* claim to discern logic or progress, they resemble a 'saying what you want to hear' style, a manipulative fashioning of conversation:

> TOMRED: [...] Tilly ... Tilly.
> TILLY: Hmm.
> TOMRED: Tilly, you do need me don't you?
> TILLY: I told you.
> TOMRED: Tell me again.

32 Carr, *Ullaloo*, p. 92.
33 Marvin Carlson, *Performance: A Critical Introduction* (London: Routledge, 1996), p. 4.

TILLY: (*Resigned*) Which answer do you want?
TOMRED: The very much one.
TILLY: I need you very much.[34]

Additionally, the words embody a particular shape or structure that demonstrates the endless cycle evident in the play. Carr allows the characters to pursue their individual line of thought, resulting in parallel conversation. While the speeches maintain some sort of rationality, the overall shape of their conversations conveys the failure of man and woman to communicate:

TOMRED: [...] My one hope! (*Rubs big toenail*) The rest of yis are a lazy shower! D'ye hear? He's streets ahead of ye! Streets!
TILLY: If you said what you should have ...
TOMRED: It's time yis got year act together! (*Measures Champ lovingly*) Never let me down, do ya?
TILLY: The night you left me you said it.
TOMRED: It was he who left you!
TILLY: And who are you?
TOMRED: I'm the one who stayed. (*Bitterly*)
TILLY: (*Absently*) That was very nice of you ... to stay ... with me ... Forever?
TOMRED: And ever!
TILLY: (*sincerely*) Thanks very much. Well I should entertain you I suppose.
TOMRED: No![35]

The dialogue of *Ullaloo* reveals how meaning imposes the kind of relationship that demands an external reality, whereby words are agents of communication that carry structure. In the Peacock production of *Ullaloo*, shortly into the first scene, Tilly and Tomred enact a first encounter with one another, in front of a screen upstage. A strobe light and music accompany the scene, carried out in slow conscious movements by the actors. Tilly puts on a red silk dress and shoes, while Tomred dons a black jacket and bowtie. They walk past each other and then back again across the

34   Carr, *Ullaloo*, p. 45.
35   Carr, *Ullaloo*, pp. 2–3.

stage, brushing 'accidentally' against one another. The following dialogue captures a small part of their relationship:

> TOMRED: So ah, what's your name?
> TILLY: Tilly.
> TOMRED: Want to know mine?
> TILLY: Not really.
> TOMRED: Well, it's Tomred.
> TILLY: Is it?
> TOMRED: Were you always such a bitch?
> TILLY: Yes.
> TOMRED: What do you do for a living?
> TILLY: This and that.
> TOMRED: Do you have any hobbies?
> TILLY: (*jeers*) That's an awful question to ask anyone, do you have any hobbies!
> TOMRED: I'm only trying to talk to you.
> TILLY: No you're not. You just want to talk about yourself and you're getting thick now, cause I won't give you the opportunity to blather on about what you've done, what you're doing, what you're going to do.
> TOMRED: Yeah, well actually, my hobbies are deep-sea diving, swimming, tennis, golf, rugby, football, mountain climbing, swimming, cinema, opera, theatre, anatomy, book reading and bird watching, and ah, I'm also writing a thesis on the alienation of the species.[36]

The ritual between couples in their first meetings, depicted by Tomred and Tilly, here reveals heightened and coded communication of behaviour and language. Tomred indulges himself in the typical small talk that takes place at the beginning of relationships, while Tilly is keen to expose the performance incorporated into such conscious behaviour. As Schechner states: 'Performances ... of ordinary life are made of "twice-behaved behaviours," "restored behaviours," performed actions that people train to do, that they practice and rehearse.'[37] For Tomred, the ritual offers reassurance and structure to the human condition, but for Tilly, it is fake and contrived, tending toward the ridiculous. Tilly and Tomred's dialogue depicts the

---

36 *Ullaloo*, Dir. David Byrne, Abbey Archive, 23 August 2004.
37 Schechner, p. 22.

Saussurian internal arbitrary logic of language but also the fragility of all linguistic structures by which they order their world of meaning. The paternal function (the symbolic order), which in the Kristevan sense, is to establish a unitary curve between the subject and object division during separation, fails. Tilly and Tomred's ritualised dialogue is an example of this failure, and depicts their attempt 'to hold on to the ultimate obstacles of a pure signifier that has been abandoned by the paternal metaphor.'[38] As Lacan had perceived, the acquisition of language continues to distance ourselves from ourselves because it separates us from the actual materiality of things.[39] The linguistic binaries of self/other exposed in Tilly and Tomred's conversations demonstrate the breakdown of meaning in language and represent how language structures over a lack, or the abject fear of loss. Kristeva outlines how language can appear to be alien to the abject subject, because of

> the ability of the sound trace to maintain and go beyond the signified, which always involves the addressee as a perception as well as the coenesthetic representation of object relation and of the relation to the discourse of the other subject.[40]

The dialogue of Tomred and Tilly's 'first meeting' connects to the opening line of the play spoken by Tilly: 'If you said what you should have said it might have made all the difference' that permeates the drama throughout.[41] Tilly refuses to engage in the ritual while Tomred persists in it, pointing up the ways in which people commonly perform in the presence of others in order to portray a particular kind of identity. Citing Erving Goffman, Schechner states: 'A "performance" may be defined as all the activity of a given participant on a given occasion which serves to influence in any way any of the other participants.'[42] Goffman distinguishes between the expression that the individual *gives* and the expression that they *give off*, referring

38   Kristeva, *Powers of Horror*, p. 51.
39   See Jacques Lacan, *Écrits*, trans. Bruce Fink (New York: W.W. Norton & Company, 2002), pp. 33–124.
40   Kristeva, *Powers of Horror*, p. 50.
41   Carr, *Ullaloo*, p. 1.
42   Schechner, p. 23.

to the gap between the subject's expression and the intention behind the meaning of the expression received.[43] Such a gap is at the core of abjection and the cyclical nature of the abject selfhood, which stems from that void and which is a typical feature of self-destruction.

As we hear the formulaic interchanges being repeated by Tomred and Tilly in *Ullaloo*, we become aware that, unable to communicate comprehensively with one another, they fall onto what they have said before. Carr's characters' desires, fears, hopes and frustrations are conveyed through repetitive devices that heighten an awareness of the pointlessness of their existence. Tilly, we come to realise, has simply stopped functioning (we assume she has died as she no longer speaks at the closing moments of the play) before the end of the play. The emotional high points of the play are achieved by bringing back elements used, in such a way that their force increases with each repetition. Tomred's final dialogue, in which he declares that he believes it is a marvellous thing to be alive, sees a man exclaiming that he has cherished the journey of his ambition, even though he has been largely frustrated and anxious throughout. His final wish places him in the impossibly contradictory position of having no one available to witness his 'immortality' once he dies. His joviality at the end of the drama exposes the hopelessness of having lived. Without ever being able to communicate with one another as to why they have spent a lifetime together, once Tilly is motionless (dead), Tomred states that he knows what he would say to her. The closing speech dramatises the retrospective desire to take hold of the universe, to handle and manipulate it in such a fashion as to take control of it. Tomred's statement is matched by the image of Tilly's still body in their shared space. Her life is over and his death is not far off. Thoughts of the past, or retrospective needs cannot beguile their present state. Carr's handling of this scene contrasts with Beckett's *Endgame* where Hamm adamantly asks to be placed in the centre of the booth-like room as 'lord' of the space, a dull space with two small high windows and blank walls. He asks Clov to inspect the universe outside using a telescope and when Clov

---

43   See Erving Goffman, 'Introduction' in *The Presentation of Self in Everyday Life* (New York: Penguin, 1959), pp. 13–27.

generally reports that there is nothing to be seen, that it is a dying world, Hamm responds, enraged for most of the time, about their predicament. Just as the act of waiting in *Godot* has been a desire for salvation as an end that never happens, a similar moment brings together the shape of the whole performance of *Ullaloo*. Tomred is at the point where he sees himself as only inches away from 'immortality' because his nails are grown almost to his head, but he has spent his life carrying out a 'dead' project. He tells Tilly what he wants himself and her to do, but she is gone:

> If she were here now, I think I would say many things. What would I say? I would go to her and I would say, 'I want to hold the universe in the palm of our hands, feel it, watch it breathe, tear it with our thumbs and our lips, and when galaxies are swallowed, when dimensions dribble down our chins, when there's not even nothing left to erase, come softly then, soundlessly, Let us Big Bang into Space.'[44]

The play abounds in images of malfunctioning bodies, a central signifier of the abject, which cancels the border between inside and outside: 'There I am at the border of my condition as a living being. My body extricates itself, as being alive from that border.'[45] Both characters strive to 'throw up everything that is given to [them].'[46] Tilly for the most part remains in bed, placing materials over her eyes, ears, nose and mouth in her efforts to stop them from functioning. She is determined to prevent her body from involvement in day to day working processes. Tomred sits, stomps and stands around the room, measuring, recording, nurturing and polishing his toenails. His antics demonstrate what he too has thrust aside in order to live, yet their daily endeavours validate their reality and existence. The 'meaning' behind their existence cannot be fully explained, as they are in a state of perpetual anxiety about their ambitions, which constantly interrupts any attempt to overcome their regrets.

The expectation of a traditional dramatic plot is forever deferred. Like Beckett, Carr's early dramatic aesthetics (and poetics) tends toward failure

---

44   Carr, *Ullaloo*, p. 90.
45   Kristeva, *Powers of Horror*, p. 3.
46   Kristeva, *Powers of Horror*, p. 6.

in the form of regret, the unattainable and the lack of fulfilment. The act of regretting is the dominant metaphor for existence in *Ullaloo*, and strongly mirrors Beckett's focus on the act of waiting in *Waiting for Godot*. To regret is to arrest the present in exchange for a desire for something from the past. Yet as Beckett notes: '[P]ermanent reality ... can only be apprehended as a retrospective hypothesis.'[47] Tomred and Tilly do not consciously make the effort to search for a permanent reality, rather all denial of a concrete reality is postponed.

In the second act of the drama, Tilly is becoming more fragile and Tomred more exasperated about his ambition. Each of their ambitions grates and conflicts with the other, and provides the clues that point towards their deterioration, clues which are strongly echoed in *Marble* (2009):

> TOMRED: Isn't it important to you?
> TILLY: No, it's not. And you're annoying me Tomred, you just won't stop taking yourself seriously. You're living your life as if it matters!
> TOMRED: It does matter. I just don't want to go ... not yet!
> TILLY: It'll be great! You and me clay, clay flesh and flesh green, and you and I umbilical again.
> TOMRED: There are so many things I want to do Tilly, after the nails!
> TILLY: The what?
> TOMRED: The nails. My nails! They're growing, really long.
> TILLY: What nails? What's growing?
> TOMRED: Tilly, why is it that every time I get to this stage, you start this racket? Pretending you can't remember! Pretending everything is nothing and nothing matters!

The development of their respective ambitions occurs for each at a different pace, as seen in their appearance in the second act of the production. Tilly is losing the will to live, while Tomred has become more debilitated by his nails.

> TOMRED: You have to fight.
> TILLY: I'm fighting stronger than ever!
> TOMRED: I don't see you fighting! Against what?

47 Beckett, *Proust*, p. 7.

TILLY: Against the start, against the end.
TOMRED: And the middle? What about you? What about me?
TILLY: The batttlefield! And Tomred, we're winning.
TOMRED: Winning? We're wasting away to nothing!
TILLY: That's your victory! Not mine.[48]

The idea of time as the reassuring provider of resolutions is eroded. This is seen through the struggle to remember:

TOMRED: But me! What about me? I was there! You were there!
TILLY: Was I? How was I?
TOMRED: You must remember.
TILLY: I remember nothing. I remember too much. A life time of remembering and not remembering, each time the time before or the time after, with nothing, nothing that is mine, nothing that is not stained with before and after.[49]

The theme builds to the articulation of anguish, when Tomred and Tilly summarise their existence in a repeat and variation of one another's words:

TOMRED: [...] Tilly ... we have spent a lifetime together ... why did we do that? I can't remember the first time we met ... Tilly, imagine that! Have we ever met? Wait! Can I remember the first time?
TILLY: We have spent a lifetime together, breathing simultaneously in adjacent spaces ... asking one another questions that die as they're asked, why did we have to do that? So much time to pass between two seconds, so much time to pass.[50]

Their retrospective past desires are affected by memory. As Beckett notes: 'Memory and Habit are attributes of the Time cancer.'[51] Neither Tilly nor Tomred can remember. Nor do they place specific reference to exactly what they are remembering. But time replaces memory with a new one. Kristeva notes: 'The time of abjection is double: a time of oblivion and thunder,

---

48 Carr, *Ullaloo*, pp. 49–50.
49 Carr, *Ullaloo*, p. 49.
50 Carr, *Ullaloo*, p. 83.
51 Beckett, *Proust*, p. 4.

of veiled infinity and the moment when revelation bursts forth.'[52] The play depicts time as predominantly 'oblivion', where Tilly and Tomred's existence is experienced by repetitious, physical and verbal routines, with momentary flashes (thunder) of memory, which challenge them in their struggle to obliterate their subjectivity. As with Estragon and Vladimir in *Waiting for Godot* (1949), the idea that over the course of time there will be a revelation gradually dissolves.

In *Ullaloo*, Tilly's 'if' factor that opens the play, 'if you said what you should have said it might have made all the difference'[53] will have some kind of an outcome, but as Tilly resists memory, she is forced to reconcile with the fact that time is a developmental process from which she cannot escape, with moments of time inextricably connected to others.[54] Carr reminds the audience that time is passing, highlighting the characters sense of missed opportunities; and similar to Beckett she does not specify what these opportunities are.

The two characters in *Ullaloo* possess some defining characteristics. Their histories and their relationship to one another are binding, yet they do not talk very much about their private memories. As Esslin states:

> Because the Theatre of the Absurd projects its author's personal world, it lacks objectively valid characters. It cannot show the clash of opposing temperaments or study human passions locked in conflict, and is therefore not dramatic in the accepted sense of the term.[55]

In fact, if the play does have a coherent meaning, then it is that men and women are not compatible as partners to sustain any kind of a significant relationship and their differences will forever render them unable to communicate with one another. This theme is elaborated upon across the spectrum of Carr's plays, shown through various kinds of partnerships men

---

52   Kristeva, *Powers of Horror*, p. 9.
53   Carr, *Ullaloo*, p. 1.
54   Carr, *Ullaloo*, ms 36,099/3/8, p. 49.
55   Esslin, *The Theatre of the Absurd*, p. 403.

and women struggle to share with one another such as parental, lover or sibling relationships.

In reading the text of *Ullaloo*, there is so much in common between Tilly and Tomred. On stage however, the characters are presented as male and female with the distinctions more observable. Their physical and temperamental differences provide material for a series of tragicomic routines and dialogues. The differences that emerge in the course of the production of the play are themselves organised as comic pairs or contrasts. Tomred tries to grow the longest toenails in the world, Tilly to find nothingness, Tomred wishes Tilly would get out of bed while she wishes Tomred to stop growing his toenails. Tomred keeps busy trying to protect and spur on the growth of his nails, rubbing vitamin E cream on them, measuring them and taking photos of them. Tilly's obsession with doing nothing is presented by her attempts to preserve her organs, covering one eye with her hand, plugging her left ear with cotton wool and not finishing her sentences. Tomred leaps about the stage shouting at his small toenail that refuses to grow at the same pace as 'Champ', his big toenail on the right foot: 'Go on. What have you got against me?' to which Tilly replies, 'Don't know where to begin.'[56] Tomred is agitated and explosive while Tilly is righteous and controlled.

Like Beckett's divisional devices, Carr employs pairings, which create a relentless perpetuation of the binary in the play. The result positions Tilly and Tomred's ongoing anguish between transcendence and delusion. The two characters are linked in a symbiotic relationship with no obvious imbalance of power, where small differences take on great significance, leading to their division of roles. Tomred is the more lively and active of the two. Intent on becoming the record holder for the longest toenails, he thinks this is a way of achieving immortality. Tilly is the more lethargic in her ambition to do nothing. She provokes a response from Tomred, giving him a sense of purpose by listening to him, and occasionally amusing him with her sardonic sayings. Tomred is the more restless, Tilly the tormentor, and both are visibly frustrated in their efforts to carry out their ambitions. The

56   Carr, *Ullaloo*, p. 3.

pairing device within the play demonstrates abjection's power to project onto the Other regularly seen throughout Carr's plays such as the twins in *Portia Coughlan*, Hester and her abandoned mother in *By the Bog of Cats*, the title roles of Woman and Scarecrow, or Man and Woman in *The Cordelia Dream*.

Yet the abject is ambiguous. It is the Other that the subject has rejected to establish its self which is at the same time the precondition of the subject's autonomy. The subject is simultaneously drawn towards and repelled by the abject and the Other that it represents. On the one hand, the subject yearns for giving the Other and the semiotic order and thereby becoming homogeneous, through reconciling the split between the self and the Other in an experience of *jouissance*. On the other hand, doing this would mean abandoning the differentiation from the Other that establishes the self which would lead to its annihilation. Hence, Tilly and Tomred are caught in a perpetual bind – repelling each other yet needing one another for self-fulfilment. The bond of abjection yields a resolute dynamic of scheming (self-)destruction with both characters abject.

The inescapable continuity of existence is placed on Carr's characters in her early dramas. Just as *Endgame* enacts the coming to an end of that which can never be reached, so *Ullaloo* acts out a continuous cycle of regret. Tilly calls upon a self-conscious 'if' enactment to Tomred: 'Maybe you should pretend to be dead for a while, we might get on better that way. Or maybe you should pretend to be dead and see if I miss you'; this demonstrates a performance that will be repeated throughout the drama. However, the existential divide between the two worlds of actors-playing-characters-playing-actors that is called upon by the play points up Carr's efforts to abandon logical constructed reasoning. The human situation in the world of fractured beliefs is a divorce between humankind and life, the actor and her/his setting, which constitutes the feeling of absurdity. *Ullaloo* illustrates disunity between the human condition and the forms in which it is expressed.

With *Ullaloo*, the same sequence of actions is repeated throughout. The nature of Tilly and Tomred's repetitious existence renders a continuum, which allows past, present and future to coexist. Repetition gives stability to existence, yet existence is always in a process of being replaced. Abject existence reinforces further such a process, because in order to consider oneself as a separate identity, it must expel what is deemed other to oneself. The banishment involved in abjection never recedes, but haunts subjectivity and threatens to unravel what has been constructed. Tomred's words at the end of the drama speak in 'if' terms: 'If she were here now, I think I would say many things. What would I say? ... I would go to her and I would say ...'[57] The very first line of the play spoken by Tilly emphasises the sense that there is something that should have been said or done. This 'if' factor, what might get said or done, sets in motion the sequence of actions that will be repeated over the course of the drama. Yet the realisation that nothing is repeatable in the play is reminiscent of Vladimir and Estragon's remembrance of a time when they were respectable in *Waiting for Godot* or Hamm's recollection of being a landlord in *Endgame*. Although aware that their existence is constructed and habitual, they continue to perform. Tilly and Tomred's repetitive rituals performed as a means of stability are also a form of betrayal, which renders continuity as an illusion. Such slippages are reminiscent of the kind of self-deception compelled by and characteristic of abjection.

Carr develops a visual aesthetic in the form of a video cassette, described in the play's directions, in the script of *Ullaloo*, which provides another kind of symbolic order, constituted by a set of language and codes different to that of the predominant genre of play. The video cassette comprises music, which underscores and visually reveals much about the couple's relationship. The fact that this new language and these new codes are not compatible for Tomred reinforces the play's pattern of repetition and prevents the confrontation of the past with the present that fails to enable him to recreate his self. Tomred looks at the content of the video that does not 'forget', which contrasts radically with his struggle to remember in the play. Carr's concern for visual iconography is detailed, evident in a four-part black and white home-movie, outlined at the end of the first scene of Act 1. The scene is accompanied by a blues song, and portrays mood and atmosphere as back projections on the stage. Carr's visuals function much like the tape reels

57   Carr, *Ullaloo*, p. 95.

used by Beckett's eponymous character in *Krapp's Last Tape* (1958), where Krapp can exercise the power to fast forward past unwanted parts of his tapes in order to listen to desirable ones. Tomred has banked episodes of his romantic life on a video machine and in the play he selects four clips. The first one contains a young attractive woman in her forties talking animatedly to a group of people and gradually becoming aware that she is being filmed. Her attention turns to the camera holder. The next clip presents a young man in the picture with a young woman: '*Both are engrossed in one another. She takes his hand, kisses it. They talk.*'[58] Clip three is a familial scene in the home, with the same couple and a three-year-old child being played with by the man. The final clip shows the man on the beach shore, with his back to the sea, looking in the direction of the camera. He beckons the holder to come nearer. The image shakes and moves in and out of focus, as the camera gets closer to him. As the camera moves up and down the man's face, it falls, and he takes it and turns it on her. It is focused on her left leg and he travels the camera from there up her body. She laughs, as the camera moves closer to her face. The clip ends abruptly, with Tomred staring fixedly at the empty screen as the video runs on in the black. The implication is that Tomred does not fill the ellipses, omissions and gaps left by the abject, but remains in the same context, outside of it and not redefined. The series of film images stands out as both the opposite and the other to Tilly and Tomred's life in terms of their abject existence as a couple. Caught up in frequent arguments in a tense and volatile atmosphere, usually centred on their individual and independent meaningless life ambitions, the film sequence contrasts with this, depicting the idyllic family unit of father, mother and child, through a loving atmosphere of quiet and calm. Such idealised familial representations, though absent for Tilly and Tomred, are nevertheless not completely absent, since the film's content filters through, specifically, to Tomred's sense of his abject being. The implication is that it is Tomred's past, because he identifies with the images not as a stranger; he seems to realise that he cannot preserve the past in the sense that the past still holds value for him. His attraction to

58   Carr, *Ullaloo*, p. 19.

these scenes suggests his disinterest in the present, which disappoints him. Tomred's prolonged stare after the series of images has ended emphasises his sense of loss, which yet hovers in another connection and another place, from his current meaningless existence. The assemblage of these images also draws the past to the present and contrasts the non-naturalistic dramatic style with the more 'realistic' recorded one. The images described for the screen in the play are juxtaposed with the present existence in the dialogue. Although the home movie is not used in the 1991 stage production, the visual dramatic aesthetic remains. Of major importance regarding the home movie is the confrontation of the past in the present, in the context of the cyclical structures of behaviour that predominantly surround family and resonate back to Scaife's question about Carr's repetitions of and attempts to avoid terrible patterns of human behaviour. Abandonment and loss are typical features across Carr's oeuvre that are triggered into awful actions of physical and emotional abuse. In *On Raftery's Hill* for example, incest is set up as a familial problem that will carry on and on. In *Ariel*, the cycle of murder, which began offstage and in the past, continues throughout the drama in the present and will possibly in the future. In *The Cordelia Dream*, the battle between father and daughter, again originating in the ancient and terrible past, brings the downfall and death of familial bond.

Carr incorporates and demonstrates Beckett's use of the repetition of statement, gestures and actions; how they come to convey the lack of purpose and meaning in the lives of her characters. *Ullaloo, Low in the Dark* and *Woman and Scarecrow* dramatise how repetition, under worsening conditions, enables the emergence of fear, self-deception and irony. In *Ullaloo*, Carr invents images which take on a condensed status, confining her characters in some physically restrictive way. Their plight is resonant of Beckett's Winnie in *Happy Days* (1961), who distracts herself from meaningful living by the ritual of manicuring her nails to mark her existence. Tomred's growing toenails in *Ullaloo* are getting progressively restrictive as every inch makes his mobility more difficult. Tilly wishes to stay lying down because she believes that this will preserve her organs. In Beckett's *Endgame*, Hamm is chair-bound and Clov has a limp while *Waiting for Godot* presents Lucky, a slave who is confined by a rope.

The objects in *Ullaloo* that surround the characters do not necessarily point to any particular room in a house or indeed to a particular place outside it. A hammock, vitamin E cream, pencil, book, camera, ball-gown and so on, are objects that can be utilised in no particular place or in any particular place. This fact points to the neutrality of the liminal setting, an empty space that is neither historically conditioned nor socially appropriated. Schechner defines a limen as:

> a threshold or sill, a thin strip neither inside or outside a building or room linking one space to another, a passageway between places rather than a place itself. In ritual and aesthetic performances, the thin space of the limen is expanded into a wide space both actually and conceptually. What usually is a 'go between' becomes the site of the action ... It is enlarged in time and space yet retains its peculiar quality of passageway or temporariness.[59]

The limen metaphorically enables an escape in theatre from the naturalistic genre, and provides a metaphor for the whole 'if' factor, within which Tilly and Tomred exist. The liminal space, analogous to the position of the abject, sees Tomred and Tilly exist between their actual presence in the space and their continual estrangement and sense of otherness represented by repetitious behaviour and dialogue. They occupy a liminal space metaphorically similar to the space between the conscious and the unconscious, between knowledge of their physical presence and the unknown of their past, between the inarticulate and the ability to communicate – between the Other, estrangement and non-verbal state of the semiotic order, and the entry into language and identity of the symbolic order. Their ambiguous dialogue and their indeterminate attributes represent a form of liminality, 'where they are not-this-not-that, neither here nor there, in the midst of a journey from one social self to another'.[60] Their silences, absences and omissions in the play reinforce their existence in a liminal space; they cannot reach one another yet they can easily talk, echoing Kristeva's notion of 'neither subject nor object', where subjectivity is drawn to a place where

59 Schechner, p. 58.
60 Schechner, pp. 57–58.

meaning collapses. The opening use of 'if' by Tilly and the closing use of it
by Tomred leaves the audience in no doubt as to whether there is anything
concrete from the outset of their relationship. The liminal space alluded to
by Tomred in the text at the closing of the play, when he repeats a variation
of Tilly's earlier speech confirms this:

> We met together after long separation. Met by no accident. Up early, where was I
> going? She watched me dress. 'I know you better now' she said. I said nothing ... If
> she were here now, I think I would say ... I would go to her and I would say 'I want us
> to hold the Universe in the palms of our hands, feel it, watch it breathe, tear it apart
> with our thumbs and our lips, and when galaxies are swallowed, when dimensions
> dribble down our chin, when there's not even nothing left to erase, come softly then,
> soundlessly, let us Big Bang in Space.'[61]

This neutral space is connected to Tomred's reference in the production of
the play to the 'Celtic wastelands' where he grew up: 'a flat land of bog and
watered-down passion.'[62] This 'no place' is a liminal space that becomes
hugely significant in *The Mai* (1994), *Portia Coughlan* (1996), *By the Bog
of Cats* (1998) and *Ariel* (2002) with their topography of boglands, lakes,
rivers and hills.

While *Low in the Dark* is also concerned with issues of the human condition, the play moves toward specific concerns such as gender subversion,
the role of storytelling, the confrontation of the past and the function of
naming in the drama. Elements of the form and content of the play can be
read as symbolically reflective of Kristeva's revival of the semiotic and the
maternal with the breaking from the constraints of a law governed symbolic
order, which violates conventional rule and 'proper' order. *Low in the Dark*
portrays moments and movements between the unconscious process and
conscious structure, between the semiotic or the symbolic, between the
material maternal and the symbolic paternal, which sometimes share and
at other times occlude one another. Kristeva maintains that there should
not be a radical cleavage between them. Rather there should be alterna-
tion between masculine and feminine, between the instinctual process and

61   Carr, *Ullaloo*, p. 88.
62   Carr, *Ullaloo*, p. 85.

structured unity. Yet the extent to which Carr demonstrates the sharing and occlusion of the semiotic and symbolic modalities, through the non-natural aspects of *Low in the Dark*, reveals the rigidity of sex and gender roles by making 'socially' and 'historically' determined stereotypes into a universal feminine or masculine essence.

The narrative is concerned with three 'female' characters and two 'male' characters' routine performance in their cycle of existence. Bender, Binder and Curtains, the 'female' characters, and Baxter and Bone, the two 'male' characters, all demonstrate some form of gender polarisation. The character named Curtains tells a story throughout the drama, which strongly echoes the growing disintegration and paralysis of Tomred and Tilly's relationship in *Ullaloo*. If there is a sense of coherence in *Low in the Dark*, it is provided by Curtains, who narrates the sub-plot of the play, which interrupts and is analogous to the central plot and which presents the audience with abject signifiers around death, the meaninglessness of living, unsuccessful male and female relationships and the tragedy of the human condition. From the onset, she narrates the story of the man from the north and the woman from the south, and their journey to complete estrangement from one another. Her tale highlights states of incompatibility between the opposite sexes, notably at the close of Act 1, from which the title of the play is derived. Curtains states:

> They agreed to be silent. They were ashamed, for the man and woman had become like two people anywhere, walking low in the dark through a dead universe. There seemed to be no reason to go on. There seemed no reason to stop.[63]

The narrative describes a collapse in the boundaries that structure the abject, the position of the abject who '*strays* instead of getting his bearings, desiring, belonging or refusing.'[64] Curtains' story describes an absence of subjectivity outlined in the man's and woman's psychic wandering, their loss of place and of being. Their abject position is congruent with the discourse produced on the borders of language: 'what is abject ... draws me toward

63   Marina Carr, 'Low in the Dark', *Plays 1* (London: Faber and Faber, 1999), p. 59.
64   Kristeva, *Powers of Horror*, p. 8. [Emphasis in original]

the place where meaning collapses.'[65] For Kristeva, the 'borderlander' is always an exile; '"I" is expelled,' or ceases to be, for, 'How can I be without border?'[66]

The condition of the borderlander, therefore, appears in, through and outside of language in the less structured, unstitched discourse which is at the limits of the symbolic. The static-ness of Curtains' tale perpetuates the demarcation of the man and woman articulated in the word and can be aligned to the symbolic realm, reinforced by Carr's description of the stage design, where stage right as the 'men's space', with tyres, walls and building blocks and stage left is the 'women's space', with bathroom, brush, toilet and shower, depicting the rigid divide between the sexes. The separation between the sexes enhances what is Other to the characters, that which has been repressed, emphasising the lack of continuity between the symbolic and semiotic.

The symbolic realm is contrasted by the performative acts of role-playing, cross-dressing and the fluidity of gender roles, outside of Curtains' story, which can be aligned to the semiotic. The blurring of gender roles and the subversion of gendered bodily functions outside of the tale represents how the abject situates subjectivity in *Low in the Dark*. Male/Female, inner/outer, the living/dead are blurred in the play, with men giving birth, babies simply appearing and the narrative sporadically beginning and stopping in cycles of apparent non-sense. The characters therefore demonstrate how consciousness has 'assumed its rights and transformed into signifiers those fluid demarcations of yet unstable territories where an "I" that is taking shape is ceaselessly straying.'[67] The fluidity of sex and gender roles in the dizygotic twin motif in *Portia Coughlan*, in the words of Damus Halion, Portia's lover, who recalls her and her now dead twin on a school tour: 'We got to Bettystown, still have the photo of the whole class, still can't tell one of them from the other.'[68]

65   Kristeva, *Powers of Horror*, p. 2.
66   Kristeva, *Powers of Horror*, p. 8.
67   Kristeva, *Powers of Horror*, p. 11.
68   Carr, *Portia Coughlan* (Oldcastle, Co. Meath: Gallery Press, 1998), p. 42.

Despite the non-naturalistic genre of *Low in the Dark*, the problematic nature of strict categories of heteronormativity with the sense of loss involved, never gets resolved, remains significant throughout Carr's plays. In relation to the non-naturalistic style of the dramatic form and content of Beckett's and Harold Pinter's works, Kristin Morrison states:

> What these narratives present is nothing less than a modern psychological equivalent of the soliloquy constituting an intrinsic part of the central dramatic action itself, the internal made external in a particularly revealing and dramatically convincing way.[69]

Narrative in both Beckett and Pinter operates in a way that 'the conflict between facing issues and fleeing them is actually dramatized. In fact ... the conflict itself is the real action of the play.'[70] *Low in the Dark* maps the disjuncture between internal dramatic action and external theatrical manifestation in a way that gives emphasis to the problems encountered in the discontinuity between the semiotic and the symbolic. Such a juncture for Kristeva depicts the skirting nature of abjection, which on one hand dodges the somatic symptom of abject subjectivity while on the other hand it sublimates it. The symptom, which Kristeva states is

> a language which gives up, a structure within the body ... *Sublimation* is nothing else than the possibility of naming the pronominal, the pre-objectal, which are in fact only a trans-nominal, a trans-objectal. In the symptom the abject permeates me. I became abject. Through sublimation, I keep it under control.[71]

Curtains' narrative is the way in which sublimation has found the language to connect with the non-symbolised loss and its effects, bringing them into articulation in the interpersonal realm of the play. Curtains opens the drama with her dialogue of the unnamed man and woman, which tentatively expands upon how a subject and speech are brought into being.

---

69 Kristin Morrison, *Canters and Chronicles: The Use of Narrative in the Plays of Samuel Beckett and Harold Pinter* (Chicago: Chicago University Press, 1983), p. 2.
70 Morrison, *Canters and Chronicles*, pp. 3–4.
71 Kristeva, *Powers of Horror*, p. 11.

Her story generates a sense of curiosity, particularly when she is asked by Binder to open her curtains. She refuses and walks off. She illustrates that she would prefer to tell a story than to engage in conversation, which is a large part of her 'action' in the play. Her next dialogue reinforces the desire to conceal herself:

> CURTAINS: I love your blinds, they really keep the light out.
> BINDER: And the shower curtain?
> CURTAINS: (*examines the shower curtain*) Yes, it's magnificent! Truly magnificent.
> BENDER: I bought it in a sale. Eh, where did you get your curtains?
> CURTAINS: (*outraged*) Don't be so impudent!
> BINDER: We told you all about our blinds and our curtains!
> CURTAINS: (*smugly*) Did I ask you about them! No I didn't!
> BENDER: Yeah, well you're always in here touching them up, looking for information about them. I even lent you one of the blinds and it came back filthy![72]

Curtains focuses on a narrated past about others rather than on an actual present, which might disclose information about herself. Her story is representative of the substitute for 'the good maternal object' where the symbolic is seduced as a symptom of self-loathing.[73] Kristeva notes:

> In abjection, revolt is completely within being. Within the being of language. Contrary to hysteria, which brings about, ignores, or seduces the symbolic but does not produce it, the subject of abjection is eminently productive of culture. Its symptom is the rejection and reconstruction of languages.[74]

In the telling of the story of the man from the north and the woman from the south, she displays a fear of self-disclosure, or self-loathing, and the paradox which it carries. As Kristeva outlines:

> That order, that glance, that voice, that gesture, which enact the law of my frightened body, constitute and bring about an effect and yet not a sign. I speak to it in myself, a world that can be assimilated.[75]

---

72 Carr, 'Low in the Dark', *Plays 1*, pp. 11–12.
73 Kristeva, *Powers of Horror*, p. 45.
74 Kristeva, *Powers of Horror*, p. 45.
75 Kristeva, *Powers of Horror*, p. 10.

Curtains creates a distance, in the sense that conventional narrative portrays the storyteller as different from the story persona itself, as observed in Carr's trilogy and *Ariel*. Carr's use of storytelling, together with the use of myth, dreams and fantasy in these works, offers realms of escape in terms of otherness for her characters. Yet if the story is analysed in *Low in the Dark* as a means of exploring Curtains' own sexuality, then significance is given to the couple in her story who become alien to one another as they roam the barren landscape. The correlation between Curtains' story and 'self' is her sexuality. Incidentally, a curtain is a piece of material suspended at the top to form a screen, typically moveable sideways along a rail and can be used to indicate the start or end of a theatrical performance. The notion of revealing and concealment emerges in the continuum of beginning and ending a play with Curtains literally opening and closing *Low in the Dark*. Curtains, as storyteller, pre-empts the role of narrator in *The Mai* where the character of Millie filters the fully subjective element of storytelling throughout. The kind of memory offered by Millie and Curtains reflects Carr's comment: 'How we tell a story is so important. It is not the facts we are looking for, it is the details, the embellishments.'[76]

The content of Curtains' narrative as a form of evasion and as a means to shield her body from the world at the same time reveals something about her abject character. This connects to the processes of abjection, which 'weary of fruitless attempts to identify with something on the outside, finds the impossible within.'[77] The irreconcilable differences between male and female that permeate Curtains' narrative constitute some of the important issues of sexuality surrounding her character and the drama as a whole, but significantly too, resonate with the thematic content in Carr's other plays. As Scaife states: 'It is in [Curtains'] story as well as the occasional

---

76 Marina Carr, 'Marina Carr' in Heidi Stephenson and Natasha Landridge (eds), *Rage and Reason: Women Playwrights on Playwriting* (London: Methuen, 1997), p. 90.
77 Kristeva, *Powers of Horror*, p. 5.

monologues by other characters that we hear an echo of the minor chord of dread that is so much a part of the later plays.'[78]

Curtains, who does not reveal externally any evidence about her body, gender or sexuality, embodies concealment. There is a source of masking from behind the narrative as well as from behind the curtains. In the stage directions, Carr outlines how Curtains *'can be any age, as she is covered from head to toe in heavy, brocaded curtains and rail. Not an inch of her face or body is seen throughout the play.'*[79] Bernadette Sweeney points out about Curtains that 'there is also perhaps an inference to the veiling of women ... In the mid-1980s, the curtaining or veiling of this character would also have suggested to Irish audiences Catholic images of the Virgin Mary.'[80] Yet the theatricality within the performative nature of Curtains' dialogue removes all sense of gender essentialism and any serious comment on enforced veiling and violence. The masking of Curtains' body can be read as the representation of someone who chooses to be excluded from the public, paradoxically giving her control over her body. In 'Visual Pleasure and Narrative Cinema', Laura Mulvey writes:

> In a world ordered by sexual imbalance, pleasure in looking has been split between active/male and passive/female. The determining male gaze projects its phantasy on to the female figure which is styled accordingly. In their traditional exhibitionist role women are simultaneously looked at and displayed, with their appearance coded for strong visual and erotic impact so that they can be said to connote *to-be-looked-at-ness*. Women displayed as sexual object is the leitmotif of erotic spectacle ... she holds the look, plays to and signifies male desire.[81]

---

78   Sarahjane Scaife in 'Mutual Beginnings: Marina Carr's Low in the Dark' in Cathy Leeney and Anna McMullan (eds), *The Theatre of Marina Carr: "before rules was made"* (Dublin: Carysfort Press, 2002), p. 14.

79   Carr, 'Low in the Dark', *Plays 1*, p. 5.

80   Bernadette Sweeney, *Performing the Body in Irish Theatre* (London: Palgrave Macmillan, 2008), p. 183.

81   Laura Mulvey, 'Visual Pleasure and Narrative Cinema' in Lizbeth Goodman and Jane de Gay (eds), *The Routledge Reader in Gender and Performance* (London: Routledge, 1998), p. 272.

Carr subverts the conventional mode of Irish theatrical female representation twofold. The female body as an image to be looked at is made visually inaccessible and the play is framed within Curtains' narrative voice.

There is a more hard-hitting version of hegemonic patriarchy and its relation to the female body in *On Raftery's Hill* examined in Chapter 3, where the youngest daughter of the Raftery family, Sorrel, suffers rape at the hands of her father. Here, the female body is the site of patriarchal physical and emotional abuse. Similarly, the octogenarian Blaize in *Portia Coughlan* implies that her life time of verbal and physical restraint was the result of a dire marital relationship with her adulterous and abusive husband: 'I spent the first eighty years of me life holdin' me tongue, fuckin' and blindin' into the pillow, and if God sees me fit to give me another eighty, they'll be spent speakin me mind foul or fair.'[82] In *Woman and Scarecrow*, the dying Woman has suffered from nine pregnancies and her ill and decaying body is the site of abjection. *The Cordelia Dream* (2008) sees the protagonist Woman sacrifice herself by hanging at the request of her father. In *Low in the Dark*, Carr empowers Curtains through concealing her body as well as enabling her as the storyteller to direct, comment on and control the narrative. The beatings she receives from Bender in Act 1, Scene 5 are consensual and pleasurable, staging an orgasm behind the curtain in Act 1, Scene 6. Carr describes the climax in the stage directions:

> *Curtains comes on with Baxter underneath her curtains. She begins moving, slowly at first, swaying back and forward. Her breathing becomes audible, the swaying increases in tempo, the breathing increases. The swaying becomes jerky. She is now gasping, and the swaying reaches its height. All the curtains are shaking. Climax. Breathing subsides. The swaying subsides to silence.*[83]

Unlike Winnie in Beckett's *Happy Days*, whose corporeality is continuously referred to yet denied because she does not possess the necessary reproductive organs and is immobile, Carr's characters in *Low in the Dark*

---

82   Carr, *Portia Coughlan*, p. 28.
83   Carr, 'Low in the Dark', *Plays 1*, p. 55.

embody erotic possibilities; *both* male and female characters can produce babies, and Curtains' sexuality is evocatively presented.

Apart from Curtains, all characters can have babies. The act of giving birth occurs either silently or audibly, as Bender demonstrates early in Act I. She quietly gives birth and then shortly after roars through her next childbirth while calling for gas or an epidural. The babies that are 'produced' throughout the play are thrown into the shower, are sat upon and are fed when the notion arises. Kristeva's discussion of the nature of the feminine is characterised by abjection in the female body through her sexuality and reproductive functions whose transgressions and deviations undermine the social order. Childbirth is the ultimate signifier of disgust because it reminds man of his desire, disgust and fear as well as his birth and death. Kristeva writes that milk binds the mother to the child thus connoting incest; this repulses Fermoy observing his pre-teen child still being breast fed by his mother in *Ariel*.[84] The maternal function is utterly corrupted in *On Raftery's Hill* by various acts of paternal deviant sexual transgressions and corporeal impropriety. As Man provocatively declaims to his daughter in *The Cordelia Dream*, 'Why should I delight in birth after birth? What have your obsessions with maternity have to do with me?'[85] The images of babies being born by both men and women in *Low in the Dark* is at the same time both threatening and subverting. While the abject can be traced to the representation of woman in the play, it is also complicated by its connection to masculinity. Now masculinity is crossing a boundary, which has to process its sexuality and reproductive function in a latest challenge to the social order. Although the play is in the genre of the absurd, it nevertheless forces an exploration of both the physical and mental manifestations of human existence. It shows what could threaten the boundaries of the self, which transgress social boundaries and it portrays the fallibility, temporality and corporeality of humankind. The paternal in this sense is questioning the discourse of feminine power, reduced to the reproductive

---

84   Kristeva, *Powers of Horror*, p. 105.
85   Carr, *The Cordelia Dream* (Oldcastle, Co. Meath: Gallery Press, 2008), p. 14.

function, and imprisoned in the narrowness of a partial representation, which aspires to universality.

Kristeva believes that feelings of repulsion emerge when confronted by images of the abject because of their ambiguity. The slippage between definitions in opposition to that repulsive body threatens to dehumanise subjectivity. The childbirth images in *Low in the Dark* literally represent the confrontation with the maternal again and again, calling up feelings of disgust, which is central to processes of abjection. But the play also presents the possibility of abjection as a primary uncanny, originated in the fertility and generative power of the father's body. Abjection as 'one of those violent, dark revolts of being' is the horror of not knowing the borders of the self located in the father's body in the play.[86] The nature of the abject subject, who is compelled to return to their crisis of loss, resulting from the early separation process, searches for what is 'desirable and terrifying, nourishing and murderous, fascinating and abject inside of the maternal [and in this case paternal] body.'[87] Such images and actions signify the maternal and paternal function and its contribution to subjectivity in the play, the realisation that the subject is separate to them and the loss incurred by such an initiation of identity. Perhaps the play is hinting that the role of the father impacts on subjectivity much earlier than that articulated by the symbolic stage of development and that the dichotomies of semiotic and symbolic need to function not in isolation to one another and definitely without hierarchy as Kristeva suggests and as is strongly argued in the discussion here on *Meat and Salt*.

The absurdity of 'the body' in the play, rebelling against itself by transforming into more than biological notions of it, and rebelling too against its physical manifestation allows the abject to surface. The body's orifices, both male and female, are objects of the abject, reminiscent of the visceral nature and the boundaries of the flesh and are confronted by presenting the flesh as independent of the body. Childbirth, childhood and its concomitant parenthood have major implications in Carr's characters.

---

86   Kristeva, *Powers of Horror*, p. 1.
87   Kristeva, *Powers of Horror*, p. 54.

Childbirth as a result of incest is a central issue in *On Raftery's Hill*, and provides the conditions by which abjection manifests in the play. Anchored by a climate of violence, as well as by collusion between family members and concealment from the public, self-loathing and the controlling force of patriarchy emerges throughout the recurring abusive incidences in the household. Woman confronts Man (her father) in *The Cordelia Dream* (2008) about his eternal desires to silence her through complicated issues that surround the 'blood bond of parent and child.'[88] The eponymous dying Woman in *Woman and Scarecrow* (2006) laments her separation from motherhood and the maternal through issues of family and home. Little Daughter, in a contemporary version of the King Lear tale, finds herself banished from Big Daddy's kingdom in *Meat and Salt* (2003) and forced to fend for herself outside of her father's dominion. Fermoy, father of *Ariel*, remembers helping his father drown his mother at the age of seven, by holding her in Cuura Lake. In *On Raftery's Hill* Carr implies that Red Raftery is the victim of sexual abuse by his mother and abandonment by his father as a child. Hester Swane suffers her mother's desertion at seven years of age and she never knew her father. Portia remembers her own and her twin's birth, 'coming out of the womb holdin hands,'[89] although her mother claims that her twin Gabriel was obsessed by her even in death: 'Came out of the womb clutchin' your leg and he's still clutchin' it wherever he is.'[90] Millie, daughter of the eponymous Mai, narrates her painful tale of being denied her mother's love throughout her life with her mother's emotional interests largely taken by Robert, the errant husband, Millie's father. A whole facet of uncertainties, built on loss, is associated with the maternal. This is precisely where self-harm, self-hate and self-destruction are encountered, which,

88   Carr, *The Cordelia Dream*, p. 23.
89   Carr, *Portia Coughlan*, p. 27.
90   Carr, *Portia Coughlan*, p. 62.

based on the feeling of abjection and all converging on the maternal, attempt to symbolise the other threat to the subject: that of being swamped by the dual relationship,
thereby risking the loss not of a part but of the totality of his living being.[91]

The function of the repetition device is therefore to prevent (albeit ironically) 'the subject's identity from sinking irretrievably into the mother.'[92]
Repetition and the dual confrontation associated with abjection culminate
in Carr's use of the pairing device.

The pairing technique in *Low in the Dark* operates similarly to *Ullaloo*
in terms of abjection, but with a heightened sense of theatricality, which
once again reinforces the destructive nature of heterosexual relationships.
The characters are presented in a dyadic unity: Bender and Binder, Baxter
and Bone, Curtains and Baxter, Binder and Bone. Pairings operate within
the play in much the same way as in *Ullaloo, Woman and Scarecrow* and
The Cordelia Dream, demonstrating abjection's power to project onto the
Other. The subject is simultaneously drawn towards and repelled by the
abject and the Other it represents. Each pair of characters in *Low in the
Dark* serves to give emphasis to the oppositional temperaments in their
relationships that cause the conflicts between them, and which also com-
plement each other's natures. The notion that a third or more person could
disrupt or destabilise the dyadic relationship in the play calls up Grandma
Fraochlán's claim in *The Mai* that she would put her nine-fingered fisherman before her children:

> There's two types of people in this worlt from whah I can gather, thim as puts their
> children first an' thim as puts their lover first an' for whah it's worth, tha nine-fingered
> fisherman an' meself belongs ta the lahher a these. I would gladly a hurlt all seven a ye
> down tha slopes a hell for wan nigh' more wud tha nine-fingered fisher man.[93]

Her remark expresses the sense of loss encountered by Carr's protagonists
as a result of the separation of a pair, depicted in the trilogy and in her more
recent works. It throws light on the subjective mechanisms that accompany

---

91   Kristeva, *Powers of Horror*, p. 64.
92   Kristeva, *Powers of Horror*, p. 64.
93   Carr, *The Mai* (Oldcastle, Co. Meath: Gallery Press, 1995), p. 70.

abjection's sense of loss. Grandma Fraochlán delineates between a 'two-sided formation' which is attributed to abjection. One aspect is the subject's visible and representable identity, which is manifested by, for example, repeating self-sabotaging actions, behaviours and gestures characteristic of the abject subject. The other aspect is the fragile and threatening non-representable subjectivity, associated with a yearning for the absent other. The use of the dyad depicted in Carr's plays literally and metaphorically demonstrates a wish for 'the archaic dyad' before subject and object division.[94] Woman yearns for Man's unity in *The Cordelia Dream*. Man himself, rejected and separated from the subject, blames the role of parents and laments the day parents get involved in their children's upbringing: 'The only thing children need to learn is passion ... Find the child's passion. Feed it. And you will have an extraordinary individual. The rest are dodos ... The walking dead nursing Mommy and Daddy's darkness.'[95] The Mai comments: '[N]o one will ever understand how completely and utterly Robert is mine and I am his, no one ...'[96] As mentioned, Portia claims that she and her twin 'came out of the womb holdin hands.'[97] In *By the Bog of Cats* Hester, whose lover has abandoned her for another woman, states: 'There's things about me and Carthage no wan knows except the two of us ... Our bond is harder, like rocks we are, grindin' off of wan another and maybe all the closer for that.'[98]

Pairing in *Low in the Dark* depicts Bender as reasonable while Binder is petulant and argumentative, Baxter carries an air of confidence and independence while Bone is needy and apologetic, Curtains is controlling and private while Baxter is open and giving, Binder is manipulative while Bone is eager to please. Elements of their personalities emerge through various acts of giving birth, cross-dressing and role-playing. Like *Ullaloo*, *Woman and Scarecrow* and *The Cordelia Dream*, the characters in *Low in the Dark* form a kind of tandem and are reminiscent of Beckett's Vladimir and

94   Kristeva, *Powers of Horror*, p. 58.
95   Carr, *The Cordelia Dream*, p. 16.
96   Carr, *The Mai*, p. 72.
97   Carr, *Portia Coughlan*, p. 27.
98   Carr, *By the Bog of Cats* (Oldcastle, Co. Meath: Gallery Press, 1998), p. 16.

Estragon, Pozzo and Lucky in *Godot*, Hamm and Clov, Nell and Nagg in *Endgame* and the dialogue of a man and his past self in *Krapp's Last Tape* (1958). The entire theatrical effect expressed in their movements, gestures, physical and vocal rhythms appears first and foremost in the way they relate to one another.

The incompatibility of the sexes continues in *Low in the Dark* with the characters struggling to live according to a conventional reality. Binder declares to Bender about sharing life as a couple, in Act 2 scene 2:

> [W]e will talk of many things, but light, and we will not stop to think, never, because *mi amore*, when you stop to think, then is *triste, molto triste*, because the universe, she is an incurable wound, blistering on the belly of the void, she is one vast unbearable grief.[99]

Void, and the continuous compulsion to fill it, renders the abject subject in a permanent state of loss similar to grief. Bender later makes a comment about living life as though one were dead, inspired in her response to the newspaper obituaries that she is reading:

> No one dies suddenly at 97! She's probably been dead for years only Jimmy didn't notice. Sure how would he? He's probably blind, deaf, toothless, crawling around, waiting himself to be struck suddenly or peacefully. Or maybe he's dead too, only they don't notice because of the upset over Mary Rose ... Sure they might never have been alive.[100]

Later Curtains similarly states: 'There are worse things than dying... There's living when you know you've never been alive.'[101] Life is evidence of how one lives and is echoed in all of Carr's works. As Auntie Ah in *Woman and Scarecrow* states: 'I like to see the finish of a life. How we die says so much about how we have lived.'[102] Life is presented as a painful experience in the plays, which must be avoided. The central metaphor in *Low*

99   Carr, 'Low in the Dark', *Plays 1*, p. 67.
100 Carr, 'Low in the Dark', *Plays 1*, p. 74.
101 Carr, 'Low in the Dark', *Play 1*, p. 84.
102 Carr, *Woman and Scarecrow* (Oldcastle, Co. Meath: Gallery Press, 2006), p. 45.

in the Dark is the notion of men and women cohabiting but not living life in any meaningful way. Such a painful existence becomes the subject matter of deeper exploration in Carr's mature works. Frances, mother of the eponymous Ariel, is accused by her family of living too much with the dead. Husband Fermoy tells her: 'Live! Live! Live! Thah's whah we're here for. Do something! Anhin! You'll have all of eternihy for pussin in the dark.'[103] Portia Coughlan spends much of her time by the river where the ghost of her dead twin commonly roams. The ghost of Hester Swane's murdered brother and the memories of her absent mother provide dramatic signifiers to the nature of Hester's loss in *By the Bog of Cats*. In *The Mai* the large window of the family's living room, which frames the panoramic view of Owl Lake, also metaphorically frames Millie's narrative as she tells posthumously the story of her mother's suicide by drowning in the lake and the collapse of the family.

In an interview with Sihra, Carr outlines why the tragic sensibility is central to her work: 'On stage there is nothing more important than looking at the arc of a life and the completion of that life.'[104] Carr refers to Eugene O Neill's response to the source of the inevitable tragedy in his work: 'I have the innate feeling for exultance about tragedy, which comes from a great reverence for the Greek feeling for tragedy. The tragedy of man is perhaps the only significant thing about him.'[105] Carr comments on this statement:

> That is beautiful. The fact that we are dying *is* the only significant thing for us all. And *how* we live and *how* we die ... I love the idea of the tragedy of man and woman. It *is* the only significant thing about us – that we are going to die, and that we all get it so wrong.[106]

103   Carr, *Ariel* (Oldcastle, Co. Meath: Gallery Press, 2002), p. 51.
104   Melissa Sihra, 'Marina Carr in Conversation with Melissa Sihra' in Lillian Chambers, Ger FitzGibbon, Eamonn Jordan, Dan Farrelly and Cathy Leeney (eds), *Theatre Talk: Voices of Irish Practitioners* (Dublin: Carysfort Press, 2001), p. 56.
105   Sihra in *Theatre Talk*, p. 56.
106   Sihra in *Theatre Talk*, p. 56.

Carr's depiction of characters and narrative in this dramatic style and form presents a disintegrated world outside of accepted legitimate principle. As Esslin states about the significance of absurdist theatre:

> It bravely faces up to the fact that for those to whom the world has lost its central explanation and meaning, it is no longer possible to accept art forms still based on the continuation of standards and concepts that have lost their validity; that is, the possibility of revealed certainty about the purpose of man in the universe.[107]

Naming in *Low in the Dark* is purposely fluid and repetitious. Babies are given the same first names making distinction between the children difficult. Bender states in relation to feeding them: 'Now, Jonathon, you'll have to wait while Jonathon and Jonathon drink first.'[108] Here, naming disables differentiation of selves and the possibility of recreating selves, values and worlds. Naming in this case makes signifiers incongruous to signifieds. Other babies are given titles that categorise their identity in a general way:

> BENDER: Where's the Pope?
> BINDER: On your mountain!
> BENDER: That's the Doctor!
> BINDER: Show?
> *Bender holds up a baby.*
> That's him.
> BENDER: I know my children! This is the Doctor! Here on my right breast is the Black Sheep! (*Points to the yellow one.*) On my left, the President! Now, where's the Pope? (*accusingly*) You have him![109]

'The Pope', as one example of the naming category in the drama, immediately refers to the religious leader of the Roman Catholic Church, to power, to celibacy and to Catholic ways of living. Carr illustrates in her early works the notion that naming can enclose identity in a particular way that can assimilate and give some kind of order to subjectivity and suggests

---

107 Esslin, pp. 399–400.
108 Carr, 'Low in the Dark', *Play 1*, p. 52.
109 Carr, 'Low in the Dark', *Play 1*, p. 54.

that the power of naming may have a self-fulfilling prophesy. Wallace notes of Carr's later dramas:

> Carr's use of naming becomes increasingly deliberate and meaningful from *The Mai* to *By the Bog of Cats*. As in folkloric traditions, names indicate character and bear multiple significances as stigma or stigmata.[110]

For Kristeva, the function of naming within language differentiates borders and 'just as it distinguishes pleasure from pain as it does all other oppositions, [it] founds the separation inside/outiside.'[111] The characters' constructed identities within names are precisely constructs dependent on rejections and differentiations from what they are not. This notion is demonstrated by Hester Swane whose brother Joseph was directly called after their mother. Hester's jealousy betrays her confused feelings about Josie's abandonment of her. Her surname echoes 'swan', the ominous dead animal whose image opens *By the Bog of Cats* and which offers symbolic significance to her fate in the play. Woman's refusal to call any of her children after her father again points to her feelings about his abandonment of her in *The Cordelia Dream*. Indeed Carr's use of pronouns or titles to refer to her characters in *Meat and Salt*, *Woman and Scarecrow*, *The Cordelia Dream* is a form of resistance to the prescribed power contained within names. Ariel lives according to the resonance of her namesake, when explored in the context of medieval demonology, which recognises Ariel as the spirit of the waters. One of the significances of Grandma Fraochlán's name is the painful reminder that she was the only illegitimate child born on Fraochlán Island, from where she takes her name in place of the name of her father.

The result of naming in *Low in the Dark* offers subversion that is a device fully embraced in her later plays. Bender states in her wish to feed 'The Pope':

---

110   Clare Wallace, 'Authentic Reproductions: Marina Carr and the Inevitable', in Cathy Leeney and Anna McMullan (eds), *The Theatre of Marina Carr: "before rules was made"* (Dublin: Carysfort Press, 2002), p. 60.
111   Kristeva, *Powers of Horror*, p. 61.

I'll feed him. I want him fat and shiny. Holy father, (*bows to the baby*) you'll pull your auld mother up by the hair of her chiny chin chin, won't you? We'll have tea in the palace and I'll learn Italian and the pair of us side by side, launching crusades, banning divorce, denying evolution, destroying the pill, canonizing witches.[112]

The image of an over-fed Pope and a general life of indulgence is far from the life of moderation and sacrifice which the Catholic Church advocates. The notion that Bender, as the Pope's mother, will be working together with the Pope managing the people, controlling science and preventing women from having control over their bodies illustrates the power of the church. When the trilogy was written, divorce and abortion were illegal in Ireland. While divorce was passed in 1995, abortion is still illegal. Father Willow in *By the Bog of Cats* comically forgets the words of the popular and well-versed prayer for any practising Catholic, the grace before meals, at the wedding celebration in the play, and he also expresses his lament for a lost love at the dinner table comically coming to remember her as Elizabeth, his mother's name. The implication suggests his regret for embracing the priesthood as well as hinting at incest. Boniface, the Monk in *Ariel*, holds a cynical view of the Church, conveying feelings that his religious vocation has been a squandered way of living. Additionally, Boniface remembers, as a child, the religious fanaticism of his mother, whose obsession stretched to her taking down her safely kept blouse, which contained the stains of Padre Pio's blood. The household in *On Raftery's Hill* is without any spiritual structure, and abuse continues as the play's tensions reach a kind of 'anti-resolution.' In *Woman and Scarecrow*, Woman believes that God has long abandoned humankind with the death of the Virgin. She states: 'and with her end came the end of God's desire for any truck with us.'[113] Catherine in *Marble* asks her husband Ben, 'Do you believe, actually believe, this sojourn here means something?"[114]

There is an identifiable direct relationship between the characters' loss of subjectivity and the role of parents in Carr's works. Parenthood

---

112   Carr, 'Low in the Dark', *Play One*, p. 55.
113   Carr, *Woman and Scarecrow*, p. 43.
114   Carr, *Marble* (Oldcastle, Co. Meath: Gallery Press, 2009), p. 59.

recurs as a through-line in all of Carr's works, particularly in relation to the idea that parents cannot fulfil the conventional roles expected of them. The primary caregivers outlined in Kristeva's abjection place the abject individual in the difficult state of being 'powerless outside and impossible inside.'[115] Subjectivity, constructed on the one hand by the painful separation from the maternal and the failure of the paternal function to provide an adequate unitary role after the division between the subject and object, produces abjection. Kristeva refers to the dynamic involved in the process as 'a strange configuration: an encompassment that is stifling, and at the same time, draining.'[116] The offspring of parents who abandon them are seen as directly conducive to the child's journey towards origins, to that place where life and death meet, where the danger and pleasure of the loss of self are intertwined.

The notion of 'mother' or 'father' as having a universally identifiable fixed role is contested in *Low in the Dark*. Bender, a mother, smokes and drinks, and the play's other characters create no sense of maternal or paternal awareness or capabilities. Scaife observes the poignant and humorous contrasts presented in Act 2 in relation to maternity and motherhood, specifically surrounding the notion that maternity is a 'natural' instinct. Scaife comments:

> [T]he notion that mothers just cannot seem to provide any real sustenance for their offspring: it seems to be part of the human condition that they are unable to help alleviate the suffering of the children that they have been instrumental in creating.[117]

In *Nationalisms and Sexualities*, Andrew Parker wonders 'why the world has come to see itself as divided along the seemingly natural lines of national affiliation and sexual attachment.'[118] He outlines how concepts of national identity have been inextricably bound up with the notion of appropriate

---

115   Kristeva, *Powers of Horror*, p. 48.
116   Kristeva, *Powers of Horror*, p. 49.
117   Scaife in *The Theatre of Marina Carr*, p. 11.
118   Andrew Parker, Mary Russo, Doris Sommer and Patricia Yaeger (eds), 'Introduction', in *Nationalism and Sexualities* (New York: Routledge, 1992), p. 2.

gendered or sexualised identity. McMullan writes about the pressures: 'Whether Catholic or Loyalist, the role of the woman is to serve and to suffer. While her image is sublimated, her voice is suppressed.'[119] John Bowlby's theory of attachment between a child and its mother claims to be as a result of infants being born with a number of interrelated built-in tendencies that make them seek direct contact with an adult, and this he stipulates is usually the mother. While not denying the innate tendencies on the child's part, the theory has been heavily contested in social development from the point of view that filial devotion is predominantly a 'motherly' bond.[120] 'Caring', 'loving' and 'protecting' do not have to be seen as specifically 'motherly traits' and Carr dramatises the alternative by presenting mothers who are unable or unwilling to perform their associated 'maternal' role. Similarly, the conventional role of fathers as 'protectors' and 'breadwinners' is subverted. In Act 2 of *Low in the Dark* Baxter is encouraging the pregnant male, Bone, to exercise, while arguing his case for wanting an abortion:

> BONE: (*still on the floor, from behind his hump*) I'm seriously contemplating an abortion.
> BAXTER: Are you crazy?
> BONE: I have a right to choose.
> BAXTER: You have not. There's a life inside you! A destiny, all of its own.
> BONE: Stop it! You're just trying to make me feel guilty. It's painless. An overnight job. I could be back building tomorrow.[121]

Bernadette Sweeney notes that 'by projecting this (abortion) debate on to the bodies of the male characters (and actors), Carr points to gen-

119   Anna McMullan in 'Irish women playwrights since 1958' in Trevor R. Griffiths and Margaret Llewellyn Jones (eds), *British And Irish Women Dramatists Since 1958* (Buckingham, UK: Open University Press, 1993), p. 111.
120   See John Bowlby's Attachment theory in *Attachment and Loss* (London: Hogarth, 1974).
121   Carr, 'Low in the Dark', *Plays 1*, pp. 79–80.

dered roles and questions the essential materiality of the maternal.'[122] She
also extends the debate around the paternal role and fatherhood, inverting
paternal and maternal characteristics as typically concomitant with fatherhood and motherhood respectively, and showing both in a state of crisis.

These early works see Carr present to her audience a theatrical shape
that comments upon itself. The openness of such an approach seeks alternative theatrical possibilities in performance. The fluidity, interchangeability
and instability of the theatrical representation of abjection are presented to
the audience for consideration. *Ullaloo* and *Low in the Dark* give us both
a human situation that draws us in as well as a reflection on the theatrical
means used to achieve this.

The foundation of Carr's concerns about gender, relationships, familial dynamics, violence and death in the early plays are continued in her
later works. Melissa Sihra notes: 'Just as the characters in *Ullaloo* reflect
upon their unfulfilled ambitions and desires as they journey towards death,
Woman, in the later play, contemplates her life: "I look over the years and
all I see is one wrong turning leading to another wrong turn. I cannot
remember a moment when it was right."'[123] Yet Carr writes abjection in
Woman and Scarecrow not only into the characters but also unequivocally into the world of the drama, establishing abjection as the stigma of
the contemporary subject, who suffers from it on numerous levels – from
family systems which centre primarily around the figure of the mother,
to social and cultural practices, to the post-modern dilemma of insecure
disassociation. The world of the play reflects the subject's disorientation
and the subject's disassociation reflects the world of the play. *Woman and
Scarecrow* re-figures and re-frames the dramatic narrative, from the context of an unrelenting abjection and 'the breaking down of a world that
has erased it borders.'[124]

---

122 Bernadette Sweeney, *Performing the Body in Irish Theatre* (London: Palgrave
      Macmillan, 2008), p. 179.
123 Melissa Sihra, 'The House of Woman and the Plays of Marina Carr' in Melissa Sihra
      (ed.), *Women in Irish Drama: A Century of Authorship and Representation* (London:
      Palgrave Macmillan, 2007), pp. 201–218, p. 202.
124 Kristeva, *Powers of Horror*, p. 4.

Woman and Scarecrow was first produced at the Royal Court Jerwood Theatre, London on 16 June 2006 and was directed by Ramin Gray with Fiona Shaw as Woman and Bríd Brennan as Scarecrow. It was later produced in the Peacock Theatre, Dublin in 2007, directed by Selina Cartmell with Olwen Fouéré in the lead role and Barbara Brennan as Scarecrow. What is witnessed during this play is again the expression of many of the themes and ideas explored in the earlier works but noticeably also a return to the imagery of the dying woman in bed, which is the central subject of *Ullaloo*. *Woman and Scarecrow* (2006) elaborates on dying, charting the story of Woman's last days of suffering. All characters in the play are referred to by either pronouns or titles – Woman, Him, Scarecrow, Auntie Ah, placing a universal slant on who they are and what they represent. Woman and philandering husband, Him, have eight children. Their ninth child, which Woman claims to still mourn, died at birth. As Woman relates her life and desires for death to alter ego Scarecrow, anguish, anger and aggression are often brought to the fore, offered through a somewhat surreal lens. Such a lens, tinged with a nightmarish quality in the world of the play, emphasises the vulnerable sensuality of death's journey.

Woman and Scarecrow presents the abject on the margins of the signifiable, constantly changing its subject position within the framework of humiliation, making the refuge of the protagonist's self difficult to explain. Carr turns the experience of estrangement in *Woman and Scarecrow* to the point where her characters concede to the dramatic narratives of origin and identity, central to the constructed imaginings of abject subjectivity. Again, the individual's quest for identity is seen to stem from family and home and once again, family and home are highly problematic and do not provide a sense of belonging. On the contrary, they destabilise identity. The characters in *Woman and Scarecrow* occupy a defeatist position in their challenges against the origins of identity in favour of the relentless preoccupation with dying and death. *Woman and Scarecrow* is susceptible to silencing the experience of the outsider, the peripheral figure of difference, with the death of the protagonist as the conclusion of the play.

As in Carr's other works, *Woman and Scarecrow* undermines the notion of a stable individual identity and places the drama of abjection at the birth of woman and the maternal. Abandoned, withdrawn, excluded,

yet inevitably there and forever to be held at bay, the abject will physically occupy and incorporate parts of the body, in that anxiety and coincidence between attraction and repulsion, which also – especially – marks
the female/maternal body. The protagonist Woman, deformed by nine
pregnancies (as well as the death of one of those nine) and by the decay
of aging and illness, has inscribed on her body the fatality of human life
and death, the inevitable process of degeneration of the flesh. As Woman
states: 'The body has betrayed me or I have betrayed it or the betrayal was
mutual. Who cares. I'm fatal. Terminal. Hopeless.'[125] Permeated with the
torture and revulsion which are often evoked by the biological processes
of reproduction, Woman fits into that 'rhetoric of abjection' retraced by
Kristeva in her analysis of Céline's texts. Disconnected and aggressive dramatic dialogue, as well as a descent into an almost purgatorial hell, *Woman
and Scarecrow* is filled with abjection, which explodes into images of decay,
abandonment and disgust.

Woman was born on the western seaboard and the play opens with
her dying wish to cross the Shannon back to her place of birth.

> WOMAN: I started out West. I'd like to finish there.
> SCARECROW: When you could've gone West you refused.
> WOMAN: No, listen to me. If I could get across the Shannon once more maybe the
>   air would perform some kind of miracle ... I might live.
> SCARECROW: You think crossing the Shannon is all it takes? Once, perhaps, long
>   ago, that would have been the thing to do.[126]

Woman is literally and metaphorically drawn back to the abject, to that
place where the separation from her (m)other took place after birth, where
she had to reject her in order to ascertain and establish her self. The idea
of crossing presupposes a border or divide. Crossing therefore signals the
uneasy conjunction of apparently divided spaces. In the play, these divided
spaces can be identified as the West, which is typically associated with
images of green, wild, barren and rugged landscapes where water (the

125   Carr, *Woman and Scarecrow*, p. 17.
126   Carr, *Woman and Scarecrow*, p. 11.

sea, lakes and rivers), mountains, remoteness and rurality are dominant. On the other hand, the East of Ireland, whose countryside is more luscious, and of which Dublin is the urban centre, is where most of Ireland's population reside. Woman believes that the open air of the West will offer her some kind of healing, and her Aunt maintains that the people of the West have a toughness about them – meaning a will to fight anything that comes against them. She tells Woman, 'And it wasn't for nothing that you were born there too [The West of Ireland]. But the eastern blood of your father diluted the limestone and softened you to this.'[127] The West symbolises the pre-Oedipal phase of Woman's life before she passed through the 'mirror phase' and entered into the symbolic order – the East – thereby enabling her to assert her own individuality by differentiating her self from the unity with her mother. Woman's desire to cross the Shannon back to the West is accompanied by abjection, which effects a frenzied dramatic narrative thrust. Countering this drive is the thwarting of dramatic narrative momentum demonstrated through repetitious expressions of self-effacement. Crossing then for Woman becomes internalised in corporeal, psychic and abject forms. Repetition and return – the constant recurrence of the terror of death (and birth) steep the drama in the imagery and processes of abjection.

Exploring the ritual of dying through the continuum of Woman's abjection, a symbolic transitory stage between self and other emerges. Dying is the means by which to explore those borders and boundaries that define the space between self and other. The journey towards death sees the horror of the outer dying world matched by that of the inner dying world. The abject world of the play is at its extreme, disorienting and fragmented, symptomatic of the wandering stray, who arrives in a territory where her desire to belong is displaced. Having been born in the Winter season, a time of dying and death, Woman, as wandering stray, lyrically describes the memory of an event where she is an onlooker when Christ passes by in a cart where she is stopped at an old house. The detailed image, surreal in its calmness, evokes Woman's experience of seeing Christ one time in Winter

127 Carr, *Woman and Scarecrow*, p. 32.

when it snowed and when a woman stopped to give her a lift. Her poetic description evokes sharp frozen images of the event as an onlooker, who is without access to it, yet the moment is memorably significant to her.

> We drove and drove through all the whiteness until finally she pulled in at a courtyard of an old house with a wooden balcony going round it. And on the wooden balcony painted scenes in that old red and gold. We sit looking at these painted scenes, the snow whirling, the darkening road, the courtyard and then Christ passes by in a cart. He's a painting and not a painting, and the woman and I stare, transfixed, as he glides past, quizzical, peaceful, and his passing is such we don't want to share it, speak of it. We refuse to look at one another, refuse to acknowledge what we have just seen, are seeing in the snow, in the courtyard.[128]

Peggy Phelan has discussed abstraction in painting and theatre:

> Painterly qualities ... as they relate to theater in general, revisit the dynamic between figure and landscape in ways that both echo and distort the Romantic movement's interest in this trope. For the Romantics, the perceiving human soul is framed by the looked-at-ness nature and anthropo-centric definitions of 'the natural.'[129]

The external 'natural' landscape referred to by Woman's memory reflects the inner topography of her mind. Death, hints of the after world and icy snow recall too the painterly qualities of the opening of *By the Bog of Cats* when Hester walks through the 'bleak white landscape of ice and snow' carrying a dead black swan whose blood trails it, the swan a portent for Hester's death.[130]

Woman's response to the event is symptomatic of abjection, because the abject appears in the play through thematic omissions, terrors and silences. That which cannot be named, and the reasons for Woman's illness are precisely what she lacks – love, her husband, her family and the

128 Carr, *Woman and Scarecrow*, p. 59.
129 Peggy Phelan cited by Cathy Leeney, 'Character, Writing, and Landscape in *Woman and Scarecrow* and Other Plays by Marina Carr' in *Princeton University Library Chronicle* (68:1–2:2006), pp. 705–719, p. 715.
130 Carr, *By the Bog of Cats*, p. 13.

loss of her dead child, reinforced by the surreal space which characterises the world of the play.

The opening scene sees Woman lying pale, gaunt and almost blind on her deathbed in her home lamenting aspects of her life to Scarecrow, while The Thing in the Wardrobe – the symbol of death – waits to take her to her end. Like Tilly in *Ullaloo*, she threatens, in a childish way to stop breathing if Scarecrow does not play Demis Roussos on the CD. The stage directions read: *'Things are calm for a while as they eyeball one another. Then both start to go red in the face. Then Woman starts thrashing around. Scarecrow clutches her throat, doubled over.'*[131] Scarecrow eventually gives in but is 'thick' [annoyed] for having to do so and puts the music on. Echoing *Ullaloo*, Tilly and Tomred have defiant ambitions related to the body before they die. Tilly wants to stop all her bodily functions from working and Tomred wants his toenails to grow so long that it will be documented in the *Guinness Book of Records*. Woman's breathing scene demonstrates her control over Scarecrow. On the other hand, The Thing in the Wardrobe is not within Woman's control, suggesting that death will come when it is ready to take her. The Thing in the Wardrobe occasionally lets out deep guttural growls and groans, mirroring Woman's suffering cries from the bed. Scarecrow and The Thing (in the Wardrobe) are aspects of the 'sublimated', labelled and named as something else so as Woman can articulate the subject matters of rejection, the death of a child, dying, illness and self-destruction. Scarecrow and The Thing in the Wardrobe are what cannot be named – the abject.

The setting denotes a purgatorial space between two symbolic realms – the living and the dead. It is a site of chaotic awareness of belonging and resisting belonging to the cycle of being, with images of damnation and salvation. It is a liminal space, which must be crossed to leave the world. As in a rite of passage, this *limen* is ambiguously connoted, as it is not-life and not-death. Victor Turner states that the subjects of a rite of passage 'are neither living nor dead from one aspect, and both living and dead from

131   Carr, *Woman and Scarecrow*, p. 14.

another. Their condition is one of ambiguity and paradox, a confusion of all the customary categories.'[132]

Abjection is found in borderline spaces, in the inbetween-ness of being, in the unstable sense of self. It finds expression in the body. Woman's ill and dying body, invaded with the abject, is the ultimate signifier of abjection. The opening of Act 2 sees her lying in her bed, blood dripping from her lips and chin, clutching a bunch of black feathers in her hands. Kristeva notes about the perpetual abject:

> Abjection preserves what existed in the archaism of pre-objectal relationship, in the immemorial violence with which the body becomes separated from another body in order to be – maintaining that night in which the outline of the signified vanishes and where only the imponderable affect is carried out.[133]

Forever threatened by the frailty of a boundary built on the originary void of loss, Woman experiences the feeling of abjection through her body. Her bodily excretions radically question her integrity and identity. The deprived bodily practices of the dying body emphasise Woman's sharp sense of exclusion.

The black feathers which Woman clutches, are strongly linked to The Thing in the Wardrobe. In the early part of the play, Scarecrow asks Woman: 'Can't you hear him sucking his oily black wings?'[134] Her words not only echo death's signifier of the black swan featured in *By the Bog of Cats* but also call to mind Selina Cartmell's production at the Peacock, with Olwen Fouéré, who wore a long white nightdress for most of the play. In Neolithic Europe, white was the colour of death [and bones] and a woman in white represented the Goddess who had as her death sign an association with animals such as carrion birds, particularly the crow/raven.[135] Carr refigures

132   Victor Turner, 'Betwixt and Between: the Liminal Period in the Rites of Passage', in *The Forest of Symbols: Aspects of Ndemba Ritual* (Ithaca, NY and London: Cornell University Press, 1967), p. 97.

133   Kristeva, *Powers of Horror*, p. 10.

134   Carr, *Woman and Scarecrow*, p. 12.

135   Marija Gimbutas, *The Civilization of the Goddess: the World of Old Europe*, ed. Joan Marler (San Francisco: Harper San Francisco, 1991).

the crow figure as a Scarecrow, which tries to keep 'the crow' at bay. This is demonstrated by Scarecrow's resistance to The Thing in the Wardrobe's venture for Woman's life, by receiving, what sounds like, a physical battering from The Thing in the Wardrobe, thereby stalling the onslaught of Woman's death.

Many of the Celtic mythology goddesses are linked with the raven or crow. These goddesses are aggressive deities associated with war and death. Badb, Macha and the Morrígan are all associated with crows and/or ravens. The wife of the Fomorian sea-god, Tethra, was said to be a crow goddess who also hovered above battlefields. In this sense, Scarecrow wards off The Thing in the Wardrobe who is linked with death, and his antagonistic behaviour to the subjects in the room is a reminder to Woman that her end is in sight. The association of birds with death and war is a reflection of its tendency to eat carrion, which is found scattered on the aftermath of battlefields. This tendency led, eventually, to the persecution of the raven, as a harbinger of doom and destruction, and also to the common notion in modern European culture that the main attribute of Crow and Raven is their connection with the Other world. Scarecrow's 'persecution' of The Thing in the Wardrobe relates to his portentous connection to the Other world together with its connotation to death.

The hospital-like quality of Woman's home – *a bed, a chair, a wardrobe and a CD player* – attest to Woman's illness, to the coming of her end and thus to her dislocation. Him and Auntie Ah attend to her as nurse-like carers, propping her pillows, fixing her bed linen and giving her medication and drinks. Him is also there for 'chitchat', which regularly turns into arguments surrounding their marriage. Auntie Ah's added 'help' for Woman comes with her religious beliefs, claiming that Woman's illness is nonsense, implying that her lack of belief in God has contributed to her current ill state. She suggests that Woman has already submitted to death and is merely waiting to be taken.[136] Accusing her of having no finishing power for life and replicating her mother's life and now premature death, Auntie Ah turns to God and asks Woman to ask for His help, solace and

---

136 Carr, *Woman and Scarecrow*, p. 31.

forgiveness: 'Oh Lord, open my lips so my tongue shall announce thy praise. The five sorrowful mysteries.'[137] Woman dismisses her wishes telling her that 'God is for the living', not the dying.[138] Yet Him and Auntie Ah are reminders of the everyday. Like the eponymous Portia who feels suffocated by her family and in-laws, Him tells Woman that her relatives continuously invade and clutter their home, making the place impossible to live in. Yet the everyday is disrupted by the other world of Scarecrow and The Thing in the Wardrobe, more ghostly figures that haunt Carr's landscapes. Gabriel is seen by Portia by the river in *Porta Coughlan*, the Ghost Fancier and Hester's brother Joseph 'ghosts' the topography of *By the Bog of Cats* and the eponymous *Ariel*'s voice is heard asking for help on her home telephone, bringing the familiar, the metaphysical and the imaginary realms onto the same plane.

The Thing in the Wardrobe further signifies Woman's longing to belong, shaped by her acute sense of abjection. The setting, together with noises from behind doors, anticipates the physical and epistemological disorientation that Woman experiences throughout her final days. She tells Scarecrow: 'In theory death is magnificent but somehow I thought mine would be different,' referring to the idea that she thought her death would be for a more worthy and passionate cause – such as love for instance.[139] Later Scarecrow tells her, 'This world's job is to take everything from you. Yours is not to let it,'[140] reminding her that she relinquished very easily everything that was given to her, living instead a 'half-existence.'[141] And Woman agrees: 'I wasn't good to myself ... I refused to be happy.'[142] Similar to Tilly in *Ullaloo* and the characters in *Marble*, Woman lived a life of regret too busy being bitter about her lot to try to change it. Scarecrow tells her: 'You're going into your grave out of bitterness, out of a sense of

137   Carr, *Woman and Scarecrow*, pp. 41–42.
138   Carr, *Woman and Scarecrow*, p. 42.
139   Carr, *Woman and Scarecrow*, p. 17.
140   Carr, *Woman and Scarecrow*, p. 18.
141   Carr, *Woman and Scarecrow*, p. 46.
142   Carr, *Woman and Scarecrow*, p. 44.

meanness ... Yes, your bitterness was a flaw in the weave. I noticed it, but I never thought it would bring us down.'[143]

Woman's repetitious chores of domestic life seem to have been her way of avoiding its harsh realities. She asks: 'Why didn't I have more sex when I could have? Scarecrow reminds her: 'You were too busy hoovering.'[144] Now, on her deathbed she argues with Him for his honesty about the kind of marriage and life they have had, echoing Tilly and Tomred's inquiry into the purpose of their relationship. Referring to the last thirty years of married life, she tells Him: 'You and I? They were exile of course. Exile from the best of ourselves ... beasts in a cave with night coming on ... no way to live at all.'[145] Yet Woman does not really want to hear the truth about her marriage to a man she loved obsessively. Loving him too much and not getting the same in return is perhaps Woman's greatest flaw and is a familiar concern in Carr's work. Woman's willingness for great love comes before everyone, including her children. Scarecrow suggests that she had children more for show or for Him than for herself, referring to them as 'unwanted gifts', thus calling into question her maternal instinct.[146] Scarecrow tells her: 'Numbers. You just wanted numbers. You just wanted to look and say, this one is mine and this one and this one ...'[147]

Owning children as objects rather than as individual people is echoed in *Low in the Dark*, where characters share the same name or whose name is a position title. Although *Low in the Dark* is in the non-natural style of theatre and is as Sihra describes 'a hilarious romp with gender,' offspring are born, simply appear or are thrown about haphazardly in a nonchalant fashion in a playful yet highly socially charged way.[148] They are treated like toys in the play. Woman's kind of love for her children also recalls the mother figures in Carr's other plays, who refuse or who cannot play the

143   Carr, *Woman and Scarecrow*, p. 19.
144   Carr, *Woman and Scarecrow*, p. 46.
145   Carr, *Woman and Scarecrow*, p. 60.
146   Carr, *Woman and Scarecrow*, p. 56.
147   Carr, *Woman and Scarecrow*, p. 16.
148   Sihra in Eric Weitz (ed.), *The Power of Laughter: Comedy and Contemporary Irish Theatre* (Dublin: Carysfort Press, 2004), p. 159.

role of mother. Grandma Fraochlán's love for her Nine fingered fisherman as well as The Mai's love for Robert in *The Mai* and Hester's love for Carthage in *By the Bog of Cats* recalls how obsessive love for one man can be soul destroying for these lovers and mothers, leaving them with no sense of being, thereby bereft of the emotional strength needed to mother their children. Him's extramarital affairs and disrespect for Woman over the years have caused her great pain and her self-defeating mentality lies in her remaining loyal to him. Scarecrow's comments about how much he loved Woman suggest that it mirrors the love Him demonstrated for Woman over the years. He tells her: 'I have loved you so long. You never returned it. Threw me a few scraps from time to time. Kept me tagging along on whims and promises. Promises that were not kept.'[149] The strength of Woman's malicious outbursts to Him from her deathbed is a measure of her hurt. She tells Him:

> Well, they'll survive you whether you remember their names or not as I survived my parents or lack of, as you survived yours. We don't really figure except as gargoyles to bitch about to their lovers. They'll have the last word on me. And if you dare make a sentimental speech at my funeral I'll rise from my coffin and rip your tongue out.[150]

Woman's self-destructive behaviour replicates her own mother's decision to marry a man simply because he asked, after being let down badly by the man 'she was wild about.'[151] Auntie Ah tells her of the impact of the rejection on her: 'I never heard the whys and hows of it but I do know it nearly killed her.'[152]

Woman's feelings toward life point to her identification with death. These feelings, evident in conversations with Scarecrow, are centred on past ventures of escape from death as well as present demands for consolations from death and death threats. The many linguistic signs that Scarecrow is engaged in can be described in terms of 'phobia – as abortive metaphor

149   Carr, *Woman and Scarecrow*, p. 20.
150   Carr, *Woman and Scarecrow*, p. 61.
151   Carr, *Woman and Scarecrow*, p. 49.
152   Carr, *Woman and Scarecrow*, p. 49.

of want.'[153] For example, the phobic person is 'a subject in want of meta-phoricalness. Incapable of producing metaphors by means of signs alone, he produces them in the very materials of drives.'[154] As the play unfolds it becomes clear that Scarecrow is Woman's phobic alter ego because he, like Woman, suffers from an acute sense of abjection. The opening scene points to the early example of this invasion of the abject in Scarecrow's defensive argument against Woman's request to avoid death, achieved she believes, by breathing fresh air in the west:

> WOMAN: I ran west to die.
> SCARECROW: You ran south and you didn't run, you crawled.
> WOMAN: I ran west. West. Why should I go south?
> SCARECROW: You got lost.
> WOMAN: I thought you were the navigator?
> SCARECROW: He found you under a bronze statue of a man with his arm pointing out to sea.
> WOMAN: Did he? ... Oh yes, and his eyes fixed beyond the horizon and I remember thinking before I passed out, if I didn't see the horizon myself at least I'm near something that can. Why didn't you help me get back west?
> SCARECROW: We're not cowboys.
> WOMAN: I started out west. I'd like to finish there.

Woman 's dismissiveness of Scarecrow is interrupted by Scarecrow's drawing attention to the contents of the wardrobe: 'He's waiting in the wardrobe. Can't you hear him sucking his oily black wings?'[155] Scarecrow's clever responses to Woman's statements about her fear of death are manipu-lative and exploitative, demonstrating his obsessional desire for belong-ing. His persistence at Woman to remember her life (a self-perpetuating destructive life) is self-defensive: his fear of being abject is turned into passive aggression and projected away from the self onto an other. In this manner, the phobic subject attempts to maintain the fragile boundaries between self and other. Scarecrow is Kristeva's abject who produces Swan

153 Kristeva, *Powers of Horror*, p. 35.
154 Kristeva, *Powers of Horror*, p. 37.
155 Carr, *Woman and Scarecrow*, p. 11.

in the wardrobe as the abject of his dislike and jealousy for Woman and his desire to kill her, which simultaneously condenses his fear and reveals his powerlessness. His passive aggressive dialogue is the frantic attempt to keep the threatening abjection of self at bay.

Yet this kind of symbolism is really a comment on the domain of abjection and its exclusion. Family and life are denied in the play in favour of confronting the embodied counterparts of conscience (Scarecrow) and death (The Thing in the Wardrobe), which will continue to haunt Woman to her end. Scarecrow and The Thing in the Wardrobe, two figures of alterity, are presented as truly subversive, since Scarecrow is her alter ego who challenges Woman on resisting living and The Thing in the Wardrobe, the symbol of death, who is hidden from view and who goads Woman to her death, represents the figure who will take her as his next victim, the play suggests, to a violent death. Both figures act as a means of reintroducing the silenced 'others' to the issue of self-destruction as a social concern, as Kristeva's flow of *jouissance* into language.[156]

> SCARECROW: What do you want the mirror for?
> WOMAN: To watch myself die. I want to see how I am. I always look in mirrors to find out what's happening to me. Please bring it to me. I want to see of I'm still here.
> SCARECROW: You want to drool over the vestiges of your beauty.
> WOMAN: Yes. Let me drool. Thank god I still have my vanity.[157]

The dialogue marks a defining moment in Woman's abject life, which harks bark to her and her mother's relationship. Woman requests a mirror to examine her body. The mirror acquires strong symbolic overtones, re-enacting at first glance the myth of Narcissus. Woman's examination of herself in the mirror shows feelings of glory for how her body has changed with time and what she believes is now ideal. She tells Scarecrow:

156 Scarecrow is Woman's projected burden, an other who confronts Woman and her sense of identity, as he contests her life choices. The Thing in the Wardrobe challenges her conscience, by provoking her about her decision to die.

157 Carr, *Woman and Scarecrow*, p. 21.

> Bones, teeth, hair, the age adores. Well I always had good teeth and despite every-
> thing, my hair is still magnificent. And now finally I have achieved bones. My dear,
> I have transformed myself into the ideal. Look at me! I am graveyard chic, angular,
> lupine, dangerous.[158]

Her gaze at her body in the mirror is extremely self-appreciative, viewing it as a male object of desire, given the context of it in the conversation between Scarecrow and Woman. Their dialogue outlines Woman's numerous male conquests, which Scarecrow believes were self-defeating acts for Him's attention: 'Your backward twisted little heart was tied, always tied to him who made little of you every opportunity he could.'[159] Yet the degree of sarcasm beneath Woman's adulation of her body belies a more clinical investment of it. The existence of 'ego drives, aimed at self-preservation' is no longer reliable in this instance.[160] The narcissistic effect, which would normally protect the self from the invasion of abjection, is redundant. Woman's experience of her body as waste continues to be outlined as an object under male gaze, demonstrated particularly when Scarecrow reminds her of the man who wanted Woman to parade naked around the room. For Catholic reasons, Scarecrow reminds her that she did not enjoy the experience. The event places Woman's body within a patriarchal gaze, denigrating her body as a site to be looked at.

Woman's self-abasement, reflected in this mirror scene, is made meaningful in the examination of a much earlier time of looking in the mirror. Her recollection of herself as a child, when shopping for a red coat and red hat with her heavily pregnant mother is the incident which pre-empts the link between Woman's loss of selfhood and the invasion of her mother's abjection. At the end of the shopping day, her mother successfully finds the coat and hat she had been searching to buy. Woman recalls being asked by her mother to look in the mirror at her new clothes. One particular glimpse by her mother at her in the mirror was the first time that she saw that she

---

158   Carr, *Woman and Scarecrow*, p. 21.
159   Carr, *Woman and Scarecrow*, p. 23.
160   Kristeva, *Powers of Horror*, p. 43.

'was that thing her mother had yearned for and found.'[161] But Woman continues: 'It is her I see now, her girth disappearing in dusty shadows, old before her time, still radiant, the white teeth flashing, the russet gold of her hair and the expression in her eyes.'[162] The mirror scene undermines Woman's identity. Looking in the mirror is an alienating experience, whose image is now her mother's reflection. This moment, the brief glance by her mother, locks Woman into the *chora*, the maternally connoted space where the child's and the mother's drives are not yet separate. Woman's experience of abjection is motivated by the symbiosis with her mother and their mutual attachment to the maternal sphere. Her mother's pregnant body also alludes to impurity and future abjection. Woman's abandonment by her mother in terms of her absence by her death at a young age, her affection, her mother's infidelities to spite her husband and her mother's uncertainty about her children's fate, all emerge in the repetitious behaviour of Woman's re-enactments of them on her own family. As Scarecrow tells Woman of her mother:

> She lived bitterly. I remember her battering the spuds into a venomous pulp for the dinner. I remember her vagueness on the beach, her refusal to play. I remember the weeping in the darkened rooms, the obsession with mass and the fawning over the priest, I remember her belief that she was somehow inferior and her living out of that belief with such conviction, such passion, such energy invested in taking second place. All of which you have inherited.[163]

The maternal abject continues to haunt Woman in different contexts in the play. Religious imagery together with notions of life and death is another stark expression of Woman's abjection. In Paris, concepts of life and death are disclosed to her 'many lifetimes ago', on her visit to an exhibition at the Louvre.[164] Using Kristeva's terms, Woman's view of Caravaggio's *Death of the Virgin*, which she saw on a daily basis during her stay, is a crying-out theme of suffering. Roaming the streets of Paris, Woman is marked by

---

161   Carr, *Woman and Scarecrow*, p. 36.
162   Carr, *Woman and Scarecrow*, p. 36.
163   Carr, *Woman and Scarecrow*, p. 50.
164   Carr, *Woman and Scarecrow*, p. 42.

her experience of the painting – life and death, death in life. The painting reflects Woman's feeling of abjection, embodied in the female/maternal body of the virgin, in Woman's journey towards origins. Such feeling calls up concerns of life and death, where the danger and pleasure of the loss of self are intertwined. In a psychoanalytic reading of the religious painting, the mother and the maternal are typically the privileged figure of the inextricable proximity of life and death, which are at the centre of the symbolic construction. In *Death of the Virgin*, the central figure of Christianity is generally regarded as a figure of worship, representing the people's trust in her powers of regeneration for future unity, as well as representing the Christian belief in afterlife. However, Woman's reading of *Death of the Virgin* subverts the notion of life after death, presupposing the nonexistent. 'The miracle is over', Woman exclaims to Auntie Ah, as though the religious narrative of *Death of the Virgin* is consolatory claptrap for an un-glorious end of 'another of those invisible women past their prime.'[165]

> WOMAN: Many lifetimes ago, I went everyday across the Seine to see the Caravaggio. *The Death of the Virgin*. Her feet were blue. Her dress was red. Everyone has their head bowed. Oh the grief ... terrible to look at ... frightening ... and do you know why Auntie Ah?
> AUNTIE AH: Why what?
> WOMAN: Because the miracle is over. Yes it is. She's going down into the clay. Not up in the blue beyond. The apostles know it. Caravaggio knows it and we know it.[166]

The dark colours of dying which surround the scene of the Virgin pre-empt the process of Woman's death. The image dramatises her initiation into the realm of death and an awareness – at once horrifying and reassuring – that death is an essential part of life; that both are inscribed in the maternal power of generation, which guarantees continuity. She tells Scarecrow about what she saw when she looked from the bedroom door at her mother dying, another image that echoes her own death observed in the painting, *Death of the Virgin*, depicting how she is locked in the *chora*:

---

165 Carr, *Woman and Scarecrow*, p. 43.
166 Carr, *Woman and Scarecrow*, p. 42.

WOMAN: Yes ... something else ... as I stand there ... a terrible realization comes
flashing through ... a picture from the future ... as I stand there I see myself here.
Now I see my own death day ... and now she wakes and looks at me. I swim in
her eye, she in mine, we're spellbound, unsmiling, conspirators too wise to fight
what has been decreed on high, long, long ago.[167]

Locked within the *chora*, Woman exists as a liminal figure, a non-
coherent figure between the signifiers and signifieds of the semiotic chaos
that dying represents and her attempts to enter into the symbolic order.
This is represented in her letter-writing near the end of the play, which
maintains a connection between the signifier and the signified. Writing,
as Kristeva outlines, becomes 'a cache for suffering'; in the unbearable
instability of the boundary between subject and object, 'the narrative is
what is challenged first'; its linearity is shattered up to the scream of a
language which resembles violence and obscenity. Woman's descriptions
of herself in the letter abound in images of a malfunctioning or broken
body (remembering that Scarecrow is her alter ego) and one of the main
reasons for her loss, which possibly contributed to her illness. Her detailed
letter is a last attempt to sublimate her traumas and maintain some kind
of identity right until the end. While her death will obviously take her
identity, how she lived might still be reconciled before her death if she
can retrieve aspects of it. As Auntie Ah tells her: 'How we die says it all
about how we have lived.'[168] Woman's sense of authority, together with her
confrontation with betrayal and death, all converge in her efforts to direct
how she will be laid to rest. She asks for what's left of her baby's coffin to
be placed on hers, for a carriage, four black horses and a coachman to take
her to the grave, to be buried wearing particular clothes, not to have her
hands crossed and wrapped in rosary beads, for people to refrain from
kissing her corpse and for the funeral party to be excessive, ensuring that
there will be lots of food and drink so that people can get drunk. She asks
that Demis Roussos's music be played while her sons take her coffin from

167   Carr, *Woman and Scarecrow*, p. 48.
168   Carr, *Woman and Scarecrow*, p. 45.

the coach to her grave. Yet her alter ego writes the other part of her letter, which betrays her hurt, loss and rejection.

Scarecrow's letter significantly attacks Him for his betrayal, deceit, cowardice, infidelities, secrets, absence, empty promises, lies and abandonment over the years of his marriage to Woman:

> SCARECROW: Heading into the dark I want to leave a trail of darkness after me. I want you to wake at three in the morning and think of me packed into the cold clay and when you think of me down there I want you to realise that you have killed me as surely as if you had taken an ice pick and plunged it to the hilt.[169]

The letter reveals the extent to which Him's painful dismissal of her caused her great distress. As a result, Scarecrow's written part of Woman's letter demonstrates how her inner world enters the symbolic order, whose writings represent how Woman did commit 'the greatest sin of all' by not being good to herself.[170] Scarecrow tells her that she is dying out of spite, that she is disappointed with life and therefore did not cope with what life dealt to her – 'The world has not yielded up all you had hoped.'[171]

Woman's strict instructions about her funeral arrangements and the bitterness at Him's treatment of her in the letter are a *crying-out theme* of abjection, a drama 'of suffering-horror.'[172] The letter is Woman's attempt to ascertain her self by literally writing herself into the symbolic order and thereby avoid being swallowed up by the loss that threatens to dissolve her identity and leave her in a state similar to that of the semiotic order: 'The abject finds expression and containment in writing. Outside of the sacred, the abject is written.'[173] Kristeva maintains that talking of 'the aesthetic task – [is] a descent into the foundations of the symbolic construct – [which] amounts to retracing the fragile limits of the speaking being, closest to its dawn, to the bottomless "primacy" constituted by primal repression.'[174]

169 Carr, *Woman and Scarecrow*, p. 54.
170 Carr, *Woman and Scarecrow*, p. 44.
171 Carr, *Woman and Scarecrow*, p. 18.
172 Kristeva, *Powers of Horror*, p. 140.
173 Kristeva, *Powers of Horror*, p. 18.
174 Kristeva, *Powers of Horror*, p. 18.

The letter can thus be seen as an exploration of the abject; 'metaphoriza-tion in order to keep from being frightened to death' so that Woman can come to life again in signs.[175]

Woman and Scarecrow presents a link between the threat of abjection and the maternal body. Within the world of the play, particularly regard-ing representations of the female body within systems of family and home, Woman is articulated as the abject other of the symbolic order. Woman's severing of links with family and home foregrounds Freud's notion of the 'unhomeliness'. The unhomely and uncanny (*unheimlich*) as the 'class of the frightening which leads back to what is known of the old and familiar' is revealed, with family and home as empty spaces, significant in terms of the distance they indicate.[176] Freud's meaning of *heimlich* conceals and keeps out of sight what is familiar while *unheimlich* brings to light what is kept within.[177] The unhomeliness of the familiar in the play calls attention to the frailty of the boundaries between self and other. Woman moves through spaces of disquiet where the displacement from the world around her is matched by her sense of self-abjection. The world presented in the play is therefore a frightening web of entrapment placing her in a permanent state of dislocation.

Perhaps Carr is responding to the phobic symbolic order presented in *Woman and Scarecrow*, which has established its position by the abjection of Woman. It may be that Carr is confronting the mythic and idealistic representation of female otherness, by presenting an otherness which reveals the strict system of gender identity and social order. Observing, engaging and responding to such structures helps in their invalidation and potential deconstruction.

175   Kristeva, *Powers of Horror*, p. 38.
176   Sigmund Freud, *The Standard Edition of the Complete Psychological Works of Sigmund Freud*, James Strachey (ed.), Vol. 17 (London: The Hogarth Press, 1955), p. 220.
177   Freud, p. 225.

Coagulated Blood, Congealed Blood and Mixed Blood

The Mai (1994), *Portia Coughlan* (1996) and *By the Bog of Cats* (1998), known as 'Carr's Trilogy', mark a shift towards the conscious struggle with individual and collective subjectivity that requires the delineation of borders between the 'self' and 'other'. These plays' obsession with loss and the manifestation of suicide evokes a process of cultural formation that is similar to Kristeva's conception of signification and cultural production. The representational dynamics of the plays relate closely to the significatory tensions Kristeva outlines. Kristeva maintains that the struggle for cultural and individual identification is marked by attempts to establish borders between what is acceptable, identified positively as attributes of the self, and what is unacceptable or abject, identified negatively as separate from the self. Equally important is Kristeva's assertion that the abject preserves what was abjected in the significatory process, remaining an essential part of the dialectical semiosis through which culture and the individual identify themselves. Carr's characters, conscious of the historical and cultural forces that shape and act upon them, reflect both individual and cultural attempts to position the self between the 'positive identifying' and the 'negative abject', specifically manifested in resistances towards the symbolic representation of the subordination of woman and her relegation to the domestic role. Kristeva also maintains that cultural formations are based on patriarchal rejections or sublimations of the generative power of the feminine and that the role of the mother in the production of culture is suppressed in patriarchal orders. Carr's trilogy, read in this way, reveals the rejection of both the female body and the feminine imagination in cultural formation.

This chapter examines the three plays together in terms of their similarities in both form and content. Although retaining non-natural and
theatrical elements of Carr's earlier works, such as the use of fantasy, storytelling and repetition, the trilogy follows a more recognisable linear narrative pattern, examining how Ireland's cultural and historical developments
are inextricably linked and embody the imprint of a vast range of social
meanings. Abjection is explored through the issues of discrimination,
bigotry, hypocrisy and violence that surround the plays' troubled familial
relationships. The Trilogy offers the female characters paths of negotiation
for femalehood, demonstrating resistances towards female subjectivity, to
what McMullan states as 'their critique of the lack of accommodation of
difference in small town or rural Ireland.'[1] The discussion will demonstrate how Carr allows her females a sense of authority and agency, which
ultimately leads to their choice of suicide.

Colonial and postcolonial theory, which examines particular kinds of
abject conditions in the production of individual and collective identities,
is used here. In terms of a collective identity, the relationship between the
colonised and the coloniser under imperialist structures reveals how the
'dominant' culture is seen as greater than its colonised. Colonial practice
ultimately sees the colonised as passive in their relationship with the coloniser. The equivalent power relation within the construction of individual
identity, sees the hierarchy of gender, aligning the coloniser with masculinity and the colonised with femininity.

Carr's plays offer a forum where the culturally coded symbolic and
actual representations of the female are given scrutiny. The representation
of woman in Irish postcolonial discourse in the context of Carr's trilogy
critically engages with the female and demonstrates the extent to which
various constructions, deconstructions, appropriations and manipulations
of her manifest in the dramas. Specifically, the role of woman within the

---

1   Anna McMullan, 'Gender, Authorship and Performance in Contemporary Irish
     Women Playwrights: Mary Elizabeth Burke-Kennedy, Marie Jones, Marina Carr,
     Emma Donoghoe', in Eamonn Jordan (ed.), *Theatre Stuff: Critical Essays on
     Contemporary Irish Theatre* (Dublin: Carysfort Press, 2000), p. 41.

Irish family is centre stage in Carr's plays. The Irish family is defined by
the Constitution within the institute of marriage by the model of father,
mother and child(ren). Marriage is validated in accordance with, the law
and the state, and is the dominant ideology by which 'family' is classi-
fied. 'Family' relates to authority and social order, and is indispensable to
the welfare of the Nation and State. Siblings within the family dynamic
fall under the control of the designated role of their parents. As Kieran
McKeown notes:

> Parenting can be seen as having two interrelated aspects: the provider or 'investment'
> role and the caring or 'involvement' role. Traditionally, the father's role was defined
> by investment while the mother's role was defined by involvement.[2]

As a microcosm of wider society, the nuclear family helped to reinforce
strict notions of gendered divisions.

The problematic notion of family in Ireland finds itself at the centre
of much dramatic action in both traditional and contemporary Irish theatre, and is also central in the trilogy.[3] 'Familism' was the term given by
American anthropologists C.M. Arensberg and S.T. Kimball to the typical
traditional Irish patriarchal socio-economic system, whereby property and
wealth were exchanged between families as part of marriage dowries, with
the female subordinated within the transaction.[4]

Carr's representation of the female as central protagonist in *The Mai*,
Portia Coughlan and *By the Bog of Cats* marks a moment of re-appropriation
and re-configuration of female representation. The trilogy contests the kind
of family structure outlined in the Constitution in various and numerous ways, and presents invented realms of 'escape' within the drama from

2   Kieran McKeown, Harry Ferguson & Dermot Rooney, *Changing Fathers?* (Cork:
     Collins Press, 1997), pp. 27–28.
3   See W.B. Yeats' *Countess Cathleen* (1899), Yeats and Lady Gregory's *Cathleen Ni
     Houlihan* (1902), J.M. Synge's *In the Shadow of the Glen* (1903), Martin McDonagh's
     The Beauty Queen of Leenane (1996) and *The Lonesome West* (1997), Enda Walsh's
     The Walworth Farce (2006) and *The New Electric Ballroom* (2008) for example.
4   C.M. Arensberg and S.T. Kimball, *Family and Community in Ireland* (Cambridge,
     MA: Harvard University Press, 1968).

the defined gendered roles of family life. Dream, fantasy, storytelling and myth are used as a kind of privileged realm of femininity, with gender roles in the family portrayed in these arenas. The characters have difficulty in playing these defined roles, specifically matriarchal and patriarchal responsibilities, and so all the energies which might in a conventional way have been invested in the family are instead engaged in wayward journeys. The exploration of the characters in these invented mythic and fantastic realms is connected to contained modes of female representation in Irish culture. Melissa Sihra observes that Carr's plays offer a valuable kind of subversion, 'where lyrical narratives of memory and flashback disrupt temporal and "historical" linearity effecting a repeated discordance between subjective "truth" and speculative invention.'[5]

Carr's women both perpetuate and subvert elements of traditional and contemporary Irish theatre, particularly the common themes of family, rural Ireland and the Catholic Church. Her plays show how women under a powerful patriarchy strive for autonomy. The chapter explores Carr's Trilogy in relation to Irish cultural notions of woman, motherhood and femininity, in order to fully engage with Kristeva's theory of abjection, particularly in relation to violence and the maternal.

Coagulated Blood

The Mai retells the past and familial relationships, with their complex dynamics, in order to project a contemporary drama of a woman's history. Events from Ireland's colonial past are brought into direct confrontation with the polyvocal, multivalent postcolonial present. As the frame and structure of the narrative is filtered through the voice of a central narrator,

5   Melissa Sihra, 'Reflections Across Water – New Stages of Performing Carr' in Cathy Leeney and Anna McMullan (eds), *The Theatre of Marina Carr: "before rules was made"* (Dublin: Carysfort Press, 2003), p. 94.

the audience is reminded that *The Mai* is a memory play. The intermittent dialogue is the arena in which the competing voices of the past and the present do battle in an 'imagistic' sequence of actions that deals with connection and disconnection, exploitation and retaliation, cultivation and neglect.

The Mai intersperses the Irish penchant for oratory, but it also dramatises the contention that events are meaningful mainly insofar as they become stories told by their participants. Meaning resides not only in what actually happens in stories, but also in who narrates and participates in them and to whom they are told. In relation to recalling events from the past, Michel Rolph Trouillot states:

> Human beings participate in history both as actors and as narrators. The inherent ambivalence of the word 'history' in many modern languages, including English, suggests this dual participation. In vernacular use, history means both the facts of the matter and a narrative of those facts, both 'what happened' and 'that which is said to have happened'.[6]

Though Millie's narrative is a personal history, the lives of the people remembered and filtered by her reveal a significant sense of loss. As Kristeva notes,

> narrative is all in all, the elaborate attempt ... to situate a speaking being between his desires and their prohibitions, whose intimate side is suffering and horror its public feature.[7]

On the one hand, the Mai sews, drinks, welcomes the women of her family into her home, and performs domestic chores. Gradually however, one becomes aware that the play is also concerned with language beyond the text. Millie's narrative distorts, builds illusions and hurts, instead of conveying 'truth', feelings and ideas. Echoing Carr's early plays, short 'throw away' lines or instances become important elements in the narrative; for

6   Michel-Rolph Trouillot, *Silencing the Past: Power and the Production of History* (Boston: Beacon Press, 1995), p. 2.
7   Kristeva, p. 140.

example, Millie's request to go with her parents into town is met by her mother's reply: 'Some other evening', to which Millie responds 'Tch'.[8] There is a discrepancy between what the family says and what it does. Millie is not simply a voyeur; she also takes part in the action of the play. The fact that the stage directions place Millie onstage throughout, points to a text beyond the verbal. A look, a silence, the music, gesture and movement in the drama become significant. In the Kristevan sense, 'the narrative yields to a crying-out theme ... of suffering and horror.'[9]

The drama explores the troubled voices that occupy Millie's memories. Her identity is shaped as much by the ghosts of the past as by the symbols and icons of the present in Irish patriarchal culture. The past is seen to impinge in various ways on the present. Trouillot notes:

> [T]he past does not exist independently from the present. Indeed the past is only past because there is a present, just as I can point to something over there only because I am here. But nothing is inherently over there or here. In that sense the past has no content. The past – or more accurately, pastness – is a position.[10]

In this sense, Millie's retrieval of *her* past calls into being four generations of the Mai's family. The play's temporal setting is Summer 1979 and Summer 1980, looking back a century to 1879, through references made by Grandma Fraochlán, and the focus is on the historical and cultural developments that have shaped Irish women's identity through this century. Millie's narration calls up the disparate characters that engage her in the forces that shape her identity, and through the filtered dramatic action, Millie becomes a voice through which a contentious image, not only of her personal identity but also of a larger cultural identity, begins to emerge.

Similar to the typical country kitchen setting common in Irish domestic drama throughout the century, with the relegation of women to the private sphere, *The Mai* takes place entirely in the sitting room of the Mai's family home, built by The Mai and located in the Midlands of Ireland.

---

8   Marina Carr, *The Mai* (Oldcastle, Co. Meath: Gallery Press, 1995), p. 27.
9   Kristeva, p. 140.
10 Trouillot, *Silencing the Past*, p. 15.

The two-act drama opens with the return of Robert, the Mai's husband, unannounced, after a five year absence, and it tells the story of the complex relationships in the Mai's family, which includes her husband and daughter Millie, Grandma Fraochlán, her two sisters, Beck and Connie, and her two aunts, Julie and Agnes. Millie is described in the stage directions as both sixteen and thirty years of age, which enables the play's time to sway forward and backward through the dramatic content and form.

Early in Act 1, Millie reveals the death of the Mai. The plot continues as a theatrical enquiry of how her death came about. Her brisk articulation of her mother's suicide points to her evasion of the effects that the event has had on her. Ernst Van Alphen refers to 'the cause of trauma as precisely the impossibility of experiencing and subsequently memorising the event' as the 'failed experience' of the past.[11] Millie's renunciation of the event reproduces and recreates her past as a means to have access to the house on Owl Lake, her childhood home and the site of her mother's suicide. Millie's difficulty in telling this past event is not located in the event itself but in the processes of the experience through her familial narrative. She demonstrates how 'the narrative is a cache for suffering.'[12] Kristeva notes that 'when narrated identity is shaken, and when the boundary between subject and object is shaken ... the narrative is what is challenged first.'[13] The displacement of The Mai's suicided body struggles to protect the individual and culture, coinciding with the separation of subject from object, as the supplanting of Kristeva's semiotic by the symbolic, of the mother's body by the Law of the Father, involves turning towards the narrative. The Mai's body metaphysically remains whole and harmonious, because her death by suicide is so succinctly revealed, and her presence in the play after her death invokes a 'unifying' drama, signifying the work of the paternal order. But it also reflects Millie's search for a lost cultural and individual childhood. Suicide, the loss of unity from the maternal and the feeling of

---

11 Ernst Van Alphen, 'Symptoms of Discursivity: Experience, Memory, and Trauma', in Mieke Bal, Jonathan Crewe and Leo Spitzer (eds), *Acts of Memory: Cultural Recall in the Present* (Hanover, NH: University Press of New England, 1999), pp. 25–26.
12 Kristeva, p. 140.
13 Kristeva, p. 141.

emptiness remain suppressed and repressed in and through Millie's narrative. In this context, emphasis is given to the forms of discourse that Millie calls upon to create a degree of distance from it. As Van Alphen points out: 'To be part of an event or of a history as an object of its happening is not the same as experiencing it as a subject ... Experience is the transposition of the event to the realm of the subject.'[14] Millie's memory narrative then is directly related to everything that is left behind by the maternal abject. Joseph Roach, writing about collective memory describes 'the three sided relationship of memory, performance and substitution in the reproduction of culture' as a process of 'surrogation':

> In the life of a community, the process of surrogation does not begin or end but continues as actual or perceived vacancies occur in the network of relations that constitutes the social fabric. Into the cavities created by loss through death or other forms of departure, survivors attempt to fit satisfactory alternates. Because collective memory works selectively, imaginatively and often perversely, surrogation if ever rarely succeeds.[15]

Millie depicts a similar process that incorporates many ruptures and calamities. Her father suddenly becomes the surrogate mother figure because of her mother's suicide, and this creates a deficit, which taps deep into Millie's prejudices and fears, provoking unbidden familial memories. Significantly, she immediately continues with the narrative after announcing her mother's death, going back to her own and her mother's response to Robert's departure when Millie was eleven: 'So The Mai and I went into town and sat in the Bluebell Hotel where The Mai downed six Paddy's and red and I had six lemon-and-limes.'[16] She denies her father, which could be construed as a failure on his part to ensure the separation between the mother and child. His literal and metaphorical abandonment from Millie's life, his blatant infidelities, his failure to recognise his daughter after a five-year absence, and his general lack of parental support represent the breakdown in the

---

14   Van Alphen, p. 27.
15   Joseph Roach, *Cities of the Dead: Circum – Atlantic Performance* (New York: Columbia University Press, 1996), p. 2.
16   Carr, *The Mai*, p. 13.

paternal function, which produces the abject. His failure to enforce the symbolic law ultimately signals its collapse. Millie's opening question to her father on his return is accusatory:

> ROBERT: Now let me see, is it Orla or Millie?
> THE MAI: Millie
> ROBERT: Millie.
> THE MAI: She's sixteen now.
> ROBERT: I bought sweets for the children – but I suppose you're too big for sweets.
> [...]
> MILLIE: Where were you?
> ROBERT: Here – there –
> MILLIE: Everywhere. We were here all the time and in the old house.[17]

Millie accommodates the central familial historical events through the process of memory, indicating the significance of what she recalls. When The Mai refuses to share Robert with Millie by taking her with them into town on the first evening of his return, Robert promises to take her the next day as a consolation but Millie states:

> Maybe we did go into town the following day, I don't remember. It is beyond me now to imagine how we would've spent that day, where we would have gone, what we would have talked about ... We're well matched, neither gives an inch, we can't, it's life and death as we see it. And that's why I cannot remember that excursion into town if it ever occurred.[18]

In the sense of defiance that permeates her relationship with her father's, echoes of Friel's memoirs resonate:

> And since there is no lake, my father and I never walked back from it in the rain with our rods across our shoulders. Have I imagined the scene, then? Or is it a composite of two or three different episodes? The point is – I don't think it really matters. What matters is that for some reason ... this vivid memory is there in the storehouse of

17 Carr, *The Mai*, pp. 12–13.
18 Carr, *The Mai*, pp. 27–28.

the mind. For some reason the mind had shuffled the pieces of veritable truth and composed a truth of its own.[19]

Like Friel's account of an event that may or may not have ever taken place, Millie's memory too flies in the face of belief.

Millie, as narrator of the play, is isolated from the other characters, making physical for the audience her emotional and at times experiential isolation from her family. In one sense, she is split from the suicide event and from her family, while she also allows her memories to be ascribed to the family. What emerges from this is the play's insistence on the subjectivity of personal identity channelled through memory. Millie experiences the connections in her world when her narrative gives way to the forces at play behind her memory. Yet as Van Alphen notes:

> Events never stand on their own. We experience events not as isolated happenings, and happenings cannot be experienced in isolation. Events always have a prehistory, and they are themselves again the prehistory of events that are still going to happen.[20]

Suicide closes off all expectations of coming events because it is so sudden and final. The Mai's family, left to cope with the consequences of it, incorporates the response of the community to the family after the event as well as the family's response to the community. Millie's narrative is progressively enhanced by the images liberated in the dreams, storytelling, monologue and myth. Framed by her, the play's historical, familial and sexual forces seek expression throughout the drama in these realms of her existence.

The play's setting, the house on Owl Lake, is the primal scene for Millie's lost and found childhood. It represents the *chora*, the maternal space where the developing child is nurtured by the mother's response to its needs in the womb. The space represents a time of plenitude between child and mother, where the child experiences the world without prescribed sense, where feelings of pleasure and pain are indefinite in terms of their

---

19   Christopher Murray (ed). *Brian Friel: Essays, Diaries, Interviews: 1964–1999* (London: Faber and Faber, 1999), p. 135.

20   Alphen, p. 33.

origin. The 'home' as a spatial boundary is where the (re)construction of Millie's subjectivity emerges. McMullan states: '"Home" in Irish theatre never seems to be a place, but a past memory or a future possibility.'[21] The house and home on Owl Lake is also the site of the self-destructive feminine, and as a memorial to the suicide of The Mai it marks the collapse of the semiotic. It induces a simultaneous fear and fascination in Millie, a return to the space of the maternal semiotic, to 'the place where meaning collapses.'[22]

The appellative origin of Owl Lake is mythically and literally associated with the turbulence and disorder of the feminine. The legend of Owl Lake takes on a retrospective ominous quality as Millie explains the origins of the lake and the family's blindness to 'gods and mortals [who] called out for us to change our course, and, not listening, we walked on and on.'[23] Abjection cries out through the story of the lake, recounting the suffering of the family. Millie recalls the tale of how *Coillte*, daughter of the mountain god, fell in love with *Bláth*, Lord of the flowers, lovers doomed by tragic destiny. *Bláth*, meaning flower in Gaelic and coinciding with the Summer season when flowers bloom, explains to *Coillte* that he must leave in Autumn to live with the dark witch of the bog, but he will return in Spring. Overwhelmed by her sense of loss, *Coillte*, determined to search for her abandoned lover, follows him, to find that he is 'frozen' by the dark witch's spell. *Coillte* lies down and cries a lake of tears, which forms Owl Lake. One night the dark witch pushes her into it and she drowns. Millie's subjectivity is connected to the mythic landscape of the lake, metaphorically entangling her in the maternal. She says:

> We teeter along the fringe of the world with halting gait, reeking of Owl Lake at every turn. I dream of water all the time. I'm floundering off the shore, or bursting towards the surface for air, or wrestling with a black swan trying to drag me under. I

---

21   Anna McMullan in 'Unhomely Stages: Women Taking (a) Place in Irish Theatre' in Dermot Bolger (ed.), *Druids, Dudes And Beauty Queens: The Changing Face of Irish Theatre* (Dublin: Arts Council, 2001), p. 72.

22   Kristeva, *Powers of Horror*, p. 2.

23   Carr, *The Mai*, p. 42.

have not yet emerged triumphant from those lakes of the night. Sometimes I think
I wear Owl Lake like a caul around my chest to protect me from all that is good and
hopeful and worth pursuing.[24]

The family all knew the tale of Owl Lake and the tale's legend of love replicates the doomed love story of Millie's parents: Coillte who drowns is
echoed by The Mai taking her life. The family's suffering bleeds beyond
the narrative, to

> a beyond made up of sense and measure. Beyond the narrative, dizziness finds its
> language: music, as breath of words, rhythm of sentences, and not only as metaphor
> of an imaginary rival where the voice of the mother and of death is hiding.[25]

The powerful presence of the past, continuously triggered by the waters
of the lake, hauntingly reminds The Mai's family of the genealogical mis-
fortune contained in its blueprint.

Born in 1879 and having lived through a century of social and cultural changes in Ireland, Grandma Fraochlán signifies the living past in
the present; the pathways of her history have brought her into the future.
She is portrayed as 'other' in the play; a woman for whom the notions
of 'home' and of 'Irishness' are unstable. She is the hybridity of the Irish
national experience caught between Declan Kiberd's debate about Irish
identity, being an 'exponent of multiple selfhood' and an exponent of 'a
pure, unitary race, dedicated to defending a romantic notion of integrity.'[26]
Grandma Fraochlán's painful process of identity resonates in the comment
that she 'was the on'y bastard on Fraochlán in livin' memory an' tha' stigma
must've bin terrible for her.'[27] Writing about nineteenth century Ireland,
Dympna McLoughlin describes how:

---

24   Carr, *The Mai*, p. 71.
25   Kristeva, p. 146.
26   Declan Kiberd, *Inventing Ireland: The Literature of a Modern Nation* (Cambridge,
     MA: Harvard University Press, 1995), p. 7.
27   Carr, *The Mai*, p. 60.

Sexual activity was affected by marital status, social and economic position, conditioning mores with their strict defined codes of respectability, and the ostracisation that would be directed at those who failed to conform in terms of chastity and virtue.[28]

Through the persona of Millie, Carr posits how forms of subjectivity are largely composed of undigested memories, which emerge in various forms of dreams, storytelling, monologue and myth, that create socially and culturally loaded concepts of identity. Such a state of subjectivity ties in with the Kristevan sense of disunity for the abject being, where what was abjected in the early stages of development continues to remain on the margins of subjectivity, constantly testing the tenuous borders of selfhood. Millie's various kinds of memory are a significant theatrical vehicle in the effectiveness of the drama. Ontological delusions and distortions continue to articulate the genealogy of The Mai's family, through these realms of undigested memory. They are the very instruments of over-determined signification, which are the symptomatic yearning for their sense of loss. For Millie, they are the avenues where her thoughts are confronted in a difficult and at times painful process of self-examination and self-criticism in the context of her family.

Millie needs to reimagine Grandma Fraochlán's past through the romantic and idealised figure of grandma's husband, the 'nine-fingered fisherman'.[29] Grandma Fraochlán's name brings to Millie's mind

a thousand memories ... She was the result of a brief tryst between an ageing island spinster and a Spanish or Moroccan sailor ... There were many stories about him as there are about those who appear briefly in our lives and change them for ever ... Whoever he was, he left Grandma Fraochlán his dark skin and a yearning for all that was exotic and unattainable.[30]

---

28 Dympna McLoughlin, 'Women and Sexuality in Nineteenth-Century Ireland', in Alan Hayes and Diane Urquhart (eds), *The Irish Women's History Reader* (London: Routledge, 2001), p. 79.
29 Carr, *The Mai*, p. 22.
30 Carr, *The Mai*, p. 18.

Grandma Fraochlán's genealogy is shrouded in dubious circumstances that forge her personal characteristics, specifically her dark skin, attributed to foreign identity.

Cultural pressure from the island community where she grew up, and disdain shown to her family because they did not conform to a common and dominant behavioural lifestyle, constantly remind her of her absent father and the ways in which her mother compensated for his absence. The early stages of how Grandma Fraochlán came to see herself in the world therefore, as a discrete subject from her mother, her father (significant in his absence) and the wider community at large, situate her between her desires and their prohibitions. The development of Grandma Fraochlán in the narrative sums up the mythic variant of abjection. Entering the island as the bastard offspring of her mother, she undertakes to purify her subjectivity. However, her body permanently carries the concentration of abjection, with her skin as the constant reminder of the loss of selfhood, the 'other that I am but will never reach.'[31]

As the scapegoat figure of 'defilement' on the island, who struggles to free herself from the burden of her ambiguous identity (symbolised by her skin) and manifested centrally in the fear and disappointment which surrounds the absence of her father and her over-compensating mother, she is the character who 'stands on the fragile threshold as if stranded on account of an impossible demarcation.'[32] Homi K. Bhabha observes how 'Skin as the key signifier of cultural and racial difference in the stereotype … is recognised as "common knowledge" in a range of cultural, political and historical discourses.'[33] Bhabha's concept of *ambivalence* in stereotypical discourse recognises within fetishistic identification that the construction of discriminatory knowledges 'depends on the "presence of difference" [which] provide a process of splitting and multiple/contradictory belief at the point of enunciation and subjectification.'[34] Bhabha suggests that stereotypical

---

31   Kristeva, p. 150.
32   Kristeva, pp. 84–85.
33   Bhabha, p. 78.
34   Bhabha, p. 80.

knowledges are recognised as a means of practical control, kept separate from the authorative justifications of them. Grandma Fraochlán embodies Bhabha's notion of ambivalence in colonial fantasy. Millie articulates her grandmother's difference, which affords her subjectivity no security in her personal and cultural identity. Grandma Fraochlán enacts what Bhabha outlines as the 'move away from the singularities of "class" or "gender" as primary conceptual and organisational categories ... that inhabit any claim to identity in the modern world.'[35] She occupies the Bhabhaian notion of 'collaboration and contestation' because her identity exists on the periphery of perceptions of 'Irishness'.[36] Her 'fixed' position as a colonial fantasy proposes a reformable teleology of colonial domination and control, while at the same time it makes visible her separation from it, signifying a disruption to stable concepts of identity.

Fantasy is a reminder of the semiotic in Millie's mental life, breaking from the constraints of a law-governed symbolic order and operating as a means of dealing with prejudice, alienation and displacement. But fantasy also connotes purpose in the lives of The Mai's family. In 'Irish Drama and the Fantastic', Christopher Murray cites Kathryn Hume's definition of fantasy in literature as, 'Any departure from consensus reality [which all relate to] ways of giving a sense to meaning.'[37] The tale of Millie's great grandmother, who is referred to by the mythic title 'The Duchess', invents a story around her mysterious paternity:

> [H]e'd hid The Duchess an' meself an Fraochlán because we were too beautiful for tha worlt. Buh in tha summer he was goin' ta come in a yach' an' take us away ta his palace in Spain. An' we'd be dressed in silks an' pearls an' have Blackamoors dancin' attindence an us an' everyone on Fraochlán'd be cryin' wud jealousy – an' I believt her an' watched an tha cliffs ever'day for the Sultan of a Spain. An' ah th'end a every

---

35 Bhabha, p. 1.
36 Bhabha, p. 2.
37 Christopher Murray in 'Irish Drama and the Fantastic' in Donald E. Morse and Csilla Bertha (eds), *More Real Than Reality: The Fantastic in Irish Literature and the Arts* (New York: GreenWood Press, 1991), p. 86.

summer tha Sultan would noh've arrived an' ah' th' end a every summer Tha Duchess'd
say, ih musta bin next summer he meant.[38]

The elaborately concocted tale of Grandma Fraochlán's father is a form of
protection from social condemnation, incorporating feelings of waiting
and yearning, two forces which in the Kristevan context point to the significance of Millie's remembered familial narratives: 'The world of illusions
(dreams, fantasy, myth) brings to light or embodies the prohibition that
has us speak.'[39] Millie's sense of loss is reinforced by the Duchess's continued belief that one Summer the Sultan will return. Dympna McLoughlin
writes about the inextricable links between gender, class, economics and
sexuality in nineteenth century Ireland:

> The daughters of the thrifty and wealthy were continuously watched and gossiped
> about. This gossip served as social control on their actions ... In this sense, sexual
> prudery in nineteenth-century Ireland had little to do with the Church and all to
> do with the economics of the emerging middle class.[40]

Sexual prudery alongside the strong hold of the Catholic Church on a
small island community in *The Mai* would have been enough to radically
marginalize the 'Duchess' and her illegitimate child. The Duchess's tales are
appropriate realms of safety against the island's oppressive social environment. Adrian Frazier argues that by the end of the nineteenth century

> the purity of Ireland's women had become a plank in the nationalist program: every
> crown colony is bound to be thought of as a slut, used at the pleasure of the Empire
> – Ireland alone, though poor, is pure. Critics may mock the status of chastity as a
> virtue, but one cannot deny its importance both to Irish nationalist thought and in
> Irish behaviour.[41]

---

38   Carr, *The Mai*, pp. 58–59.
39   Kristeva, p. 133.
40   McLoughlin in *The Irish Women's History Reader*, p. 85.
41   Adrian Frazier, *Behind the Scenes: Yeats, Horniman and the Struggle for the Abbey
      Theatre* (Berkeley: California University Press, 1990), p. 135.

If, as Grandma Fraochlán argues, 'we repeat and we repeat, the orchestration may be different but the tune is always the same', then Millie's family is trapped in a cycle of repetition created by the legacy of their forbearers. Here, the present struggles to free itself from the powers of the past, and demonstrates the persistent tendency to replay the past. In line with this, Millie embodies her Grandmother's contention. An unmarried mother with a five year old son, Joseph, who 'expects far too little of me, something I must have taught him unknown to myself,'[42] Millie's constructed fantasy echoes the Duchess's story of Grandma Fraochlán's 'Spanish Sailor'. Millie tells Joseph that his father was 'an Elsalvadorian drummer who swept me off my feet when I was lost in New York.'[43] Although single parenthood is now very common in contemporary Ireland, Millie demonstrates the emotional and romantic burden that is so much a part of her matrilineal history.[44] Her psychological constructs are the attachments she has to her family history. Her life strongly parallels those of the other women in her family, above all, the difficult relationship with lovers that is reflected as one of the play's major themes. The Duchess, Grandma Fraochlán, The Mai and Millie construct lovers more 'other' than in reality because of their need to escape their painful and pressurised situation. They all hunger for something more valid and valuable in terms of their intimate relationships. Their abject 'gap' is created when life's facts do not coincide with their desires, resulting in an abject loss that all the characters struggle to come to terms with.

Dreams operate in the play according to Freud's theory in *Interpretation of Dreams*, that is, as unfulfilled desires that offer avenues of contact between the conscious and the unconscious (see the discussion on *Marble*). The characters' dreams mark a distinction between the imaginative and the actual realms of the narrative. The rigid categories of femininity and masculinity within the institution of marriage in the *The Mai* are broken down.

42　Carr, *The Mai*, p. 56.
43　Carr, *The Mai*, p. 56.
44　1 in 6 parents are lone parents. Most lone parents are women. See Dept of the Taoiseach, *Census of Population of Ireland* (Dublin: Irish Central Statistics Office, 2008).

Declan Kiberd outlines the reasons for the illumination of dreams in Synge's *Playboy*, which seem to apply to *The Mai* too. Kiberd states that where

> the facts seem more brutal than ever, the dreams [become] even more unreal. Instead of closing with one another in a dancing dialectic, they move further apart, leaving society unredeemed and apparently unredeemable.[45]

Worlds of otherness proliferate and supplement a harsher reality in the absence of solid relationships.

In The Mai and Robert's dreams, both are chasing one another. Dreams, which are the centre of the drama in *Marble*, articulate what Colin Graham calls 'the need for the "unrealizable and faraway"'; where 'a plethora of images creates a fantasy of a "projected utopianism which acts as a bait and a promise."'[46] Mai and Robert chase the bait, but that goal disappoints them and leads them into empty and broken promises. Both Robert and The Mai are searching for points of connection between competing needs and desires, some of which would normally be prohibited in reality. In Robert's dream of the Mai he is 'running, running, running over water, trees, mountains, though I've long lost sight of the carriage and of you.'[47] In the dream he comes to see her funeral cortege on the water. His dream image of The Mai as dead, 'my cello case was your coffin and a carriage drawn by two black swans [which] take you over a dark expanse of water' is significantly prophetic.[48] Robert's visual image of The Mai's death in the dream is associated with the responsibility he feels for her suicide. His dream images act as realms of liberation from rules and codified behaviour associated with the symbolic. Indeed the position of men in the Republic of Ireland in the 1937 Constitution sees 'man' and 'father' used interchangeably, with an overarching notion of paternal roles as head of the household and central 'breadwinner'. In Robert's dream he is free from all strict categories of masculinity, unable to play the role of the contemporary father

---

45   Kiberd, *Inventing Ireland*, p. 170.
46   Graham, *Deconstructing Ireland*, p. 5.
47   Carr, *The Mai*, p. 25.
48   Carr, *The Mai*, p. 25.

figure and husband. The guilt he feels for having abandoned The Mai for five years comes out in his recurring dream of her death. Like Woman who returns to Man in *The Cordelia Dream* as a result of a dream, Robert states that losing sight of The Mai in the dream caused him to return to her at Owl Lake: 'And I wake, pack my bags, take the next plane home.'[49] The play opens with his return:

> ... *Silence. For the first time Robert looks at her [The Mai], cello bow in his hand.*
> ROBERT: Well – Well – Well.
> *He taps her on shoulder, hip bone, ankle, on each of the 'Wells'.*
> THE MAI: Just look at you.
> ROBERT: You're as beautiful as ever.
> THE MAI: Am I?
> *Now he plays the cello bow across her breasts. The Mai laughs. Softer*
> ROBERT: Like this? Hmm?
> THE MAI: Yeah.[50]

The image reconfigures the lived relation with other subjects in the exchange of psychic energies. Psychic energies, such as desires and demands, are always potentially transferable onto an 'other'. For Robert, The Mai's body is the site of sexual desire (and death), communicating as the physical 'other', whereas for The Mai communicates as the mental other. Mind and body in this instance disconnect, with Robert disengaging from the affective part and displacing his desires and demands onto The Mai. He needs her as a sort of waste bin so that she becomes a kind of castrated 'other'.

The sexual energy in the image of Robert playing The Mai's body, the cello shape closely resembling the female body, is linked to the fatal drive presented in the dream of her cortege, complete with the cello case coffin, and drawn by Carr's common portentous death motif of the swan.[51] The

---

49　Carr, *The Mai*, p. 25.
50　Carr, *The Mai*, pp. 11–12.
51　The black swan is also featured in *By the Bog of Cats* as a death motif and is the origin of the name of protagonist Hester Swane. Additionally in an interview Marina Carr discusses ghosts as well as the significance of swans in relation to her own mother's death. Carr describes the swan as 'the soul bird'. See Clíodhna NiAnluain (ed.),

cello case, a symbolic reminder of Robert's failed music career as well as of his elusive lifestyle, is connected to his murderous thoughts of The Mai. The images of the bed and the coffin are merged in his dream, placing his efforts as a husband alongside his inability to fulfil this role. Robert's murder of The Mai in his dream liberates him from his role as her husband, by literally killing her.

Similarly, the Mai describes for Robert, at his request, her dream of him dying. It is significant that her only dream of his death by her murder, happened 'the night before we got married.'[52] In Act 2, The Mai describes the dream she had when she was a young girl: 'I used to dream that a dark-haired prince would come across the waves on the wings of an albatross and he'd take me away to a beautiful land, never seen or heard of before and he'd love me as no girl had ever been loved.'[53] The fairytale, which commonly outlines rigid notions of male and female categories (see the discussion on *Meat and Salt*) frames The Mai's innocent willingness to run away to live this kind of lifestyle. The same dream moves to when The Mai and Robert were children and the elusive Robert passes her, which The Mai takes as a sign to follow him to 'a black cavern and I know it leads nowhere. And I start walking that way because I know I'll find you there.'[54] The wish in The Mai's girlhood fantasy is actualised in a lesser idyllic reality in adulthood, with her visual imagery of the dark haired prince, albatross and the sea substituted for Owl Lake, Robert and the black swan of death. In expressing how hilarious she finds the dream scene of Robert dying, where she watches 'an old woman put a knife though your [Robert's] heart and you die on the grey pavement,' The Mai demonstrates subversiveness in terms of the role of mother and wife.[55] In the unrestricted world of dreams, she strives for a more valid form of relationship with her husband, even though she knows

---

Reading the Future, Interview with Mike Murphy. Further discussion of ghosts is discussed in this chapter in relation to *Portia Coughlan*.

52   Carr, *The Mai*, p. 25.
53   Carr, *The Mai*, p. 54.
54   Carr, *The Mai*, p. 26.
55   Carr, *The Mai*, p. 26.

it is inevitably destructive and 'leads to nowhere.'[56] Failing the validity of her relationship to Robert, her inability to fulfil the conventional role of mother and wife emerges and ultimately ends with her suicide.

Unfulfilled subjectivity continues with The Duchess's unmarried status, which caused her to invent 'Fraochlán' as her daughter's surname, a name that has no association with their family history. Indeed Fraochlán Island serves as a backdrop to the questions of genealogy and identity. The origin of Grandma Fraochlán's name, as is a common trend in all Carr's plays, carries with it the topography of the landscape where she was reared, as well as metaphorically exemplifying the isolation felt as a result of her 'illegitimacy'. The natural flora and fauna of the Island gives its Gaelic name to Inis Fraochlán, translated as 'the island of heather'. The name reflects the social and cultural burden placed upon Grandma Fraochlán's identity because her mother was unmarried and therefore did not have her father's title. Wallace notes:

> Carr's exploration of the ambivalences of identity is powerfully communicated within the structures she has chosen. Destiny is articulated and implied on a number of levels, through naming, genealogy, memory and storytelling.[57]

Wallace observes: 'For instance Grandma Fraochlán's name emerges as a cipher to a whole family's intricate and unfortunate history of (self) deception.'[58] Similarly the name 'The Mai' indicates strength and authority; her name readapts 'the Irish tradition of adding "the" before the last name of the (male) head of a clan.'[59] Significantly too, the play's temporality indicates that The Mai built her house some time in the 1970s. Like itinerant Hester in *By the Bog of Cats*, the Mai subverts the typical custom

---

56   Carr, *The Mai*, p. 26.
57   Clare Wallace, 'Authentic Reproductions: Marina Carr and the Inevitable', in Cathy Leeney and Anna McMullan (eds), *The Theatre of Marina Carr* (Dublin: Carysfort Press, 2003), p. 60.
58   Wallace in *The Theatre of Marina Carr*, p. 61.
59   Mary Trotter in 'Translating Women into Irish Theatre History', in Stephen Watt, Eileen Morgan and Shakir Mustafa (eds), *A Century of Irish Drama: Widening the Stage* (Bloomington: Indiana University Press, 2000), p. 168.

of male-owned property prevalent in Ireland at that time. In *History Men and History Women: The Politics of Women's History*, Mary Cullen writes how historically women's identity was placed outside of the laws, regulations and customs when they didn't conform to the behaviour patterns prescribed by society, which were predominantly at the hands of men:

> Titles and property passed to sons in preference to daughters. The home was seen as the 'woman's sphere', yet, to take a representative example, under English common law, in force in Ireland, when a woman married her legal identity merged into that of her husband.[60]

The play consistently reveals the ways in which practices of subversion or resistance to dominant patriarchal ways of living mark the family's sense of 'otherness'.

The diminished role of the Catholic Church is taken to parodic lengths in the figures of Grandma Fraochlán's two daughters, Julie, seventy-five and Agnes, sixty-one. In the lives of The Mai's family, the discrepancies between conservative Catholic mores and the experiences of otherness of the characters are exposed; a point echoed and discussed in *By the Bog of Cats, Ariel*, and *Woman and Scarecrow*. Julie's and Agnes's sister Ellen died in childbirth and had to forfeit her education at Trinity College Dublin and her medical career because she became pregnant out of wedlock. Urged into marriage by Grandma Fraochlán, Ellen was deprived of a sense of personal achievement and independence. Her liminal position, between the women's liberation movement, with the prospect of a career that would enable her to be financially independent, and becoming a mother, was short lived:

> CONNIE: [...] She was the only woman in her class doing Medicine the year she entered the Dublin university, and she did it all be herself. I had nothin' in those days –
>
> GRANDMA FRAOCHLÁN: Shame on ya mockin' ya'ar own mother! And thin thah summer in Dublin, half way through her college degree on a wild nigh' of drink an' divilment, me darlin' girl goh pregnant be a brickie.

60   Cullen in *The Irish Women's History Reader*, p. 16.

CONNIE: Ara give over.

GRANDMA FRAOCHLÁN: (*lost in memory*) Oh lord, nineteen years of age, she had to marry him, what else could she do, it was nineteen-thirty-eight.[61]

Grandma Fraochlán, who was the offspring of an unmarried mother, and who experienced all the social stigmas and pressures attached to it, strongly urged Ellen to conform to the social conventions of the day. Dutifully, Ellen got married and had her child but unfortunately she died during childbirth. The narrative gives emphasis to the pressures of the complex dynamics of the Catholic Church, which Kristeva outlines in relation to biblical teachings, that concern 'the structuration of the subject's identity [regarding] the cathexis of maternal function – mother, women and reproduction.'[62] Ellen's circumstances, reminiscent of Grandma Fraochlán's subjectivity and later Millie's identity, demonstrate a departure from biblical (Catholic) precepts in performing

> the tremendous forcing that consists in subordinating maternal power (whether historical or phantasmatic, natural or reproductive) to symbolic order as pure logical order regulating social performance as divine Law.[63]

Millie's two aunts contrast radically with their opium smoking and sexually liberated mother. Unlike Fraochlán, who is symbolically and literally a figure of subversion, Julie and Agnes, keen to maintain and perpetuate the patriarchal social system, present their version of Catholic orthodoxy. Millie narrates how her two aunts arrive at Owl Lake, 'armed with novenas, scapulars and leaflets on the horrors of premarital sex'; assuming that Beck, their niece, is pregnant and is in the process of getting a divorce.[64] However, there can be little doubt as to the sincerity of the aunts' religious zeal, whose comments range from 'I hope to God she's not pregnant' to 'God forbid! A divorcee with a child born after the divorce' to 'with the luck

---

61   Carr, *The Mai*, p. 19.
62   Kristeva, p. 91.
63   Kristeva, p. 91.
64   Carr, *The Mai*, p. 32.

of God she'll miscarry.'[65] As Terence Brown put it: 'the social patterns and attitudes of the latter half of the nineteenth century was ... dominated by a social and cultural conservatism.'[66] Julie and Agnes's attitudes, together with Grandma Fraochlán's failed attempts to resist such attitudes, make sense in light of Brown's portrayal of the repression of the era, particularly surrounding the policing of the female body and behaviour.

For Millie, it is the act of her memory narrative which constantly explores and rediscovers that part of herself that figures loss, namely as the daughter of a mother who has committed suicide and a father who has abandoned her. Millie traces the condition of abjection for The Mai, as her story depicts the gradual development of her mother as an abject subject. The stories of the Mai's family represent possible situations, views of life and ways of coming to terms with the repercussions from the past that Millie is able to envisage. Ultimately, she struggles to play out certain possibilities in terms of her memories. Her subjectivity coagulates within territories of abjection, instead pursuing identifications that might repair her empty and destructive selfhood.[67] The fact that her narrative simply tails off implies that such a journey of abject selfhood is a malaise that will continue in the future.

Congealed Blood

Carr's next drama, *Portia Coughlan*, explores the many conflicting voices of female subjectivity in the contemporary Irish context. The complex nature of Irish female identity, and particularly the seminal influence of

65   Carr, *The Mai*, p. 34.
66   Terence Brown, *Ireland: A Social and Cultural History 1922–1985* (London: Fontana Press, 1985), p. 17.
67   Adrenalin actually causes blood to coagulate. The blood becomes solid and is similar to blood in the dying state.

the mother figure, is explored on stage. The drama examines the troubles occupying Portia, whose problematic identity is shaped as much by the ghost of Gabriel, her dead twin, as by the social ideals of motherhood. Carr presents her version of female subjectivity through Portia, whose life is populated by her disparate familial characters. It is only by engaging in the 'other' world of her dead twin, Gabriel, that Portia can escape from and attempt to come to terms with the forces that shape her identity. Gabriel acts as a symbol of Portia's 'split self', torn between the confines of her home and wanting to escape, between living and wanting to be dead. Her 'split self' is something that repeatedly haunts her throughout. In the semiotic stage, the figure of the exile that identifies with the maternal and yet must separate from her, becomes a wandering stray, seeking love and deprived of her psychic space. Kristeva reminds us that, 'Abjection ... is a kind of narcissistic crisis.'[68] Portia's narcissistic crisis is twinned to the threat of death on the one hand and to the threat of living on the other, to separation and belonging. Her sense of her own ontology is bound up with the ghost and the river, outside of language and of the Symbolic.

Set in the Midlands of Ireland, the eponymous character sits by herself drinking brandy in her living room at ten o'clock in the morning. But she is not alone for long, as her husband Raphael comes back to check on her, under the guise of bringing her birthday present – an expensive but vulgar diamond bracelet. The dialogue opens with him questioning her about the domestic duties:

> RAPHAEL: Ah for fuck's sake. Ten o'clock in the morning and you're at it already.
> PORTIA: Thought you were at work.
> RAPHAEL: I were.
> PORTIA: Come back to check on me.
> RAPHAEL: Not especially. (*He holds up brandy bottle, examines level and looks at her.*) And there's dishes in the sink as hasn't seen a drop of water this week nor more.[69]

68   Kristeva, p. 14.
69   Carr, *Portia Coughlan* (Oldcastle, Co. Meath: Gallery Press, 1999), pp. 11–12.

In fact his intrusiveness is matched by her extended family's unannounced invasion of her home. Carr uses the birthday as the dramatic motif for the family to gather in Portia's home and to reveal the extent to which Portia is smothered by them. 'Home', officially the integral space of 'femalehood' and 'family' as defined by the 1937 Constitution, becomes a major subversive motif in *Portia Coughlan*. It operates as a 'female space' of entrapment, reinforcing heightened and sustained feelings of dislocation. The sections in Article 41 of the Constitution, as Liam O'Dowd states 'combined with the prohibition on divorce, idealised women as unpaid homemakers and mothers while doing little to improve the day-to-day lives of women without the home.'[70] McMullan utilises Luce Irigaray's term 'déréliction'[71] in order to express the sense of exile

> experienced by women who have not been adequately represented or 'housed' within culture except through the maternal function and can find no place within the dominant currencies of symbolic exchange.[72]

Shortly after Raphael's return to the home, her Aunt Maggie May and husband Senchil arrive with '*a three foot white delft horse on its hind legs*', their tasteless present for her.[73] Later that day, her father and mother, Sly and Marianne, and her paternal grandmother Blaize Scully, when the doorbell is not answered, come into her home to investigate, judge and advise her on how to improve the 'feminine' domestic role that they feel she fails to

70   Liam O'Dowd, 'Church, State and Women: The Aftermath of Partition', in Chris Curtin, Pauline Jackson and Barbara O'Connor, *Gender in Irish Society* (Galway: Galway University Press, 1987), p. 5.

71   Luce Irigaray discusses the existence of woman as already living in a dérèlict position because she is always without adequate 'housing' in the symbolic order. The tension lies in her lacking mediation within the symbolic and her struggle to construct an alternative female symbolic. Outside of the symbolic, she cannot find a language to communicate her gender. See *An Ethics of Sexual Difference*, trans. Carolyn Burke and Gillian C. Gill (Ithaca, NY: Cornell University Press, 1993) and *Je, Tu, Nous: Toward a Culture of Difference*, trans. Alison Martin (New York: Routledge, 1993).

72   Anna McMullan, 'Marina Carr's Unhomely Women', in *Irish Theatre Magazine*, 1.1 (1998), p. 16.

73   Carr, *Portia Coughlan*, p. 15.

play. Portia's radical and dislocatory impulses are employed in the pursuit of repositioning some kind of adequate alternative female subjectivity and space, expressed by the twin motif, outside the home.

The home, as a measurement of 'femininity', reveals received notions of femininity. Marianne queries why the household chores have not been carried out and observes angrily: 'You'd swear you were never taught how to hoover a room or dust a mantle; bloody disgrace, that's what ya are ... And where's your children?'[74] Yet Portia implies that the drowning of her twin Gabriel fifteen years earlier was due to Marianne's gross negligence as a mother; that Marianne played a first hand role in his death. Portia tells her: '[D]on't you bluster in here and put a death wish on my sons just because you couldn't save your own. My sons'll be fine for if I do nothin' else I leave them alone and no mark is better than a black one.'[75]

Maggie May and Senchil, in their appearance and behaviour, echo 'the playful romp with gender stereotypes and clichés' portrayed in *Low in the Dark*.[76] Maggie May, who offers support and friendship to Portia, plays more of a surrogate mother role, but she is far from the emulated and idealised social model of the mother figure that has traditionally been valorised by the Church and State. Described in the stage directions as '*an old prostitute*' and wearing a '*black mini skirt, black tights, white high heels, sexy blouse, loads of costume jewellery* [and a] *fag in her mouth*' she is childless; her female/maternal body/is a site of promiscuous carnality. Playing with excess, Maggie May is at the same time a critique and an overcoming of the situation she represents as 'female' and prostitute. 'Mother' is the negative figure of a female reduced to the reproductive function; she is a discourse of power imprisoned in the narrowness of a partial representation which aspires to universality. Senchil, who is described in the stage directions as '*half the size of her, skinny, fussy, lovely*' brings gender subversion to parodic lengths.[77] He performs Marianne's description of the 'appropriate

---

74 Carr, *Portia Coughlan*, p. 26.
75 Carr, *Portia Coughlan*, p. 27.
76 See Melissa Sihra, 'The House of Woman and the Plays of Marina Carr' in *Women in Irish Theatre: A Century of Authorship and Representation*, p. 205.
77 Carr, *Portia Coughlan*, p. 14.

female', carrying out the nurturing, caring behaviours and domestic duties
traditionally associated with woman.

The play sees Portia regularly fleeing to the river to where the ghost
of her dead twin Gabriel can often be found, and whose 'being' intermit-
tently 'ghosts' the dramatic action of the play throughout. Portia's home
is metaphorically the phobic object, which has led her to 'the strongly
structuring power of symbolicity,' where she confronts

> with a limit [her] speaking being into a separate being who utters only by separating
> – from within the discreteness of the phonemic chain up to and including logical
> and ideological constructs.[78]

Her withdrawal from her home allows us to witness the painful dawning
of her abject selfhood through various forms of fear, aggressivity and the
projection onto the other (the ghost of Gabriel and the river) in the play.
The ghost and the river symbolise both loss and abjection, representing the
risk of difference to which the Symbolic is permanently exposed. Kristeva
locates abjection within the realm of desire: 'I endure it [abjection], for I
imagine that such is the desire of the other.'[79] This abject both safeguards
and annihilates. Its banishment consolidates the I, but its acknowledgement destroys the I. More specifically, the abject must remain in its place
of 'non-existence and hallucination' in order to keep intact the illusion of
a unified subjectivity.

The measure of the Coughlan family property is the site for destabilising complex hegemonic patriarchal invasions, and in Portia's dislocation, the
private and public worlds, the semiotic and the symbolic, are made visible.
Portia's guilt for not possessing the 'womanly' qualities of motherhood is
articulated by her fears of harming her own children, failing to conceive
herself as a subject with a Symbolic economy. She tells Raphael:

78   Kristeva, *Powers of Horror*, p. 46.
79   Kristeva, *Powers of Horror*, p. 2.

PORTIA: [...] I'm afraid of them, Raphael! What I may do to them! Don't you understand! Jaysus! Ya think I don't wish I could be a natural mother, mindin' me children, playin' with them, doin' all the things a mother is supposed to do! When I look at my sons, Raphael, I see knives and accidents and terrible mutilations.[80]

Portia's relation to deprivation, manifested in her resistance to motherhood, sees her struggle accompanied with 'the aggressivity of drives, which consequently never presents itself a "pure" state.'[81] As Kristeva asks: '[D]oes not fear hide an aggression, a violence that returns to its source?'[82] Portia's declaration of the violence she would do to her children brings want, deprivation, violence and the death drive into the arena, where her fear and aggressivity, which are there to protect her from some not yet localisable cause (the abject selfhood), are projected and come back from the outside (her family), signifying her feelings about the threatening abject.

However, Portia is keenly aware of her predicament, although seemingly unwilling to search for self-empowerment. McMullan observes Carr's 'powerful articulation of her female protagonists' [in their] 'lucid perception of their own alienation, their evocation with mythical forces, and their critique of the lack of accommodation of difference in small town or rural Ireland.'[83] Portia's heightened sense of awareness manifests in her challenges to patriarchy before her suicide, which, as in *The Mai* takes place in *media res*, creating the illusion of a 'unified' narrative that marks the work of the symbolic order. Remembering, abjection also serves to stabilise the social order by siphoning off all bodies, all sexualities that exceed the limits imposed by cultural mandates.

Yet the women's relationships in Carr's plays challenge cultural boundaries, characterised by repeated references to matrophobia, violence and death. These concerns directly relate to what Kristeva describes as the 'fear of the archaic mother [which] turns out to be essentially a fear of her generative power. It is this power, a dreaded one, that patrilineal filiation

---

80   Carr, *Portia Coughlan*, p. 49.
81   Kristeva, p. 39.
82   Kristeva, p. 38.
83   McMullan in *Theatre Stuff: Critical Essays on Contemporary Irish Theatre*, p. 41.

has the burden of subduing.'[84] Any sense of female generative power in relation to the mother turns towards self-destruction.

Prescribed definitions of woman, culturally central yet socially subordinate, are persistently ruptured throughout. *Portia Coughlan*, challenging received notions of femininity, gender and motherhood, contests the binary categories of male and female as biologically, socially or historically determined. Unable to play the role of wife and mother, women/mothers acting against their 'natural' instincts, within the patriarchal context, bring about their deaths. In an interview, Carr comments on the possibility for woman defined beyond the traditional notions of motherhood:

> I don't think the world should assume that we are all natural mothers. And it does ... The relationship between parent and child is so difficult and so complex. There's every emotion there. We mostly acknowledge the good ones. If we were allowed to talk about the other ones, maybe it would alleviate them in some way.[85]

Portia is condemned to continually resist the socially prescribed roles. Carr, aware of the dangers of the fixity of female identity within the calcification of Irish traditional patriarchal culture, demonstrates how the celebratory romance of the past or the homogenising history of the past in the present strengthens the entrapment of female subjectivity. *Portia Coughlan* explores McMullan's belief that:

> Irish women come under pressure from both Catholic and Protestant ideologies to retain the domestic role as their primary function ... Whether Catholic or Loyalist, the role of the woman is to suffer and to serve. While her image is sublimated, her voice is suppressed.[86]

The male and female divisions of gender take a new ordering in the split motif of the dizygotic twins in *Portia Coughlan*. The divided or split self has

---

84   Kristeva, p. 77.
85   Carr in *Rage and Reason*, pp. 150–151.
86   Anna McMullan, 'Irish Women Playwrights Since 1958' in Trevor Griffiths and Margaret Llewellyn-Jones (eds), *British and Irish Women Dramatists Since 1958: A Critical Handbook* (Buckingham, UK: Open University Press, 1993), p. 111.

a particular application to contemporary Irish theatre (Friel's *Philadelphia Here I Come!*) as a means of demonstrating the manner in which homogeneous subjectivity can be challenged and theatrically actualised. But the twin motif is also construed as an arrangement of differences in terms of the speaking subject in the abject sense. This arrangement regulates Portia, who is internally divided, and who through her physical, linguistic and emotional affiliation to Gabriel does not cease purging herself of him. Her relationship to him demonstrates the interiorisation of abjection, something permanent which comes from within. As Kristeva outlines, the abjection of self 'attempts to identify with something on the outside [but] finds the impossible within.'[87] The 'fluid' nature of identity between the twins is illustrated on a number of levels, compelling the recognition of abjection in a particular way. Damus Halion, Portia's lover, and Fintan Goolan, the barman at the High Chaparral, recollect the physical, emotional and social bond shared by the twins, on the evening that Portia's dead body is pulled from the River Belmont:

> DAMUS: Remember the school tour? [...] Portia and Gabriel sat up in the front of the bus in red shorts and white T-shirts.
>
> FINTAN: Aye.
>
> DAMUS: [...] when the time came to get back on the bus Portia and Gabriel was missin'. [...] The pair of them found five mile out to sea in a row boat. They just got in and started rowin'. Poor auld Mrs Sullivan in an awful state, 'What were yees at, children, what were yees at at all?' 'We were just goin' away,' says one of them. 'Away! Away where, in the name of God?' says Mrs Sullivan. 'Anywhere', says the other of them, 'just anywhere that's not here.'[88]

The 'split' self is a *crying-out theme* of suffering, marked by life and death, death in life. Life and death meet, and the danger and pleasure of loss are intertwined in Freud's notion of the 'uncanny'. Freud's 'uncanny' describes the class of frightening things that leads us back to what is known and familiar, revealing what is private and concealed, not only from others

---

87 Kristeva, p. 5.
88 Carr, *Portia Coughlan*, pp. 41–42.

but also from the self.[89] This notion of 'unhomeliness' is inherent in the stage directions:

> *Two isolating lights up. One on Portia Coughlan in her living room. [...] The other light comes up simultaneously on Gabriel Scully, her dead twin. He stands at the bank of the Belmont River, singing. They mirror one another's posture and movements in an odd way; unconsciously.*[90]

The play's *mise en scène* is intrinsically concerned with the dialectical interrelationship between inner and outer worlds, between the home and notions of 'other', the symbolic and the semiotic. In relation to incest and the pre-verbal, Kristeva notes:

> In that anteriority to language, the outside is elaborated by means of a projection from within, of which the only experience we have is one of pleasure and pain. An outside in the image of the inside, made of pleasure and pain.[91]

Literally and metaphorically, inside and outside is regularly non-distinctive. The three spaces that overlap one another: *the living room of Portia Coughlan's house; the bank of the Belmont River; the bar at the High Chaparral*, signify the potential fluidity.[92] As Fintan O'Toole notes: 'The landscape of Marina Carr's plays is both literally and metaphorically watery. Her Midlands ground is soft underfoot, boggy and unstable, bounded by lakes and rivers.'[93] The stage directions denote the spilling over between the spaces that become significantly fluid throughout, allowing Portia a kind of transcendence. The river, a place of subversion and escape, is given to Gabriel's ghostly presence and is the source of Portia's refuge, the allocated realm of 'otherness' in the play. Wallace notes the irony in the archangel's

---

89   Sigmund Freud, 'The 'Uncanny', Collected Papers, Vol. 4, trans. Joan Riviere (New York: Basic Books, 1959), pp. 368–369.

90   Carr, *Portia Coughlan*, p. 11.

91   Kristeva, p. 61.

92   Carr, *Portia Coughlan*, p. 8.

93   Fintan O'Toole, 'Portia Coughlan, by Marina Carr' in Julia Furay and Redmond O'Hanlon (eds), *Critical Moments: Fintan O'Toole on Modern Irish Theatre* (Dublin: Carysfort Press, 2003), pp. 164–165.

name Gabriel 'who in Hebrew legend personifies the power of healing.'[94] The play's portrayal of Gabriel's presence is soothing to Portia. The exterior space of flowing waters associated with her dead twin, is Portia's place of sanctuary and escape, which contrasts with the interior domestic space that is anything but secure and tranquil, and which is structured according to 'rules' and daily routines, as signified by the symbolic order.

Turning to Freud's discussion of the uncanny (the unhomely), Bhabha interprets subjectivity from the perspective of the marginalised or exiled which underscores the ambivalence of the margin and also the threat it poses to identity. Bhabha gives emphasis to the position of the liminal which fissures the unity of identity. The communication between the twins, across different spaces, provides a way of capturing the separating sense characteristic of Bhabha's 'unhomeliness'. Portia's 'home' is made 'meaningful' by her parents, husband, children and aunt. Her displaced sense of self is revealed in the move from her familial home territory to relocate in Gabriel's realm along the river. Portia enacts Bhabha's liminal strategies of selfhood, found in the notion of the beyond:

> The negating activity is indeed the intervention of the 'beyond' that establishes a boundary: a bridge where 'presencing' begins ... To be unhomed is not to be homeless nor can the unhomely be easily accommodated in that familiar division of social life into private and public spheres.[95]

Portia's connection to the supernatural Gabriel ruptures the sense of determinate female gender. In *Fantasy: The Literature of Subversion* Rosemary Jackson states: '[T]he ghost is neither dead nor alive, [it is] a spectral presence, suspended between being and nothingness.'[96] The dizygotic nature of the twin's identity symbolically contests female 'oppression [and] challenges the transparency of social reality, as a pre-given image of

---

94   Clare Wallace, 'Tragic Destiny and Abjection in Marina Carr's *The Mai, Portia Coughlan* and *By the Bog of Cats*', in Anthony Roche (ed.), *Irish University Review*, 31:2:2001, p. 441.

95   Bhabha, *The Location of Culture*, p. 9.

96   Jackson, *Fantasy: The Literature of Subversion* (London: Routledge, 1998), p. 20.

human knowledge.'[97] Bhabha advocates Frantz Fanon's strength in liminal discourse who 'speaks most effectively from the interstices of historical change ... from deep within the struggle of psychic representation and social reality.'[98] For Bhabha, fixed identities give the illusion of stability, an image that can never be actualised or reached in any real sense, therefore their power can alienate us from ourselves. The twin motif offers freedom from such estrangement and is a way of privileging liminality as a means of undermining solid 'authentic' identities in favour of unexpected and fortuitous kinds.

Gabriel's 'ghost-being' is felt by Portia but can only be seen by the audience at certain moments in the drama. His existence takes us out of fixed notions of 'reality' and into the realm of fantasy. Portia is split between a disenchanted figure in the 'real' world and an 'other' being from a non-real world. The 'other-being', spiritualised in nature, constitutes the sign of imminent loss. According to Lucie Armitt, 'one explanation for the particular pleasures offered by the literary fantastic derives from a prevalent awareness of loss.'[99] Portia, aware of her sense of loss, is drawn to the banks of the river. Her loss symbolically exists in the image of the omnipresent and omniscient Gabriel. Armitt goes on to state that 'all fantastic fictions of otherness become projections of the uncanny derived from the primary site of boundary negotiation which marks us all as aliens and exiles.'[100] Jackson believes that literary fantasy is made and determined by its social context and cannot be understood in isolation from it. The finite 'real' is directly related to the infinite world of fantasy. She states:'[F]antasy characteristically attempts to compensate for a lack resulting from cultural constraints: it is a literature of desire, which seeks that which is experienced as absence and loss.'[101] Carr's relationship to 'presences' or ghosts is 'a way

---

97   Bhabha, *The Location of Culture*, p. 41.
98   Bhabha, *The Location of Culture*, p. 40.
99   Lucie Armitt, *Theorising the Fantastic* (London: Arnold Hodder Headline Group, 1996), p. 8.
100   Armitt, *Theorising the Fantastic*, p. 8.
101   Rosemary Jackson, *Fantasy: The Literature of Subversion* (London: Routledge, 1998), p. 3.

of seeing the world.'[102] In stating her belief in existences beyond life, Carr laments: 'People don't believe in things anymore. They go to the theatre and they want two episodes of a soap opera. They don't want to be told about a ghost.'[103] The presence of the ghost body of Gabriel is challenging in terms of presenting other possible realms or categories of existence. As Jackson states: 'The fantastic ... reveals reason and reality to be arbitrary, shifting constructs, and thereby scrutinizes the category of the "real".'[104] On stage the ghost body breaks narrow categories of definitions, by providing witness (Portia) to the public manifestation of 'otherness' (Gabriel) for the contemporary world (the audience).

The figure of Gabriel is connected to suicide and incest. During the scene where Portia's body is being hoisted from the water, Gabriel is described as standing detached on the other bank. According to the stage directions

> *Portia is raised into the air and suspended there, dripping water, moss, algae, frog-spawn, waterlillies, from the river. Gabriel stands aloof on the other bank, in profile singing.*[105]

His detachment, visible to the audience, implies a smug kind of success over Portia's soul. Portia's suicide follows Gabriel's suicide by drowning fifteen years later, and effectively can be read as a resignation of herself to the dead. Gabriel has kept his revengeful word; that he will keep coming back until he has Portia. Carr elaborates on this kind of death, personifying it in Freudian terms as an impulse that seeks to draw you into it. She describes it as 'wanting a little piece of my life. [The Presence] is dead, and the dead are jealous of the living.'[106] In *Sacred Play: Soul-Journeys in Contemporary Irish Theatre*, Anne F. O'Reilly understands Irish theatre as addressing the loss of soul. She considers:

---

102 Cliodhna Ni Anluain (ed.), *Reading the Future: Irish Writers in Conversation with Mike Murphy* (Dublin: Lilliput Press, 2000), p. 51.
103 Ni Anluain (ed.), *Reading the Future*, p. 51.
104 Jackson, *Fantasy: The Literature of Subversion*, p. 21.
105 Carr, *Portia Coughlan*, p. 40.
106 Ni Anluain (ed.), *Reading the Future*, p. 49.

soul as the impulse towards the embodiment of spirit. Where spirit soars, soul descends. Where spirit aspires towards light, soul grapples with the dark. If spirit transcends, soul remains rooted to the earth, in the messy place of birth and embodiment. Where spirit seeks the non-engagement and the ultimate liberation in death, soul calls us back towards life to the daily realities of relationship, love and commitment.[107]

In this sense Gabriel has not completed his journey and is caught in the inbetween space of body and spirit. His 'being' is merged with Portia's being. The soul on earth as the 'messy place of birth and embodiment' can be connected to Marianne's description of the twin's birth. She tells Portia: 'Came out of the womb clutchin' your leg and he's still clutchin' it from wherever he is.'[108] It is radically different to how Portia remembers her birth coming out of the womb holding hands with her twin. Abjection, as the horror of not knowing the borders of the self, is a primary uncanny originated in the fertility and generative power of the mother's body. Like abjection, pregnancy and the pre-natal period are borderline phenomena, they are a space-time of con/fusion, bodily co-existence (coincidence) of identities linked in a vital and deadly relation, but at the same time preparing for separation and distinction.

The commitment to incest between the twins when Gabriel was alive calls upon prohibition and 'mostly concerns matters that are capable of enjoyment.'[109] The social and cultural aversion and taboo that surrounds incest, is firmly reinforced in the contradiction that Marianne represents, revealing her and Sly as half brother and sister. The repression of the pleasure/pain dialectic, which accompanies incest, further removes a reconciliation which might accompany the acknowledgement of it. The separation of Gabriel's and Portia's bodies from the womb once born into life, followed by the separation from the mother which takes place during the processes of abjection and culminating in the traumatic abandonment of one twin by the other fifteen years later, because Portia reneged on a suicide pact,

---

107   Anne F. O'Reilly, *Sacred Play: Soul Journeys in Contemporary Irish Theatre* (Dublin: Carysfort Press, 2004), pp. 8–9.
108   Carr, *Portia Coughlan*, p. 62.
109   Kristeva, p. 59.

continues to haunt Portia, Gabriel and their parents in different ways. Birth, incest and death are brought onto the same plane. For Portia and her mother, they evoke

> this insuperable drama in the journey when sexual pleasure is drowned in a pool of blood during the confrontation between the sensual daughter and her jealous, deadly mother.[110]

Already signified in religions and myths, the mother and the maternal are the privileged figure of the inextricable proximity of life and death at the centre of the symbolic construction.

Gabriel's suicide and Portia's suicidal tendencies threaten the social order of the play, dramatising suicide as predominantly something that cannot be discussed. Sly, Portia's father, articulates his humiliation about Gabriel's suicide, asking her to forget about Gabriel who shamed him, foregrounding the stigma attached to it. Sly's feelings of disgrace, caused by his son's suicide and his wish to silence the issue, are linked to the Catholic Church's position on the subject. In relation to sacrifice and taboo, Kristeva notes that 'some religious texts stress taboo [in order to] seek protection from sacrificial interference.'[111] According to the Church, suicide was not acceptable. In the bible, suicide is linked with betrayal and shame. Though the bible contains numerous references to suicide, the most explicit reference to it in the Old Testament is in The Second Book of Samuel 17:23: 'When Ahithophel saw that his advice had not been followed, he saddled his donkey and went back to his own city. After putting his affairs in order, he hanged himself.'[112] Similarly, the case of Judas Iscariot in the New Testament, where Judas acknowledges his sin: "'I have sinned by betraying an innocent man to death" ... then threw the coins down in the Temple and

---

110 Kristeva, p. 159.
111 Kristeva, p. 95.
112 2 Samuel 17, *Good News Bible: Today's English Version* (London: Collins, 1976), p. 319.

left; then he went off and hanged himself.'[113] Kristeva's semiotics of biblical abomination outline the persuasive nature of biblical impurity, which

> encounters fear in the face of a power (maternal? Natural? – at any rate insubordinate and not liable of being subordinated to Law) that *might* become autonomous evil but *is not*, so long as the hold of subjective and social symbolic order endures.[114]

Biblical impurity, specifically in relation to the issues of incest and suicide in the play, is concerned with the separating and ordering of social performance. Wallace writes how Gabriel also shares the name of an archangel, 'though one associated with the manifestation of Divine justice and punishment.'[115] In this way, Gabriel's suicide together with his ghost roaming the banks of the lake acts as a kind of public warning to the community in the play against taking a life. The Catholic Church's contemporary views on suicide have not left the past fully behind, in that it deems the suicidal individual as being of unsound mind and therefore not capable of conscious sin but it has calmed its punitive attitudes of previous generations. Noteworthy was the prohibition of suicide victims' burial on consecrated ground and excommunication from the Catholic Church as a punishment for attempted suicide.

Portia's withdrawal from her family, and her suicidal tendency, is prefigured in the various ways in which violence is presented in the play. Signs of the abject are marked on the body which confirm the very edges of language, and contest boundary failure.

The physical disfigurement of the rural populace of Belmont Valley, bearing injury and deformity, is reminiscent of John Millington Synge's rural community in *The Playboy of the Western World* where 'Red Linahan has a squint in his eye, Pacheen is lame in his heel … Daneen Sullivan knocked the eye out of the peelers and Marcus Quinn got six months

---

113   The Gospel According to Matthew, *Good News Bible*, p. 41.
114   Kristeva, p. 90.
115   Wallace in *Irish University Review*, 31:2:2001, p. 441.

for maiming ewes.'[116] The deformities are indicative of the wider painful aberrations that exist in the community. As Kristeva suggests, the only method of reasserting difference once one has already emerged from the maternal matrix, is by laying bare its abject marks: 'With material, visceral gestures, subjects return to the bar of the signifier, "killing substance to make it signify."'[117] In *Portia Coughlan*, Stacia Doyle, nicknamed the 'Cyclops of Coolinarney', wears an eye patch to cover an injury. Stacia favours publicly exhibiting the injury, in an imaginative brave display to the world that women are victims of abuse: '[S]ometimes I think if I had me eye gouged out, I'd wear ne'er a patch at all.'[118] Raphael too, referred to by Damus Halion as 'Hopalong' because he lost half his foot, allegedly disfigured himself in order to get compensation. While Portia dismisses it as all lies, Damus claims to 'know plenty as may for half a million.'[119] The play depicts the body as the bearer of the physical imprint of abusive economic misdemeanours. The symptoms of abuse in the drama are made visual, while the facts about them remain ambiguous.

The relationship between parental rearing and abusive genealogy is persistent in the drama. Family quarrels, some leading to violence, are essential elements of sex and power presented in Carr's family life. Childhood and parents emerge as subjects of loss, as seen in figures of absent spouses, the prostitute, the withdrawn mother or the enraged wife. Kristeva understands that the human investment in signs makes it desirable to equate disunity, and pre-lingual arenas, with the womb. Abject power hovers threateningly in the background of the play, which simultaneously gives of that power an image of downfall, emotional poverty and self-humiliation articulated in the spoken word. As Kristeva notes, talking 'is a descent into the foundations of the symbolic construct – [which] amounts to retracing the fragile limits of the speaking being, closest to its dawn, to the

---

116 John Millington Synge, 'The Playboy of the Western World' in John P. Harrington (ed.), *Modern Irish Drama* (New York: W.W. Norton & Company, 1991), p. 74 & p. 75.

117 Kristeva, p. 30.

118 Carr, *Portia Coughlan*, p. 22.

119 Carr, *Portia Coughlan*, p. 19.

bottomless "primacy" constituted by primal repression.'[120] Blaize, Portia's grandmother, who no longer has the power of her legs and is in a wheelchair, is exposed as having been the victim of domestic violence for years. In an aggressive exchange of words between her and Maggie May, after Portia's funeral, Maggie May reminds Blaize how her husband repeatedly beat her, how she wouldn't appear out of the house because of her bruised face. The restrictive space of the home, not just reflected physically, but also verbally, finds a sense of release in the freedom the widow Blaize finds speaking profane language:

> I spent the first eighty years of my life holdin' me tongue, fuckin' and blindin' into the pillow, and if God sees me fit to give me another eighty they'll be spent speakin' me mind foul or fair.[121]

Stacia tells Blaize of her husband's disrespect and hypocrisy: '[D]id I ever tell you about the time I gave your husband a quick one down Mohia Lane?'[122] Blaize's unconventional stance in relation to her gender and age seems all too late, as she is now close to death, having spent most of her life under patriarchal control.

The traditional patriarchal barter of the female is prominent in the drama. Portia's sense of place is positioned within the masculine boundaries of material possession. Sly reminds her that it was his hard work and toil that built up the Belmont farm, which made her a commodity and thus a 'value' to Raphael in the monetary transaction. However, Damus Hallion alleges that Sly made capital from getting old Tim Lahane drunk and stealing his land off him. Sly's 'advice' to marry Raphael was, according to Portia, an order, forcing her to forfeit her college place. Sly's property and wealth implies a certain kind of social respectability, but how it was acquired infers his seemingly aberrant nature. This is further emphasised by the watchful eye he keeps on Portia. Portia's sense of being spied upon is confirmed by Sly's admonishment at her hanging around with Damus

---

120 Kristeva, p. 18.
121 Carr, *Portia Coughlan*, p. 28.
122 Carr, *Portia Coughlan*, pp. 46–47.

Halion: 'More than talkin' I seen! I'm tellin' ya now, put a halter to that wayward arse of yours.'[123] She feels that her father's spying is inappropriate behaviour, and displays what Laura Mulvey terms 'scopophilia', an expression which sees the voyeur as 'taking pleasure in using another person as an object of sexual stimulation through sight.'[124] Portia's feeling of being watched adds to her growing claustrophobia in the play, and also contributes to her abject state manifested in her dispossession and alienation from her family and the community. Gabriel as 'other' infuses with Portia's identity as interchangeable and part of each other, to posit her displacement at the borders between home and 'other'. The narrative ends not simply with her suicide, but with the notion that strictly defined categories of gender are not sustainable. They exist outside of such definitions, in alternative subjectivities, of that referred to as 'otherness'. The idea of a 'congealed' identity, as a neither-solid-nor-fluid identity, conforms to the notion of an 'inbetween' subjectivity most prevalent in the twin motif. Disruptions of stable identity in the narrative hover and tend towards states of abjection. In the process, Carr demonstrates the mechanisms of subjectivity and the ways in which abjection's power is based.

Mixed Blood

The final play of The Trilogy, *By the Bog of Cats*, predominantly explores abjection in terms of the cultural forces which impinge on subjectivity. The point of departure for the discussion on abjection reveals the ways in which the abject protagonist, Hester Swane, responds to the social environment of the drama. While Hester is a theatrical representation of the Travelling

---

123 Carr, *Portia Coughlan*, p. 30.
124 Laura Mulvey in 'Visual Pleasure and Narrative Cinema' in Lizbeth Goodman and Jane deGay (eds), *The Routledge Reader in Gender and Performance* (London: Routledge, 1998), p. 271.

community, her response to the settled community is examined against
the cultural context of legislation, authority and control in Ireland in relation to the two communities. Government decisions on social policy in
relation to Travellers and how these have influenced changes in traveller
culture are dramatised. The 'realist' elements of the play provide illumi-
nating representations of how cultural 'exclusion' operates, revealing the
journey towards abjection.

Hester's relationship with the community and vice versa examines her
confrontation with her abject state, as a result of the early abandonment of
her mother and her absent father. The difficulties involved in the separation
process from parental authority have already been discussed in *The Mai* and
Portia Coughlan, which share similar features to Hester's failed separation
from her parents and the uncertainty of meaning and subjectivity which
accrue. The focus on Hester's decisions and compromises are animated by
her abject sensibility and demonstrate her reactions to cultural pressures,
which privileges 'those violent, dark revolts of being, directed against a
threat that seems to emanate from an exorbitant outside.'[125] Hester is abject
because of her obsessive appeal to ideals that no longer exist, manifested
by her irremediable anger, which erupts in various ways throughout the
play. She is angry because her mother left her when she was seven years
old, because her father rejected her but maintained a relationship with her
brother Joseph (whom she killed as a result) because Carthage, her lover,
discarded her after their fourteen-year relationship, which also included
a wedding agreement, and because the dominant community want her
ousted from her home.

The play explores and considers the complexities involved in the recognition of an indigenous cultural minority, particularly in relation to
female representation. Carr examines the construction of social hierarchies
both within and between communities and explores Irish cultural anxiety
and resistance to difference. The position of existing between cultures and
the ways in which the dominant culture seeks to place mixed subjectivity
with its minority 'other' is complex. Hester Swane's genealogy identifies

125   Kristeva, p. 1.

her mixed origin in the drama. Her father, Jack Swane of Bergit's Island, is a member of the 'settled' community, while her mother, Big Josie Swane, is a Traveller. Yet Hester is reminded of her 'tinker' background by the reluctance of the settled community to acknowledge and identify her settled heritage or to allow her to exist or co-habit with them as a Traveller.

By the Bog of Cats tells the story of Hester Swane, a woman abandoned by her lover and the father of her child, Carthage Kilbride, in favour of the younger Caroline Cassidy. This marriage will increase Carthage's economic position, his openly stated ambition. Set in the boggy midlands of Ireland in the present day, the story is based on Hester's resistance to her enforced exile. Her position as a half-Traveller, half-settled member of the community complicates things further, by exposing the kind of relationship that the two communities have with one another.

The play is loosely based on Euripides's *Medea*, who fell in love with Jason. In disobeying her father, Medea was forced to flee Colchis, and become an exile with Jason at Corinth. Here, despite the oaths that Jason had vowed to Medea, he forsakes her and marries the daughter of Creon, King of Corinth, in order to strengthen his economic status. Hester, like Medea, refuses to accept the inevitable state of banishment and degradation that will ensue following the marriage.

Hester's refusal is revealed in its disruptive potential as a force of criminality in the play. When the drama begins, she has already murdered Joseph and her reign of destruction throughout the narrative sees her burn Carthage's house and livestock, kill her child and then finally kill herself. The power of abjection is seen in Hester's actions, which do not in any way create an order more authentic than that of the community to which she is opposed, but rather she seizes on the inconsistencies of her actions and their mutual resemblance. She exploits the very attempt to assign symbolic value to her deeds and she taunts them with the threat of collapse. As Kristeva reminds us, what is abjected in the early stages of development 'is radically excluded and draws me toward the place where meaning collapses.'[126]

126 Kristeva, p. 2.

By the Bog of Cats examines the link between an identifiable cultural hegemony and its inferior 'other' embodied in the Travelling community, as well as the ideological legitimisation of female subordination. Edward Said's notions of 'imagined geography' are employed to interrogate this link. Said's colonial and post-colonial theory, as articulated in *Orientalism* (1978) can be employed to investigate the ways in which the dominant Settled Community gains its identity and power from setting itself against its surrogate other, the Travelling Community. Said's East/West construction of Orientalism morally evaluates the colonial relationship as 'one of fundamental inequality.'[127] The ambiguity of cultural representation as a political process and the fraught position of the minority culture in relation to female representation in the drama can be considered through the work of cultural theorists Bhabha and Antonio Gramsci. Extending Said's cultural diagnosis, Bhabha's notion of '"liminal spaces" of colonial discourse, marginal areas, where the ultimate opposition of coloniser and colonised breaks down through irony, imitation and subversion,' gives agency to the colonised to work against colonial ideology.[128] Bhabha resists the construction of dominant ideology in his notions of the discursive gap in Said's colonial configuration.

Gramsci's theories emerge from his studies of the Italian *Risorgimento*, and focus on the concerns of authority and the struggle for ideological hegemony. For Gramsci, the 'subalterns' are a categorisation of 'diverse social groups, which are subordinate to the rule of the dominant class and the state.'[129] Gramsci suggests that the 'subaltern classes, by definition, are not unified and cannot unite until they are able to become a "state"; their history, therefore, is intertwined with that of civil society, and thereby with

---

127   Colin Graham, *Deconstructing Ireland: Identity, Theory, Culture* (Edinburgh University Press, 2001), p. 82.

128   Graham, *Deconstructing Ireland: Identity, Theory, Culture*, p. 86.

129   See Antonio Gramsci, *Selections from the Prison Notebooks* (London: Lawrence and Wishart, 1971), p. 104. The term 'subaltern' has achieved critical currency primarily from Gramsci's 'Notes on Italian History' in *Selections from the Prison Notebooks*. With the advent of the Indian Subaltern Studies group the term has gained greater valency to include members of minority race and gender groups.

the history of states and groups of states.'[130] Carr's play explores the ways in which Travellers, as the subaltern class, become 'intertwined' with the wider community.

In *By the Bog of Cats*, differences between the Travelling and the Settled Communities are identified by the 'psychologically' nomadic and 'psychologically' fixed attitude to home respectively.[131] Specifically, the position of Hester Swane, whose sense of place lies both between and outside of the Irish settled and the Irish travelling communities, is examined. Her liminal position between the two cultures means that she does not fully belong to either culture and that she is part of both, placing her literally, in the abject sense 'at the border of [her] condition as a living being.'[132] Despite Hester's origin of mixed blood genealogies, the one-sided settled perspective given by the characters in the play is presented as a lack of acknowledgement and understanding of the Travellers. It manifests as suspicion, and as an anxiety and threat to the dominant settled community, where Hester's right not to be discriminated against is never a consideration. Her abject self is doubly abjected by her position as female, and by her relationship with the dominant society, which forces her to be part of them yet refuses her the same sense of belonging.

Orientalism discusses the complex relationship between the West and the 'Orient'. Said states: 'the Orient is not an inert fact of nature. It is not merely *there*, just as the Occident itself is not just *there* either.'[133] He also states that 'both geographical and cultural entities – to say nothing of historical entities – such locales, regions, geographical sectors as "Orient" and "Occident" are man made.'[134] How one culture (usually the dominant one)

---

130 Gramsci, *Selections from the Prison Notebooks*, p. 52.
131 The terms 'psychologically' nomadic and 'psychologically' fixed refer to the differences between Travellers and Settled people's notion of home respectively. Travellers like to believe that they are not tied to their home. Their state of mind finds comfort in the idea that they can leave it at any time. Settled people see their home as more of a permanent fixed place that remains constant in their lives.
132 Kristeva, p. 3.
133 Edward W. Said, *Orientalism* (London: Penguin, 1978), p. 4.
134 Said, *Orientalism*, p. 5.

comes to 'know' and 'speak' about its (lesser) 'other' forms a kind of strategy that constructs the us/them divide. That the 'Orient' is a construction by the West is central to Said's argument, but significantly the political, economic and cultural interdependence between the two cultures emerge, where the West is seen as superior to the Orient.

The relationship between the settled and the travelling cultures in Ireland in the production of different levels of authority, domination and hegemony to some extent parallels this strategy. According to Said, the forces at work in constructing the Orient use the principle of 'binomial' opposition, a mode of categorical comparison that stems from

> the culturally sanctioned habit of deploying large generalizations by which reality is divided into various collectives: languages, races, types, colors, mentalities, each category being not so much a neutral designation as an evaluative interpretation.[135]

Said argues that 'theirs' is dependent on and therefore inferior to 'ours'. What follows from the practice of categorisation is a distinction between received wisdom, or systematic modes of understanding on the one hand, and more independent, imaginative approaches to the Orient on the other. One category perpetuates the various stated views about Oriental society, languages, literatures, history, sociology, and so forth; the other is less explicitly defined, but it is based on a collective shared set of preconceived images and attitudes that are less informed by conventionally held notions.

Considering the Travelling community as a cultural minority in *By the Bog of Cats*, the drama explores what it means to be a Traveller in terms of historical, cultural, social and linguistic characteristics. The application of Saidian notions of Orientalism to the drama sets about interrogating the difficult relationship between representation and 'truth' in the play and the distinction between government administration, what is researched and written by various scholars and non-specialists and the set of predispositions and theorisations about Travellers that come to make oppositional claims about their community separates the settled community from the

135   Said, *Orientalism*, p. 227.

travelling community. In Saidian terms, Travellers are predominantly seen as a homogeneous entity 'incapable of defining itself; therefore it is assumed that a highly generalized and systematic vocabulary for describing the Orient from a Western standpoint is inevitable and even scientifically "objective".'[136]

The title 'Traveller' is somewhat misleading with regard to the idea that all travellers are on the move from one place to the next, and have no fixed sense of home. Michael McDonagh, a Traveller representative, cites the 1963 European Commission synthesis report, *School Provision for Gypsy and Traveller Children*, which claims that Irish Travellers have a mobile mentality. This, he sees, as the link that Irish Travellers have with Travellers (Gypsies, Roma) elsewhere: 'Nomadism is as much a state of mind as a state of fact.'[137] Having a mobile mentality, McDonagh believes, is important, because the option to move from place to place reduces the claustrophobic feeling of having to stay in one place. This concurs with Hester's claim, that moving from living in a caravan to a house does not make her feel 'settled' there. The Ghost fancier asks Hester: 'You live in that caravan over there?' She replies: 'Used to; live up the lane now. In a house, though I've never felt at home in it.'[138] Later she demonstrates her indifference to owning bricks and mortar when she burns down the house Carthage bought for her, telling her neighbour Monica Murray: '[Its] only an auld house, it should never have been built in the first place. Let the bog have it back. Never liked that house anyway.'[139] In Act 2, Carthage reminds Hester of an agreement she made with him, which involves her moving away from the Bog of Cats:

136 Said, *Orientalism*, p. 301.
137 Michael McDonagh in 'Nomadism In Irish Travellers' Identity' in May McCann, Séamus Ó Síochain and Joseph Ruane (eds), *Irish Travellers: Culture and Ethnicity* (Queen's University Belfast: 1994), p. 96.
138 Carr, *By the Bog of Cats*, p. 14.
139 Carr, *By the Bog of Cats*, p. 63.

HESTER: [...] I know every barrow and rivulet and bog hole of its nine square mile. I know where the best bog rosemary grows and the sweetest wild rue. I could lead yees around the Bog of Cats in me sleep.

CARTHAGE: There's a house bought and furnished for ya in town as ya agreed to –

HESTER: I've never lived in a town. I won't know anywan there –[140]

McDonagh writes: 'In some cases, Travellers have become physically sick and very depressed when they move into houses, and they never adjust psychologically to living in the one permanent place. Many Travellers have left houses for these reasons.'[141] But the bog is also the space of loss and desire, amplified by the community's wish for her to leave. It is the object of desire that affects Hester's sense of personal identity, and is related to her salvaging her full sense of self. Her mother is invoked towards the climax of the narrative, triggering her longing, embodied by the topography of the bogscape: 'I can't lave – you see me mother said she'd come back here.'[142] As Kristeva observes:

---

140   Carr, *By the Bog of Cats*, p. 56
141   McDonagh in *Irish Travellers: Culture and Ethnicity*, p. 96. Note: Having a 'fixed' address for Travellers makes it less complicated in getting benefit from State Support or Social Welfare from Social Services, which is an essential part of their livelihood today. One reason for this is the suspicion in which the government hold to Travellers because of their family custom to genealogical loyalty to being named after their kin. In the play, Josie Swane is named after her Grandmother Big Josie Swane, and is distinguished from her by the adjective 'Big'. In reality, it would not be unusual, for example, to have three or four 'Michael Stokes', all cousins for example, and around the same age claiming social welfare. According to Tom Stokes, a Traveller 'settled' in the North West of Ireland: 'they [the authorities] want us to be settled. A lot belonging to us, our kids have the same name, because that was me father's name or his father's name. Same with the women. So when you're goin' to collect the money [social welfare], they'd [the authorities] be thinkin' that'd you'd already got it.' (Tom Stokes, Personal Interview, 10 December 2004.)
142   Carr, *By the Bog of Cats*, p. 57.

> Abjection preserves what existed in the archaism of pre-objectal relationship, in the immemorial violence with which the body becomes separated from another body in order to be – maintaining that night in which the outline of the signified vanishes and where only the imponderable affect is carried out.[143]

Hester's destructive actions are also a cultural rage than simply an act of rage towards Carthage. She is repeatedly reminded of her 'otherness' in scenes that reveal the ways in which exclusionary practices delimit and mark the subjectivity of the minority 'other'. Her actions are a statement against the increased pressures to assimilate to dominant ways of community life. Such a feeling is a justifiable reality in contemporary Ireland, as the housing authorities would desire her to remain in fixed accommodation. The 1963 Report of the Commission on Itinerancy, set up by the Irish government to investigate Travellers' Rights, demonstrates the ignorance the government held towards Travellers and also its 'colonial' tendency to 'fix' the conditions of the Traveller's lifestyles. The report has helped form the view that Travellers are an undesirable minority group:

> [A] substantial amount of the state and local authority assistance ... given to those itinerants who have not settled down in a fixed abode or who are not ... on an approved camping site provided for them ... should be paid in voucher form exchangeable for food and clothing so as to overcome abuse by dissipation on intoxicating liquor ... Those who settle down should, after a probationary period ... be paid and treated in every way the same as members of the settled population.[144]

The approaches to the Travelling community embody Said's notion of a '*textual* attitude', where the Settled community relies on constructions and images of Travellers which are not derived from empirical evidence or experience, but from other books or texts: 'The idea is that people, places, and experiences can always be described by a book, so much so that the

143 Kristeva, p. 10.
144 Dept of the Environment, *Report of the Commission on Itinerancy* (Dublin: Stationery Office, 1963), pp. 76–77.

book (or text) acquires a greater authority, and use, even than the actuality it describes.'[145]

The 1963 report points up the firm mindset held by the government towards the Travelling community, what Gramsci refers to as 'cultural–social unity' forged 'on the basis of an equal and common conception of the world' for the subaltern class by the dominant class.[146] The primary aim of the report is to 'colonise' the Travelling Community by providing incentives, to encourage a more 'homogenised' and therefore 'settled' way of living. The secondary aim in the report, to help Travellers 'to overcome abuse by dissipation on intoxicating liquor,' presents a 'contradistinction' to the general way of Irish culture, as though this cultural trait serves to further divide the Travellers from the Settled Community. In 1983, the discriminatory elements of the 1963 report were removed and/or rectified.

Central to Gramsci's paradigm of the subaltern as a diverse social group, subordinate to the rule of the dominant class and the state, is his elaboration of the concept of 'hegemony' as political dominance based on ideological control and achieved through the manufacture of popular consent. Significantly, the 1996 census shows that the Irish Travellers' culture is eroding, particularly their nomadic way of living; where the majority of their population is assimilating into permanent housing and to some extent the larger way of living.[147] The 2002 census continues to illustrate this trend, with statistics demonstrating that the Travelling people of Ireland are predominantly living in permanent dwellings.[148]

145   Said, *Orientalism*, p. 93. [Emphasis in original]

146   Gramsci, *Selections from the Prison Notebooks*, p. 349. Gramsci defines cultural social unity as the formation of a 'national collective will' commonly experienced as nationalism and its vicissitudes, in which the hegemonic class can 'nationalise itself' as the embodiment of the people–nation: 'It is in the concept of hegemony that those exigencies which are national in character are knotted together.' See pp. 130 & 241.

147   Dept of the Taoiseach, Census of Population of Ireland, 1996, Irish Central Statistics Office, Dublin.

148   Dept of the Taoiseach Census of Population of Ireland, 2002, Irish Central Statistics Office, Dublin. While the overall statistics show that the majority of Travellers are unemployed, the kinds of areas where they do work in are on the whole male-oriented

Considering the various theories offered about the origins of Irish Travellers, a number of characteristics of their life-style have been identified with other nomadic groups, namely English or Welsh Gypsies and Scottish Travellers, which continue to reflect the 'us' and (inferior) 'them' divide. According to anthropologist Judith Okley, 'They share a resistance to wage labour, a multiplicity of self-employed occupations, often a need for geographical flexibility and an ideological preference for trailers and caravans.'[149] Travellers' preference for this type of employment, together with their tendency for 'mobility' makes it difficult for the dominant social groups to negotiate their cultural ways. As a result, Travellers are accused of indolence or of not contributing to the larger society. In *By the Bog of Cats*, Mrs Kilbride, Carthage's mother, essentialises Travellers and demonstrates on a number of occasions the stereotypical intolerance she has of them. She tells Hester: 'I've had the measure of you this long time, the lazy shiftless blood in ya'[150] and 'All tinkers know is the open road and where the next bottle of whiskey is comin' from.'[151] In relation to stereotype, Bhabha states:

> [I]t is the force of *ambivalence* that gives the colonial stereotype its currency: ensures its repeatability in changing historical and discursive conjunctures; informs its strategies of individuation and marginalization; produces that effect of probalistic truth and predictability which, for the stereotype, must always be in *excess* of what can be empirically proved or logically construed.[152]

---

and are on the increase. These include the areas of manufacturing, construction, and wholesale and retail industries.

149 Judith Okley's 'An Anthropological Perspective On Irish Travellers' in May McCann, Séamus Ó Síochain and Joseph Ruane (eds), *Irish Travellers: Culture and Ethnicity* (Queen's University Belfast: 1994), p. 8.
150 Carr, *By the Bog of Cats*, p. 54.
151 Carr, *By the Bog of Cats*, p. 56. Similarly in *The Mai*, Julie, Mai's sister, describes her notion of aborigines: 'They live in caves, don't they, and they're black, black as the ravens with teeth of snow. Sure didn't I see it on the telly.' Carr, 'The Mai', p. 140.
152 Bhabha, *The Location of Culture*, p. 66. [Emphasis in original].

The 'civilizing' validation of the colonial duty is disconnected from the stereotype. A (positive) normality is assumed along modes of inferior differentiation. In the play, the 'prophetic ability' associated with Travellers has been both curiously welcomed and feared by the settled community. The blind Catwoman has much in common with the Travelling community; she is considered 'dirty' because of her physical appearance, she lives on the bog and talks to the ghosts of the dead and she is in attendance at Caroline's and Carthage's wedding party in Act 2, clad from head to toe in feline-like fur. Mrs Kilbride asks Xavier Cassidy, the bride's father, 'Why did you have to invite her?' to which he replies 'Ya know as well as me it's bad luck not to invite the Catwoman.'[153] A similar attitude is shown to Catwoman and Big Josie Swane. Monica Murray tells Hester: 'There was a time round here when no celebration was complete without Josie Swane ... And it wasn't so much they wanted her there, more they were afraid not to have her.'[154] Monica's ingrained cultural fear of the Travelling people reveals more about the mind set of the settled community towards the travelling people. In the drama, Mrs Kilbride continues to form and uphold the kind of discourse associated with cultural domination. In Act 2, she tells Hester, 'that savage tinker eye ya turn on people to frighten' represents a rigid view held by the 'settled' community of the 'travelling' community.[155] Hester tells Monica Murray of the fearful fascination of the 'settled' community with her and her mother, Big Josie Swane, when they would be invited to sing at weddings, funerals, christenings, birthdays, and harvest celebrations.

> HESTER: [...] And they never axed us to stay, these people, to sit down and ate with them, just lapped up her songs, gave her a bag of food and a half a crown and walked us off the premises, for fear we'd steal somethin', I suppose. I don't think it bothered her, it did me – and still rankles after all these years. But not Josie Swane, she'd be off to the shop to buy cigars and beer and sweets for me.[156]

153   Carr, *By the Bog of Cats*, p. 50.
154   Carr, *By the Bog of Cats*, p. 65.
155   Carr, *By the Bog of Cats*, p. 54.
156   Carr, *By the Bog of Cats*, p. 65.

The association of Travellers with the gift of insight or a sixth-sense way of seeing is common and has origins in a time when the practice stemmed mostly from the need for Travellers to make money. George Gmelch cites Nan Donaghoe on her fortune telling days:

> If I was short of money and maybe I'd have nothin' to sell, I'd go along and ask did they want their fortune told. Well I'd read the cups and tell them all I could. I'd nearly know what to tell them. If it was a young person I'd tell them that they were going to be married or they were goin' to get money from friends across the water or they were fallin' into a bit of luck. Anything just to get a livin'.[157]

Good fortunes were almost invariably offered to their clients. However, bad fortunes, known as 'the tinker's curse', were cast upon a select few of the settled community who refused to offer some kind of help or subsistence to the begging Traveller. According to Bhabha, 'the analytic of ambivalence questions the dogmatic and moralistic positions on the meaning of oppression and discrimination' as a way to understand the process of subjectification through stereotypical discourse.[158] Bhabha interrogates specifically each individual stereotype, because while stereotypes function in similar ways, their differences disable and expose the nature and source of their production. Said's diagnosis of the West's view of the Orient as something both familiar and unknown parallels the conventional stereotyped view of Travellers presented in the play: 'The Orient at large, therefore vacillates between the West's contempt for what is familiar and shivers of delight in – or fear of – novelty.'[159]

The loss of Travellers' language and dialect patterns, known as 'cant' or 'gammon' or academically as 'shelta', is also evident in the drama. Xavier describes a time when Big Josie Swane was roaming on the bog, 'and the fields covered over in stars and her half covered in an excuse for a dress and her croonin' towards Orion in a language I never heard before or since.' According to Dónall P. Ó Baoill, 'it would seem from the linguistic evidence

---

157 George Gmelch, *The Irish Tinkers: The Urbanisation of an Itinerant People* (Menlo Park, CA: Cummings, 1977), p. 20.
158 Bhabha, *The Location of Culture*, p. 67.
159 Said, *Orientalism*, p. 59.

that the mother tongue of Irish Travellers is a combination of Cant and some form of Irish English.'[160] Ó Baoill locates its origin 'at a time when its original speakers were bilingual, having a knowledge of both Irish and English. This would seem to date the creation as sometime in the last 350 years or so.'[161] According to Alice Binchy: 'The 25,000 Travellers in Ireland all speak a language spoken by no one who does not belong to their group.'[162] Although Hester does not speak Cant in the play, it is likely that the Cant speech has had an influence in the production of words pronounced in Irish English of those around her in the play. Cant is an oral, as opposed to a written, language form and is passed on in this tradition. The idioms and rhythms of the Travelling people, along with the flat guttural influences of the Midlands accent, produce a particular kind of dialect which Carr captures in the phonetical dialogue in the drama. Frequent words in the play such as 'tould', 'wan', 'auld', 'lavin' and 'ax' instead of 'told', 'one', 'old', 'leaving' and 'ask', demonstrate the substitution of the broader and flatter vowel sound for the standard rounder one. Specific varieties of Irish English help to locate people to places, and the Cant language is a defining characteristic of the Travellers' culture, but it is not taught in Travellers' schools and is, according to Ó Baoill, in danger of becoming extinct.

The Saidian construction of a systematised form of exclusion of the East by the West, which comes to be seen as 'naturalised' and 'logical', is evident in the Traveller/Settled relationship in the drama. A number of arguments between the two communities in relation to employment, marriage, family, class and gender interrelate in the play along the lines of a hierarchal hegemony. But Said reminds us that the notion of Orientalism focuses on the exteriority of the representation of the Orientalist text, because the Orientalist, that is the poet or the scholar, articulates what is said. Carr's representation of the Settler/Traveller relationship is articulated in relation

---

160   Dónall P. Ó Baoill, 'Travellers' Cant – Language or Register?' in May McCann, Séamus Ó Síochain and Joseph Ruane (eds), *Irish Travellers: Culture and Ethnicity* (Queen's University Belfast: 1994), p. 156.

161   Ó Baoill, 'Travellers' Cant – Language or Register?', p. 160.

162   Alice Binchy, 'Travellers' Language: A Sociolinguistic Perspective', in *Irish Travellers: Culture and Ethnicity*, p. 134.

to what she says about the 'Travelling' community in her representation. Said's version of 'truth' is the visible representation of the Orient/Occident relationship, paralleling the Travelling/Settled relationship. The accuracy of Said's representation is incidental to how the Orient/'Other' [Traveller] is represented: 'The things to look at are style, figures of speech, setting, narrative devices, historical and social circumstances, *not* the correctness of the representation or its fidelity to some great original.'[163]

In exploring the social circumstances in the play, the settled community's obsession with ownership of land as one of the central means of social advancement is reminiscent of much of Ireland's drama throughout the century. Having land, or the prospect of gaining more land as an extension of wealth, has been the source of much conflict represented in Ireland's theatre.[164] In *By the Bog of Cats* Carr presents material possession as a means of affirming identity and of raising social status. Hester tells her rival, Caroline, that it was her money that bought Carthage the land that raised his social standing from a labourer's son. This is a reversal of the traditional notion of Travellers as landowners, particularly female Travellers:

> HESTER: [...] Let's get one thing straight, it was me built Carthage Kilbride up from nothin', him a labourer's son you wouldn't give the time of day to and you trottin' by in your first bra, on your half-bred mare, your nose nudgin' the sun. It was me who tould him he could do better. It was my money that bought him his first fine acres.[165]

Having given Carthage this kind of start, as well as having a child, Josie, with him, Hester is defiant in announcing her 'rights' to Carthage. Carthage's aspirations, however, achieved by his marriage to Caroline, are to increase his property holdings, social standing and financial gain. He will acquire Xavier Cassidy's farm, as well as attaining access to Caroline's inheritance, which she receives on the morning of the wedding. Carr dramatises the consequences for women of a traditional Catholic marriage, as written into

163 Said, *Orientalism*, p. 21. [Emphasis in original]
164 See for example W.B. Yeats's and Lady Augusta Gregory's *Cathleen Ni Houlihan*, John B. Keane's *Sive* and *The Field*, Brian Friel's *Translations*.
165 Carr, *By the Bog of Cats*, p. 30.

the 1937 Irish Constitution, which defines the vocational role of woman within the home and marriage:

> In particular, the State recognises that by her life within the home, woman gives to the State a support which the common good cannot be achieved ... The State shall, therefore, endeavour to ensure that mothers shall not be obliged by economic necessity to engage in labour to the neglect of their duties in the home.[166]

Material security is a fiercely contended battleground, where control and agency are acknowledged by varying degrees of male hegemony. Carthage articulates the value of property in admonishing his daughter's future prospects were she to stay and live as a Traveller. Compensating for his own sense of insufficiency, he states: 'Look Hetty, I want Josie to do well in the world, she'll get her share of everythin' I own and will own. I want her to have a chance in life, a chance you never had and so can never understand.'[167] Carthage has a great fear of being laughed at by 'the whole neighbourhood' if Josie lived in a caravan.[168] Hester reinforces the relationship between property and male power, telling Xavier, 'It's only your land and money and people's fear of ya that has ya walkin' free.'[169] She implies that if Xavier was not a substantial landowner and therefore not a man of social standing, he would be imprisoned for his 'illegal' behaviours, which she implies, amount to sexual abuse. She tells him: 'G'wan home and do whatever it is ya do with your daughter, but keep your sleazy eyes off of me and Josie.'[170] Throughout the play Xavier speaks for his daughter Caroline; he tells Hester: 'Ya see I married me daughter today! Now I don't care for the whinny little rip that much, but she's all I've got and I don't want Carthage changin' his mind after a while.'[171]

---

166 J.M. Kelly, *The Irish Constitution*, Article 41.2.1, 41.2.2 (Jurist Publishing Co., UCD, 1980), p. 48.
167 Carr, *By the Bog of Cats*, p. 35.
168 Carr, *By the Bog of Cats*, p. 42.
169 Carr *By the Bog of Cats*, p. 38.
170 Carr *By the Bog of Cats*, p. 38.
171 Carr *By the Bog of Cats*, p. 71.

Here, the relationship between female identity and material economy is bound together, where they form a gendered barter object. Caroline's inheritance, Josie's potential inheritance, and Hester's lack of material ownership are perpetual conflicts throughout. Their identities are subject to commodification, to maintain the male economy in the drama. Caroline's marital status will legitimise her position within the family, under the patriarchal control of Carthage, a transition from having been under the paternal hegemony of her father. Josie's future in terms of property will potentially benefit too, creating a legitimate sense of 'being' and 'place'. Critically, however, it is the position of Hester, as a landless, liminal outsider, that threatens the 'stable' settled people, and her exile from the Bog is repeatedly called on. Not disguising his wish for land ownership, Carthage demands that Hester move 'onto another haltin' site'[172] and later at the wedding he tells her to 'go home ... and pack your things'.[173] The wedding guests, specifically Xavier Cassidy and Mrs Kilbride, who want to obliterate Hester's existence, receive her drunken imposition at the wedding with general contempt: 'We'll burn ya out if we have to' threatens Mrs Kilbride, which contains the all encompassing 'we', with which no-one else at the wedding takes issue.[174] Gramsci emphasises that political dominance does not rely solely on physical coercion, but must also achieve popular consent:

> [T]he supremacy of a social group manifests itself in two ways as 'domination' and as 'intellectual and moral leadership'. The social group dominates antagonistic groups, which it tends to 'liquidate', or to subjugate perhaps even by armed force; it leads kindred and allied groups. A social group can, and indeed must, already exercise 'leadership' before winning governmental power (this indeed is one of the principal conditions for the winning of such power); it subsequently becomes dominant when it exercises power, but even if it holds it firmly in its grasp, it must continue to 'lead' as well.[175]

---

172 Carr, *By the Bog of Cats*, p. 35.
173 Carr, *By the Bog of Cats*, p. 55.
174 Carr, *By the Bog of Cats*, p. 57.
175 Gramsci, *Selections from the Prison Notebooks*, pp. 57–58.

Indeed, the dominant patriarchal hostility towards the loss of land and its inextricable synonymy with the paternal family name is exposed. Xavier's comment about the loss of the name on his land refers to the practice in Irish Catholic marriage, where the woman typically takes her husband's surname, but where, even if she does not, their children will acquire his name. He states bitterly to Hester, that the political implications of Carthage and Caroline's marriage will allow him to retain his property:

> He [Carthage] loves the land and like me he'd rather die than part with it wance he gets his greedy hands on it. With him Cassidy's farm'll be safe, the name'll be gone, but never the farm. And who's to say but maybe your little bastard and her offspring won't be farmin' my land in years to come.[176]

Carr's commitment to place and its inextricable link to family is intense. The sense of displacement, created by tensions between the self and its relationship to constituency act out the conditions of identity in the drama. The focus on naming serves as key to a range of identities in the play. References to belonging and exclusion are riddled with irony and 'proper' acts of naming, challenging the secure ground which will allow identity to be more than the arbitrariness of language. For Carr, naming reaches the point of redundancy, particularly in relation to Mrs Kilbride, whose father, she comically differentiates, was a 'wandering tinsmith' as opposed to 'a tinker'.[177] Carr pits birth against language's promise to encapsulate identity. In *By the Bog of Cats*, whether one is a settler or a traveller, a name gives the position of the individual in relation to community, society and hence, culture. In keeping with the dominant 'settled' social context in the play, a person accredited higher social status is identified more with the work they do than with their name. Xavier and Carthage, as 'farmers', who place great importance on property, contrast with Hester as Traveller, whose identity stems from her family name. As McDonagh points out: 'Ask a Traveller, "What are you?" and the answer will be, "I'm a

---

176   Carr, *By the Bog of Cats*, p. 328.
177   Carr, *By the Bog of Cats*, p. 56.

McDonagh" or "one of the Joyces" or "Collins".[178] Carthage's mother, Mrs Kilbride, refers to her granddaughter Josie as a Swane and not a Kilbride, because a 'Swane' is first and foremost one of the 'tinkers', and a member of the minority group: 'Swane means swan' Catwoman tells Hester, when she explains how Big Josie Swane abandoned her and left the infant Hester in the black swan's lair.[179] The name is linked to the ominous image of the dead black swan at the opening of the play. Added to this is Josie's illegitimacy. Sihra makes the connection of the name 'Hester' with Nathaniel Hawthorne's *The Scarlet Letter*, where the protagonist, Hester Prynne, is 'the fallen woman with an illegitimate child'.[180] In the eyes of the Catholic Church and Irish State, as well as with Mrs Kilbride's patriarchal 'peace of mind', Carthage's marriage to Caroline will give at least some sense of legitimacy to young Josie:

> MRS KILBRIDE: [...] I bet ya can't even spell your name.
> JOSIE: And I bet ya I can.
> MRS KILBRIDE: Gwan then, spell it.
> JOSIE: (*spells*) J-o-s-i-e- K-i-l-b-r-i-d-e.
> MRS KILBRIDE: Wrong! Wrong! Wrong!
> JOSIE: Well that's the way the Teacher taught me.
> MRS KILBRIDE: Are you back-answerin' me?
> JOSIE: No Grandmother.
> MRS KILBRIDE: Ya got some of it right. Ya got the 'Josie' part right, but ya got the 'Kilbride' part wrong, because you're not a Kilbride. You're a Swane. Can ya spell Swane? Of course you can't. You're Hester Swane's little bastard. You're not a Kilbride and never will be.[181]

Irish theatre has always been familiar with this notion. The works of Brian Friel have explored the extent to which language is an agent of communication and the complexities that this presents. In *Translations*

178　McDonagh in *Irish Travellers: Culture and Ethnicity*, p. 98.
179　Carr, *By the Bog of Cats*, p. 22.
180　See Melissa Sihra, 'A Cautionary Tale: Marina Carr's *By the Bog of Cats...*' in Eamonn Jordan (ed.), *Theatre Stuff: Critical Essays on Contemporary Irish Theatre* (Dublin: Carysfort Press, 2000), p. 261.
181　Carr, *By the Bog of Cats*, p. 25.

(1980), Owen's efforts to suppress the importance of a name and the fact that the English officers have got his name wrong heighten the value in a name. He states to his brother Manus: 'Owen – Roland – what the hell. It's only a name. It's the same me, isn't it? Well, isn't it?'[182] The resigned tone in his statement, together with the double questioning, begs rather than affirms that there is nothing in a name, and demonstrates the contrary. Richard Pine points out the significance of naming in relation to Friel's biographical context: 'Without a name, a place, like a person, is incapable of fully discussing its identity, conducting its business, knowing its identity; while it can perceive itself, it cannot celebrate itself, except by subverting simile, metaphor and analogue, by pressing imagination into mendacity.'[183] The attempt to simplify the complexities involved in names, and by implication the act of naming, is played out in *By the Bog of Cats*. Whether a Kilbride or a Swane, the play depicts names as signifiers of cultural acceptance or cultural resistance by the dominant community to its lesser other. Naming signifies the assignment of boundaries in sense and selfhood.

The cultural authority of the Catholic Church is used to oppress the marginalised figures in the play. The dominant community's self-appointed stance sees its members holding an ambivalent and self-serving view of the Church in its relationship to the marginalized community. Despite Mrs Kilbride's grudging relationship with Father Willow and Hester Swane, she declares her desire for her granddaughter Josie to have some sense of legitimacy in the eyes of the Catholic Church through her son's wedding. Nevertheless, in an unchristian way she wants to break Josie's [tinker] spirit 'and then glue ya back the way I want ya.'[184] The Catholic Church, represented by the figure of Father Willow, is brought to parodic lengths in his behaviour at the wedding. Carr's directions describe him entering the wedding party with arms linking Catwoman: '*Father Willow has snuff*

182   Brian Friel in 'Translations' in John P. Harrington (ed.), *Modern Irish Drama* (New York: W.W. Norton, 1991), p. 342.
183   Richard Pine, *Brian Friel And Ireland's Drama* (London: Routledge, 1990), p. 16.
184   Carr, *By the Bog of Cats*, p. 49.

on hand, pyjamas showing from under his shirt and trousers, hat on, adores the Catwoman.'[185] Their alliance symbolises his difficulties in committing to the Catholic Church's traditions and conventions as a priest, as well as portraying the church's relationship with the wider community in a number of ways. He indulges in Catwoman's flirtatious dialogue, which suggests not just the sense of loneliness he feels, but also the lack of sexual fulfilment due to his vows of chastity as a Catholic priest:

> CATWOMAN: We should go away on a holiday, you and me, Father Willow.
> FATHER WILLOW: Ah, ya say that every winter and come the summer I can't budge ya.
> CATWOMAN: I'll go away with ya next summer and that's a promise.
> FATHER WILLOW: Well where do you want to go and I'll book the tickets in the mornin'?
> CATWOMAN: Anywhere at all away from this auld bog, somewhere with a hot sun.
> FATHER WILLOW: Burgundy's your man then.[186]

Additionally, his companionship with Catwoman may be linked to the lament for a lost love, as he is about to say the prayer before the meal. Confused by his memory and failing to recall the prayer, as well as calling some of the members of the bridal party by their incorrect name, Father Willow mistakenly substitutes his mother's name for his fiancée's:

> XAVIER: And now Father Willow, ya'll say grace for us?
> FATHER WILLOW: It'd be an honour, Jack, thank you –
> MRS KILBRIDE: Who's Jack?
> *Father Willow gets up. All stand and bless themselves for the grace.*

185 Carr, *By the Bog of Cats*, p 49. Note: The priest has more in common with a cross between the characters of Fr Jack and Fr Dougal in the Irish television sit-com, *Father Ted*. The television series is based on the lives of Irish Catholic priests living together in a house on Craggy Island. Although *Fr Ted* predominantly relies on humorous jibes pointed at Catholic conventions and sensibilities, it also comments specifically on issues of isolation, Catholic vows of abstinence and celibacy, penance and an inability to communicate with the wider society.

186 Carr, *By the Bog of Cats*, pp. 49–50.

FATHER WILLOW: In the name of the Father and of the Son and of the Holy
   Ghost, it may or may not surprise yees all if I tould yees I was almost a groom
   meself wance. Her name was Elizabeth Kennedy, no that was me mother's name,
   her name was – it'll come to me, anyway it wasn't to be, in the end we fell out
   over a duck egg on a walkin' holiday by the Shannon, what was her name at all?
   Helen? No.[187]

Significantly too, Catwoman's unconventional lifestyle is not consistent with the church's practices and values. Presented as a marginalised character who has more in common with the Travelling community
than with the settled, she is defined by her physical demeanour, her residence in the bog and her spiritual ability to commune with the dead.
The response of the community to Catwoman is expressed for the most
part by Mrs Kilbride. Her grievances over Catwoman's attendance at the
wedding party, as well as her irritation at her alliance with Father Willow
are clearly stated:

MONICA: Hasn't she as much right to walk God's earth as you, partake of its pleasures too.
MRS KILBRIDE: No, she hasn't. Not til she washes herself. The turf-smoke stink of
   her. Look at her moochin' up to Father Willow and her never inside the door of
   the church and me at seven Mass every mornin' watchin' that auld fool dribblin'
   into the chalice. And would he call to see me? Never. Spends all his time with
   the Catwoman in her dirty little hovel. I'd write to the Archbishop if I thought
   he was capable of anythin'. Why did ya have to invite her?[188]

Shortly following Mrs Kilbride's outburst at Catwoman's presence at the
wedding, Father Willow, who is largely a peripheral figure in the play, is
presented as weak, in his inability to appease the community's taste for conflict. Representative of the Catholic Church's failure to understand its role
in the community, his presence brings the play to melodramatic levels:

MRS KILBRIDE: Would you say the grace, Father Willow and be –
FATHER WILLOW: The grace, yes, how does it go again?

187   Carr, *By the Bog of Cats*, p. 53.
188   Carr, *By the Bog of Cats*, p. 50.

MRS KILBRIDE: Bless us, oh Lord, and these thy gifts which of –
FATHER WILLOW: Rowena. That was it. Rowena Phelan. I should never have ate
that duck egg – no – (*stands there lost in thought*).[189]

Father Willow's final piece of dialogue is presented as ambivalent and conflictual. In response to Hester's desperate plea for rescue from being expelled from Mrs Kilbride's violent threat to burn her out of the Bog of Cats and Xavier's rhetorical question commanding her to leave, Father Willow openly rejects her:

HESTER: I can't lave the Bog of Cats –
MRS KILBRIDE: We'll burn ya out if we have to –
HESTER: Ya see –
MRS KILBRIDE: Won't we, Xavier –
XAVIER: Ya can lave me out of any low-boy tactics. You're lavin' this place today, Swane, aren't ya?
HESTER: I can't lave – Ya see me mother said she'd come back here. Father Willow, tell them what they're doin' is wrong. They'll listen to you.
FATHER WILLOW: They've never listened to me, sure they even lie in the Confession Box. Ya know wha I do? I wear ear-plugs.[190]

Ironically, the narrative reveals Mrs Kilbride's genealogical connection with the Travelling community. The irony is further deepened by Mrs Kilbride's defence to this information, in which she distinguishes her grandfather as 'a wanderin' tinsmith.'[191] In relation to the origin of Travellers, George Gmelch notes:

[...] the name *tinker* was derived from the sound of the craftsman's hammer striking metal. As early as the fifth century, smiths travelled the countryside making personal ornaments and weapons in exchange for food and lodgings. By 1175, *tinker* and *tynkere* began to appear in written records as trade names or surnames.[192]

---

189 Carr, *By the Bog of Cats*, p. 53.
190 Carr, *By the Bog of Cats*, p. 57.
191 Carr, *By the Bog of Cats*, p. 56.
192 Gmelch, pp. 8–9.

However, popular belief in Ireland is that they descended primarily from families dispossessed during the Great Famine of 1845–48. Irish Travellers themselves favour this local origin, because sharing a historical connection to the dominant society arguably forms a more 'positive' discrimination for both. Consequently, it tends toward a 'sympathetic' view of their symbiotic economic and social relationship with one another. According to Okley, Travellers acquiesce to a title and origin in exchange for a desirable recognition from the dominant society, as a form of protection 'and freedom from enforced similation or persecution.'[193] Okley suggests that this kind of relationship 'both reflects and enforces their current political position.'[194] Bhabha's cultural interstitial perspective incorporates cultural difference 'without an assumed or imposed hierarchy.'[195] He cites Renée Green, who 'reflects on the need to understand cultural difference as the production of minority identities that "split" – are estranged unto themselves – in the act of being articulated into a collective body.'[196] Mrs Kilbride, as 'estranged unto herself' also portrays Gramsci's notion of how subalterns form their own counter hegemony in order to displace the hegemony of the dominant class. Mrs Kilbride enacts Gramsci's belief that subaltern groups affiliate themselves to dominant groups. This affiliation reaffirms Kiberd's notion of why the colonised imitate their oppressor.

Cultural difference is represented in *By the Bog of Cats* in the various degrees of political, social and economic discourses, providing the dominant rhetoric over Travellers by the Settled Community. Just as 'the relationship between the Occident and the Orient is a relationship of power, of domination and of a complex hegemony' the Travellers' enforced assimilation to the settled ways of life is articulated as though it is a shared and collective concept.[197] The 'production' of Travellers by the Settled culture sees Travellers struggle to affiliate themselves to the dominant group in the drama. The closing moments of the play demonstrate Hester's abjection

193   Okley in *Irish Travellers: Culture and Ethnicity*, pp. 6–7.
194   Okley, pp. 6–7.
195   Bhabha, *The Location of Culture*, p. 4.
196   Bhabha, *The Location of Culture*, p. 3.
197   Said, *Orientalism*, p. 5.

within the oppressive world, where Hester slits her daughter's throat and then kills herself. The 'maternal' mother as the 'caring' and 'nourishing' figure is at the same time confirming her journey towards the loss of self-hood. The force of Hester's abject resistance is the plight placed upon her by the Settled community. She has been beaten down, gradually succumbing to the gratification of violence, to the deadening of emotion and to her own sense of powerlessness, as the only viable response to her liminal position as half traveller–half settled woman. The murder of her child depicts what Kristeva describes as 'absolute degradation'[198]:

> Abjection then wavers between the fading away of all meaning and all humanity, burnt as by the flames of a conflagration, and the ecstasy of an ego that, having lost its Other and its objects, reaches, at the precise moment of this suicide, the height of harmony with the promised land.[199]

The play dramatises the need for society to confront representations of difference with respect. In order to achieve this, the Settled community needs to embrace what Said calls, referring to Raymond Williams, a cultural process involving 'the unlearning' of 'the inherent dominative mode.'[200] While Hester is neither a Traveller nor a Settled person, she is both a Traveller and a Settled person. In acknowledging her subjectivity, society could then begin to hear her void of selfhood, her cries of abjection, rather than wanting to expel what they don't understand.

---

198 Kristeva, p. 18.
199 Kristeva, p. 18.
200 Said, *Orientalism*, p. 28.

The One Blood

This chapter examines the fragile borders of subjectivity in *On Raftery's Hill* and *Meat and Salt*, plays responding to the collapse of social and patriarchal values, which no longer offer meaning, so that the characters need to draw on their capacity to create boundaries, draw lines, affirm differences in order to both create and maintain some kind of order. The binaries which underlie this boundary-making activity, by which order is demarcated from disorder, dirt from clean, pleasure from pain and so on, are ambiguous. What lies along or between the spectrum of the binary – the irregular, anomalous, or unnatural – still exists but may not be selected as acceptable for how humans experience their existence. Therefore the threat to existence in terms of 'order', 'the proper' and 'the clean' for example, gives potential power to its binary other and to what lies along and between the spectrum – in the context of 'disorder', 'the improper' and 'the unclean'.

This chapter examines the conditions and the nature of individual and cultural boundaries in terms of abjection in *On Raftery's Hill* and *Meat and Salt*, showing how the processes of abusive power relationships are built around individually appropriated value systems and revealing the destructiveness of abjection. *On Raftery's Hill* is the most explicit of all of Carr's works and unlike most of her other plays, it lacks any mythic framework which might tender some sense of hope or accountability for the tragic and traumatic events dramatised in the world of the play. Carr resists an explanatory metanarrative that might 'frame' the violence of the play and thereby keep the uncanniness of the invaded body at bay. The chapter examines how relationships in the abject sense embody a vast range of social meanings relating to the society which the plays literally or symbolically represent, and specifically, how difficult social concerns are subsumed through forms of individual denial and avoidance. The fact that no one dies in either play offers different meanings in terms of their form and content. In *On Raftery's Hill*, incest and abuse are perpetuated by patriarchal power but in *Meat and Salt* patriarchal power is apprehended and reformed by the successfully resistant female protagonist, enacting Cathy Leeney's statement: 'Only the crossing of a boundary makes that boundary visible.'[1]

Julia Kristeva's notion of abjection is used to interrogate Carr's structure of boundaries in terms of identity, related to family, home and 'kingdom' in the plays, presented through issues of power and abuse. Kristeva's concepts of 'inside', 'outside', 'inclusion', 'exclusion', her questions of origin related to the maternal, and the Law of the father in relation to abjection illuminates the construction of boundaries in the plays. Subjectivity in the context of abjection is revealed as unstable and ambiguous, a particular kind of derelict identity that emerges from individual self-abasement. Abjection is a state in which 'the twisted braids of affects and thoughts I call by such a name does not have, properly speaking, a definable object ... The abject has only one quality of the object – that of being opposed to I.'[2] Kristeva's process of anti-self can be thought of in terms of the journey towards self-destruction in *On Raftery's Hill* and the resistance to authority in *Meat and Salt*.

Set in the Midlands of contemporary Ireland, the plot of *On Raftery's Hill* centres on four generations of the Raftery family. The play opens to the sound of Ded, the only son of patriarch Red Raftery, playing fiddle music, which echoes through the house from the open door of the kitchen that leads to where Ded lives in the barn outside. It is evening and Sorrel, his youngest sister of eighteen, beckons Ded to come into the house for his dinner, which Dinah has prepared. Ded is terrified to come in and is described in the stage directions as '*a huge man, beaten to the scut*'.[3] When

1   Cathy Leeney, 'Ireland's "exiled" women playwrights: Teresa Deevy and Marina Carr' in Shaun Richards (ed.), *The Cambridge Companion to Twentieth Century Irish Drama* (Cambridge University Press, 2004), pp. 150–163, p. 150.

2   Julia Kristeva, *Powers of Horror: An Essay on Abjection*, trans. Leon S. Roudiez (New York: Columbia University Press, 1982), p. 1.

3   Marina Carr, *On Raftery's Hill* (Oldcastle, Co. Meath: Gallery Press, 2000), p. 13.

the play opens, Red is out hunting but, according to Ded, he could 'slide back in like a geenie.'[4] From the outset, abuse is evident in the Raftery home. The central plot reveals that Sorrel is Dinah's daughter by her father Red, and that Ded, her brother, delivered her. Dinah, the older sister, plays the roles of 'mother' and 'wife' in the home. Shalome, their paternal grandmother, also lives in the house. She is aware of the ongoing incest and she has also been subject to patriarchal authority in the past; that of her father and of her now dead husband, Brian Raftery.

The inter-play of past and present in *On Raftery's Hill* shapes the dramatic content and form, and the narrative moves between the 'real' and the unnatural. The absent, elusive or romantic male in Carr's previous works, such as Robert or the Nine Fingered Fisherman in *The Mai*, or Gabriel Scully in *Portia Coughlan*, is now a fully fleshed figure, characterised by sexual possessiveness and violence. Matt O'Brien notes in relation to Carr's dramas that 'the legendary and fanciful offstage [male] figure in the other plays – is actually on stage, in the person of Red Raftery. [W]e see the Fantasy Male here – and he's horrifying.'[5] Commenting on the significant absent and present characters in Carr's works, O'Brien observes how 'Red's need for self satisfaction, his domination of the situations and rooms he enters, his disregard for the feelings and needs of his children is perfectly in line with Big Josie Swane, and for all we know, Grandma Fraochlan's nine-fingered fisherman.'[6]

Patriarchal control is a dominant and destructive force and that destruction is self-perpetuating. Carr explores this legacy as it affects the lives of the Raftery family. While patriarchal control is also at the centre of destruction in *The Cordelia Dream* (2008), *Meat and Salt* (2003) and *Ariel* (2002), the Greek myth that frames *Ariel*, the fairytale and playfulness of *Meat and Salt*, the dreamlike King Lear connections to *Meat and Salt* and *The Cordelia Dream*, make the plays less harsh and realist and

4   Carr, *On Raftery's Hill*, p. 13.
5   Matt O'Brien, in 'Always the Best Man, Never the Groom: The Role of the Fantasy Male in Marina Carr's Plays' in Cathy Leeney & Anna McMullan (eds), *The Theatre of Marina Carr* (Dublin: Carysfort, 2003), p. 214.
6   O'Brien, p. 214.

more theatrically imaginative than *On Raftery's Hill*. The current social background makes the events of *On Raftery's Hill* even more chilling.

The interfamilial sexual relationships, dominated by the father, are an ongoing force to be contended with. Shalome speaks of an 'immortal' patriarchy that refuses to die. Referring to her own dead father, she tells her son Red, 'Daddys never die, they just fake rigor mortis and all the time they're throwing tantrums in the coffin, claw marks on the lid.'[7] This observation acts as a framing metaphor for the central action of the drama depicted in male authority, which is seen through the relationships between father and daughters, father and mother, and father and forefather.

For Carr, the cycles of abuse are an inevitable process of abjection, a legacy that she confronts in this play. In placing a male figure centre stage and employing typical elements and themes of the Irish theatrical canon, such as marriage, parents (usually the father) and their offspring, sexuality, rural Ireland and the Catholic Church, *On Raftery's Hill* questions both male authority and the ways in which female subjectivity is represented in contemporary Ireland.[8] Carr's plays are dramas of cultural exposition and resistance to traditional representations of the idealised female in Ireland in both private and public spheres, supported by Church and State and reinforced by the 1937 Irish Constitution.

The focus on Red's behaviour in the Raftery family gives emphasis to the nature and character of sex roles and definitions of masculinity and femininity in the household. Red is more characteristic of a traditional than of a contemporary father figure in rural Ireland, as observed by Eliott Leyton: 'In the mid 1970s in Ireland, the dominant male position within the family typically dictated and shaped many aspects of family values and

---

7   Carr, *On Raftery's Hill*, p. 57.

8   *On Raftery's Hill* has remnants of John B. Keane's *The Field* (1965), which dramatises the conflict between the 'rightful' ownership of the land and the possibility of losing its possession to a more ambitious youth. There are traces of Keane's drama *Sive* (1959), which is concerned with how sexuality is used as a commodity. There are echoes of Brian Friel's *Philadelphia Here I Come* (1964), which centres on the alienating conditions in the relationship between a parent and child because of the inability to communicate.

family discipline, including sexual behaviour.'⁹ The traditional notions of woman, with her feminised domestic duties in the home and man with his role of authority and breadwinner outside of it, are presented by the Rafterys.

While the contemporary notion of family is difficult to define, given its multidimensional concept, it has shifted from the traditional family paradigm of two parents; a father and mother, and their child and/or children. Finola Kennedy refers to some of the changes to family, which include babies born to unmarried mothers and marriage partners having more third level education, which combined with improved job opportunities, have enabled women to find employment.¹⁰ Additionally, given that the Irish State gives financial support to single mothers, the agency afforded to women in contemporary Ireland is not seen in *On Raftery's Hill*. Yet as Melissa Sihra states: '[I]n a society where historical processes of female oppression have only begun to be seriously acknowledged in the social, political and academic fora of the last decade or so, painful narratives need to be addressed.'¹¹

The man/masculine/father figure and woman/feminine/mother figures in the play are complex. The play reveals that there were rumours in the past about Red and Shalome's relationship, which caused Old Raftery to quit the hurling team. By implying that Red is also a victim of sexual abuse, the relationship between victim and aggressor is blurred and complicated. Eamonn Jordan notes: 'Carr points to Red's origins not to downgrade Red's responsibility but to establish the complex cycle of abuse from which he has been the by-product, and to hint, as is often the case, that offspring of incestuous relationships have been genetically predisposed to some sort

9   Eliott Leyton, *The One Blood: Kinship and Class in an Irish Village* (St John's, Canada: Memorial University of Newfoundland, 1975), p. 35.
10   See Finola Kennedy in *Ireland in Transition*, pp. 91–100.
11   Melissa Sihra, The House of Woman and the plays of Marina Carr' in Melissa Sihra (ed.), *Women in Irish Drama: A Century of Authorship and Representation* (Basingstoke, UK: Palgrave Macmillan, 2007), pp. 201–215, p. 214.

of maladjustment or madness.'[12] Dinah too is having an ongoing sexual relationship with Red. Added to this, their daughter Sorrel highlights their relationship as mother and father. The breaking and blurring of these boundaries and roles in the household raises immense concerns not just about parent–child relationships but also about the generic and cultural meaning of parenthood as a whole. This incorporates the domestic responsibilities of the Raftery family and how the home and family are divided up, which reflects much about male and female power relations in the family. Kristeva notes that 'abjection is elaborated through a failure to recognise its kin; [where] nothing is familiar, not even the shadow of a memory.'[13] Edged by the abject, Red rejects familial boundaries and social rules, by having sexual relations with his family, thereby driving his family by his abject laws within his abject territory. Nothing is familiar for Red in the Kristevan sense of acknowledging social and moral boundaries.

The opening moments of *On Raftery's Hill* portray Ded, described as '*a man in his mid-thirties, big shouldered, long-haired, bearded, filthy; cowdung all over his clothes*,' terrified of his father, Red.[14] Ded has never recovered from participating in the birth of his sister/niece, Sorrel, eighteen years ago in the cowshed:

> DED: Me stomach hurts fierce and me head and me eyes.
> DINAH: Ya just had wan a your fits.
> DED: Whah?
> RED: A'ya calmed down now a ya?
> DED: Whah planet am I on?
> DINAH: You're on planet Raftery.[15]

12   Eamonn Jordan, 'From Context to Text: A Construction of Innocence and Sexual Violation in Contemporary Irish Theatre' in *Bullan – An Irish Studies Journal*, Vol. VI. 1 Summer/Fall (2001), p. 57.
13   Kristeva, *Powers of Horror*, p. 5.
14   Carr, *On Raftery's Hill*, p. 13.
15   Carr, *On Raftery's Hill*, p. 48.

Ded's behaviour and personal hygiene enacts Kristeva's notion of filth which disturbs 'identity, system, order.'[16] Red asks Dinah to take Ded back to the shed and like an animal she leads him there and settles him down on the hay. Shalome blames Red's parenting skills for the way Ded lives: 'You didn't give him a proper rearing Red.'[17] The trauma of Sorrel's birth has left Ded living and behaving like an animal outside in the shed. Red tells him at one point, while threatening him into silence and keeping the family's behaviours a secret: '[S]top blinkin will ya. You're noh a hare a' ya.'[18] Red's authority is enough to generate confusion in Ded's mind, convincing him that he 'should be puh away.'[19] As Jordan notes: 'The capacity of the authority figure to demand and insist upon contradictory things is firmly established.'[20] Ded asks Red: 'So am I to smoke or not to smoke? Whah? Am I to come in the house or noh? Whah? Am I to drink your whiskey or noh? Whah ya sayin, Daddy? Just lay down the rules, don't keep changing them. Don't. I don't know whah to do to make you happy.'[21] Ded's animal behaviour sees him being regarded as 'lesser than' the other Rafterys. Philo and Wilbert note:

> [There is] a long-standing human belief in a basic distinction between what is often termed the 'civilised' or 'rational' being who can think and act in the world (the human) and what are often identified as the base passions and instincts which allegedly obliterate a being's potential for agency ... From this distinction arises the widespread use of terms such as 'animal' and 'bestial' to describe groups of people perceived to engage in antisocial, possibly inhumane activities ... Sometimes human groups may be regarded as lesser or marginal to other more dominant groups, and may thereby be associated with animals.[22]

16 Kristeva, *Powers of Horror*, p. 4.
17 Carr, *On Raftery's Hill*, p. 50.
18 Carr, *On Raftery's Hill*, p. 26.
19 Carr, *On Raftery's Hill*, p. 26.
20 Jordan, in *Bullan – An Irish Studies Journal*, Vol. VI. 1 Summer/Fall, p. 55.
21 Carr, *On Raftery's Hill*, p. 27.
22 Chris Philo and Chris Wilbert (eds), *Animal Spaces, Beastly Places: New Geographies of Human–Animal Relations* (London: Routledge, 2000), p. 15.

In the 'Improper/Unclean', Kristeva outlines filth as a form of self-loathing, which paradoxically protects the self.[23] It is the simultaneous process of establishing and abjecting oneself and it is the very condition for the abject self-hood to emerge. The self is consciously and unconsciously expelled from the being, and the state of abandonment is the reinstatement of a new identity where, 'I am at the border of my condition as a living being ... where the border has become an object ... It is something rejected from which one does not part, [and] from which one does not protect itself as from an object.'[24] For Ded, the memory of delivering Sorrel is the last-ditch crisis resulting from father/daughter incest. Kristeva's association of fertility with bodily filth, and its equation with suffering and exhaustion, is manifested in Ded's behaviour following the delivery of Sorrel: 'The corpse (or cadaver: cadere, to fall) ... upsets even more violently the one who confronts it as fragile and fallacious chance. A wound with blood and pus, or the sickly acrid smell of sweat, of decay ... show me what I permanently thrust aside in order to live.'[25] Ded's state of mind at experiencing abjection presents the borders of himself, threatened and disoriented, trying to fathom his participation in the birth, how and why Dinah became pregnant, why no-one came to help him, wondering what it all means to him and what he means. Though the grandmother Shalome and Red were close at hand in the house during Sorrel's birth, no one came to help Ded. As he tells his father and grandmother: 'I was the wan had to do ih all. Daddy came to me and says, you're to go down to the cowshed wud Dinah ... And there's blood and every fuckin thing comin ouh a Dinah.'[26] The experiences of the Raftery family on the hill are beyond the intervention of the Catholic Church and State, and outside of society, as Red says with 'no stupid laws houldin us down or back or in.'[27] Ded espouses an abject self, living as the outcast in the shed, literally and metaphorically skirting

23   Kristeva, *Powers of Horror*, pp. 2–3.
24   Kristeva, *Powers of Horror*, pp. 3–4.
25   Kristeva, *Powers of Horror*, p. 3.
26   Carr, *On Raftery's Hill*, p. 48.
27   Carr, *On Raftery's Hill*, pp. 31–32.

along the periphery of his family. He declares that he will only live in the house when Red dies.

On Raftery's Hill traces the shadowed existence of the household, specifically the women, living on a remote hilltop, and complying to live a cloistered existence at the cost of their personal safety. Red Raftery has become something of a Big Daddy figure similar to *Meat and Salt*; he is 'the king of his castle' on the hilltop overlooking the valley below. Just as the topography of Carr's Midland bogscapes, rivers and lakes in her 1994–1998 trilogy is significant to both the form and content in the dramas, so too the hilltop in *On Raftery's Hill* provides a symbolic resonance of topographical prominence and social isolation in the play. Shalome's comment to Dara Mood, an ambitious but small farmer from the valley below and Sorrel's fiancé, acknowledges the geographical and symbolic position of the family's isolation: 'we are strange creatures up here on the Hill.'[28] Their location on the hilltop provides another means by which to promote the family's abject existence. Kristeva points out in 'An exile who asks where?',

> For the space that engrosses the deject, the excluded, is never *one*, nor homogenous, nor totalizable, but essentially divisible, foldable and catastrophic. A deviser of territitories, languages, works, the *deject* never stops demarcating his universe, whose fluid confines – for they are constituted of a non-object – the abject – constantly question his solidity and impel him to start afresh.[29]

The abject marks out its territory. Foreignness is incorporated into its terrain in exchange for feelings of estrangement, which identify the inner subject. Abjection stresses a loss, which establishes being-a-subject, and is reflected in the space around the subject. The location of the Raftery's home is a reflection of this space, and is a way for the Rafterys to be separated from the public, fencing their being inside the boundaries of the house and securing Red's abusive patriarchal role within the home. The currency of his being oscillates between his fear of himself and his protective constructed abject self. In 'A Fortified Castle', Kristeva metaphorically

28   Carr, *On Raftery's Hill*, p. 50.
29   Kristeva, *Powers of Horror*, p. 8.

describes how the subject's 'constituting barrier between subject and object has here become an insurmountable wall. An ego, wounded to the point of annulment, barricaded and untouchable, cowers somewhere, nowhere, at no place than the one that cannot be found.'[30] Red's abjection of self, projected towards his family in the form of incest and abuse, is his 'link to the world ... A stifled aspiration towards an other as prohibited as it is desired – abject.'[31] Carr subverts the hilltop as the familiar cultural site of beauty in the play. The hills of Ireland are frequently associated with an idealised (Catholic) pastoral rural vision, yet the beauty of the hills can often conceal the harsher realities of Ireland's landscape:

> From the hills of holy Ireland we can look down and admire the deep valleys, the yellow fields of corn, the circling rivers and cattle-dotted meadow; yet to all of Irish birth can never be hidden the crumbling walls of empty farmsteads, the brier grown graveyard, with roofless abbey and broken cross, the gallows hill, the decaying towns with huge barracks and ponderous jails, and the ever-present workhouse, where no work or industry is ever taught, and from whose walls no good ever came.[32]

Here the panoramic landscape is contrasted against the more severe situation of poverty, loss, emigration and death, the blighted social circumstance. The juxtaposed images presented retain yet some kind of overall tranquillity, but emphasising the sacredness of the landscape subsumes the cultural problem viewed clearly from the hilltop. A parallel can be drawn between what is presented by *The Hills of Holy Ireland* and the panorama presented in the play; a particular perspective enables certain aspects to be seen, while shadowing or masking others. Many of the hills of Ireland were the locations of ancient myths, legends, medieval churches, towers and the sites of great battles lost and won. Seán P. Ó Ríordáin writes of the Hill of Tara in County Meath: 'There is no doubt that the hilltop situation and also the prospect it commanded were factors in the selection of the site at Tara in ancient times and people innocent of modern ideas of geology

---

30   Kristeva, *Powers of Horror*, p. 47.

31   Kristeva, *Powers of Horror*, p. 47.

32   Ardrigh, [pseudonym], *The Hills of Holy Ireland* (Dublin: Catholic Truth Society of Ireland, not dated), p. 4.

were nevertheless influenced by features developing from the geological development of the area.'[33] In describing the rich soil and the impressive view of Tara, Ó Ríordáin states that it is 'a fitting dwelling place for royal rulers who looked down on the source of their wealth – some of the richest pasture land in Europe.'[34] Red's surveillance of his wealth from the hilltop is primarily in terms of his family. Protecting his 'wealth' means protecting 'his kingdom', the system that allows him to continue abusing his family and farm in the way that he does. In keeping a watchful eye on his family, he is also keeping the community away from the sexual violations that he performs on his family in the home and the animal cruelty he performs on the farm.

The position of the hilltop in the play has other idyllic and sinister realities related to it. Red's lands of decomposing animals have destabilised the kind of ordering he tried to establish over his farm, enacting Kristeva's notion of bodily confrontation. For Kristeva, death's charge of abjection is borne out, not in linguistic or graphic representation, but in the physical body. This confrontation takes place in the fields, which have become a graveyard for animals. The amplified smell of animal corpses trigger the detachment felt by Red towards his father. Red's father, Old Raftery, kept the farm impeccably, as Shalome states: 'Far be it from me to say anything good about old Raftery, but I will say this much. He kept this farm clean. You could eat your dinner off the yard if you were that way inclined.'[35] Red's farming method has created a 'spatial externality' where the stench of the bodily wastes of his animals has diffused beyond the bounds of the farm, penetrating and polluting the valley below.[36] Red cannot fully control his land and his animals. In death, the animals' rotting carcasses seep and leak beyond his fenced boundaries. As Chris Philo and Chris Wilbert state:

33 Seán P. Ó Ríordáin, *Tara: The Monuments on the Hill* (Dundalk: Dundalgan Press, 1964), p. 5.

34 Ó Ríordáin, p. 6.

35 Carr, *On Raftery's Hill*, p. 31.

36 Philo and Wilbert, *Animal Spaces, Beastly Places*, p. 2.

a complex human–animal relation is established which does not operate solely through the physical proximity of humans and animals, but rather entails a spread-out geography through which animals are able to have an effect on human at-a-distance. Wider questions about private property, the byproducts of economic activity, and the duty of the state to regulate agricultural activities in the interest of preventing pollution ... are deeply implicated.[37]

Extending beyond the boundaries of the farm through wind and streams, animal abuse has implications that extend to the wider society. Isaac tells Red: 'Ud's not the hares has the land ruined and you wud a stinkin carcass in every field. You'll turn this beauhiful farm into an abattoir.'[38] Yet the play offers no intervention from the community. Raftery's hill and farmlands are allowed to stink the community below and no one complains.

The lack of social intervention or engagement between people in the community also emerges in the subplot of the narrative. Dara Mood, and Isaac Dunne, a neighbour and Red's hunting partner, tell the news of a tragedy in the community as a result of incest. Dara is an eyewitness to the death of Sarah Brophy, a peer of Sorrel's from the valley below, who died shortly after digging her dead child's grave and clinging to the coffin. The story reveals that Sarah's son was the offspring of her relationship with her father and when word goes out that she is missing, she is

found by her father in the small hours, sittin on the coffin tryin to fade the child, couldn't say which a them bluer. Brophy throws hees coah over her and tries to take her home buh she refuses to go wudouh the child. Eventually they geh her into bed wud the corpse a the infant and she goes into some sourt a fih and dies this afternoon.[39]

Later, Brophy kills himself by drinking weed killer in an asylum in Ballinasloe, Co. Galway. Red disbelieves the story, claiming that it is all based on hearsay. He tells Dara: 'Don't belave ud. Don't believe wan word of ud. Sarah Brophy goh whah was comin to her. Now I'm sorry the child

---

37   Philo and Wilbert, *Animal Spaces, Beastly Places*, p. 2.
38   Carr, *On Raftery's Hill*, p. 19.
39   Carr, *On Raftery's Hill*, p. 23.

had to die, wouldn't wish thah on anywan. Buh blamin Brophy's all wrong. Ya don't know whah you're talking abouh, young Mood. Ud's gossips like you distriys a man's good name and reputation.'[40] Red's repudiation that such events could have occurred is a denial and a rejection of responsibility for his own incestuous behaviour. If the event did occur, Red's sense of morality believes that Sarah Brophy 'goh whah was comin to her.'[41] That the Brophy story did not reach the community until after the tragic deaths of the mother and child were discovered is significant. The silence of the community in the play acts a metaphor for Ireland's tendency to resist and conceal distasteful issues. It is only in the last fifteen years that Ireland's hidden histories of abuse in many families and state institutions are being exposed. Jordan notes:

> Since the mid-80s people have been shocked by stories in the public domain of abuse against children and vulnerable adults. The activities of predatorial, serial abusers and rapists have been reported along with details of child prostitution and paedophile rings ... It is not just individuals, but institutionally structured violation also needs to be considered ... The failing of care institutions like the Goldenbridge home for children, investigations into sexual abuse at both Madonna and Trudder houses and the horrors of the Magdalene laundries and of some industrial schools all came to light and gave rise to huge anger.[42]

As in Carr's other works, the animal kingdom becomes a way to critique a kind of social order. *On Raftery's Hill* examines how animals are defined as food, pets or pests by the various characters and how they are 'placed' in spaces such as farms, fields and homes. Animals are bound up with humans in the uses that humans make of them. Repeated references to animals such as swans, cats and hares as dramatic signifiers of love, luck and death in *The Mai* and *By the Bog of Cats* recur in *On Raftery's Hill* with hares, cats and cattle – as pets and pests.

The ways in which Red relates to the world of animals metaphorically echo the wielding of an oppressive power within the human relations of

40 Carr, *On Raftery's Hill*, p. 23.
41 Carr, *On Raftery's Hill*, p. 23.
42 Jordan, in *Bullan – An Irish Studies Journal*, Vol. VI. 1 Summer/Fall, p. 47.

the Raftery family. Red rapes Sorrel on the kitchen table, trapping her in a dismal abject situation. The act of rape is accompanied by Red's commentary on how to gut a hare, a sign of man-as-hunter, a powerful image that reinforces Sorrel's trauma:

> RED: Did you gut them hares, did ya?
> SORREL: I don't know how to gut a hare.
> RED: Donten ya? Alrigh, I'll show ya how to gut a hare.
> *Grabs her suddenly and holds her in a vice grip. Sorrel struggles pointlessly against the strength of him.*
> SORREL: Ow! You're hurting me, Daddy.
> RED: (*cutting the clothes off her with the knife*) First ya skin the hare ...
> SORREL: Daddy! Stop!
> RED: Ya do that slow and aisy ...
> SORREL: Whah're ya doin! Whah're ya doin!
> RED: (*holding her in a vice grip, all the time cutting the clothes off her*) Ya do that slow and aisy so ya don't nick the flesh ...[43]

Red treats his family and animals as one and the same. The only hope of escape from the patriarchal cycles of abuse is Sorrel, but this is quenched by her rape, which results in her breaking off her engagement to Dara. Red enacts Laura Mulvey's appropriated notion of Freud's scopophilic gaze, which preludes the rape. Red has been standing on the stairs watching the lovers Dara and Sorrel part, with Sorrel as the object of his gaze. In the context of the traditional gender binary categories, Mulvey's scopophilia outlines 'woman as image [and] man as the bearer of the look.'[44] She notes that the 'determining male gaze projects its phantasy on to the female figure which is styled accordingly. Women are simultaneously looked at and displayed, with their appearance coded for strong visual and erotic impact so that they can be said to connote "*to be looked at ness.*" Women displayed as sexual object is the leitmotif of erotic spectacle.'[45] In 'The Decline of the

43   Carr, *On Raftery's Hill*, p. 35.
44   Laura Mulvey in 'Visual Pleasure And Narrative Cinema' in Lizbeth Goodman & Jane deGay (eds), *The Routledge Reader in Gender and Performance* (London: Routledge, 1998), p. 272.
45   Laura Mulvey, 'Visual Pleasure And Narrative Cinema', p. 272.

Panoptic Principle' Martin Jay describes the power of surveillance 'from punishment to pleasure and the psychological mechanisms on which that is based' stating:

> Freud came to believe that the very desire to know, rather than being innocent, was itself ultimately derived from an infantile desire to see, which had sexual origins. Sexuality, mastery and vision were thus intricately intertwined in ways that could produce problematic as well as 'healthy' effects. Infantile scopophilia could result in adult voyeurism or other perverse disorders such as exhibitionism and scopophobia (the fear of being seen).[46]

The play suggests that Red was abused in the past, and like his mother, 'his desire to know' regarding sexuality, was probably imposed on him rather than discovered by him. Thus, his sexual growth had its origins in a perverse awareness, corrupting a healthier journey to his sexual development. The abject drew him back to a confusion regarding the boundaries between the self and the mother's body: 'The abject confronts us, on the one hand, and this time within our personal archaeology, with our earliest attempts to release the hold of maternal entity even before ex-isting outside her, thanks to the autonomy of language.'[47] Red's confusion of his self with Shalome, his mother's body, causes his unease in terms of the self's ability to function productively (as farmer or father) or reproductively (as an autonomous adult in a healthy sexual and emotional relationship).

The symbolic frailty of the hare is linked to Sorrel's defencelessness when the rape act takes place. Sorrel is anti-hunting and when Red asks her to gut the hares she refuses: 'I will noh. Nowan ever tell you ud's bad luck to shooh a hare never mind two?'[48] Red's kind of hunting becomes a violation of nature. David Matless outlines a particular version of animal–human consideration conceived through 'visceral eyes', which 'highlights a particular conjunction of body and sight' in the pursuit of the animal

---

46   Peter Weibel in 'Pleasure and the Panoptic Principle' in Thomas Y. Levin, Ursula Frohne and Peter Weibel (eds), *CTRL [Space]:Rhetorics of Surveillance from Bentham to Big Brother* (Karlsruhe, Germany: ZKM, 2002), p. 219.
47   Kristeva, *Powers of Horror*, p. 13.
48   Carr, *On Raftery's Hill*, p. 19.

whether for pleasure, profit or food.[49] Red's hunting techniques can be considered through the visual relationship between landscape and nature. Matless outlines how this version of animal–human

> rests on a metaphoric connection of eye and guts, in three senses: that one sees in order to kill in order to eat; that the deadly dead-eye of a good shot brings his visceral human closer to the visceral animal through the act of killing; that guts signify a courageous and hardy masculinity in the field.[50]

Reminiscent of Red's scopophilic look before he rapes Sorrel, his technique for hunting animals in Matless's terms can also be considered in relation to humans. Red visually spans the area, (kitchen) locates his target (Sorrel) and then 'shoots' his prey (rapes) – the ultimate power of 'owning' his victim.

The blurring of boundaries between humans and animals continues throughout the play. Red treats Shalome as an expendable animal because she is old and therefore no longer of use to anyone. He tells her: 'If you were a cow or a sick dog ud'd be perfectly lagle to put ya ouh a'your misery, but you're an auld woman and ya can do nothing to women these days.'[51] His claim that the law protects women, echoes the Constitution's insistence on protecting the family as the central unit of Irish society, which is ironic in terms of the individual reality of the females in the Raftery family. The final scene, where he brings Shalome back into the house, is accompanied by his hunting commentary of having 'caught' her. Dinah asks: 'Did ya ketch anything?'[52] Red replies: 'Only this auld bird. I nearly shoh her.'[53]

Isaac Dunne too blurs and subverts the relationship between animals and humans. Isaac describes how his old cat Rosie has taken the place of his dead wife in the bed. He states:

49   David Matless, 'Versions of Animal–Human' in Philo and Wilbert, *Animal Spaces, Beastly Places*, p. 116.
50   Matless, p. 116.
51   Carr, *On Raftery's Hill*, p. 31.
52   Carr, *On Raftery's Hill*, p. 57.
53   Carr, *On Raftery's Hill*, p. 57.

Nothin would do her [Rosie] last nigh only hop me ouh on the fluur and her with the whole bed to herself. And would thah sahisfy her? Noh a bit of her ... So I says, Rosie ya cranky yoke ya, you're noh getting me cap as well, and she goes into a tantrum, tears rollin off a her whiskers and poundin the pilla.[54]

Red accuses Isaac of liking animals better than humans. When Rosie dies Isaac declares: 'I'm thinking of havin a waistcoat made ouha her' so, as Dinah suggests, he can continue to stoke her from time to time.[55] Isaac's cat, like Red's cattle, questions the agency of animals, and the extent to which animals can destabilise human ordering. According to Philo and Wilbert, this involves an intricate 'conjoint conceptual–physical placement' of animals by humans, which implies that 'some species should properly be proximate to us while others should properly be remote.'[56]

Red's farm and animals are depicted as a commodity to be controlled as he sees fit. On his farm, he preys upon both animal and human flesh. His farmland reveals a type of space, wherein his livestock live and die as part of a highly unequal human-animal relation predicated on the utility, adaptability and expendability of the animal so incarcerated and highlighting the brutality and inhumanity within the home. The stench of rotting carcasses surrounding the household and farmland accentuates some of the horrific realities in the drama. Red's lack of humanity is foregrounded through the pitiless imagery of his treatment of animals. Isaac describes Red's cruel hunting behaviour on one particular occassion:

ISAAC: And he went into the lair after them and strangled the leverets. Seven little babbys all huddled in a ball. Ya don't hunt fair, Red.
RED: They've the land ruined.
ISAAC: Ud's not the hares has the land ruined and you wud a stinkin carcass in every field. You'll turn this beautiful farm into an abattoir.
RED: Would ya drink thah and stop bendin me ear.[57]

54 Carr, *On Raftery's Hill*, p. 22.
55 Carr, *On Raftery's Hill*, p. 43.
56 Philo and Wilbert, *Animal Spaces, Beastly Places*, p. 11.
57 Carr, *On Raftery's Hill*, p. 19.

Isaac implies that they have a right to live free from interference from humans, at least until they have reached some kind of sporting chance in the hunting game. Dara describes Red's abuse of his cattle, warning Sorrel of his violent potential:

> SORREL: Daddy doesn't have perverse rages, does he?
> DARA: I seen him cut the udders off a cow noh two wakes ago. Down in the River Field. And then he shoh ud, and then he dragged ud to the river wud a rope, a job should take three men to do. And then he pushed ud over the bank and into the river. Cows is the most beauhiful creatures, gentle and trustin and curious, and they've these greah long eyelashes. This wan walked up to him and starts nuzzlin him and he goes ah her wud a knife.[58]

Perversity reaches horrifying heights in *On Raftery's Hill*, particularly in relation to the domain of the female and of motherhood. The act of cutting off a cow's udders, the vessels that permit milk, a vital life-giving source to an animal's young, signifies a deeply ingrained level of abhorrence towards the female, and the maternal. Kristeva's analysis of biblical abominations encounters milk as a dietary prohibition in Judaism because it is a 'food that does not separate but binds' mother to the child.[59] Carr's *Ariel* broadly centres on the extent to which the maternal and the feminine are regarded as 'unclean' by protagonist Fermoy, who is revolted at his ten-year-old son being breast fed by his mother. Milk does not exemplify the logic of separation in both plays; for Red Raftery it connotes incest. The act of shooting the animal after the barbaric deed tends towards psychopathic phobia. The butchered animal described in Dara's graphic imagery, is mobilised and connected to Dinah's pregnancy all those years ago, as the condition wished on the unborn child. No one came to help Ded deliver Sorrel because no other family member wanted her to live, especially Red. Dara is both literally and metaphorically describing Red's annihilation of maternity. Kristeva connects the abject to perversity in the following way:

---

58   Carr, *On Raftery's Hill*, p. 33.
59   Kristeva, *Powers of Horror*, p. 105.

The abject is perverse because it neither gives up nor assumes a prohibition, a rule, or a law; but it turns them aside, misleads, corrupts; uses them, takes advantage of them, the better to deny them. It kills in the name of life ... it lives at the behest of death ... it curbs the other's suffering for its own profit ... it establishes narcissistic power while pretending to reveal the abyss ... Corruption is its most common, most obvious appearance. That is the socialized appearance of the abject.[60]

The fact that the rape takes place in the Raftery's home on the kitchen table is significant, in terms of demonstrating the collapse of the traditional metanarrative as a means of elucidatation. The rape enacts Kristeva's notion of abjection: 'What does not respect borders, positions, rules.'[61] The 1937 Irish Constitution presents 'home' as a social and spatial boundary of 'goodness', implying it to be a safe place. Margaret Llewellyn-Jones describes the connection between woman, mother, family, and home in the Constitution: 'Iconography of woman as pure, yet paradoxically as Madonna-like self sacrificing motherhood is also rooted in the Constitution of the Irish State through articles that also recognised the family.'[62] Woman, absorbed somewhere within the notion of the 'family', will be cared for by the state: 'The state, therefore, guarantees to protect the Family in its constitution and authority, as the necessary basis of social order and as indispensable to the welfare of the Nation and the State.'[63] Articles 41.1.1 and 41.1.2 explicitly frame women as responsible for both the reproduction of the population and the transmission of national identity through the practice of mothering, in order to secure a 'common good'. References to women in the family are in terms of 'her life within the home' upon which the 'common good' depends, and the state's duty to ensure that mothers are not 'obliged by economic necessity to engage in labour to the neglect of their duties in the home.'[64] The problem that faces woman is the discovery that an

60 Kristeva, *Powers of Horror*, pp. 15–16.
61 Kristeva, *Powers of Horror*, p. 4.
62 Margaret Llewellyn-Jones, *Contemporary Irish Drama and Cultural Identity* (Bristol, UK: Intellect Books, 2002), p. 67.
63 J.M. Kelly, *Irish Constitution* (Dublin: Jurist Publishing Co., 1980), Article 41.2.1 and 41.2.2, p. 48.
64 Kelly, *Irish Constitution*, p. 48.

'image' of her in the family and the nation precedes her. Not only does the Constitution advocate a homogenous and rigid notion of womanhood, but it also frames woman within the definition of family. Regarding the Constitution, Kieran McKeown and Harry Ferguson observe: 'Both men and women are diminished by a system that over-identifies women with motherhood and under-identifies men with fatherhood.'[65] Carr subverts the ideologies of gender defined by the State, and presents the family as a site of servitude, submission, and suffering.

The concerns about Irish identity in the public and private spheres, in the context of the State, Church and family, converge on the issues of sexuality in *On Raftery's Hill*. Red exploits his patriarchal authority, giving him licence to construct his own sexual values in the home. Jeffrey Weeks states:

> Sexual Values are important not because they are either rooted in the 'natural' or some revealed truth or foundational given, but because they provide the basis of social or cultural identification which makes possible a meaningful individual and social life, and where appropriate, moral–political struggles.[66]

The patriarchal structure of the Rafterys reveals a gendered hierarchy within the family, where female agency becomes subsumed within the family unit. The drama blurs and complicates the roles of mother, wife, sister, daughter, son, husband and father. The women emerge as passive victims trapped within the family. Dinah performs the typical traditional female roles as outlined by the Constitution, showing no knowledge of any alternatives outside of these narrow confines. Her nameless and dead mother refused to engage in sexual relations with Red, forcing the child to take her place.

---

65   Kieran McKeown, Harry Ferguson & Dermot Rooney, *Changing Fathers?* (Cork: Collins Press, 1997), p. 156.
66   Jeffrey Weeks, *Invented Moralities: Sexual Values in an Age of Uncertainty* (Cambridge: Blackwell Publishers, 1995), p. 9.

DINAH: [...] I never had anywan looking ouh for me the way I looked ouh for you.

SORREL: Some lookouh you are and ya listenin behind the duur to the whole thing.

DINAH: For eigheen years I watched you and minded you and kept ya safe! Ya know how many wishes and drames thah is brushed aside. Eigheen years, the best part of me life and noh wan bih a grahitude from you! No, ya go and fling ud in me face. I had me whole life before you came along missus, nowan ever stood up for me. Ya know whah me mother done? She sent me in to bed beside him. I was lanin on the fridge in the pantry and she comes in behind me and says ouh a nowhere, you're to slape in wud your father tonigh. She didn't want him so she sends in me. I was twelve.[67]

The drama highlights cultural issues with abuse. Dinah has no one to look out for her, because her position as a daughter and 'wife' is absorbed within the family as a unit. Playing the conventional maternal role, she does not neglect her home duties by engaging in outside work. Dinah, who describes her mother as 'allas sick, long as I can remember anyway … lyin in the back parlour wud a dish cloth on her head' becomes the surrogate mother to the family, not just because her mother died, but because her mother refused to or was unable to play any kind of role.[68] Dinah breaks the boundaries between mother and daughter roles by engaging in a sexual relationship with her father:

RED: Stay a while.
DINAH: I'm in no mood for ya tonigh.
RED: G'wan then ya contrary rip ya.
DINAH: (*pauses on the stairs*) Don't touch Sorrel.
RED: I won't ever … I swear.
DINAH: Nigh so.[69]

For most of the play's narrative, Sorrel believes that Dinah is her sister and not her mother. Dinah, as mother figure, also fails to protect Sorrel's

67 Carr, *On Raftery's Hill*, p. 55–56.
68 Carr, *On Raftery's Hill*, p. 40.
69 Carr, *On Raftery's Hill*, pp. 30.

safety within the home, repeating the past in her knowledge and collusion. Indeed the Constitution promotes female subservience as the domestic and sexual expectation in the home, enabling a hierarchal order of power relations. The play sees Red command Sorrel to gut the hares: 'Skin them now, young wan, and gut them. I want hare soup for me breakfast', and he also demands that Sorrel serves his dinner, regarding the female role as a domestic one.[70] Weeks cites Janet Finch on the 'negotiated order'[71] of the family:

> [T]he shared meanings of the family generate a 'hierarchy of obligations' – to spouse above all, to children, to siblings and others, in which women rather than men emerge as carers. The obligations spring from the accepted common sense of everyday life and are sustained by a vague public opinion, expressed through gossip, reputation, family pride, scandal and so on ... The family is a contested space, where there is room for manoeuvre, but also explicit and implied limits.[72]

The Raftery's 'hierarchy of obligations', rooted in incest, is dictated by Red. With no room for manoeuvre, familial incest becomes part of the shared meanings of the family. The Rafterys are not playing the roles as outlined by the State, nor are they representative of Eamonn De Valera's famously cited idyllic representation of Ireland, replete with the family as a microcosm of the nation, emulating safety and security. Ded and Sorrel are constantly under threat of Red's sexual and violent abuse. The Constitution and its laws narrowly define and differentiate mothers, fathers and their children within the institution of marriage.

The Irish state facilitates the vulnerability of individual family members by advocating the 'Family', constructed along the specific kind of heteronormative and essentially gendered citizen. This poses a dilemma when the problematic and complex notions of family conflate. A rape case of 1992, known familiarly as the 'X Case', exposed a particular crisis in Irish social policies. The Irish High Court in 1992 prevented a fourteen-year-old rape victim from travelling to Britain for an abortion, which remains a criminal act. Weeks explains how 'social movements, around sex, gender,

---

70   Carr, *On Raftery's Hill*, p. 19.
71   Weeks, *Invented Moralities*, p. 134.
72   Weeks, *Invented Moralities*, p. 134.

race, the quality of life have significantly changed the political agenda –
and in doing so have shifted the boundaries between the public and the
private.'[73] In relation to the X Case, the boundaries that have shifted are
the public ones, which further dictate how private lives are to be lived.
The structure of the family as an institution in the Irish State sees 'family
values' and beliefs as inextricably linked to Irish cultural values. The State's
intervention in the X case family highlighted the hegemony of the State
as the upholder of justice and 'morality', and its intrusion into the private
sphere of the family.

The role of the State is seen in the context of how abuse operates in
the play. Red, as father and therefore head of the household, enables Sorrel
and Dinah as the victims of rape and incest. The family's collusive psychological climate exposes individual subjective complicity as the result of a
larger family system. At the time of the rape, the rest of the family (Dinah,
Shalome and Ded) were in the house and the cries and yells from Sorrel
echoed through the home. The presence and absence of the family, whose
silence enabled the rape, leave the room isolated and the household 'without the mantle of humanity':[74]

> SORREL: Ya heard me callin, Ded ... why didn't ya come?
> DED: Ya see now, Daddy, I'm just a little bih wary of him, but same as you were to
> remove him, ya wouldn't know me.
> SORREL: Then why don't ya remove him?
> DED: I've a crowbar filed if he comes near me. I'm no girl to be played wud.
> SORREL: I don't think Daddy's choosy. He just wants to bate us all inta the dirt.
> DED: Ud's Dinah decides everythin round here anyway. Dinah's Daddy's cattle dealer.
> You and me is only the cattle, Sorrel.
> DINAH: (*coming down the stairs with a wedding dress*) Am I now?
> DED: First thing I'll do when I get this farm is peg you off of ud.
> DINAH: Why'd'n you just fuck back to the cowshed where ya belong?
> DED: I'll go when I'm good and ready.[75]

73   Weeks, *Invented Moralities*, p. 136.
74   Jordan, in *Bullan – An Irish Studies Journal*, Vol. VI. 1 Summer/Fall, p. 54.
75   Carr, *On Raftery's Hill*, pp. 37–38.

Given that Dinah has been abused for twenty-seven years since the age of twelve and has allowed it to continue, seems to offer little hope that change in this household is imminent. The play demonstrates abuse victims' tendency 'to transfer or pass on the pain.'[76] Jordan states:

> The long term impact of sexual abuse depends on a whole host of factors, from the type of abuse (consensual/non consensual, penetrative/non penetrative) to the degree of cohesive violence involved; from the frequency of the abuse to the prior relationship with the abusive person; from the way the child has been 'groomed' for the assault to the ability of the abuser to admit fully to his/her crime; from the age of the abused person to the relationship that individual has or had with the abusive person; and from the support provided to the victim after the termination of the event to the individual personality of the victim of abuse.[77]

Red's long-term sexual abuse of his family, his superiority in terms of physical strength and monetary control, the climate of abuse in which he himself grew up and his denial of his abusive behaviour, are all factors which promulgate the abuse of sexual power from family member to member.

The level of power assigned to 'man' in the Constitution is extensive, and illuminates the link between the Catholic Church and the State. McKeown et al. state:

> One of the most influential images of fatherhood for many centuries has been the patriarch, which literally means 'father and ruler' ... In this imagery, God is the father and ruler of heaven and earth; the king is the father and ruler of his people; the priest is the father of his flock and the man is the father and head of his family. Throughout the generations, this imagery and, more particularly, the structures which support it, has conferred status on men, or at least some men, in the public spheres of work, politics and religion.[78]

Interestingly, the father in the Christian tradition is connected to the traditional esteem of fathers as signifiers of power, yet, in terms of domestic or emotional responsibility, fathers play an understated role towards the

---

76   Jordan, in *Bullan*, p. 60.
77   Jordan, in *Bullan*, p. 58.
78   McKeown et al., p. 14.

children and the duties in the home. McKeown links the decline in the belief in God in contemporary Ireland (who cannot be separated from Western iconography of a masculine God), the shift from God as a person to God as a spirit or life force, to 'the decline in the symbolism of the father, and possibly vice versa.'[79] The father figure in the Raftery household is all-powerful, largely due to his financial position and the level of power afforded him as head of his family. The family live in Red's farm on Raftery's Hill. His work and his home are one and the same and this enables him to exert ultimate control over everything that takes place. The farm is Red's livelihood and he organises the finances of the household, which enables him to orchestrate his incestuous behaviour and to command the family's silence. Red also tells Dinah: 'I'm thinking a signin the farm over to ya[80] ... Ya want to go into town some day this week?'[81] 'For whah', she asks to which Red replies: 'I d'n know, buy a dress, get your hair done, whahever ud is yees women likes spending money on.'[82] Dinah's response is one of resignation to her situation: 'Whah do I want wud a hair do or a new dress except you to ogle ud off a'me.'[83] Alcohol is her crutch in the intolerable aspects of the life she lives. She tells Red, 'A cuurse I was drinkin upstairs, how else could I face the lug a you.'[84] Regarding his rape of Sorrel, Red states: 'I was only putting manners on her, someone had to, you've her leh run wild ... here. (Gives her a wad of money) G'way and spend thah for yourself.'[85] In relation to Sorrel's wedding, Red offers Dara, who is not aware of what took place, 'the deeds of fifty acres and a cheque for twenty grand.'[86] When Dara turns it down, the frustrated Sorrel tells him to take it, stating. 'They're mine and dearly paid for.'[87] Dinah tells Sorrel regarding

79   McKeown et al., p. 15.
80   Carr, *On Raftery's Hill*, p. 25.
81   Carr, *On Raftery's Hill*, p. 30.
82   Carr, *On Raftery's Hill*, p. 30.
83   Carr, *On Raftery's Hill*, p. 30.
84   Carr, *On Raftery's Hill*, pp. 29–30.
85   Carr, *On Raftery's Hill*, p. 45.
86   Carr, *On Raftery's Hill*, p. 50.
87   Carr, *On Raftery's Hill*, p. 51.

her wedding: 'Daddy says we're to spare no expense, he wants you to have an astoundin day ... he can be very good, Daddy, can't he now?'[88]

While the contemporary conception of the family involves different and changing patterns to the rural family, the Rafterys have characteristics which cannot aptly be fitting by either model.[89] The limits of the family observed earlier by Elliot Leyton, particularly with regard to the family dominated by patriarchy, have broken down in many respects since the 1990s. McKeown et al. list some of the factors that have led to the changing roles of fathering in Ireland from 1971 to 1996. These include the number of women, especially married women, working outside of the home, the growth in the number of one parent families, which is due mainly to the breakdown of marriage, births outside of marriage, and the change in expectations as to what constitutes a 'good father':

> Parenting can be seen as having two interrelated aspects: the provider or 'investment' role and the caring or 'involvement' role. Traditionally, the father's role was defined by investment while the mother's role was defined by involvement. However, involvement is increasingly perceived much more highly than investment, particularly by children, but often, by both fathers and mothers themselves ... These developments place fathers, particularly those who are the sole breadwinners, in an awkward psychological position because investment without involvement no longer carries the esteem that it once did ... At the same time, there appears to be a growing receptivity to the idea that the breadwinner role should not be the sole defining characteristic of a man's worth as a man and a father.[90]

Yet Carr's play demonstrates that none of these factors are prevalent in the Rafterys. Ireland's major changes during the 1990s revealed a climate of revelations regarding the Church and other State institutions, as well as an explosive accumulation of economic wealth not previously seen in the Republic. The play indicates that the Rafterys are financially secure and

---

88   Carr, *On Raftery's Hill*, p. 39.
89   See Finola Kennedy, 'The Family in Transition', in Liam Kennedy (ed.), *Ireland in Transition* (Cork and Dublin: Mercier Press), pp. 91–100. Kennedy mentions some of the pre-1960s characteristics of the family, which include older age for marriage, an average lower rate of formal schooling and high fertility with marriage.
90   McKeown et al., pp. 27–28.

that they were also well off in the past. Red remains as the traditional type, where his involvement in the family is as the financial provider, enabling him to manipulate and break boundaries in order to perform illicit sexual roles within his family. He stretches McKeown's notion of investment (financial) role to incorporate emotional abusive investment in the home.

The Raftery family's status with regard to land and wealth in the past creates hierarchical relationships with those in the valley. Red states in a begrudging exchange to Dara Mood: 'Raftery's Hill fed yees all through the Greah Hunger, sould yees yeer fifty acre a scrub and marsh, 1923. You'll take me River Field young Mood, and me churchyard field and me daugher, for the Moods was ever opportune and you're wan a' them.'[91] Eliott Leyton suggests that the significance of kinship in the mid-1970s 'lies in the nature of the resources controlled by families in a given area.'[92] The unequal distribution of wealth, according to Leyton, leads 'to the creation of class "groups" whose interests do not invariably coincide.'[93] Alexander J. Humphreys defines the strength of the Irish rural family:

> its ownership, control, and direct operation of the principal form of productive property in the community – the farm itself. The control and operation of economic production give the family its own intrinsic measure of independence from non-familial organisations. For it makes the family farm a collective productive unit and thereby makes the homestead the prime centre of each individual's total activity, economic and otherwise.[94]

Humphrey's reference to 'family farm' as one unit makes the two terms mutually dependent and subsumes individual agency. The Rafterys' incest and rape is concealed within the ostensible productivity of Red's self-sufficient farm.

91 Carr, *On Raftery's Hill*, p. 52.
92 Leyton, *The One Blood*, p. 2.
93 Leyton, *The One Blood*, p. 3.
94 Alexander J. Humphreys, *New Dubliners: Urbanisation and the Irish Family* (London: Routledge, 1966), pp. 12–13.

Class, according to Leyton, has three dimensions: 'prestige, wealth and authority.'[95] Red refers to Dara's family as 'scrubbers from the valley', whose proposal of fifty more acres will enable Red to 'see how well you'll manage now you've a hundred acre to work.'[96] Dara twice refuses Red's offer stating, 'I'll noh touch your River Field, Red Raftery, noh if ud was harvestin nightingales and gold'.[97] He goes on to say: 'You'll never see my plough on your cursed land.'[98] In rejecting Red's property, Dara gives precedence to the moral axioms of the society. Red's contradictory fears that he will be left with no 'competent' heir for his 'three hundred acre of the finest land this side a the Shannon and west of the Pale', calls again on a moral lament from Dara at the state of Raftery's 'finest land'. He tells Red, 'Ya should clear them fields, boss, the wind takes the stink all over the Valley.'[99] Shalome tells him:

> I wanted to send you away to the Jesuits, away from this terrible Hill ... You could have amounted to something, Redmond, if old Raftery had let me have my way. Please don't think I'm a snob, I've nothing against the people round here, they're just not our sort Redmond, never were.[100]

Shalome is quick to disassociate the Rafterys from the rest of the valley, even though they would have needed the surrounding community for their livelihood and for the farm's survival.

In relation to years of sustained economic growth in Ireland during the 1990s, Colin Coulter writes: 'Increasingly, there are signs of atomisation among people who were formerly renowned for their sense of connectedness. As individuals in the twenty six counties have grown less attached to one another, they have inevitably grown more attached to things.'[101]

---

95   Leyton, *The One Blood*, p. 17.
96   Carr, *On Raftery's Hill*, p. 51.
97   Carr, *On Raftery's Hill*, p. 52.
98   Carr, *On Raftery's Hill*, p. 52.
99   Carr, *On Raftery's Hill*, p. 21.
100 Carr, *On Raftery's Hill*, p. 28.
101 Colin Coulter and Steve Coleman (eds), *The End of History? Critical Reflections on the Celtic Tiger* (Manchester: Manchester University Press, 2003), p. 24.

Predominant readings of the Celtic Tiger consider it to be a singularly positive social phenomenon but this denies the complexity and exclusions that accompany such major social and economic change. Coulter states: 'In the course of their evolution, human societies tend to get both better and worse at the same time ... The dislocation and casualties of the modernisation process are understated or even air-brushed out of the picture altogether.'[102] Coulter is referring to the fact that although some people gained capital affluence during the 'tiger' period, whether or not the quality of their lives has improved is very debatable. Red regards his land, home, family and livestock as his commodified 'things'.

In locating the play in a household owning substantial amounts of land, and against the backdrop of a mature Celtic Tiger, Carr places the Raftery family in a socio-economic bracket 'typically regarded as transparent and unproblematic.'[103] Jordan notes: 'It is often easier for a spectator to think that abuse happens predominantly outside his or her social class. Working-class housing estates are too often the location for plays that contain sexual abuse.'[104]

Red's aversion to the female is directly linked to his rape of Sorrel and the continuing incest in the Raftery home, as demonstrated and hinted at in his relationship with his own mother. A common feature of Carr's plays, the grand matriarch typically shoulders and merges her past experiences with the present. Shalome Raftery first '*enters across the landing and down the stairs. She wears a nightdress, a straw hat and struggles with a suitcase and an armful of flowers*.'[105] Typically for Carr, the names of the characters are significant. In Jewish society, the word 'shalom' is used as a salutation at meeting or parting.[106] In the drama, Shalome is seen as constantly 'leaving' the house, though Sorrel points out that 'she never gets further thah the

---

102 Coulter and Coleman (eds), p. 17.
103 Coulter and Coleman (eds), p. 13.
104 Jordan, in *Bullan*, p. 54.
105 Carr, *On Raftery's Hill*, p. 15.
106 *The New Shorter Oxford English on Historical Principles Dictionary*, Lesley Brown (ed.) (Oxford: Clarendon Press, 1993), Vol. 2 N–Z, p. 2809.

end of the lane.'[107] Her opening dialogue of six lines contains five goodbyes: 'Goodbye Raftery's Hill … Goodbye disgusting old kitchen and filty stairs … Goodbye Slieve Bloom … Sorrel my darling Goodbye.'[108] Shalome embodies the stifling confines and sense of entrapment of the Raftery home. Her memories of travel indicate a desire for freedom. Anna McMullan writes about 'characters in plays who are trapped in their circumstances … myth is placed in this everyday context to emphasise the narrow confines of the world of the play and to give significance to the quotidian struggle for survival.'[109] Shalome's struggle for survival is enacted in her invented stories of alternative times and places. She tells Dinah and Sorrel about her time in India:

> And mother came and saw me in the arms of the gorilla and was terrified it would harm me and shouts at the man and the gorilla runs down the verandah with me gripped tightly in its armpit. Next thing myself and the gorilla are looking down at Mother and the old man. We're up an orange tree. We pick orange blossom, and throw them down on Mother and the old man. Nothing will make us come out of that orange tree … it was a wonderful time.[110]

According to Shalome, after her mother died, the family returned from India to Kinneygar. And it is to there that Shalome wishes to return throughout the play in order to 'make him [her father] account for his actions.'[111] Although she refers to her father's 'vicious barb' in response to her marrying Brian Raftery, there are also implications of sexual violation and overtones of an injurious past:

> Once a man with a gorilla came to our house and the gorilla licked me all over as if I were its baby and the old man told me about the language of gorillas, how they encompassed the poetry of the sea … I didn't know what he meant … still don't. Girls! Sorrel! Dinah! Do you know what he meant?[112]

---

107   Carr, *On Raftery's Hill*, p. 18.
108   Carr, *On Raftery's Hill*, p. 15.
109   McMullan in *Druids, Dudes And Beauty Queens: The Changing Face of Irish Theatre*, p. 83.
110   Carr, *On Raftery's Hill*, p. 18.
111   Carr, *On Raftery's Hill*, p. 17.
112   Carr, *On Raftery's Hill*, p. 17.

Shalome's belief that 'Daddys never die', spoken at the end of the play in Sorrel's spoiled wedding dress, displays the impact of patriarchal control, even after the death of her father all those years ago.[113] Red states: 'Don't ya remember hees funeral? Ya took me, I must a been whah? Twelve, thirteen, the army blowin their bugles.'[114] Yet she persists in enquiring about her own father: 'Do you think will Daddy recognise me after all these years?'[115] Ded reinforces the fact that Shalome is the victim of sexual abuse when he asks her of her whereabouts during Sorrel's rape. Agitated that she has evaded his question, he offers his own theory: 'I'll tell you where you were, up in your bed, dramin a your Daddy. Perverts the loh a' yees.'[116] Jordan points out how 'Carr dramatises not only the horror of incest but she also captures in this instance a cycle of violation that complicates somewhat the relationship between victim and aggressor.'[117] The narrative also implies abuse in Shalome and Brian Raftery's relationship. Red asks Shalome: 'Who was me father? I want to hear you say ud?'[118] Shalome replies: 'Your father, Redmond, was a beautiful looking man with soft brown eyes and the gentlest of ways.'[119] He asks again: 'No, really, who was he?'[120] When she is pressed by Red about who his father was, she conjures up a 'beautiful', 'gentle' and 'loving' man, far removed from Old Raftery. Earlier she had referred to Old Raftery as 'rough' and 'ignorant' ... 'with his dirty hurler's hands and the stink of cowdung off him.'[121] Her insistent claim that 'he never laid a hand on me' suggests the direct opposite.[122] Red's conversation with Shalome about his father implies that as her husband, Old Raftery did not fulfil her desires, a consequence of her self-destructive relationship

---

113   Carr, *On Raftery's Hill*, p. 57.
114   Carr, *On Raftery's Hill*, p. 57.
115   Carr, *On Raftery's Hill*, p. 57.
116   Carr, *On Raftery's Hill*, p. 48.
117   Jordan, in *Bullan*, p. 54.
118   Carr, *On Raftery's Hill*, p. 28.
119   Carr, *On Raftery's Hill*, p. 28.
120   Carr, *On Raftery's Hill*, p. 28.
121   Carr, *On Raftery's Hill*, p. 28.
122   Carr, *On Raftery's Hill*, p. 28.

with her father and now with her son. His aloofness in the home made Shalome retaliate in a vindictive way, which caused Old Raftery misery. She remained emotionally detached from him. She tells Red:

> Poor Old Raftery. I'd watch him from here, scouring the yard and all I could think of was how much I hated the shape of his back. I was cruel to him, Red, crueller than necessary to keep him at bay. And the crueller I was, the bigger and sadder his eyes. In the end, he just stood in ditches and stared, died that way, standing in the ditch, staring at God knows what.[123]

John N. Briere states that 'various forms of cruelty and deprivation [sexual, physical, psychological and emotional] provide a vast store of negative childhood experiences that, in turn, have significant – frequently overlooked – impact on the later mental health of millions of people.'[124] The stage directions describe Shalome as '*a bit gone in her mind*'.[125] The directions also indicate that she has '*flashes of accidental lucidity*', although whether they are 'accidental' or not is thrown into doubt on a number of occasions in the play.[126] Dinah's complaint that she has no time for herself is met with the loaded retort from Shalome, 'You manage time a plenty for your sly pursuits', which references the sexual relationship between father and daughter.[127] In Act 2, when Dinah pulls Shalome back into the house, en route to Kinneygar, the old woman acknowledges her annoyance at this and admits to having heard the rape of Sorrel: 'You're not as nice to me as Sorrel, poor little Sorrel, I wanted to stop it. Is she still alive?'[128] Yet, because Shalome wavers in and out of lucidity, she is never fully culpable.

Red has undergone his own crisis as a direct result of the inadequate role played by his parents. His uncertainty of self is manifested both by his continuing commitment to incest and by the fact that he has a sexual

---

123 Carr, *On Raftery's Hill*, p. 31.
124 John N. Briere, *Child Abuse Trauma: Theory and Treatment of the Lasting Effects* (Thousand Oaks, CA: Sage Publications, 1992), p. 15.
125 Carr, *On Raftery's Hill*, p. 15.
126 Carr, *On Raftery's Hill*, p. 15.
127 Carr, *On Raftery's Hill*, p. 17.
128 Carr, *On Raftery's Hill*, p. 46.

relationship with his mother. It is the separation from the mother which enables, as Kristeva describes, the development of identity. The image of Red bringing his mother back into the house in Sorrel's stained wedding dress literally recalls the process of abjection in the failed attempt at differentiation from his mother. The father enters as part of the separation process of subjectivity by accompanying the emergence of the subject into language. Yet Red does not recall much about the role of his father in any aspect of his childhood. Although Old Raftery died when Red was twelve years of age, up to then, his father had not been present, even in the metaphorical sense, in order to engage symbolically with either his or Shalome's desire. The short-lived father figure does not seem to have played an adequate role in his life. Red's need to know who his father is reiterates this. He tells Isaac that he remembers his father sitting in his car for hours, smoking and doing nothing: 'me father, now come the winter'd sih out there in hees Morris Minor, member ud? [...] Called ud hees smoking saloon, he'd sih there for hours, looking at nothing ... dya know I can't ever remember talking to him.'[129] His existence is characterised by 'exile' from the presence or memory of his father and from proper symbolic functioning codes. His insufficient selfhood in the abject sense is founded in the paradoxical desire for self-identification. His attempt to ascribe guilt to the female figures is no accident, and this is really an effort to assuage his own guilt. Weeks after the rape and with much tension in the house, Red thinks that time will dilute the impact of his crime:

> RED: (*Shouts to Sorrel*) Young wan!
> SORREL: Whah?
> RED: High time you goh dressed and joined the land a the livin.
> SORREL: I'm noh well.
> RED: We'll let bygones be bygones young wan. Just apologise to me now and we'll say no more abouh ud.
> SORREL: Apologise to you!
> DINAH: Uds high time yees were greah agin, come down and make ud up wud him, I'm the wan stuck atwane yees tryin to keep the pace.[130]

129 Carr, *On Raftery's Hill*, p. 41.
130 Carr, *On Raftery's Hill*, pp. 45–46.

The alternative options for Carr's characters in *On Raftery's Hill* are difficult to imagine. Dinah struggles to overlook the fact of rape, yet persists in her efforts to do so. When Ded threatens to tell the police about her sexual relationship with her father, she responds 'Gwan, get the guards. Gwan get them! And I'll tell them what ya done to me while yu're ah ud.'[131] She is quick to take advantage of Ded's confused sense of self, moulded by years of paternal bullying. Red tells him that he is as mad as a man from the Valley, Alfie Horgan. 'And what happened to him?' asks Red. Ded replies, 'He choked on his tongue in the lunatic asylum.' Red threateningly reinforces this then: 'Thah's righ, he choked on hees tongue from telling too many lies. Would you like to end up like thah, would ya?'[132] Sorrel depicts a similar mindset, demonstrated by her confused allegiance, that oscillates between Dara and Red. At one point she states to Dara: 'There's natin' wrong a Daddy. Ud's you! Think you know eveythin about everywan!'[133] At another point her condemnation of her father quickly turns into loyalty: 'He's good at the back of ud all, leastways his instincts are, and for you to be putting him down to his daughter is wrong!'[134] Finally the event that ends the play reveals that Sorrel has called off her engagement, claiming that Dara has ruined everything. She states: 'The world's gone out like a ligh and I can't see righ about anything any more.'[135] This reiterates Dinah's earlier statement that she is unlikely to expose the family secrets, exclaiming that 'she's a Raftery, a double Raftery, well versed in subterfuge.'[136] Jordan observes the ways in which Carr

> confirms for an audience how a negative bond can be as strong as a positive one, how family victims of violation can be antagonistic, almost rivals towards each other, and seldom allies, and how the victim of abuse through processes of internalisation and identification can accommodate him/herself, on one level, to situ-

---

131   Carr, *On Raftery's Hill*, pp. 38.
132   Carr, *On Raftery's Hill*, p. 26.
133   Carr, *On Raftery's Hill*, p. 53.
134   Carr, *On Raftery's Hill*, p. 53.
135   Carr, *On Raftery's Hill*, p. 53.
136   Carr, *On Raftery's Hill*, p. 46.

ations and circumstances even as self-esteem is slowly peeled away through a sense of powerlessness.[137]

The unequivocal authority of Red Raftery in the family and the rape of Sorrel signify that the Rafterys life within a patriarchal culture will remain subjected to the discursive and social practices that require obedience. They maintain the incestuous system through collusion and silence, and as such they promote their own oppression, and ultimately self-destruction. Weeks notes in 'Inventing Realities':

> A battered wife or an abused child ... may have a theoretical set of choices – to leave the domestic hearth, to go to a refuge or, in the case of children, to appeal to others to run away. But we know that in practice such choices are difficult. Loyalty commitments, dependency and fear all block the free play of choice. Moreover, choice has consequences with which we have to live: Women living in poverty as single parents, children in institutional care, separated from those who may actually love them.[138]

The domestic trappings of the Raftery home are pervaded by violent language and passive, physical, and emotional cruelties. Compliance with incest is evoked in the context of violence against the weak, the helpless human and animal. The threat of violence reduces the Rafterys inclination to expose the sexual abuse in the home or indeed to stray too far away from the boundaries of the home. Roxanna Carrillo states: 'Women experience violence as a form of control that limits their ability to pursue options in almost every area of life from home to school, work-place and most public spaces.'[139] The language of violence depicts a failed attempt to subvert male authority in the play, and reinforces the Rafterys' inability to change the destruction that goes on in their home. Verbal attacks, particularly employed by Ded and Dinah, are an emotional defence that further exposes their lack of self-assurance and security. When Dinah overhears Ded tell

---

137   Jordan, in *Bullan*, pp. 53–54.
138   Weeks, *Invented Moralities*, p. 60.
139   Charlotte Bunch and Roxanna Carrillo, *Gender Violence: A Development and Human Rights Issue* (Dublin: Attic Press, 1992), p. 17.

Sorrel that she Dinah, makes all the decisions in the home and that she is 'Daddy's cattle dealer', she responds by threatening Red on him:

> DINAH: Why'd'n you just fuck back to the cowshed where ya belong?
> DED: I'll go when I'm good and ready.
> DINAH: Ya'll go now or I'll tell Daddy ya were in here guzzling hees whiskey and causin trouble.
> DED: You tell him anythin' about me and I'll puh a mate hook through the turkey neck a ya.
> DINAH: And I'll ring the lunatic asylum and they'll take ya away and squaze ya like a bull calf and cut bits ouha your head.[140]

Ded occupies a position of vulnerability and impotence in the play, emphasised by his alleged store of farming equipment, which will act as harmful weaponry if Red comes in range of his living quarters. He tells Sorrel that he has a 'crowbar filed if he comes near me.'[141] When Dinah forgets to include Red's hunting partner Isaac in the dinner, Red responds physically to her (*knocks her on the head*) and states: 'What's in there? Wool? Friggin moths?'[142] Further irritated by Ded's agitated behaviour in the kitchen and his wish to go back to the shed, Red '*hits him a slap on the head.*'[143]

The other Rafterys are predominantly all talk and no action. Passive violence, demonstrated by their silence, is ultimately an act of self-destruction. The family members do little more than respond to the control and fear he inspires in them. They passively accept their life as victims, enacting Shalome's comment that they are 'entirely blameless' for their (in)actions.[144]

Kristeva claims that incest is 'dealing with imprecise boundaries in that place, at that moment, where pain is born out of an excess of fondness and a hate that, [in] refusing to admit the satisfaction it also pro-

---

140 Carr, *On Raftery's Hill*, p. 38.
141 Carr, *On Raftery's Hill*, p. 38.
142 Carr, *On Raftery's Hill*, p. 20.
143 Carr, *On Raftery's Hill*, p. 27.
144 Carr, *On Raftery's Hill*, p. 31.

vides, is projected toward an other.'[145] Kristeva's comment suggests that the satisfaction found in that moment of incest stems from self-hate. The power of self-hate entraps others by projection, particularly those within close proximity. This not only accounts for Dinah's continued willingness to commit incest with her father, but for the entire family's collusion with it. Their persistence forms the incestuous dynamic that comes to define them, revealing the conditions of abjection that penetrate all the Rafterys. Dinah rationalises the rape as an accident stating to Sorrel in the last scene: 'We're a respectable family, we love wan another and whahever happened ya happened ya be accident. D'ya honestly think we'd harm wan another?'[146] Kristeva notes: 'Abjection is above all ambiguity. Because, while releasing a hold, it does not radically cut off the subject from what threatens it – on the contrary, abjection acknowledges it to be in perpetual danger. But also because abjection itself is a compromise of judgement and affect, of condemnation and yearning, of signs and drives.'[147]

On Raftery's Hill presents man as responsible for 'purity', demonstrating McMullan's comment on incest in the play: 'All difference and heterogeneity are excluded.'[148] Traditionally, Irish representations of woman carried the paradoxical burden of being either symbolically pure or socially dissolute. As Maryann Valiulis notes: 'Purity was primarily cast as a woman's responsibility, a woman's crowning glory. Women were thus critical to Irish self-definition and any rejection of traditional standards of purity endangered Ireland's definition of self.'[149] The play depicts the subversion of traditional notions of female purity, produced by masculine definitions. Before the rape, Red Raftery links his notions of purity to virginity and innocence, implying that morality and sexual behaviour adheres to certain agreed norms of behaviour and types of activity: 'D'ya know whah uh manes to be young Dara Mood? Do ya? Manes your slate is clane, manes the muck

145 Kristeva, *Powers of Horror*, p. 60.
146 Carr, *On Raftery's Hill*, p. 56.
147 Kristeva, *Powers of Horror*, pp. 9–10.
148 McMullan in *Druids, Dudes And Beauty Queens: The Changing Face of Irish Theatre*, p. 82.
149 Valiulis, p. 154.

on your boots stays on your boots and don't sape up to your unploughed soul. Manes ya know fuck all abouh the dirty world, how and why men and women fall.'[150] Red's construction of morality and sexual behaviour in the play reveals his idea of 'dirty world', which relates to sex and carnal knowledge. He regards people, particularly women, who know about this sexual and 'dirty' world as fallen, that is, plummeting in some kind of value. Ironically, his choice of the word 'fallen' suggests that women choose to have sex, rather than be forced. His moral and sexual understandings shift within his constructed values, contexts and situations.

The 'pure' insularity of the Raftery family, high up on the hill and physically separated from the community in the valley below, is further emphasised in the sub-plot of the drama where incestuous relationships are rife. 'Pure' is defined as 'not mixed with anything else, not adulterated.'[151] The Catholic Church interprets sexual chastity with purity as the ultimate state that all followers should strive for. The scriptures state: 'Blessed are the pure in heart,' Christ said in his Sermon on the Mount, 'for they shall see God.'[152] Kristeva notes how the bible conceives heterogeneity as a form of 'impurity: intermixture, erasing of difference [and a] threat to identity.'[153] She notes that Rabbinical legislation pronounces the relations between morals and impurity, referencing '"impure seed" to be understood as "incestuous".'[154] For her, Biblical abomination, with all its prohibitions, taboos, sacrifices and purifying acts, imposes 'the logic that sets up the symbolic order.'[155] In this context, Red reveals the repressed nature of prohibitions and taboos of sexual incest and abuse, inside the Kristevan notion of horror and beyond the verbal.

As in *Portia Coughlan* and *By the Bog of Cats*, characters in the drama have no access to a safe place but unlike these plays, where the protagonists

---

150   Carr, *On Raftery's Hill*, p. 24.
151   Judy Pearsall (ed.), *The New Oxford Dictionary of English* (Oxford University Press, 1998), p. 236.
152   *Good News Bible* (England: Collins, 1982), p. 194.
153   Kristeva, *Powers of Horror*, p. 101.
154   Kristeva, *Powers of Horror*, p. 105.
155   Kristeva, *Powers of Horror*, p. 110.

find refuge in realms of 'otherness' outside of the home, the characters in *On Raftery's Hill* have no access to an alternative safe place. Sorrel breaks off her engagement to Dara, refusing to live 'in a poh of lies'.[156] This harmful irony is further reinforced by Dinah's response: 'Ud's noh lyin, ud's just noh telling him things. Ud's just sayin the opposite of whah your thinking. Most goes through their whole life sayin the opposite a whah they think.'[157] Dinah, when younger, forfeited her opportunity to escape incestuous abuse by marrying Dara's brother, Jimmy and she tells Dara that 'things were rickety for me that time', implicitly indicating the early existence of her abusive relationship with her father and the typical consequence of being unable to form a trusting long term adult relationship.[158] The play highlights the fact that victims of incest, who may have the option of a healthier heterogeneous relationship, are likely to abandon this possibility. In 'Associated Problems for a Child who has been Sexually Abused', David Jones and Paul Ramchandani's state that 'about half of the children studied, who had been sexually abused experienced depression, post-traumatic stress disorder[159] ... or disturbed behaviour or a combination of these.'[160] The consequences of sexual abuse, beginning at a young age, radically decrease the chance for an optimistic and healthy lifestyle as an adult.

Indeed the play presents marriage, which might have been Sorrel's strategy of escape from abuse as perpetuating it. Red regards marriage as a sexual licence to be used as he sees fit. Of his dead wife, he claims

---

156 Carr, *On Raftery's Hill*, p. 56.
157 Carr, *On Raftery's Hill*, p. 56.
158 Carr, *On Raftery's Hill*, p. 54.
159 Post-traumatic stress disorder is described as a 'disorder which can follow the experiencing or witnessing of a number of events including violence, disasters and child abuse of all forms. Three types of symptoms occur. First, the traumatic event is re-experienced in the form of intrusive images or dreams. Second, places and objects associated with the event are avoided, and third symptoms of over-arousal such as sleep disturbance and poor concentration are experienced. PTSD is commonly experienced by children who have been sexually abused.' See pp. 112–113 in David P.H. Jones and Paul Ramchandani, *Child Sexual Abuse: Informing Practice from Research* (Abingdon, UK: Radcliffe Medical Press, 1999).
160 Jones and Ramchandani, *Child Sexual Abuse*, p. 14.

that he 'married a lunatic with an antique violin and an eternal case of migraine. If Christ heeself slid onto the pilla she'd plead the migraine.'[161] The Constitution implies that the father's relationship with the child's mother is often used as a way to examine his standing with his children. In the context of the play, Red reveals a destructive relationship with his children based on the image of his relationship with his wife. Shalome tells Sorrel that her mother used to entertain in the house when she first came to the hill but 'your father put a stop to all of that. I don't know why it is, Sorrel but he never liked to see people enjoy themselves a big smuth on him when everyone else was happy. Daddy was the same.'[162] Dara's own parents don't speak to one another, and the father is described as 'full a stingy silences.'[163] Against her father's wishes, Shalome married a man she never loved: 'It was all just one terrible mistake.'[164] The play implies that Shalome married the 'wrong man' out of spite for her father, who it is suggested was a dictator, reinforced by a lifetime spent in the army. Sorrel's later statement to Red and the final line in the play reveals that her relationship with Dara is irredeemably finished: 'Oh I sourted him ouh Daddy, don't you worry, I sourted him ouh for evermore'.[165] Her statement consolidates Shalome's earlier observation to Dara: 'You'll make someone very happy Dara Mood, but it won't be Sorrel because you see we are strange creatures up here on the Hill. And strange creatures, aberrations like us don't make for lifetime companions.'[166]

In *On Raftery's Hill*, the wedding dress becomes symbolic of a range of insidious violations – sexual, physical, psychological and emotional. The traditional wedding dress in Catholic Ireland, an iconic signifier of chastity, virtue and celebration, is subverted in Carr's dramas. Reaching satirical heights in the appearance of '"four" wedding dresses' at Carthage, and Caroline's wedding in *By the Bog of Cats*, the one wedding dress in *On*

---

161   Carr, *On Raftery's Hill*, p. 31.
162   Carr, *On Raftery's Hill*, p. 16.
163   Carr, *On Raftery's Hill*, p. 33.
164   Carr, *On Raftery's Hill*, p. 16.
165   Carr, *On Raftery's Hill*, p. 57.
166   Carr, *On Raftery's Hill*, p. 50.

Raftery's Hill offers a more dismal symbolism. In *By the Bog Of Cats* Mrs Kilbride, who presents herself at her son's wedding in *what looks extremely like a wedding dress, white, a white hat, with a bit of a veil trailing off it, white shoes, tights, bag, etc,* exposes a competitive resistance to her son's bride taking centre stage in his life.[167] Mrs Kilbride, like Red, takes an unhealthy interest in her child's romantic relationship. Carthage's daughter, dressed for her first Holy Communion as a fetishised bride, and Hester, his lover, in a wedding dress signifying jealous vengeance, complicates the icon further and verges towards parody. Significantly, Sorrel's wedding dress gets worn and soiled by her Grandmother as she attempts in the final scenes of the play to flee the Raftery house but is escorted back by Red. The stage directions read *Enter Red with Shalome on his arm, muddied wedding dress.*[168] As one of the closing events in the play, Red's act of bringing Shalome back into the house in the grimy dress consolidates his power and the likelihood of his continuing incest within their home.[169]

On Raftery's Hill presents the unromantic world of rural Ireland without a space for refuge. Carr offers no release from the immediate savagery that is presented in the drama. Sihra notes: 'By not bowing to the option of death, the characters are consigned to a kind of purgatorial entrapment and stasis, with no possibility for change or transformation.'[170] As Carr states, none of the characters 'earned their death in the play.'[171] Hypocrisy, abuse, silence and deceit are continuous throughout. Carr's trilogy, which employs fantasy, myth, story telling and memory, creates escapist shadow worlds for the fatalistic protagonists. The ancient multi-layered mystery of the bogscape in *By the Bog of Cats* with the mystical characters of Ghost Fancier and Catwoman, the lakes in *The Mai* and *Ariel*, the renewable

---

167 Marina Carr, *Plays One*, 'By the Bog of Cats ...' (London: Faber and Faber, 1999), p. 303.
168 Carr, *On Raftery's Hill*, p. 57.
169 Jordan, in *Bullan*, p. 60.
170 Melissa Sihra in 'Marina Carr in conversation with Melissa Sihra' in Lillian Chambers, Ger FitzGibbon, Eamonn Jordan, Dan Farrelly and Cathy Leeney (eds), *Theatre Talk: Voices of Irish Theatre Practitioners* (Dublin: Carysfort, 2001), p. 60.
171 Sihra in 'Marina Carr in conversation with Melissa Sihra', p. 60.

moving waters in *Portia Coughlan* and the fantastic perspective presented by Grandma Fraochlan's nine fingered fisherman, Beck's prince on a white horse, Connie's 'chariot with golden bells that could sing my name'[172] in *The Mai* have all but disappeared in *On Raftery's Hill*. The mention of incest between Zeus and Hera in *On Raftery's Hill* is brief and mainly used to set up the argument between Red and Isaac as to whether incest is a predisposed maladjustment. Red's comment, 'And doesn't your god make monsters too, for all the world to look down on?', is met by Isaac's response 'Monsters make themselves.'[173]

Cathy Leeney and Anna McMullen observe that, Carr's 'work suggests rather than explains' and they imply that Carr leaves the audience to find their own answers to the concerns raised in the plays.[174] In simultaneously acknowledging and perpetuating their state of abjection, the Rafterys form a continuing abusive cycle. But their situation is horrifying and the play paints such a dismal ethical picture that no different morality is imaginable within the constricted world of the play. Neither Carr's women nor the Irish State nor any authority cannot get beyond Red's power.

Yet in emphasising the horror of the abject, constituted through destructive boundaries and which maintain power and incest, Carr exposes the control exerted by it. Abjection need not mean the end of the Rafterys, whereby present and future are lost. If abjection were to remain hidden as it is in *On Raftery's Hill*, it only empowers it but it also contains, through oblivion, the codes that sustain the other side of social, ethical and ideological constructs. Those codes are revealed in *Meat and Salt* to be just as destructive as the Raftery's private ones. However in *Meat and Salt*, the realm of the semiotic (feminine) and the symbolic (masculine) in the Kristevan sense, occupy a balanced dialectic without privileging one over or at the expense of the other, which makes for a more meaningful and stable subjectivity. In the return of the abject, where the origins of it can be traced and processed, Kristeva observes:

172   Marina Carr, *The Mai* (London: Faber and Faber, 1999), p. 163.
173   Carr, *On Raftery's Hill*, p. 43.
174   Leeney and McMullan (eds), *The Theatre of Marina Carr*, p. xv.

The abject is the violence of mourning for an 'object' that has already been lost. The abject shatters the wall of repression and its judgements. It takes the ego back to its source on the abominable limits from which, in order to be, the ego has broken away – it assigns it a source in the non-ego, drive, death. Abjection is a resurrection that has gone through death (of the ego). It is already alchemy that transforms death drive into a start of life, a new significance.[175]

Given this perspective, Carr's presentation of the disintegration and degeneration of abjection in the Rafterys carries the dynamic possibility of a new and healthy transformation, which is symbolically presented in *Meat and Salt*.

In *Meat and Salt*, the female holds the power because she wanders as the abject beyond the confines of her father's kingdom, the position that destabilises aspects of the monarchy. In Carr's kingdom the 'natural' order of feminine roles is destabilised and women refuse to enter the office of femalehood. *Meat and Salt* sees Carr exaggerate concepts of masculinity and femininity to reveal their artificiality and construction. Judith Butler opposes the notion of an essentialised self, arguing that the discourse of compulsory heterosexuality determines the self and gender. There is no 'authentic' self or gender, no genuine 'womanliness' but rather, compulsory heterosexuality is a 'repetition that can only produce the effect of its own originality ... "Man" and "woman" are theatrically produced effects that posture as grounds, origins, the normative measure of the real.'[176] Carr's tale theatrically exposes socially instituted notions of gender in both the familial and political realm. Harvey O'Brien posits 'patrimony as a mindlessly ordering force' and the female as a determined individual will of strength[177] but in the tale, consenting to the rules of one's family and/or community is represented as far from a 'natural' process. Once again, Carr conceives

---

175 Kristeva, *Powers of Horror*, p. 15.
176 Judith Butler in Linda Nicholson (ed.), 'Imitation and Gender Subordination', *The Second Wave: A Reader in Feminist Theory* (New York: Routledge, 1997), p. 307.
177 Harvey O'Brien, 'culturevulture.net 26 January 2003', cited by Bernadette Sweeney in *Performing the Body in Irish Theatre* (Basingstoke, UK: Palgrave Macmillan, 2008), p. 191.

the idea that it may be better to abandon one's family and institutions altogether, in the hope of gaining a more stable subjectivity.

In mapping the female protagonist's trajectory towards maturity, *Meat and Salt* is an abject representation of the specific rites of passage that she must undergo in order to accede to selfhood with its treatment of boundary crossing, and its construction of the maternal figure as the fearful feminine. Carr lays claim to a contemporary young audience with references to mobile phones, Westlife, pizza, Levi jeans, Eminem and Harry Potter, but to read *Meat and Salt* as aimed at a younger audience only, or to consider it as an 'ancient' and 'simple' tale short-changes the digressions and complexities of the work, particularly in the context of Carr's other works.

Meat and Salt is not published but is available to view on DVD at the Abbey Archive. Although originally written in 1999, it was produced at the Peacock Theatre in 2003, alongside Jim Nolan's *The Road to Carne*, under the heading *Sons and Daughters*. Both plays, directed by Andrea Ainsworth, are coming of age tales, which trace the emotional and social development of teenagers. Andrew Bennett, Emma Colohan, Matthew Dunphy, Caroline Lynch and Ruth Negga played various characters throughout both plays and Vivienne Long provided the music for the production. Quotes from *Meat and Salt* are based on this production of the play.

Meat and Salt is written in the fairy tale genre, and although there is no mention of fairies in the story, it does contain a talking moon and talking wolves and it introduces the Prince towards the end who transforms the original character configuration of Big Daddy and his three daughters to the Young King and Little Daughter at the close of the tale. Equally, it follows the structure of the fairy tale genre, if in subversive and oppositional ways, tracing what Roz Chast illustrates as the 'Once upon a time' element to 'suddenly …' moving to 'luckily …' and finally the 'happily ever after' ending.[178] Elizabeth Wanning Harries' definition of the fairy tale genre befits *Meat and Salt* as 'tales that include elements of folk tradition and magical or supernatural elements, tales that have a certain predictable

---

178 See Elizabeth Wanning Harries, *Twice Upon a Time: Women Writers and the History of Fairy Tales* (New Jersey, Princeton University Press, 2001), p. 8.

structure.'[179] Carr creates strong and independent females not constrained by the gender norms of a patriarchal, regal society. *Meat and Salt* resists the fairy tale genre, operating against what Cristina Bacchilega outlines as the fairy tale's magic:

> The fairy tale's magic fulfils multiple desires. As literature for children, fairy tales offer symbolically powerful scenarios and options, in which seemingly unpromising heroes succeed in solving some problems for modern children. These narratives set the socially acceptable boundaries for such scenarios and options, thus serving, more often than not, the civilising aspirations of adults.[180]

If, as Bacchilega states, 'fairy tales have served as a secular means of instruction about diligence, moderation, cleanliness and obedience to parents and institutions,'[181] then *Meat and Salt* seizes upon such inclinations. Carr's play sets about contemporising and democratising the fairy tale genre into an emancipated and progressive framework centred on female identity and independence.

Echoing the *King Lear* saga, a vitriolic Big Daddy opens *Meat and Salt* with commands of a love test, what he calls 'a riddle', shown to him by his three daughters; Big Daughter, Middle Daughter and Little Daughter. As in *King Lear*, the tale makes the connection between tongue and heart, a return to Carr's interest in what is not said but meant and on what people declare to be but are not.[182] Carr omits the Lear abdication and auction of wealth as the central reward for satisfying the test, but she does suggest the threat to Little Daughter's safety upon being disinherited from Big Daddy's Kingdom once he deems her 'performance' of love unsatisfactory. Just as Cordelia tells Lear, 'I love your majesty according to my bond,'[183] Little

179 Harries, p. 6.
180 Cristina Bacchilega, *Postmodern Fairy Tales: Gender and Narrative Strategies* (Philadelphia, University of Pennsylvania, 1997), p. 5.
181 Bacchilega, p. 8.
182 *Ullaloo, Low in the Dark* and *Woman and Scarecrow* have particular examples of the relationships between tongue and heart, which is discussed in Chapters 1.
183 George Hunter (ed.), William Shakespeare, *King Lear* (London: Penguin, 2005), p. 8.

Daughter, tells Big Daddy that she loves him 'as meat loves salt.'[184] This response, read as deviant and disobedient, causes her to be flung out of Big Daddy's castle. He literally abjects her by throwing her out of his kingdom. The intolerable body, Little Daughter, violates the 'clean and proper', the Kingdom, making the boundaries of the self ambiguous.

Big Daddy's test might have stemmed from a deep psychological need, but because it purposefully lacks a concrete motivation, it renders it arbitrary and ridiculous. Andrew Bennett's Big Daddy held a tannoy for 'speaking' to his daughters in the Abbey production and his infuriation at Little Daughter's (played by Ruth Negga) unacceptable response to his love test caused him to stomp and step outside of the golden casket, which was protecting his painted gold feet, a symbol of the ways in which male power and wealth operated. Big Daddy's throne and casket were positioned upstage and centre and his family and people used a circular space around the throne, reflecting the extent of his power and wealth. His golden feet, most of the time locked into the casket for 'he lived in mortal fear of someone stealing them', are reminiscent of Tomred's long toenails in *Ullaloo*, both representing the struggle to maintain the borders of the Symbolic and the sense of fragility over an abject identity.[185] Big Daddy's obsessive need to guard his golden feet points to a boundary being threatened in the Kristevan sense. In Big Daddy's kingdom, the 'natural' order is maintained as long as females signify their compliance and willingness to perform the prescribed roles of femalehood.

However, what Little Daughter discovers outside the wall of her father's kingdom is not so much a world of danger but a place where she can establish her own sense of being. Outside the kingdom resembles Kristeva's more sensual maternal semiotic constituted by the subject's drives and private articulations, where the subject's bodily instincts are given more expression. Carr depicts a determined and wilful Princess who expresses her critique of a patriarchal society that assumes a socially accepted and acquired femininity. She proactively undergoes her own journey, a crisis of sorts that she

184   Carr, *Meat and Salt*, Dir. Andrea Ainsworth, 2003, Abbey Theatre Archive.
185   Carr, *Meat and Salt*, Dir. Andrea Ainsworth, 2003, Abbey Theatre Archive.

masters in order to consolidate her own values, which are not the norms of her father's kingdom. Significantly, beyond the walls of the Kingdom, Little Daughter is chased by a pack of wolves over the mountains and into the trees. She loses her slippers, tears her silver dress and cuts herself in the process but despite her terror, she whispers to herself, 'This is living. This is what happens when you leave Big Daddy's Kingdom.'[186] There are echoes of Shalome in *On Raftery's Hill*, who for most of the play tries to leave the Raftery house to return to her 'Daddy's' home in Kinneygar. Instead she is returned to the Raftery's under the watchful authority of Red. The audience sees Shalome coming back into the house in her torn and soiled dress, with Red brandishing his gun, ensuring her 'safe' return. Carr dramatises the destruction of living under abusive patriarchal rule inside the confines of the home or the kingdom, suggesting that the freedom and safety of the female and the maternal lies beyond constructed masculine boundaries.

In *Meat and Salt*, the semiotic and the symbolic should have been continuous with one another and not discrete entities – inside the kingdom, outside the kingdom. Little Daughter's exclamatory joy at turning away from convention acknowledges her joy in the semiotic, which had been supplanted by the symbolic. When she cannot run any longer, she leans against a tree and turns to face the wolves. Unexpectedly the wolf prince appears and asks for her hand in marriage. Although 'Little Daughter is tempted, for the wolf prince had great allure and spoke to some ancient thing in her that longed to be a wolfish bride' she refuses, telling him that 'she cannot be something that she is not.'[187] She persistently rejects the confined roles of marriage and institutions and because of this she both attracts and fascinates suitors. Her desire and fear suggest that boundaries are threatened. Her longing for, yet resisting the wolf prince's hand in marriage resembles that of a subject trying to establish a separate identity but as Kristeva outlines, 'with the constant risk of falling back under the sway of a power as securing as it is stifling.'[188] Since this 'falling back' threatens

186 Carr, *Meat and Salt*, Dir. Andrea Ainsworth, 2003, Abbey Theatre Archive.
187 Carr, *Meat and Salt*, Dir. Andrea Ainsworth, 2003, Abbey Theatre Archive.
188 Kristeva, p. 13.

Little Daughter's identity and boundaries, she is repelled by this power, the abject, but while it causes fear, it also attracts.

According to Celtic tradition, the wolf is the pathfinder, the forerunner of new ideas who can help take control of one's life. Because the wolf's desires are just below the surface of the consciousness, it is strongly allied to the Moon, which symbolises the unconscious and holds the secrets of knowledge and wisdom.[189] Thus Little Daughter in Kristeva's pre-conscious or unconscious instinctual early phase is confronted by the Moon, by the wolves and by her mother.

The Moon who has 'been all alone since time began' warns her to be careful of the wolves 'for I'll drive them mad tonight'; this is a caution for the return of the repressed, what was left behind in the process of separation in order to become individualised.[190] Little Daughter's mother was abjected from her husband's kingdom, for 'turning on lights and forever putting coal on the fire'; because he dislikes her horse's feet, he 'had to get rid of her.'[191] She represents elements of the abject, which threaten codes of behaviour inside the kingdom. Similar to Little Daughter, she exists outside of the symbolic and in the semiotic. The abject is what is repressed and suppressed within and through the symbolic. Her mother sits on a stone, reading and does not recognise her, long banished because of her 'defiance' to Big Daddy. When Little Daughter says, 'Oh Ma, I've missed you', her mother responds 'I've missed myself', suggesting her own loss of selfhood.[192] 'I was a lot of things', she tells Little Daughter.[193] The abject mother is more radical than the semiotic in terms of her powerful non-compliance of regulation by the symbolic. The mother literally could not be brought under the control of the symbolic. Offspring, who are of the same flesh as the mother, are in a sense the double of the mother and they testify to her power. For the daughter, the meeting of her mother literally

---

189   See Jules Cashford, *The Moon: Myth and Image* (London: Cassell Illustrated, 2003) and Barry Cunliffe, *The Celtic World* (London: Constable, 1992).
190   Carr, *Meat and Salt*, Dir. Andrea Ainsworth, 2003, Abbey Theatre Archive.
191   Carr, *Meat and Salt*, Dir. Andrea Ainsworth, 2003, Abbey Theatre Archive.
192   Carr, *Meat and Salt*, Dir. Andrea Ainsworth, 2003, Abbey Theatre Archive.
193   Carr, *Meat and Salt*, Dir. Andrea Ainsworth, 2003, Abbey Theatre Archive.

represents the mirror stage of development, where the extension of self is seen through the (m)other. Once her mother leaves, Little Daughter re-experiences boundary separation from the maternal.

Little Daughter's mother, surviving banishment well, echoes the mother figures in many of Carr's plays, who withdraw from or who refuse to conform to the prescribed role of motherhood. Mai in *The Mai* is distant and resentful to her children; Portia Coughlan cannot pretend that motherhood is a position that she cherishes; Hester Swane kills her daughter because she could not deal with the rejection of her lover, the father of their child; the dead mother in *On Raftery's Hill* is posthumously referred to as having been absent in the role of motherhood and she also played a compliant part in maintaining the incestuous situation in the family home. Frances, the mother in *Ariel* yearns too much for her dead child and is bitter as a mother because of her husband's infidelities. In *Woman and Scarecrow*, Scarecrow tells Woman that she had nine children to make up numbers and for no other reason. Both Catherine and Anne in *Marble* play functional roles as mothers with no emotional sense given to it. Little Daughter's mother in *Meat and Salt* succeeds in finding herself, re-connecting with the loss of self and the conditions surrounding that loss from which she had long been separated.

Meat and Salt, therefore, can be posited in terms of the abject, where the semiotic and the symbolic lack a continuous relationship. Where they begin to inhabit a world that shares a dialectic is portrayed in Carr's most drastic departure from *King Lear*, which subsequently destroys its tragic conclusion. The tragicomedy of this version of *King Lear* winds up with the aged king begrudgingly attending Little Daughter's wedding banquet at another royal household. He observes her independence, restored by her own making and without his permission. The priority of the Symbolic Order is portrayed in the Young King's kingdom and his initial rage at Little Daughter's attitude. 'How dare you speak to me like this?' is met with Little Daughter's semiotic energy and creativity, 'I have nothing left except my pride. Goodbye.'[194] However, while Little Daughter agrees to marry the

---

194 Carr, *Meat and Salt*, Dir. Andrea Ainsworth, 2003, Abbey Theatre Archive.

Young King, she does so on her own terms. She tells him, 'Alright, I will stay with you for I have reached rock bottom. I will stay with you but I will not pretend that you are my meat, you are my salt until you have proved yourself so.'[195] The tale ends with Big Daddy stomping out of the banquet hall never to be seen again and Little Daughter, now reigning as Queen, lives her life as she sees fit.

The story of Little Daughter exposes the fairy tale's overused form and content, reworking its narrative system in a way that questions the kind of production that constructs naturalised subjectivity. Little Daughter's attitude to all of the men she meets on her journey is challenging and confrontational. Carr's use of the fairy tale undoes its power. Specifically, Big Daughter, Middle Daughter and Little Daughter are sources through which to explore the typically naturalising strategies of gender. Big Daughter and Middle Daughter tell Big Daddy how much they love him in hyperbolic mockery, and their manipulative behaviour gets them what they want. Little Daughter's genuine answer displeases Big Daddy and in his banishment of her, she displays independence and strength throughout.

While Carr's other plays might be accused of restoring patriarchal order through the death of the female protagonists, making it difficult to enter critical dialogue on the displacement of the abject onto the female, the King in *Meat and Salt* is unable to restore patriarchal authority and the central females do not die but rather re-assert their own independence. This might be read as one of the means to reconfigure mechanisms of the abject in a way that frees woman from internalising masculinity's desire to abandon her.

The tale too has different meanings both culturally and socially within the fairy tale genre. It warns how bright young girls can be expelled from their homes for their honesty. It cautions outspoken girls in the presence of royalty to remain loyal and courteous at all costs. It demonstrates how power in the hands of male stupidity is self-defeating or how power in the hands of stupidity does not command common sense and respect. It shows

195   Carr, *Meat and Salt*, Dir. Andrea Ainsworth, 2003, Abbey Theatre Archive.

how independent-minded girls who defy authority can continue to exist and remain loyal to their values and beliefs.

If the moral of the traditional fairy tale is to discipline women into obedient daughters and wives, showing that women's unruly desires must be tamed by constant policing, then *Meat and Salt* rebels against this. Carr's tale is a clear-eyed subversion of what is thought of as the 'fairy tale' pattern. The tale may in fact be a transparent allegory of the desired position of Carr's women in terms of family, home, political institutions, submissive female behaviour and marriage. *Meat and Salt* therefore is not simply a reversal of the traditional fairy tale genre when read through notions of the abject.

It seems that to achieve a generative transformation in the context of abjection, the hidden aspects of it must be confronted in public, which is the case in *Meat and Salt*. Examining the nature of repression as both constitutive and disruptive of the social order, is a way to understand it and thereby transform it.

In the next chapter's discussion on *Ariel* (2002) and *The Cordelia Dream* (2008), abjection is predominantly examined in terms of family but it has further implications as it circulates on the periphery of the public realm. It shows how the subject's encounter with forms of 'otherness', internal and external, establishes heightened and extreme individualism. The chapter suggests that this needs to be reconciled within a sense of mutual responsibility between individuals and society.

CHAPTER 4

Sacrificial Blood

On Raftery's Hill and *Meat and Salt* demonstrates how the male protagonists set their boundaries, their relation to their territory, their 'empire',
to which their family and 'the kingdom', pay the toll of isolation, and in
On Raftery's Hill, also abuse. *Meat and Salt*, in the fairy tale genre, depicts
patriarchal authority and its power of self-destruction but also demonstrates
female resistance to that authority. The absence of myth in *On Raftery's
Hill* makes the drama of abuse all the more painful and confrontational
and the fact that no one dies in the play proposes that incest will continue
without intervention. In *Meat and Salt*, the lack of any death might be seen
as offering less of a cultural impact, given the fairytale framework, with its
sense of charm and playfulness. That there are no deaths in these plays is
significant also given that in Carr's trilogy the female protagonists die.

This chapter looks at Carr's return to the death of the protagonist(s)
and to mythical and classical frameworks, in *Ariel* and *The Cordelia Dream*.
These plays, in the context of abjection, operate differently than *On Raftery's
Hill* and *Meat and Salt*. With *Ariel*, the male protagonist casts the net wider,
across personal, familial and social boundaries, but in doing so catches
himself. He designs his boundary without fully knowing what he is doing,
almost validating a Faustian pact without fully knowing what he is signing.
Perhaps, as Michael Billington states in *The Guardian*, *Ariel* is 'thematically overloaded', with Carr struggling to fit too much of the political and
cultural world of the *Oresteia* into this much smaller world,[1] or as Lisa
Fitzpatrick argues in 'Nations and Myth in the Age of the Celtic Tiger:

---

1   Michael Billington, *The Guardian*, 5 October 2002, http://www.guardian.co.uk/
     stage/2002/oct/05/theatre.artsfeatures1, accessed 13 February 2004.

Muide Éire', the lack of a shared sense of commonality and community, so much a part of classical myths, fails to signify in this instance:

> Irish dramatic (and nationalist) tradition is familiar with the sacrifice of a son for the sake of the nation; such sacrifices appear in legend, in the writings of revolutionary figures, and in the plays of the dramatic canon. But nowhere is the sacrifice of a daughter mythologized. The daughter, on the contrary, has generally functioned as a symbol of the nation, Cathleen Ní Houlihan, who demands the blood of her sons and lovers; or as a supportive daughter, girlfriend, wife or mother of the nationalist hero.[2]

Ariel replays the destructive outcome of the original myth, with the protagonist engaging in his own undertaking for his own sake but the myth disables and fails to be convincing in a wider contemporary context. Thus, *Ariel* as a micronarrative is consumed, and when examined in the context of abjection, offers an imploding process of subjectivity.

In *The Cordelia Dream*, sacrifice also signifies an all-consuming micronarrative. As in *Ariel*, the father/daughter relationship is central to the narrative and the protagonist's confrontation with the past in terms of the present is dramatised. Once again, death (and murder), with the self-sacrifice of the female, is necessary for the triumph of the male. This sacrifice of the female is dramatised as self-contained, confined as an individual trauma, having no connections to a broader context. Kristeva's boundaries of abjection, through repetition, the return of the repressed, the 'maternal' and the symbolic, are in this instance, reactionary micro dramas in the plays.

The world premiére of Marina Carr's *Ariel* (2000) was staged at the Abbey Theatre on 2 October–9 November 2002, directed by Conall Morrison. It was the fifth of her plays staged by the Abbey. It is set once more in the present in the Midlands of Ireland, and is a loose reworking of Euripides's *Iphigenia at Aulis*, a return to the dialectical structure used in her 1994–1998 dramas. Initially called *Destiny*, the play emphasises

---

2   Lisa Fitzpatrick, 'Nations and Myth in the Age of the Celtic Tiger: Muide Éire' in Patrick Lonergan and Riana O'Dwyer (eds), *Echoes Down the Corridor* (Dublin: Carysfort Press, 2007), pp. 169–179, p. 176.

the timeless predictability of the human condition.[3] *Iphigenia at Aulis* charts the story of a predestined corruption that surrounds the House of Atreus, involving power, murder and retribution. The play transposes the House of Atreus into an Irish context, giving it a contemporary language and investing it with a power-lust. The Agamemnon-figure is protagonist Fermoy Fitzgerald, played by Mark Lambert, initially encountered as a middle-aged father, husband, politician and cement factory owner, who desires ultimate power as the leader of Ireland.

The central plot sees Fermoy fatally sacrifice his sixteen-year-old daughter, the eponymous Ariel, played by Elske Rahill, in exchange for political power, followed by his murder at the hand of his wife Frances, played by Ingrid Craigie, culminating with Frances's murder by their daughter, Elaine (the older Elaine played by Eileen Walshe). Carr re-imagines Agamemnon's oldest daughter Iphigenia as Ariel, the offspring of a greedy father, against the background of a mature Celtic Tiger Ireland. Carr's Iphigenia is an optimistic young fledgling caught up in political and cultural events in the drama, an innocent victim in the midst of familial and civic hatred and hypocrisy. Fintan O'Toole has observed:

> It may well be that *Ariel* is the kind of play we will have to get used to: a meander into an unknown landscape where we see some breathtaking views and stumble into some treacherous bogs ... It takes vision and generosity to accept the task of trying to find public myths for a society that no longer knows what anything means.[4]

The narrative of *Ariel* charts Fermoy's obsession with the idea of power, motivating him to murder Ariel in exchange for ultimate political status as Ireland's leader, the Taoiseach. In declaring that this is his fate he states: 'I'm on this earth to rule. Was born knowin ud. Timidihy has held me back till now. It'll hould me back no longer. I refuse to spind any more of me life on the margins.'[5] He takes Ariel for a drive in her car, his birthday

---

3   See interview 'Marina Carr in conversation with Melissa Sihra' in Lillian Chambers, Ger Fitzgibbon & Eamonn Jordan (eds), *Theatre Talk: Voices of Irish Theatre Practitioners* (Dublin: Carysfort Press, 2001), p. 56.

4   O'Toole, p. 188.

5   Marina Carr, *Ariel* (Oldcastle, Co. Meath: Gallery Press, 2002), p. 19.

present to her, and her disappearance, with his concurrent aspiration to political success, opens tales of an ancient skirmish that has tainted the family's geneology. Like the bogs, lakes and landscapes in Carr's earlier works, here, Cuura lake holds the (g)hosts of Fermoy's familial past. The bodies of Fermoy's mother and others connected to his heritage reveal that his past is tainted by murder. Such a history takes its course in the development of the narrative. Boniface, his brother, played by Barry McGovern, is a monk, and reminds Fermoy that their blood 'is streaked', outlining the apprehension he has that their family carries the genetic blueprint of destruction.[6] Fermoy's father murdered his mother by drowning her in Cuura Lake, when he was seven years old, and forced him to hold her down. Meanwhile, his Aunt Sarah was, according to Fermoy's daughter Elaine, 'warming me granddaddy's bed' at the time.[7] Boniface resents Sarah's replacement of their mother so soon after her death. He remembers one time when 'Auntie Sarah was sittin ah the table wearin Ma's clothes, the hair up in wan of her slides, prancing round the kitchen like ud was hers.'[8] Boniface's guilt for abandoning Fermoy to the situation in the home after their mother's death recurs in his slippages back into alcoholism, triggered by his realisation that Fermoy murdered Ariel. Frances, Fermoy's wife, encounters her husband's confrontations with his past, in his openly verbal abuse and disloyalty, seen not just in the killing of their daughter, but explicitly in his infidelity and general betrayal of her. Their other children, Elaine and Stephen, bear the hallmarks of the situation in the home. Elaine transgresses the impact of Fermoy's abject self by mirroring his behaviour in both his actions and words. Stephen responds to it by initially finding solace through over-dependency on his mother, but later by rejecting his family outright. Outside the family, in the public realm, Fermoy is competing with Hannafin, his rival in the up and coming election. Fermoy's success as a candidate in the elections coincides with

6   Carr, *Ariel*, p. 19.
7   Carr, *Ariel*, p. 24.
8   Carr, *Ariel*, p. 17.

Hannafin's defeat, which is linked to the dubious circumstances that surround his subsequent suicide.

Fermoy's confrontation of the traumatic past in terms of the present and its concomitant impact on all those caught up in his world emerges in his abject self. Fermoy can be understood in terms of Julia Kristeva's analysis of the subject's process of self-individuation (see Kristeva's theory of abjection in the Introduction). Kristeva's view of the mother during this process can be seen in Carr's elaboration of the mother figure in *Ariel*, both absent and present. The subjective self is always haunted by the possible return of the abject that was part of the pre-subjective experience.

For Fermoy's subjective identity, this threatened return, that would dissolve his self into undifferentiatable parts, is posed by representative triggers which he connects to his past. Breastfeeding, eating, women (especially mothers), are both desired and feared by him in the play. Fermoy's reinstatement of a fractured self becomes a site of a series of negotiations and transmissions, both disputing and affirming his identity. Through abjection, his signifying function of self eludes rationally comprehensible meaning and yet, apprehending the role of the self is central to its location. Kristeva's theory also foregrounds the subject's process of identification to the maternal sphere, in a space she refers to as the 'chora'.[9] Fermoy's parents, particularly his mother, as well as his own parental role, play a significant part in his journey towards abjection.

The notion of abjection in *Ariel* calls into question a particular kind of subsumed subjectivity, in relation to Fermoy's selfhood, which throughout the course of the drama, has been made invisible or is in some way appropriated. This chapter's concern is not simply to articulate the final destination of the protagonist's state of abjection but also to locate the condition of abjection throughout the play. Betrayal and injustice are typical features of *Ariel*, found not only between families such as Fermoy's political opponent, Hannafin or Frances's previous husband and their child, but even worse, within the Fitzgerald family itself. Applying the Kristevan notion

9   See specifically Kristeva, under rubric 'The Chora', Receptacle of Narcissism, pp. 13–14.

of abjection, issues of power, authority, corruption and murder become the very conditions that infect Carr's protagonist, where the antagonistic selfhood is symptomatic of Fermoy's kind of anti-self, which emerges in the play. Fermoy's movement along the signifiable depths of abjection reveals his abject self as both belonging and excluded.

Ariel points to a profound link between individual excess and the social order, and exposes loss as the excessive currency that pervades the world of the play. Neither the danger of death, nor the horror often arising from such excess is avoided. The full realisation of loss is veiled, in Fermoy's political aspirations and corruption in Frances's mourning of her previous dead husband Charlie and their child James, in Boniface's alcoholism, in Elaine's obsession with Fermoy and in Stephen's obsession with and later withdrawal from his mother and family. The economy of loss gives reign to a logic of destruction that signifies their abject identity.

The various forms of corruption and excess in the drama, namely the murder of Ariel and the dubious circumstances of Hannafin's suicide (coinciding with Fermoy's progression towards power) destabilise all social and moral order. Corruption is the most common 'socialised appearance of the abject.'[10] Fermoy's self-justification denies responsibility for his actions; his self-abasement is illuminated from the beginning of the play in his belief that the only obstacle in the way of his gaining power is not his political opponent Hannafin, but himself. He tells Boniface:

> Ah, ud's noh Hannafin's the crux ah all, ud's meself, allas meself. Hannafin's a gombeen, like the rest of em. Why do they all want to be nice? What's so great about bein liked? Am I missin somethin here? Swear it was all beauhification they were after and em all cut-throats in their own kitchens. [...] I swear to God I'm goin to bring in a new religion, no more guilt, no more sorrow, no more good girls and good biys, just the unstoppable blood pah a the soul.[11]

According to Fermoy, God has commanded him to murder in order for him to embrace political power to the ultimate degree. His religious fun-

---

10   Kristeva, *Powers of Horror*, p. 16.
11   Carr, *Ariel*, pp. 17–18.

damentalism is the basis for action. Yet as Kristeva notes: 'There is nothing like abjection of self to show that all abjection is in fact recognition of the *want* on which any being, meaning, language, or desire is founded.'[12] Fermoy's 'want' is the desire to fill the void left as a result of his mother's absence and his implication in the murder, which resulted in the enforced separation from her. Fermoy's response to his emotionally absent mother is articulated through a feigned nonchalance. Her inadequacy permeates this dialogue with Boniface:

> FERMOY: She was never the suurt was goin to die in her bed.
> BONIFACE: She'd a died in her bed if she'd been leh ... I remember goin Auntie Sarah was sittin ah the table wearin Ma's clothes [...].
> FERMOY: Someone had to wash the dishes.
> BONIFACE: Now it's comin ouh.
> FERMOY: Whah?
> BONIFACE: Thah I didn't lave the novitiate to look after ya.
> FERMOY: Auntie Sarah looked after me fine, fierce good to me, a packeta biscuits and a bottle a red lemonade every nigh before I wint to bed, whah more coud ya ask for?[13]

His mother's absence and murder has left a longing in him that causes him to disregard any consequences for his actions. Specifically, the act of filicide questions one of the most basic human moral precepts, the nurturing and protecting of children. This perverse act derives from the murder of his mother, an event that goes against the social conventions of humanity. Fermoy buys Ariel a car for her sixteenth birthday, the vehicle that takes her to her death. Using the Chekhovian distinction, the play differentiates between the venial and the mortal sin. Venial sins are 'like killing yourself by the spoonful,' minor petty misdeeds, which erode our humanity over time.[14] Mortal sins are 'preordained', committed as 'a stroke of destiny'.[15] Fermoy portrays no concept of the suffering which he will cause to his

---

12   Kristeva, *Powers of Horror*, p. 5. [Emphasis in original]
13   Carr, *Ariel*, pp. 16–17.
14   Sihra, *Theatre Talk*, p. 58.
15   Sihra, *Theatre Talk*, p. 58.

family as a result of Ariel's sacrifice, and he fully justifies, in an ambiguous way, his reasons for her murder:

> FERMOY: The mortal sins is back in fashion. Welcome back, we missed yees. Age of compassion had uds turn and never took rooh. Well, way past time to banish the dregs to heaven's dungeon. The earth is ours wance more and noh before time.
> BONIFACE: If thah's your manifesto I may start prayin ya don't geh in.
> FERMOY: Ud'h mine for the takin, I know ud is, all ud nades on my part is a sacrifice.
> BONIFACE: Whah suurt of a sacrifice?
> FERMOY: A sacrifice to God.
> BONIFACE: Buh whah suurt?
> FERMOY: The ony suurt he acknowledges. Blood.[16]

Fermoy's declaration that the earth is his for the taking is portrayed in a number of forms throughout the play.[17] His logic for sacrificing his daughter finds itself in a cul de sac, where according to him, his God has presented him with no other options, believing that the earth belongs to God: 'blood and more blood, blood till we're dry as husks, then pound us down, spread us like salt on the land, begin the experiment over, on different terms next time.'[18]

Fermoy's self-justification is 'perverse' because it effectively complies with his own oppressive power of self-debasement, which goes against the natural will to survive. This begins in the debate on the origins of his identity, culminating in an ironic embrace of determining social and religious authorities. The strategy is a powerful one, responding perversely and illogically to the stigmatising accusation of his perceptions of his genealogy, and making of its shame the stuff of liberation in the form of power. Fermoy is self-appointed as a natural ruler who 'was born knowin ud', as though 'knowing it' were an actual event during his childhood. For Fermoy, self-knowledge exemplifies the incident of his mother's murder, predicated on a highly problematic attribution of it. His early childhood

---

16   Carr, *Ariel*, p. 18.
17   Carr, *Ariel*, p. 18.
18   Carr, *Ariel*, p. 19.

experiences have come to express his ideas about existential choice, the nature of power and the unspeakable trauma of his past. His statement to Frances about remembering and forgetting, 'I remember everything, don't you fear, buh ud's important to forget too,' illustrates the capacity of abjection to undermine apparently secure binary oppositions and to show up each term's interpenetration with its opposite.[19] His attempts to suppress the memory of the murderous event of his mother by his father fail every time:

> BONIFACE: Ya talking abouh Ma, a'ya?
> FERMOY: No, I'm noh talking abouh Ma. Why d'ya have to brin her up every time?
> BONIFACE: Do I brin her up every time?
> FERMOY: Withouh fail.
> BONIFACE: And is thah a crime?
> FERMOY: Was thirty-five year ago, Boniface. She's gone, she's gone.[20]

Shortly after refusing to engage in the conversation about his mother's death and before taking Ariel for a drive, he describes his father's response to the act. Significantly, he outlines not simply the behaviour of his father after the deed, but also the responsibility he still feels for his part in it. He tells Ariel:

> FERMOY: He [His father] lih a cigarette, puh me on his shoulders, all the way up from the lake, across the fields to the Sea Dew Inn. We sah at the counter, him drinkin four Jemmies, the eyes glihherin, glancing from me to the glass to the fluur, then lanin over and whisperin 'Time to be turning ourselves in.'
> ARIEL: And what did you say?
> FERMOY: Don't remember if I said anhin ... All I remember is looking ah him, the low sounds of Sunda evening drinkin, the barmaid putting an lipstick and him smiling, yeah, smiling. How can ya describe thah to anywan?
> ARIEL: He shouldn't a said 'we'.
> FERMOY: Ya think noh?

19 Carr, *Ariel*, p. 31.
20 Carr, *Ariel*, p. 16.

ARIEL: A cuurse noh.

FERMOY: No, we was righ. I was there too. And though I was ony seven, an excuse
on this earth, I was ony seven thousand and seven millin, for the soul is wan age
and mine just stood and watched. [...].[21]

While Fermoy defends his will to power, he also defends his role in
the circumstances of his mother's death. The neglected child who was
brought to witness and take part in her murder moves from abandonment
to self-abandonment to crime. Although crime, for Fermoy, is rationalised
as an inevitable sacrifice in the murder of Ariel, the play's concern is his
response as an individual subject to the oppressive predicaments in his
past. Kristeva outlines how abjection does not obey or follow rules or
boundaries of any sort:

> The traitor, the liar, the criminal with a good conscience, the shameless rapist, the killer
> who claims he is a saviour ... Any crime, because it draws attention to the fragility
> of the law, is abject, but premeditated crime, cunning murder, hypocritical revenge
> are even more so because they heighten the display of such fragility ... Abjection, on
> the other hand, is immoral, sinister, scheming, and shady: a terror that dissembles,
> a hatred that smiles, a passion that uses the body for barter instead of inflaming it, a
> debtor who sells you up, a friend who stabs you.[22]

Abjection corresponds to a fundamental hypocrisy in morality and
politics. Fermoy's hypocritical moral principles oscillate between the sly
and unpredictable at one time and the secret flouting of them at another,
lacking moral consistency. Thus, the ironic reassertion of his sense of self
in the play repudiates the agency of social determination, and deliberately
side steps its value schemes, by embracing the lowest possible status, 'I swear
to God I'm goin to brin in a new religion, no more guilt, no more sorrow,
no more good girls and good biys, just the unstoppable blood pah a the
soul.'[23] The ambiguous transition from the passive to the powerful means

---

21   Carr, *Ariel*, p. 36.
22   Kristeva, *Powers of Horror*, p. 4.
23   Carr, *Ariel*, p. 18.

of liberation, is important as a marker of indeterminacy, and as such, the failed separation at the heart of abjection.

Carr conflates childhood with failed separation, signified in the image of ten-year-old son Stephen on his mother's lap looking for her breast milk:

> FRANCES: (*To Stephen who stands beside, looking at her*) I said no, Stephen, you're not getting ud.
> STEPHEN: Just a sup.
> FRANCES: I'm noh a lollypop.
> STEPHEN: (*Climbing onto her knee*) Come on and don't be manchey wud em. (*Going for her breast*)
> FRANCES: I said, no. (*Stops him*) No, Stephen, no. (*A Struggle*)
> SARAH: Ah, leh him suck away. If there was wan goin I'd be suckin' on ud too.
> FRANCES: (*Struggling with him*) No way, Stephen. Whah would your Daddy say?
> STEPHEN: Don't you dare tell him!

In the Kristevan sense, the threat of separation from the mother is met with a second symbolic threat presented by the father. The mother figure is a risk to the child's sense of self, though as the primary source of survival, the child cannot release itself from her. Yet the father as the main prohibitor is already inherent in the child's coming of being in the process of learning to speak. In relation to the substitution of a bodily discourse that is maternal, along with the introduction of a specific kind of a masculine discourse, Kristeva notes: 'A representative of the paternal function takes the place of the good maternal object that is wanting. There is language instead of the good breast.'[24]

Like *On Raftery's Hill*, *Woman and Scarecrow* and *The Cordelia Dream*, the maternal is associated with disgust in the drama, a standpoint which is actualised and symbolised in the annihilation of maternity, by the murder of Fermoy's mother and by the aversion to various aspects that directly relate to the female, particularly the mother. Fermoy's enforced abandonment of his own mother has been deeply engrained at the early age of seven years. The image of the female body in its mothering practice of breast-feeding in

---

24   Kristeva, *Powers of Horror*, p. 45.

the abject sense, does not participate for Fermoy in the recognisable functioning subjectivity. Fermoy asks Frances: 'Was he on ya agin?' to which she
replies, 'He's ony sittin on me knee.' Fermoy states: 'Know your lyin. Can
smell the milk.'[25] Kristeva explains the source of Fermoy's fear: 'Fear of the
archaic mother turns out to be essentially fear of her generative power.'[26]
In patriarchal patrilineal societies, men define their genealogical identity
against this power, which they must control if they wish to preserve that
identity. According to Kristeva, the differentiated subject fears 'his very
own identity sinking irretrievably into the mother.'[27]

The sacred and the profane, as apparently separate domains, are fused in
the characteristics of abjection, triggered for Fermoy by the scene of the 'pre-
oedipal child' at the threatening gift of milk. Kristeva portrays the bodily
interdictions and prescriptions placed on the subject in early infancy, as a
means of approaching the larger functions of the protagonist's responses to
the interventions of social authority in subjectivity, responses which bring
about the breakdown in symbolic modes in the play. For Fermoy, the body
and corpus are continually blurred and destabilised, where eating and drinking perpetuate the confusion around 'proper' and 'improper'. He sees his
ten-year-old son who is still being breast-fed with the utmost horror. The
scene articulates Kristeva's notion of loathing an item of food as a form of
protection. For Fermoy, ingestion repeatedly figures the construction of a
degraded consciousness that comes to constitute his subjectivity. The scene,
which follows the breastfeeding one, depicts the deliberate sexual gesture
where Fermoy smashes the birthday cake and declares to Boniface 'Hate
cake, so does the kids.'[28] The smashing of the cake offers Fermoy revenge
for the outrage and sense of violation inflicted on him in the previous
breast-feeding act. Frances admonishes his action and states: 'Ya know I
love cake.'[29] Destroying the cake also signifies the murder of his mother,
echoing the act of striking her, then leaving her in a state of no return. The

25   Carr, *Ariel*, p. 27.
26   Kristeva, p. 77.
27   Kristeva, p. 64.
28   Carr, *Ariel*, p. 21.
29   Carr, *Ariel*, p. 27.

symbolism of the cake is underwritten with Frances' withdrawal of sex in their relationship, withdrawn until as Frances says, 'you learn to trahe a woman righ and noh before.'[30] Although the cake is an object of desire for Fermoy, the association of it with the maternal repositions it in the realm of the rejected. Fermoy's reply forms a connection between the cake and sex, when he says to Frances: 'And ya love withholdin ud. I'm married to nun, Boniface, a born agin virgin. Ud's noh every man can say he's hitched hees cart to the reverend mother.'[31] His response is one of loss, as the cake splinters into the denunciation of motherhood. The cake occupies both the symbolic and the real, visually transforming words into pejorative feelings and acts towards the maternal. For Fermoy, his ten-year-old breast-feeding son and the cake (symbolic of sexual rejection) become synonymous with one another. Fermoy tells Frances in the presence of Boniface:

> Sure, the ony rason I married ya was so I could have ud on demand. And all she does is talk abouh ud, talk abouh ud wud this lad here latched onto her. Look at hees teeth, he's whah? Ten, and he still has hees milk teeth.[32]

In the 'Improper/Unclean', Kristeva states: 'Food loathing is perhaps the most elementary and most archaic form of abjection. When the eyes see or the lips touch that skin on the surface of milk ... I experience a gagging sensation [which] cause forehead and hands to perspire.'[33] The nausea created by food, particularly breast milk, is the very reason for separation from the caregiver who provides it. The rejection of food is denouncing their desire, which, as Kristeva points out, 'is not an "other" for "me", who am only in their desire, [therefore] I expel *myself*, I spit *myself* out, I abject *myself* within the same motion through which "I" claim to establish *myself*.'[34]

---

30   Carr, *Ariel*, p. 28.
31   Carr, *Ariel*, p. 27.
32   Carr, *Ariel*, p. 28.
33   Kristeva, *Powers of Horror*, p. 2.
34   Kristeva, *Powers of Horror*, p. 3. [Emphasis in original]

The play's narrative of abjection is implicated more closely in the bodily experiences of motherhood. Frances is rejected because she represents the burden of deprivation felt by Fermoy as a result of his mother's absence and his fear of the maternal. Kristeva links deprivation and aggressivity as logically coextensive: '[D]oes not fear hide an aggression, a violence that returns to its source, its sign having been inverted?'[35] The maternal, as the disturbing presence, is linked to abjection, where all things related to her have been constructed through abjection. For Fermoy, triggers in the play that associate with the maternal and motherhood mean that his fears are likely to return, just as insistently, as the process of abjection that perverts from within.

Fermoy's manifestation of abjection emphasises his sharp sense of self-perpetuated exclusion, while simultaneously unveiling an inner turbulence that supersedes his abject condition and significantly marks his sense of abandonment, which he recognises as beginning at the age of seven. Fermoy is uncomfortable to discuss the subject, telling Boniface: 'No, I'm noh talking abouh Ma. Why dya have to brin her up every time?', but the narrative demonstrates his failure to ignore it and the consequences of the event on him and by association on his family.[36] Fermoy's abject condition is the circumstance which advances an ironic elevation; a new identity is born from his derelict state of abandonment when he was a child. His movement towards abjection is seen as part of the rhetorical project, whose resources are mobilised around his power-lust in the larger political scheme outside his family.

Carr's transposition of Aeschylus into the twenty first century, somewhat removed from the tragedic forms of ancient Greek writing, reflects some of the disimprovements of contemporary Irish life brought about by power and greed. Carr is more interested in contemporising the original plot than in making the audience aware of the Greek conventions that the play explores. This is apt, as *Ariel* could not hold up the large cultural signifiers which Agamemnon and Troy had to. The family, rural Ireland and

---

35   Kristeva, *Powers of Horror*, p. 38.
36   Carr, *Ariel*, p. 16.

the Catholic Church are brought on stage in Carr's diluted Agamemnon-figure, Fermoy, who is driven by an irrational force for political control, in his brother, the Monk, Boniface, and in the Fitzgerald family. Fermoy's drive for power, he tells Boniface, is his journey to the 'blood pah a the soul', meaning the blood sacrifice he will make.[37] Fermoy's act of child killing has a major impact on his family throughout the narrative: Elaine's hatred for her mother intensifies; Frances re-focuses her energies on her grief over the deaths of her previous husband and their son; Stephen, Fermoy's only son, comes to abandon his family, and Boniface queries his religious faith and retreats once again to alcoholism, due to the fact that he is withholding information that would possibly lead to Fermoy's conviction for murder. Through issues of murder, infidelity, familial hatred, political corruption and power, Carr's protagonist subverts all moral conventions, in exchange for ostensible self-wholeness.

Individual difficulties in the play speak to a contemporary Irish audience weighed down by the collapse of institutions, particularly since the 1990s. This includes scandals in the Catholic Church, revelations of political corruption, the breakdown of the notion of family as defined and constituted by the Church and State, and the impact of the 'Celtic Tiger', the familiar term given to Ireland's booming economy. Eamonn Jordan points out:

> From a late [nineteen] nineties perspective, many of the major cultural aspirations and much-sought after freedoms of the recent past are now taken as given … The heightened productivity alongside labour and technological alienation, new concerns about ownership and belonging, a growing redundancy of faith, an increasingly assertive intercultural penetration and a previously unknown dynamic economy have all led to a society in serious transition. Effectively, the confusions and confidences delivered by a period of social liberalism, the collapse of political difference with the demise of the influence of politically correct ideology have ensured that difference has been submerged and the impact of oppositional energies diluted.[38]

---

37 Carr, *Ariel*, pp. 17–18.
38 Eamonn Jordan, 'Introduction' in Eamonn Jordan (ed.), *Theatre Stuff: Critical Essays on Contemporary Irish Theatre* (Dublin: Carysfort, 2000), p. xiv.

The kind of classical tragedy that might have served to represent conflict and betrayal at their origin falters in *Ariel*, in the context of scandals in
Ireland. Carr gives emphasis to emotions and themes such as jealousy, rage,
revenge, betrayal, deceit and violence, altered more in terms of their context
than in their content, making 'epic' decline into repetitious arguments. As
Sihra points out: 'In *Ariel*, Carr shows how patterns in the Grand Design
emerge, as we spin our own fates ... We repeat the past at will, because we
imagine our twist of fate will be different. But it cannot be, if we do not
take stock of history.'[39]

The late 1990s in Ireland saw productions and versions of Euripides'
Iphigenia in Aulis by Irish writers. Edith Hall argues: [40]

> [W]hat they have in common is less a shared stance on Ireland, religion, gender or
> even theatrical aesthetics, than a conviction that mendacious political rhetoric has
> in recent years become more effective, and that the rise in spin-doctoring has been
> made possible only by the epistemological and metaphysical vacuum situated at the
> centre of the Western collective psyche.[41]

In relation to Irish versions of Greek theatre, Marianne McDonald writes
how the classics can offer a literature of protest: '[T]hey are plays that
focus on human rights more than on fate and identity. The result is not
simply a political tract protesting abuse, but a passionate expression of
hopes and fears.'[42]

---

39   Melissa Sihra, 'Writing in Blood', Abbey Theatre Programme Note of *Ariel*, 2002,
     p. 3.
40   Colin Teevan *Iph...* (1999), Kate Mitchell directed Euripides' *Iphigenia at Aulis* in
     2001 for the Abbey Theatre, Marina Carr's *Ariel* (2002) and Edna O Brien's *Iphigenia*
     (2003).
41   Edith Hall, 'Iphigenia and Her Mother at Aulis: A Study in the Revival of a Euripidean
     Classic' in John Dillon and S.E. Wilmer (eds), *Rebel Women: Staging Ancient Greek
     Drama Today* (London: Methuen, 2005), p. 3.
42   Marianne McDonald, 'Classics as Celtic Firebrand: Greek Tragedy, Irish Playwrights,
     and Colonialism' in Eamonn Jordan (ed.), *Theatre Stuff: Critical Essays on
     Contemporary Irish Theatre* (Dublin: Carysfort, 2000), p. 16.

The circumstances of death and dying in the play are inextricably linked to Kristevan notions of abjection. The way in which Fermoy's mother died echoes Kristeva's sense of the corpse and its connection to self-loathing. Fermoy remembers when he was seven years of age how his father was a 'man in a navy raincoah that butchered me mother.'[43] Like Red Raftery in *On Raftery's Hill*, who outlines how to gut a hare while raping his daughter, and connects the maltreatment of animals with humans, Fermoy equates the drowning of his mother with having previously seen his father drown kittens. He tells Ariel: 'I'd seen him drown a bag of kittens, blind, tiny pink tongues and fairy teeth. Really this was no different.'[44] Boniface tells Frances of his fears regarding Fermoy and their father: 'He'd [their father] the charm of forty devils alrigh. They allas do, buh back of the charm was the stuck-up rebellis heart of all a Lucifer's crew.'[45] He recalls the murder of their mother by drowning and Fermoy's role in it and tells Frances: 'Auld fella med him [Fermoy] hould Ma down.'[46] Boniface believes that such an event 'is bound to take uds toll on a person's view of the world.'[47] In relation to dead bodies, Kristeva notes: 'The corpse, seen without God and outside of science, is the utmost of abjection. It is death infecting life.'[48]

Fermoy exerts scathing control over the dying landscape of his world and the dramatic narrative is invested in the relentless debasing of this world: 'The earth's over, paple knows thah in their bones, ozone layer in tahhers, oceans gone to sewer, whole world wan big landfill a dirty nappies. We're goin to lave this place in ashes like the shower on Mars.'[49] He rationalises his murder of Ariel by drowning as a necessity in itself. Elaine tells Stephen that Fermoy told her when at a conference in Venice:

43   Carr, *Ariel*, p. 36.
44   Carr, *Ariel*, p. 36.
45   Carr, *Ariel*, p. 26.
46   Carr, *Ariel*, p. 26.
47   Carr, *Ariel*, p. 26.
48   Kristeva, *Powers of Horror*, p. 4.
49   Carr, *Ariel*, p. 18.

Ariel was the stroke a destiny, he said, woven into him from the beginning ... And he tould me abouh Necessity. How before ya come to the world, Necessity and her sisters weave a carpet for ya ... And then you're flung to earth wud this weave and this twist in the weave thah some calls fate.[50]

Fermoy tries to live as if he were immortal, as if he has an eternity to fulfil his life's tasks. Carr claims that 'how we die says so much about how we live'[51] and Sylvia Plath's notion of death in her collection of poems entitled *Ariel* corresponds analogously to Carr.[52] Plath's *Lady Lazarus* describes how feelings of suicide and death permeate the subject's life, as though the subject is really a living dead spirit. The poem states: 'Dying/Is an art, like everything else./I do it exceptionally well.'[53] Significantly too, the poem *Ariel* presents an abject status in the form of female rebelliousness, where the speaking subject struggles to confiscate an outer self in an effort to form a truer sense of self. In Plath's *Ariel*, the subject's suicidal mission seeks to 'unpeel –/Dead hands, dead stringencies' so as to rid the fraudulent self[54] from the return of the repressed: 'Berries cast dark/ Hooks –/Black sweet blood mouthfuls/Shadows.'[55] Plath's *Ariel* commemorates death and draws a parallel between dying and the process of early separation from the mother. Steven Gould Axelrod points out that Plath labelled this moment of separation from the mother as 'the awful birthday of otherness.'[56] In relation to how people live and die, Sihra has suggested to Carr: 'The ways in which we try to arrest the physical signs of the ageing process seem to belie an attempt on some level to resist or deny our mortality and imperfection,'[57] to which Carr responded:

---

50   Carr, *Ariel*, pp. 61–62.
51   See Sihra, *Theatre Talk*, p. 56
52   See Sylvia Plath, *Ariel* (London: Faber and Faber, 1976).
53   Plath in 'Lady Lazarus', *Ariel*, p. 17.
54   Plath in 'Ariel', *Ariel*, p. 36.
55   Plath in 'Ariel', *Ariel*, p. 36.
56   Steven Gould Axelrod, *Sylvia Plath: The Wound and the Cure of Words* (Baltimore: Johns Hopkins University Press, 1990), p. 5.
57   Sihra in *Theatre Talk*, p. 56.

I love people who fight death, because, that is what it is. I think you can surrender slowly, that's a very different thing. I think sometimes we surrender too quickly here. I like a little battle. I like people who fight, who take pride in how they look, because it comes into everything – to take pride in how one behaves and to take pride in what one says. It is not even simply a matter of pride, it's about *being* aware of what is going on with yourself, on *every* level, physically and psychologically.[58]

In the abject condition, Fermoy's resistance to death is embraced by his notion of eternity, which portrays his heightened awareness of his being on every level. His existence is characterised by 'exile' from the presence of his mother, his father, his family, and from properly functioning symbolic codes. Kristeva notes: 'The corpse (or cadaver: *cadere*, to fall), that which has irremediably come a cropper, is cesspool, and death; it upsets even more violently the one who confronts it as fragile and fallacious chance ... refuse and corpses show me what I permanently thrust aside in order to live.'[59] Ariel's murder reinforces Fermoy's self-disgust and the significance of her death on the day she turns sixteen, as Sihra points out, 'effects an implicit transformation'[60] ... which is 'frequently linked to death.'[61] Sihra considers that, 'In terms of its function as a point of passage, the birthday evokes qualities intrinsic to [Victor] Turner's concept of liminality, which, he says, "is frequently likened to death, to being in the womb, to invisibility, to darkness, to bisexuality, to the wilderness, and to an eclipse of the sun of moon."'[62]

Fermoy's inward subversion of maternal deprivation, essentially allied with abjection, holds particular relish for him and manifests through the rest of the Fitzgerald family. Abjection in this sense is closely allied to the apparent loss of all social and moral authority, or to the symbolic leap, which takes place in the fusion of two systems or orders. The betrayals and

58   Sihra, p. 56. [Emphasis in original]
59   Kristeva, *Powers of Horror*, p. 3.
60   Melissa Sihra, ' "For She A Jolly Good Fella": Transformative Moments of Being and Becoming in the Theatre of Marina Carr,' Lecture, Synge Summer School, Co. Wicklow, Ireland, 1 July 2005.
61   Sihra, 'For She A Jolly Good Fella.'
62   Sihra, 'For She A Jolly Good Fella.'

abandonment of the past, which have caused the vacuity for Fermoy are the occasion for a larger, self-conscious gratuity, which directly impacts on others who come in contact with him. 'Ud's [the earth] mine for the takin,' he tells Boniface.[63] The abject reinvests identity in the network of Fermoy's relationships. The offspring are always necessary victims in the crossfire between parents, perpetuating the unrelenting cycle of abjection dominant in Carr's plays.

Significantly, it is Elaine who exemplifies the 'perverse' wilful obedience to Fermoy, her unrecognised oppressor in the play. Her role as his PR manager is a concentrated expression of the subversion of the power relations between them. Like Fermoy, who comes to model his own father, Elaine's mode of behaviour depicts the repetition and embracing of the abject levelled at herself, as she repeats, with ritualistic fervour, the 'crime of eternihy' in killing her mother.[64] She distinguishes between the ways in which Ariel and Fermoy died, recalling Fermoy's justification as to why and how Ariel had to die. She tells Frances: 'Whah my father done to Ariel had the grandeur of God in ud. Pure sacrifice. Ferocious, aye. Buh pure. Whah you done to him was a puckered vengeful, self-servin thing wud noh a whiff of the immortal in ud.'[65] Elaine's understanding of Ariel's death is deliberately exploited to announce the parody of power, founding her sense of self in the antagonistic yet mutually dependent relationship of *jouissance* and abjection's plunge of loss, thereby mirroring Fermoy's sense of the abject. Like Fermoy, Elaine's rejection of the maternal is disjunctively wedded to a kind of religious redemption, and it is through this that she justifies Fermoy's murder of Ariel, describing it as 'a crime of eternihy' as distinct from Frances' murder of Fermoy as 'a low, blood splahhered, knife frenzied revenge.'[66] She tells Frances: 'Whah my father done to Ariel had the grandeur of God in ud. Pure sacrifice.'[67] Murder, aligned with religious imagery, subverts the policing of socially acceptable behaviour, as

63   Carr, *Ariel*, p. 18.
64   Carr, *Ariel*, p. 64.
65   Carr, *Ariel*, p. 64.
66   Carr, *Ariel*, p. 64.
67   Carr, *Ariel*, p. 64.

the central gravity of the play's narrative, and pushes Ariel's death as the catalyst for the resurgence of both Elaine's and Fermoy's sense of self. The evasion of imposed social worlds continues, as Elaine flagrantly confuses the properly consumed with the properly expelled. She commits perjury in the Courts, claiming to have been witness to Frances' murder of Fermoy, in order that Frances is found guilty and not allowed off on insanity for his death. Elaine's eulogy for Fermoy celebrates his political manifesto, as well as his general beliefs and behaviour. Her narrative models the ways in which the conventionally debased and rejected self can be reclaimed as something to be celebrated.

Elaine's imitation of Fermoy is an ironic fulfilment of maternal rejection and it is also a way of expressing her feelings of abandonment towards Frances, who she believes dedicated her life to the dead rather than the living. Instead of assuming the fully oppressive position of parental abandonment, which should also include Fermoy, her growing state of abjection escapes the old order which would object to him. Her abject being demonstrates how much she has been 'swallowed up' by Fermoy. She states to Stephen:

> You never seen him the way he seen himself, the way he was born to be seen, the way he could work a room, the way he held himself when he spoke, the big mellifluous vice, ya'd hear a pin drop. He was goin to run this country. He was goin to catapult this whole nation ouha sleaze and sentimentality and goobeenism. I'm going to take this country to the moon, he used say to me, and he would've ony for her.[68]

Kristeva describes offspring who are consumed by their parents through whom the abject exists:

> What he has swallowed up instead of maternal love is an emptiness, or rather a maternal hatred without a word for the words of the father; that is what he tries to cleanse himself of, tirelessly. What solace does he come upon within such loathing? Perhaps a father, existing but unsettled, loving but unsteady, merely an apparition but an apparition that remains.[69]

---

68   Carr, *Ariel*, p. 63.
69   Kristeva, *Powers of Horror*, p. 6.

Elaine's envelopment of her own criminal values figures liberation. The stigmatising of her family's genealogy entices her into the ironic inward rebellion whereby she psychologically transcends her predicament. In trying to find out what Elaine knows about Ariel's death, her mother states: 'You and your father, swear ya were married to him. You tell me whah you know!'[70] In knowing too much about her grandfather's death, and Sarah's replacement of her grandmother's role, the rebellious child Elaine is called a 'babby witch'[71] and is told to 'lave your mother alone.'[72] Stephen suggests that Elaine has an unhealthy obsession with Fermoy, even in death. He tells her: 'You shouldn't have puh up thah headstone, her [Ariel] name noh even on ud. You're like an alsatian the way you guard hees grave.'[73]

Elaine reinforces Stephen's belief that the ghosts of the dead rather than the living provide the stimulus for Frances' existence, and therefore her hatred of her. Even at the age of twelve, Elaine reminds her mother that breast-feeding Stephen upsets her father, a symbol of refusing to let go of her dead child James, but this also implies that she herself resents it because of the attention Stephen gets in trying to be a substitution for the dead son. When Stephen is asleep on Frances' knee, Frances looks at the locket hanging around her neck containing photos of her dead Charlie and their son James, looks at Stephen and says 'You've a look of him alrigh. The eyes, yees boh have my eyes. Buh ya don't have hees black curls [...].'[74] The event reminds Elaine that she is a bystander in the mother–daughter relationship. What is apparently no more than a childish outburst actually becomes her abject mission of transforming her humiliation into a new identity. At twelve years of age Elaine's response to her mother putting her outside the back door is revelatory: 'Ya think it bothers me goin ouhside the duur? Love ud ouh there. Can't waih to be ouhside your duur forever.'[75]

70   Carr, *Ariel*, p. 53.
71   Carr, *Ariel*, p. 24.
72   Carr, *Ariel*, p. 25.
73   Carr, *Ariel*, p. 62.
74   Carr, *Ariel*, p. 25.
75   Carr, *Ariel*, p. 24.

Elaine's feelings of maternal abandonment manifest in numerous ways in the play. The confrontational way with which she talks openly about her murdered Grandmother is a symptom of her earlier disturbance in maternal care:

> ELAINE: She's ah the bottom of Cuura Lake where me granddaddy puh her, in a bag wud a boulder, nowan ever found her.
> FRANCES: If ya know why're askin?
> ELAINE: Want to hear her say ud. She's ah the bohhom a Cuura Lake where me granddaddy puh her. Love the sound a thah.[76]

For Elaine, murder and death are used as exploitative tools. Elaine's advice to her father to use Ariel's death as a public sympathy stunt shows the emergence of the jealousy, which she experienced in childhood. Working as Fermoy's PR, she advises him what to 'perform' at the forthcoming television interview: 'Ariels's your trump card. Play ud. Ya nade to go wud the emotion of ud more. Thah's whah paple wants, details of your personal life. Don't be afraid to give ud to them. Don't be afraid to give them Ariel.'[77] Her comment, at twelve years of age, that she didn't enjoy Ariel's sixteenth birthday because, 'Birthdays is ony interestin when they're your own,' is not so much a sibling rivalry shown toward Ariel or Stephen, as it is her struggle to exist outside of the maternal. On Ariel's birthday, Fermoy tries to get rid of Elaine's need for attention from him. When she asks him: 'Sing a song to me, Daddy, song sweet sixteen to me', he refuses.[78] Persistent in seeking his interest, she asks: 'Will you give me a puff of your cigar if I go? [...] And a swig of your brandy', to which he says he will.[79] As Kristeva notes:

> The child can serve the mother as a token of her own authentication; there is, however, hardly any reason for her to serve as go-between for it to become autonomous and authentic in its turn. In such close combat, the symbolic light that a third party, eventually the father, can contribute helps the future subject, the more so if it happens

76 Carr, *Ariel*, pp. 23–24.
77 Carr, *Ariel*, p. 45.
78 Carr, *Ariel*, p. 12.
79 Carr, *Ariel*, p. 12.

to be endowed with a robust supply of energy, in pursuing a reluctant struggle against what, having been the mother, will turn to an abject. Repelling, rejecting; repelling itself, rejecting itself. Abjecting.[80]

The power of the maternal, which pre-exists a separation of (our) self and other, also provides the mother's unique identity, heightening the struggle for authentic subjectivity between the child and mother. The successful imposition of the symbolic order in the separation process is accompanied by the abject, confounding boundaries for the child. Elaine's conflictual relationship with her mother and her identification of herself in her father, reflects the 'violent, clumsy breaking away' during her early separation.[81]

Elaine's continuing resistance toward her mother is the kind of abjection that has fashioned her, that is, the ways in which she becomes homologous to her father and forms a secondary self. Regarding her relationship with Elaine, Frances states: 'This skirmish betwane us is ancient. Y'ever feel thah? Seems to me we been battling a thousand year.'[82] Elaine's hostility toward her mother is something she cannot find the origin of, yet in the abject status, language substitutes for the object world, therefore Elaine's hatred is a fear. The hatred is crystallized into the nature of her experience, which wants to know herself and to know everything; to know in particular, what seems to be lacking in her mother or could be lacking in herself:

> SARAH: There's divil the size of a whale inside you. Where in God's name is this hatred a your mother comin from?
> ELAINE: If I knew thah … I can't look at her for too long or me head swims. She appals me, allas has. (*Shudders*) Her eyes, her shoulders, everythin abouh her. I look ah her and I think there's something missin. I don't know is ud in me or in her.
> SARAH: And whah is ud ya think is missin?
> ELAINE: I think she has no soul.[83]

80   Kristeva, *Powers of Horror*, p. 13.
81   Kristeva, *Powers of Horror*, p. 13.
82   Carr, *Ariel*, p. 66.
83   Carr, *Ariel*, p. 71.

Elaine's rebellious behaviour, similar to that of Fermoy, is a return of the abject, a return to its source, where want, deprivation and the violence of rejection have been nurtured from the beginning. Her aggressive manner towards Frances is a form of protection, and is projected outwardly, which comes back at her in feelings of threat. In the misfire of identification with her parents, the result is Elaine's total rejection of her mother and the unstable replication of her father's acts and behaviours. As Kristeva notes:

> From the deprivation felt by the child because of its mother's absence to the paternal prohibitions that institute symbolism, that relation accompanies, forms, and elaborates the aggressivity of drives, consequently, never presents itself as a 'pure' state ... Aggresivity *appears* to take us as a rejoiner to the original deprivation felt from the time of the mirage known as 'primal narcissism'; it merely takes revenge on initial frustrations.[84]

Fermoy, the paternal figure, whose symbolic role was the early separation of Elaine from her mother, conflicted with Frances' desire craving an 'other'. Due to Fermoy's and Frances's contradictory roles in Elaine's early development – that of primary repression and the instability of the symbolic function – helped to bring Elaine into the realm of abjection. Kristeva depicts the early view of the abject as: '*Too much strictness on the part of the Other*, confused with the One and the Law. *The lapse of the Other*, which shows through the breakdown of objects of desire.'[85]

Stephen responds differently to Elaine in his feelings about being abandoned by his parents. His response is a resigned rejection of Fermoy associated with Fermoy's own self-abasement, inverting his sense of want and deprivation in the face of his father's abandonment. Kristeva notes that the father is the source of inverting negative emotions during the process of separation from the maternal:

> The fantasy of incorporation by means of which I attempt to escape fear (I incorporate a portion of my mother's body, her breast, and thus I hold on to her) already dwells in me on account of my learning to speak at the same time. In the face of this

---

84 Kristeva, *Powers of Horror*, p. 39.
85 Kristeva, *Powers of Horror*, p. 15. [Emphasis in original]

second threat, a completely symbolic one, I attempt another procedure: I am not the one that devours, I am being devoured by him; a third person therefore (he, a third person) is devouring me.[86]

However Stephen only acknowledges his mother's abandonment later. As a student, he comes to acknowledge that all his life she had exchanged the land of the living for the land of the dead. In relation to himself and Elaine, he tells Frances: 'we ran among your tombstones like they were swings.'[87] Stephen rejects his mother for the ten years during which he claims he was pretending to be her dead son, James, a son he felt he could never compete with. In relation to Frances's murder of their father, he tells her:

> Ya did it for Ariel. For James. There was ony two chambers in your heart, Ma, two dusty chambers, me and Elaine tryin to force our way in. Our playground was a graveyard, Ma, [...] we played hop, skip and jump on the bones a your children, your real children, while we whined for ya like ghosts.[88]

He refuses to embody the 'living dead'. This manifests in the film he made for his degree course, based on a mother and son's intimate relationship, and which won him a prize. The central plot of the film is the difficulty of separation between a mother and child, depicted in a mother breast-feeding her adult-son. Stephen pressures Frances into the situation of telling the film's storyline to the family stating: 'Ma'll tell ya, she's fierce proud of ud.'[89] Frances tells them: 'Ya've this mother and her son and ud's the son's weddin day and then the son goes missin, and the bride is looking all over the hotel for her new husband. And where does she find her new husband? In the bridal suihe, on the bridal bed, bein breast-fed be the mother.'[90] Frances asks Stephen: 'Then why did ya call the mother Frances in your film? Why was she dressed like me? Why was she drivin an auld Merc?'[91] Stephen realises

---

86   Kristeva, *Powers of Horror*, p. 39.
87   Carr, *Ariel*, p. 68.
88   Carr, *Ariel*, p. 68.
89   Carr, *Ariel*, p. 53.
90   Carr, *Ariel*, p. 54.
91   Carr, *Ariel*, p. 54.

that he had exchanged his sense of self for the dead James, in order to compensate and alleviate Frances' loss of her child. The film is Stephen's way of forcing Frances to confront her dedication to the dead and to address the impact that this has on the family. Frances never acknowledges Stephen's feelings of surrogacy. This culminates in him renouncing her at the crucial time of Ariel's funeral and Frances' forthcoming murder trial.

Fermoy's and Frances's relationship is contingent on the historical forces in their past and on the diversity of their needs in the Fitzgerald household. Sihra notes: 'The past is never far away in Marina Carr's plays, its secrets weep and bleed into the present, like wounds refusing to heal.'[92] Death, stemming from the past, plays a radical role in both Frances's and Fermoy's beings. For Fermoy, death is hijacked into the public realm, while for Frances it is separated into her private world. Fermoy's fear of the maternal increases in the play, and forces Frances to recoil more into her world in the past with the dead. Death is paired with loneliness and guilt for Frances. She claims that she is descended from 'a gintle people,'[93] and in marrying Fermoy she moved to a place unsuitable for the memory of her previous husband Charlie and their son James and also unsuitable for her and Fermoy's daughter Ariel; it is a place she describes as 'a nest a hooves'.[94] Her unease at being married to Fermoy is seen in the guilt she feels towards abandoning Charlie and James, the 'two she loved'.[95] Her visions are clearly focused on the past on what she calls the 'beauhiful dead'.[96] She highlights the poverty of responses to death and the fear of extinction that marks the Fitzgerald's lives. Instead of coming to terms with death she lives under its shadow with death as a guilty secret she contends with alone. Symbolically she wears it around her neck in the form of a locket containing a picture of the dead Charlie and James. Frances in some way blames Fermoy for James' death, 'wud black thinking and wishin him away.'[97] She sees their deaths

92   Sihra, Abbey Theatre Programme Note of *Ariel*, 2002, p. 3.
93   Carr, *Ariel*, p. 59.
94   Carr, *Ariel*, p. 59.
95   Carr, *Ariel*, p. 25
96   Carr, *Ariel*, p. 25.
97   Carr, *Ariel*, p. 29.

as some kind of retribution for her committing infidelity: 'Facts are me goin with you cost me me husband's life, me son's life and forever more me peace of mind.'[98] Fermoy accuses her of dwelling too much in the land of the dead, of being attracted to 'tombstones, headstones, graveyard excitement and the promise of funerals to come.'[99] He states to her on Ariel's tenth anniversary: 'Everythin thah happens to Frances Fitzgerald has to be momentous, spectacular. Her jiys could never be the same as anywan else's and her grafes must be inconsolable. Live! Live! Live! Thah's whah we're here for. Do something! Anhin! You'll have all of eternihy for pussin in the dark.'[100] But language soars with abjection, when boundaries of the self and other become blurred, because abjection is the pre-eminent state of 'living-death' where subject and object stage their epistemic panic. A state of 'living-death' is created in *Ariel*, in the criss-cross between the living and the dead. Frances asks: 'Why will no wan in this house leh me talk abouh James?'[101] Her preoccupation with death enters into life and animates it. Frances talks to her sleeping ten-year-old son Stephen, comparing him to the dead James: 'Buh ya don't have hees black curls, you've Fermoy's hair. James had the most beauhiful head a blue black curls. [...] Whin a'ya goin to cut thah child's hair, they'd ask? Never, I'd say, never, and I never did. Five years a black curls wint inta thah grave and me wud em.'[102] For Frances, death is the harbinger of life.

The resurgence of the abject selfhood in *Ariel* is played off in a variety of ways, against the unstable relationship of the Catholic sacred and the Catholic sacrilegious in the play and the depicted conception and transgression of social prescriptions. The drama is concerned with how identity may persist in the disturbances and coincidences wrought in and between Catholic Church values and the social, through abjection. Boniface tells of his mother's love affair with Padre Pio of San Giovanni. He reminds Fermoy:

98   Carr, *Ariel*, p. 31.
99   Carr, *Ariel*, p. 59.
100 Carr, *Ariel*, p. 51.
101 Carr, *Ariel*, p. 24.
102 Carr, *Ariel*, p. 25.

Her party piece was Padre Pio hearin her confession. And at the end of ud he puh hees hand through the curtain and the stigmaha bled onta her blouse. She had the blouse folded in tissue paper wud lavender sprigs all over ud. And if ya were really good she'd take down the blouse and leh us trace our fingers over the blood. Thah's eternity you're touchin, she'd say. Thah's eternihy, be careful wud ud.[103]

Boniface, in a cynical way believes: 'I goh the full benefih a Ma's christianity,' which led him into the novitiate at seventeen.[104] He tells Fermoy: 'Ya know it never occurred to me to go agin her. At least ya were spared thah [...].'[105]

The play's notion of obsessive power assumes a borderline position in the systems of belief which outline the fusion and divergence that take place between the abject and the symbolic systems it encounters. The extrapolation and loading of religious belief systems allow the resuscitation of characteristics of the Fitzgerald family, particularly relating to Fermoy's manipulation of power. His sense of self emerges simultaneously with the religious or socially forbidden order in the drama, exploiting power throughout.

Obsessive power occupies a crucial unstable position in relation to these value systems, and is the central dramatic strategy in *Ariel*. Fermoy's capacity to conspire with God for power is frightening in its own right; it is a kind of 'pre-articulate' desire for power. His motivation for power is not innate, but is a self-constructed justificatory value-system. He states to Frances in relation to Ariel's sacrifice: 'She rode ouha God from nowhere and to God she returned.'[106] He sequesters Ariel's death into the public zone, exploiting her anniversary as a political publicity stunt. Frances states to Fermoy: 'You're here because the press has descended like crows on the church to phohograph the big bronze lug a ya glowerin inta your daughter's empty grave. Ariel's a good phoho opportunihy.'[107] Exclusiveness and self-righteousness is not part of the Christian gospel imperatives and

---

103 Carr, *Ariel*, p. 27.
104 Carr, *Ariel*, p. 17.
105 Carr, *Ariel*, p. 17.
106 Carr, *Ariel*, p. 58.
107 Carr, *Ariel*, p. 46.

yet, as a member of the Catholic Church, he sees no contradiction in his behaviour. As Kristeva points out: 'Abjection accompanies all religious structurings and reappears to be worked out in a new guise, at the time of their collapse.'[108]

Fuelled by a power-frenzy, Fermoy is an irrational despot who will use people, including his immediate family, as tools for his self-aggrandisement. The offence *par excellence* against the Midlands society in the play, undermining social values and a hierarchical order based on belonging, lends itself to both sacrilege and sanctification, one has only to think of Fermoy's doctrine for gaining leadership – 'all ya nade to geh by in this world is horse since and God.'[109] That leadership is a flashpoint between social and religious order is indicated in the importance placed on control in both the political and catholic arenas in the drama, constituting in the extreme form, and according to Fermoy, one of the necessary qualifications for him to be Taoiseach of Ireland. Fermoy's standpoint, between activity and self-degradation, is a perverse strategy, which perpetuates oppression and actually interferes with the legislations and prescriptions placed on the self, by parental authority and by a pre-existing social and religious code.

The dual position of the abject protagonist in *Ariel*, both 'least' and 'most' powerful, is thus predicated on the uncertain differentiation of the sacred and the transgressive. Fermoy's formulations of 'God' illustrate the permeability of order in the drama, on which trust, faith and dominance must be founded, religious value implying a continual transgression, which resists its implantation in any rationalised scheme. Fermoy's belief that God will guarantee his political power, pending a blood sacrifice, resonates from antiquity, with the notion that the transaction with God can lead to acts of power. His belief in winning the up and coming election is unwavering: 'I've God behind me and what's a little civil war coven compared to God backing ya [...].'[110]

108   Kristeva, *Powers of Horror*, p. 17.
109   Carr, *Ariel*, p. 17.
110   Carr, *Ariel*, p. 14.

Early in the drama, Boniface and Fermoy argue as to what kind of God each sees:

BONIFACE: My God is an auld fella in a tent, addicted to broccoli.

FERMOY: No, my God is young. He's so young. He's on fire for us, heaven reelin wud hees rage at not bein among us, the eternihy of eternihy hauntin him. Times manes natin to him. He rises from an afternoon nap and twinty centuries has passed.

BONIFACE: No, no, no, he never slapes. Christianity is based on God never slapin. You're wrong there, God does noh slape.[111]

While Boniface's God is identified with having an addiction, similar to his, he nonetheless holds the Christian conviction that God is for the benefit of all humankind at all times. Fermoy's concept of God, on the other hand has power, is exclusionary and is protector of 'his chosen ones'. Synonymous with assent to dogma, Fermoy holds claim to finality or to an absolute certainty when speaking about God. His God's notion of eternity is a reeling with rage at not being among his people in this world. Fermoy's and Boniface's different responses to the notion of the Divine lie in their different insights into their mother's kind of Catholic devotion in their home while growing up. Fermoy belatedly considers his mother's influence over him as negative, articulated in his response to Stephen's abandonment of Frances. Boniface outlines his belief that there are liberating benefits to not having a mother. Like Fermoy, he holds his mother responsible for abandoning him and acknowledges to a much lesser extent his father's active part in it. Boniface, really speaking about himself, commends Stephen's discard of his mother, '[...] Mammy's off the menu forever more. Thah's how it's done. [...] Seems to me everythin worth looking ah in this world has ne'er a Ma ah all, ud's just there be udself in a flowerin gorgeousness, orphaned and free.'[112]

Fermoy refuses to enter into conversation about their mother's religious fanaticism: 'Furthest thing from me mind righ now. I've an election to win.'[113] The strength of the Catholic Church in relation to women, from

111   Carr, *Ariel*, p. 16.
112   Carr, *Ariel*, p. 69.
113   Carr, *Ariel*, p. 17.

the 1920s to the 1950s was particularly vigorous and prestigious. In 'Godly Burden: Catholic Sisterhoods in Twentieth-Century Ireland', Margaret MacCurtain describes how devotional Catholicism peaked after the civil war in 1923:

> The establishment of new religious feasts – in particular the cult of Mary – and the encouragement of pilgrimages to her shrines received papal approval. Novenas such as the Miraculous Medal, the Nine Fridays, and sodalities were assiduously promoted at parish level. The culmination of this highly charged, emotional Catholicism was the promulgation in 1950 of the dogma of Mary's assumption into heaven, followed in 1954 (the year decreed by Pius XII as the 'Marian Year') by an epidemic of shrine building all over Ireland.[114]

Carr portrays humankind in a process of eternity, which is a version of Fermoy's logic in the drama: 'We are of time, but also beyond it. And to forget that we are beyond it is the problem. Everyone forgets that they are also outside of time – that they are both within it *and* outside it. And actually that the next world has a claim on us, and when we arrive there we must confront that.'[115] However, Fermoy's eternity is an each-for-his-own type of doctrine that is 'noh for the herd'.[116] His God is used simply as a means to his individual end, with no thought or empirical intention or obedience to Catholic mores. Fermoy dogmatically states that he knows why he is on this planet: 'I'm on this earth to rule.'[117] He shows an arrogant hollowness towards Christian values, seen particularly in the sacrifice of his daughter and manifested once he holds political power.

The television interview which opens Act 2 displays Fermoy's flippant cynicism towards the people he has politically represented, a lack of sincerity around Hannafin's suicide, the blatant exploitation of Ariel's death for

---

114 Margaret MacCurtain, 'Godly Burden: Catholic Sisterhoods in Twentieth-Century Ireland' in Anthony Bradley and Maryann Gialanella Valiulis (eds), *Gender and Sexuality in Modern Ireland* (Amherst: University of Massachusetts Press, 1997), pp. 247–248.
115 Sihra, in *Theatre Talk*, p. 57. [Emphasis in original]
116 Carr, *Ariel*, p. 20.
117 Carr, *Ariel*, p. 19.

political publicity and an imposition of his personal views of the Church as a necessary change in the current education curriculum. As Minister for Education, Fermoy's Paper on 'The Nature of Christ' reveals a particular position contrary to the Catholic Church's advocacies:

> I was talking abouh the sullen nature a Christ, somethin thah has been hushed up for centuries. Somethin I'd long suspected and was brough home to me by a particular paintin by Pierro Della Francesca. His 'Resurrection'. Puts manners on them thah tries to tell us thah deah a Christ was for us. Thah the resurrection a Christ was for us. Leh's noh mix words here. The deah of Christ was by us, noh for us, and the resurrection a Chrish was for heeself.[118]

While politics and the Catholic Church have an uneasy alliance in the earlier part of the drama, now with Fermoy as the country's current Minister for Education and tipped as the next Taoiseach, they are identified separately.

Fermoy exploits Boniface's alcoholism, using it to weaken the refuge that Boniface takes in the Catholic Church. He seizes on Boniface's feelings of desertion, aware that he has felt guilty at leaving Fermoy to enter the noviciate at age seventeen. Boniface accurately suspects that Fermoy's taking part in the drowning of their mother at seven years of age 'is bound to take ud's toll on a person's view of the world.'[119] Fermoy helps to advance Boniface's withdrawal and inwardness in response to the oppressive dilemma in which he finds himself. Kristeva outlines: 'Contemporary literature acknowledges the impossibility of Religion, Morality, and Law – their power play, their necessity and absurd seeming. Like perversion, it takes advantage of them, gets around them, and makes sport of them.'[120] Boniface lapses back into alcoholism and focuses increasingly on his own subjectivity. His drinking carries the dramatisation of the bodily dialectic of exterior and interior, making it a powerful tool in the staging of the rejection of imposed conceptions of bodily propriety and behaviour, particularly in relation to the general Christian philosophy of living in moderation. The association of

118 Carr, *Ariel*, p. 44.
119 Carr, *Ariel*, p. 26.
120 Kristeva, *Powers of Horror*, p. 16.

excessive alcohol with depression and with strategies of abjection draws closer. He desperately struggles to make Fermoy see what he has done:

> Do you aven realise whah ya've done! Why didn't ya listen to me when I tried to stop ya, though I didn't know whah I was tryin to stop. Why didn't ya listen? All we have in this world is the small mercies we can extend to wan another. The rest is madness and oblivion. Haven't ya learnt that much? Haven't ya learnt thah much on your travels?[121]

His return to alcohol, triggered by the realisation that Fermoy killed Ariel, is an act of ironic resistance pushed to the limit, and is exemplary of the apparent withdrawal of will trapped into the narrative of abjection. His drinking deflects from the agency of his subjectivity, particularly in relation to his Christian position. He tells Fermoy:

> BONIFACE: No. No. Listen. Listen. Listen. I can't stop drinkin. Can't slape, can't ate, garden be moonligh, go to bed in the morning. I'm afraid I'll tell me psychiatrist, thah it'll just spill ouha me. [...] Burst a blood vessel in me eye, bled blood down me face for two days, they couldn't stop ud. You're the wan should be in Pat's. You're the wan should be bleedin from the eyes.[122]

Boniface has become aware that Fermoy has blindly contributed to his return to the state of the abject. His knowledge that Fermoy committed Ariel's murder brings him back to his own mother's murder. He retreats back to alcoholism as the rich source of evasions of social and Christian legislation, particularly important to his confined predicament. His drunken state ascribes him an unaccountable position, which denies the possibility of human interaction and enables the medical staff in the rehabilitation centre to think that he is a religious 'nut'. His sense of guilt for abandoning Fermoy as a child emerges in his inability to expose Fermoy as Ariel's killer.

The subversion of Christian imagery grows more disparaging throughout the narrative, in the representation of the monks portrayed by Boniface:

---

121   Carr, *Ariel*, p. 50.
122   Carr, *Ariel*, p. 50.

And Bonaventura is in intensive care, thanks be to the lord God. [...] gev him a Padre Pio relic and he flings it back ah me. Whah do I want wud Padre Pio's britches, says he. [...] And then he goes into a swirl abouh being cremahed, thah he's noh a Catholic anymore, thah he never belaved in the first place, and him takin chunks ouha the chalice his whole life.[123]

The subversion crosses the spectrum from cynicism to satire. It demonstrates Boniface's being as bordering on the periphery of an abject selfhood. The drama shows the ways in which the monks are experiencing a crisis of faith. At the beginning of the play, Fermoy accuses Boniface and the monks of being 'the most cynical, mathemahical shower I ever cem across whin it comes to God.'[124] Boniface replies: 'Facts are he hasn't been seen for over two thousand year, for all we know he's left the solar system. [...] There's many belaves wasn't him med the earth ah all, thah it was Satan and hees fallen armies, thah we were masterminded in hell, only Lucifer's pawns to geh ah God.'[125] With Boniface as the youngest monk and all the others senile, old or ill, any sense of renewal and dedication to the Catholic Church is denied. Boniface describes the other members of the monastery in a way that challenges ideas typically associated with monks. He tells how the other aged monks' illnesses manifest in various forms of physical and social inabilities such as incontinency, aggression, and senility. Kristeva notes about the body:

> The corpse ... upsets more violently the one who confronts it as fragile and fallacious chance. A wound with blood and pus, or the sickly, acrid smell of sweat, of decay does not *signify* death ... No, as in true theatre, without makeup and masks, refuse and corpses *show me* what I permanently thrust aside in order to live.[126]

The drama suggests that the Christian model of the saintly caring for the sick involves a fetishistic, sensual thrill at bodily filth and borderline material. Notions of sainthood within Christian doctrine are themselves

---

123   Carr, *Ariel*, pp. 13–14.
124   Carr, *Ariel*, p. 15.
125   Carr, *Ariel*, p. 15.
126   Kristeva, *Powers of Horror*, p. 3.

presented as unstable, and the standpoint that the play takes is far more complicated than at first appears. Boniface derives a perverse pleasure in his own description of his tending to the sick, which depicts an identifiable Catholic satirisation. He says, 'despihe their lunacy ... [they] know ud's all over and they goh ud all wrong and still they hang on.'[127] The imagery of the monks is constituted according to the ambivalent exclusion and reinstatement of the sacred, like those of abjection. Abjection here identifies strength when the perverse embraces weakness, poverty and degradation. While Fermoy's version of religion is allied to criminality, specifically the murder of his daughter, Boniface represents Christianity as a monk figure, specifically predicated on the memory of his mother's religious extremism, and on the act of his father's murder of his mother. Both articulate religious imagery and debate and confirm in the play's narrative the deliberate splintering of unity.

Carr's order of the systems of beliefs over one another presents the foundations of the abject selfhood dramatised in *Ariel*. This abject selfhood never achieves representation within fixed systems of beliefs, but inhabits precisely that space designated by its continual expulsion. Inner desertion is identified in *Ariel*, where the characters' neglect of interests and value in subjectivity lies ironically in the abdication of authority and coherence in the play.

If, as Boniface believes, Fermoy has come to embody their father, then Fermoy also emulates Boniface's statement that their father had the charm of forty devils but at the back of the charm he had 'the stuck-up rebellis heart of all a Lucifer's crew' in his political world.[128] In the context of the election, when Hannafin and Fermoy threaten to interfere and sway public opinion by exposing their respective family's history, Hannafin tells Fermoy: 'The pipe drames of the self med. You were forged in a bloodbah, Fitzgerald, and the son allas carries the father somewhere inside of him.'[129] Hannafin continues to emphasise Fermoy's potential corruption. He que-

127   Carr, *Ariel*, p. 14.
128   Carr, *Ariel*, p. 26.
129   Carr, *Ariel*, p. 33.

ries the circumstances as to 'how the cement and gravel empire goh off the ground,'[130] but the building industry soared in Ireland during the Celtic economic boom period, which could account for the Fitzgeralds' opulent home. Frances tells Stephen: 'Me and your father built thah cement up from wan lorry smuggled in from England, an auld shed and the lase of a quarry.'[131] Hannafin tells Fermoy and Frances: 'Yees think the wind is in yeer favour just because yees built the big house wud the Grake columns and the fountains goin full blast and the lions roarin on the gates and the money pourin in from the cement and gravel.'[132] In relation to growth and employment during the Celtic Tiger, Steve Coulter has pointed out: 'Gains in employment were mostly within the construction and service sectors, which expanded as some of the effects of the manufacturing growth finally filtered through to the rest of the economy.'[133] Nevertheless, Fermoy's success and ability as a businessman, which inevitably includes risk-taking and leadership skills, is also seen in his political career.

The rivalry between Fermoy and Hannafin sheds light on each other's genealogy; their argument raises the question as to whether people judge according to familial history or individual meritocracy. Hannafin initiates this argument by calling to the Fitzgerald home, in order to ask Fermoy to concede his chances of gaining his seat off him in the election. According to the polls, Hannafin says that he himself is favourite, and that Fermoy's heritage is something that will guarantee Hannafin winning the election. Hannafin tells him: Sure they're [the people of the country] ony laughin at ya. The murderer's son for this county. That'll never happen.[134] While Hannafin believes that 'ud's time the paple beyond this parish knew the gruesome blacksmith hommered you to earth', Fermoy is defiant and argues: 'Laineage manes natin anymore.'[135] What Fermoy describes as 'hoh air'

130 Carr, *Ariel*, p. 34.
131 Carr, *Ariel*, p. 67.
132 Carr, *Ariel*, p. 32.
133 Colin Coulter and Steve Coleman (eds), *The End of History?: Critical Reflections on the Celtic Tiger* (Manchester University Press, 2003), p. 41.
134 Carr, *Ariel*, p. 33.
135 Carr, *Ariel*, p. 33.

in relation to his lineage, also includes the fact that his great grandfather allegedly ate a child during the famine. However, Hannafin's personal background according to Fermoy is not so pure either. Fermoy suggests that his father committed lewd acts with sheep, his mother is a petty coffee thief, his grandmother committed suicide at eighty-seven years of age and that their family piggery has been funded in an underhanded way.

The level of insults directed at one another depicts the pervasive climate of corruption in the world of the play, as well as the candidates' kind of strategy for winning the forthcoming election. In a 'realist' reading of the play, a form of Irish 'pork-barrelling' is alluded to, a term that describes the relationship between people holding positions of political power and the expectations of the public towards them. Neil Collins and Mary O'Shea cite B. Geddes and Ribeiro Nato's use of this term which draws on an older understanding of American corruption, to include 'the exchange of resources for political support,' while noting that in the Brazilian context of their study, this 'is often legal but violates norms of fairness and efficiency.'[136] In the play, Fermoy alleges that Hannafin, as a political figure, has inappropriately used his political position for personal gain. He tells Hannafin: '[T]hat new asbestos plant, there's noh a lake or a river we can swim in anymore, thanks to you. And thah piggery, who's been fundin that all these years? There's lots of questions to be asked concernin you.'[137] Boniface too believes that personal gain comes before political allegiance in old school politics and he alleges that Hannafin comes from this kind of school. Boniface says that Hannafin would 'sell the whole country down the Swanee for an extension to hees bungalow and a new jape.'[138] When Fermoy enquires about a Mr Alloni who runs the Health Board, but who was once the Minister for Health, Boniface alleges Alloni put one of his children in hospital and made 'them take ouh her appendix, noh a thing wrong wih the girl.'[139] Fermoy's response indicates his belief in the advantages of power:

136   Neil Collins and Mary O'Shea, *Understanding Corruption in Irish Politics* (Cork University Press, 2000), p. 11.
137   Carr, *Ariel*, p. 34.
138   Carr, *Ariel*, p. 26.
139   Carr, *Ariel*, p. 21.

'I suppose if ya run the health buurd ya can have the whole family operahed on for free.'[140] Hearing that Alloni 'bates his wife' consolidates for Fermoy the sense of self-degradation in the world of the play, demonstrating the gap between individual beliefs and social behaviour.[141] Fermoy articulates this in his incongruous comment that the new generation 'judge a man for whah he is in heeself, noh where he came from. We judge a man these days be hees own merit, as if he'd ne'er a smithy bar God heeself.'[142] He maintains that he can manipulate Alloni in order to sway the old folk's votes in hospitals, nursing homes and day centres in his favour, if he knows the 'pisin' about Alloni's family.[143]

The political corruption in the play, read against a socio-political background, rooted in Ireland in the present, is revealing. Neil Collins and Mary O'Shea note: 'It is clear that each country's legal norms, historical experiences and cultural understandings influence definitions of corruption.'[144] Recent political controversies in Ireland since the 1990s, involving significant financial rewards in exchange for political favours, government structures which allow for excessive bonuses paid to already high-paid Executives and lavish spending by Ministers, have emerged.[145] Although previous decades may have successfully silenced political controversies, Collins and O'Shea state: 'There has been a distinct increase in both major and minor examples of political corruption disclosed in the last decade.'[146]

---

140 Carr, *Ariel*, p. 21.
141 Carr, *Ariel*, p. 21.
142 Carr, *Ariel*, p. 33.
143 Carr, *Ariel*, p. 21. Note: What's 'his pisin' translates as What's 'his poison', referring to the dirt (corruption) on Alloni.
144 Collins and O'Shea, p. 10.
145 See Collins and O'Shea, pp. 20–39 for details of some of the political controversies, including The Beef Tribunal, The McCracken Tribunal, The Moriarty Tribunal, The Flood Tribunal and The DIRT enquiry. See www.Irishtimes.com, accessed 9 October 2009.
146 Collins and O'Shea, p. 20. See pp. 20–39 for an outline and detail of some of these controversies – specifically The Beef Tribunal, The McCracken Tribunal, The Moriarty Tribunal, The Flood Tribunal, The DIRT Inquiry.

As an elected politician, Fermoy's attitude escalates in his feelings towards people who are overly conscious about what other people think, and whom he speculates are probably 'cut throats' in their homes. Condemning this kind of two-faced 'democratic' society in favour of a capitalist one he states:

> All [politicians] chirpin the wan tune like there's no other – equal wages, crèches in the work place, no ceilin on the women, the pace process, a leg up for the poor, the handicapped, the refugees, the tinkers, the tachers, the candlestick makers. In Sparta they were left on the side a the hills and that's where I'll lave em when I've the reins.[147]

The interview of Act 2 sees Fermoy after ten years in politics and it identifies further his dissolution into the abject. While the interview implies that Fermoy has some obscure belief that divine grace aided his rise to political success, coinciding with the downfall of Hannafin's political career and suicide, it significantly demonstrates his power as unstable. His position is undercut with further revelations of the opposition towards his political principles. These include, as the interviewee Verona suggests, how 'a sizeable portion of the public is alarmed by the last three Papers your party has pushed through,'[148] and how 'the Church has spoken out against you on several occasions.'[149]

Act 2 opens on the tenth anniversary of Ariel's death, and it reveals that Fermoy has held three ministerial posts since her disappearance: Minister for Arts and Culture, Minister for Finance and Minister for Education. The interview implies that Fermoy was behind the 'no-confidence' motion in the present Taoiseach, and it demonstrates some of his political motivations:

> There's an optimum moment for everywan, few recognise it and fewer still recognise when the moment is gone. Never to return. The Taoiseach was jaded. The party had lost direction and the party cannoh be sacrificed to wan individual, whahever our privahe estimations of thah individual may be. And belave me when I say I held him

---

147   Carr, *Ariel*, pp. 17–18.
148   Carr, *Ariel*, p. 43.
149   Carr, *Ariel*, p. 43.

in the highest esteem and will always. Hard decisions cost us all and I know more than most the price a those decisions.[150]

Fermoy presents himself as ruthlessly fearless in both his private and public life. His callous drive places suspicion as to how long either he or the public can sustain such courage. He undergoes a process of disintegration in the course of his journey to power, until as an experienced Minister aspiring towards being the next Taoiseach, he has lost the capacity for human interaction, declaring his success as 'all a drame'.[151]

Although often in denial, Fermoy is continuously forced to confront the circularity of betrayals and abandonment from his traumatic past. His subjectivity reinvests his debased sense of self with an abject value at every stage of its being, commuting a failed sense of selfhood. He embodies Kristeva's notion of the apparent contradictions that characterise the abject self and how this abject selfhood maintains its grasp on the individual:

> [A]bjection is above all ambiguity. Because, while releasing a hold, it does not radically cut off the subject from what threatens it – on the contrary, abjection acknowledges it to be in perpetual danger. But also because abjection itself is a composite of judgement and affect, of condemnation and yearning, of signs and drives.[152]

Fermoy's ambiguous subjectivity reveals his failure to come to terms with his past. His obsession with political power is directly related to this, and his belief that 'the earth's over' is an escape, to order his chaotic self.[153]

Ariel's voice from the grave is a dramatic disruptive device which calls Fermoy momentarily back to his life 'before the dream'. Echoing Man's reaction to the ghost of Woman in *The Cordelia Dream*, Fermoy shiftily responds to the sound of Ariel's voice, after an initial split second of disbelief, 'Oh Ariel ... you're alive ... you're alive.'[154] To Frances, Fermoy is

---

150 Carr, *Ariel*, p. 40.
151 Carr, *Ariel*, p. 44.
152 Kristeva, *Powers of Horror*, pp. 9–10.
153 Carr, *Ariel*, p. 68.
154 Carr, *Ariel*, p. 55.

destructively fixated on power, and will 'say anthin for company in your carnage.'[155] In the end, Fermoy's power reasserts itself through abjection, making vain all his efforts at its exploitation. His relationship with Frances and the process of their estrangement is not explored. Act 1 reveals that they have been with one another for seventeen years, predominantly outlining the Fitzgerald genealogy and placing Fermoy's lust for power central to the plot. Act 2 is ten years later, where the drama discloses that they are no longer living as a married couple, as well as revealing more about Fermoy's gaining and maintaining political power, and his and her adulterous affairs. The final Act dramatises Frances' murder of Fermoy and her Elaine's murder of Frances, presenting their destruction as inevitable. Fermoy's power-lust, driven from his bloody past, and Frances' refusal to give up the dead represent their wish to return to and recapture the past.

Significantly, their sexual relationship, from the outset of the play is seen as emasculating. Early in Act 1, Boniface asks Frances if Fermoy talks much about their father. Frances' replies: 'Me and thah man doesn't talk ah all. Wance you go past hello wud Fermoy he wants to kill ya.'[156] Fermoy's sexual un-fulfilment manifests in his defensive statement that he is married to a nun, while claiming that 'the ony reason I married ya was so I could have ud on demand'[157] and his abhorrence at Frances, who only talks about sex 'wud this lad [Stephen] latched onto her.'[158] Stephen reminds Fermoy of his own childhood and of the fact that he was left without his mother. His murder of Ariel is really a comment on his failure to come to terms with his father's murder of his mother. Thus, his power-lust is an illusion, a realm to latch on to, where ironically he tries to escape death in order to politically control the 'dying' world.

In finding Ariel's body in Cuura Lake, located near the Fitzgerald house, Boniface tells Frances that the divers also found more bodies, and implied that they were members of, or had something to do with, the

---

155 Carr, *Ariel*, p. 59.
156 Carr, *Ariel*, p. 26.
157 Carr, *Ariel*, p. 28.
158 Carr, *Ariel*, p. 28.

Fitzgerald family: 'The divers found the remains a seven people and they draggin the lake. Wan wud a boulder tied round the skeleton of a wrist. Most of them just an assortment a bones.'[159] The play reveals that Cuura Lake has held the body of Fermoy's mother, the same lake that holds the body of Ariel. The lake has gathered the (g)hosts of the dead, and in Kristevan terms is identified as the site of horror and desire. Anthony Roche states: '[T]he return of the dead to haunt the living, their refusal to stay dead, is the loophole by which the fantastic is admitted to the predominantly naturalistic Irish stage, an influence which once admitted works to transform the nature of that space.'[160] Christopher Murray cites Katherine Hume's simple definition of fantasy as 'any departure from consensus reality'.[161] Murray states in relation to the integration of the fantastic to a realistic mode of representation: 'The general purpose is twofold; to dramatise a consciousness at odds with authority or dominant social ideas; and to criticise or attack that same authority or those same dominant social ideas.'[162] Ariel's ghost is subversive, and operates within the framework of realism and heightened realism, which offers the audience another kind of space. Ariel's ghost pleas with Fermoy to rescue her: 'Come and get me, will ya? Ud's awful here, ud's awful. There's a huge pike after me, he lives in the belfry, two rows a teeth on him and teeth on his tongue, bendin back to hees throah. [...] (*Sounds of terrible weeping*) [...] I want to go home ... I just want to go home. Please, just brin me home.'[163]

The resurrection theme of Ariel establishes her ghostly being as a dramatic destabilising motif, not bound by the laws of nature and probability. This centuries old sacrificial story occurs in the Bible, in Abraham

---

159 Carr, *Ariel*, p. 66.
160 Anthony Roche, 'Ghosts in Irish Drama' in Donald E. Morse and Csilla Bertha (eds), *More Real Than Reality: The Fantastic in Irish Literature and the Arts* (New York: Green Press, 1991), p. 44.
161 Chistopher Murray, 'Irish Drama and the Fantastic' in Donald E. Morse and Csilla Bertha (eds), *More Real Than Reality: The Fantastic in Irish Literature and the Arts* (New York: Green Press, 1991), p. 86.
162 Murray in Morse and Bertha (eds), *More Real Than Reality*, p. 94.
163 Carr, *Ariel*, p. 56.

and Isaac in Genesis, where Ariel's return comes from somewhere below: 'Then deep from the earth you shall speak. From low in the dust your words shall come; your voice shall come from the ground like the voice of a ghost, and your voice shall whisper out of the dust.'[164] Parallels of meaning and similarities in imagery give richness and depth to Carr's *Ariel*. The stage directions: *Let Ariel's voice come from everywhere*[165] and the location of her body in Cuura Lake, are made significant when read with the knowledge that in medieval demonology, Ariel is a spirit of the waters.[166] Sorcerer's books, studied by renaissance scholars, found the names of 'seventy-two divine names, all ending in el', an angelic epithet.[167] In *Portia Coughlan*, Portia tells her mother: 'The only reason I married Raphael was because of his name, a angel's name, same as Gabriel's, [...].'[168] According to Fermoy, Ariel was not human, but an angel, whose shoulder blades he describes as wings. She 'didn't belong here so we gev her back', he tells Frances.[169]

It is interesting to associate the Bible passage with other possibilities concerning the nature of Ariel. For a Renaissance audience, Ariel in Shakespeare's *The Tempest* functions generally as the sole agent of Prospero, easily recognised as a familiar spirit of witchcraft. There were two main traditions in relation to the spirit world: the medieval one, where all magic and miraculous powers were due directly to either God's or Satan's hands; and the occultist's pursuit of the unity of the spiritual with the divine.[170] Nevertheless, Shakespeare possibly drew upon and linked a range of source concepts, from esoteric magic, popular traditions and Christian demonology. *The Tempest*'s Ariel is shown as elemental, composed of spiritual matter, as well as having a personality. However, if, as Edith Hall maintains,

164   Mark Patrick Hederman, Abbey Theatre Programme Note of *Ariel*, 2002, p. 11.
165   Carr, *Ariel*, p. 55.
166   Isaac Landman (ed.), *The Universal Jewish Encyclopedia* (New York: 1939), I, 472.
167   Courtenay Locke, trans., *Witchcraft Magic and Alchemy* (London: Houghton, 1931), p. 104.
168   Carr, *Portia Coughlan*, p. 27.
169   Carr, *Ariel*, p. 56.
170   See *Shakespeare's Philosophical Patterns* (Baton Rouge: Louisiana State University Press, 1937), pp. 186–188.

in relation to contemporary Ireland 'the rise in spin-doctoring has been made possible only by the epistemological and metaphysical vacuum situated at the centre of the Western collective psyche,' then Ariel's ghost in Carr's play is Fermoy's hallucination.[171] As no other character hears her, it is Fermoy that prompts Ariel's presence at the significant time of her anniversary. Her ghost erupts his guilt, which he had thought was safely buried in the past. The death anniversary works in the same way as Sihra's consideration of the birthday motif, that is, 'as a heightened moment of existential reflection and awareness for each protagonist which leads directly towards death.'[172] Sihra points out:

> This opens up the key dramaturgical through-line of Carr's theatre: the sense of our being firstly, our becoming through life, and finally our movement towards death and beyond. [Ariel's] birthday leads organically towards [her] death day, offering a sense of dramaturgical circularity or unity, from birth to death.[173]

The dramatic tension becomes powerful for the audience, as it grows aware of the degree of pretence involved in Fermoy's image of himself and senses, though momentarily, the relentless revelation of a once-submerged horror. But the climax is never reached in his confrontation of past and present; the thing that he has fled from does not corner him. He simply continues to retreat further into delusion, even at the moment of his murder.

The close connection of life and death, living and dead, again calls up the abject. Echoing the graveyard scene, where Hamlet picks up the skull of Yorick and philosophises on youth, abhorrence of dead bodies and the cycle of life, Elaine reminisces on the fragility of life. She calls up Fermoy's ghost while talking to Ariel's skull, demonstrating how, despite the fact that both Ariel and Fermoy are dead, she continues to be haunted by them. This demonstrates how she still competes with Ariel for her father's attention: '(*To skull*) I drame abouh you all the time. Strange, wakin there's no

171 Edith Hall, 'Iphigenia and Her Mother at Aulis: A Study in the Revival of a Euripidean Classic' in John Dillon and S.E. Wilmer (eds), *Rebel Women: Staging Ancient Greek Drama Today* (London: Methuen, 2005), p. 5.
172 Melissa Sihra, Lecture at Synge Summer School, 1 July 2005.
173 Sihra, *'For She A Jolly Good Fella'*, Lecture at Synge Summer School.

animosity, we're friends, friendly as sisters can be, but aslape we're enemies, enemies til the end a time.'[174] The end of Elaine's speech, which queries whether Ariel struggled with Fermoy during her murder, sees the appearance of Fermoy's ghost. She asks the skull: 'Did ya go aisy, Ariel? Or did ya figh him ah the end? Or did ya think it was all a game, smoking hees cigar and swillin hees brandy as the stars leant down to watch?'[175] Fermoy's ghost tells Elaine that he is searching for the 'yella cuurtyard',[176] the place he had told Frances of his dream where he asked God for the loan of the 'girl wud wings', who appeared by God's side.[177] His ghost seems to be hovering in limbo, a concept which although now abolished by Vatican II, retains interesting resonance in the context of the play. His ghost existing between two worlds is an in-between place, outside of both the living and the dead. The Catholic encyclopaedia outlines that 'the name [limbo] is applied to the temporary place or state of the just who, although purified from sin, were excluded from the beatific vision until Christ's triumphant ascension into heaven.'[178] The encyclopaedia continues: 'In literary usage the name is sometimes applied in a wider and more general place or state of restraint, confinement, or exclusion, and is practically equivalent to "prison".'[179] Although Fermoy and Ariel are dead, Elaine is still jealous of Ariel's relationship with her father, and Fermoy's final words, which insist in finding Ariel, trouble her. He states three times to Elaine: 'There's a girl there [the yellow courtyard] I have to meeh, I have to geh there, I have to meet this girl.'[180]

The play's final scene sees Elaine stab her mother to death, in the sitting room, where Ariel's body lies. The image powerfully demonstrates the culmination of the process of abjection in the play. Strikingly, Elaine's

---

174   Carr, *Ariel*, p. 73.
175   Carr, *Ariel*, p. 73.
176   Carr, *Ariel*, p. 74.
177   Carr, *Ariel*, p. 57.
178   http//www.newadvent.org/cathen [Catholic Encyclopedia Dictionary available on line], accessed 20 October 2005.
179   http//www.newadvent.org/cathen
180   Carr, *Ariel*, p. 74.

act of murder encounters the same ambivalent forces which surrounded the 'body politic' of Fermoy. Her ambiguous standpoint sharply recalls Fermoy's rejection of the maternal and engagement with his exclusion, through power, resulting in Ariel's death. Frances rejects her family in exchange for her dead spouse and their child, resulting in Fermoy's death. Stephen totally rejects his parents. The course of abjection questions the individual's subjectivity to function as resistance to the overturning of self-expulsion. The indeterminacy of the characters' subjectivity in *Ariel* is symptomatic of the destabilisation of binary logic, which takes place through the development of abjection. *Ariel* presents the Fitzgerald family's processes of subjectivity made indeterminate by an abject sickness, which spreads through each generation, but here it also has implications in the public realm.

Ariel examines the estrangement that Fermoy feels within himself and which is the catalyst for the sacrifice of *Ariel*, which comes with its own repercussions. His sense of displacement has implications beyond the realm of family and home to others in the world around him, but with no satisfactory conclusions. The connections to a wider world in the play are weak and ineffectual, making the sacrifice of the female in *Ariel*, at the hands of the male, redundant. Kristeva implies that living with abjection is not simply a personal problem. The subject encounters boundaries and borders in society as well as within itself. The kind of boundary failure represented in *Ariel* makes it impossible to reassert the possibility of confronting and coming to terms with abjection as a whole, meaning that confronting individual problems has to be relevant to the transformation of society in general.

Sacrifice in the context of abjection in *The Cordelia Dream*, though having similar outcomes to *Ariel*, offers different resonance in terms of family and home and what it means in relation to the abject 'other'. Although both are located in a fated abject destiny, sacrifice in *Ariel* is at the hands of the male, whereas in *The Cordelia Dream* it is woman's self-sacrifice that proliferates Man's process of dying and death.

The Cordelia Dream, directed by Selina Cartmell, was first produced in London in 2008 at Wilton's Music Hall by the Royal Shakespeare Company, with Michelle Gomez as Woman and Michael Hargreaves as Man. The play, as the title implies, draws references to Shakespeare's *King Lear* and tells the story of an estranged father/daughter relationship. As in *Ullaloo*, *Low in the Dark*, *Meat and Salt* and *Woman and Scarecrow*, naming in the work points to gender. The Beckettian pairing of characters in *The Cordelia Dream* is also a regular feature of Carr's plays. The daughter, referred to as 'Woman', is urged to go to her father, Man, after a five-year absence, as a result of a dream (of life and death) she has had about them. An apocalyptic dream of last judgement and redemption hovers over *The Cordelia Dream* but unlike *King Lear*, where the dream is forever deferred, here the dream is realised.

Kent and Edgar in *King Lear*, as bystanders to the conclusion of the father/daughter tragedy, watch the howling Lear with the dead Cordelia in his arms:

> KENT: Is this the promised end?
> EDGAR: Or image of that horror?[181]

Their questions raise issues around the fate of the parent/child relationship and the representation of what lies ahead for the 'Lear–Cordelia' bond, which frames the drama. In an interview with Eileen Battersby, Carr explains:

> It's my response to King Lear, a play I love and one which I re-read about twice every year, the same as I do with Hamlet. There is a huge amount going on in King Lear, and I decided to concentrate on the four howls and the five nevers in Act V. I've always considered Cordelia to be confrontational; here is Lear, facing his big day, about to divide his kingdom and she is looking for a fight, she refuses to play the game, to do the expected party piece in public.[182]

Both rival music composers, Woman returns to her father who asks 'And what has brought you here? A Dream of Lear?', to which she replies,

---

181   George Hunter (ed.), William Shakespeare, *King Lear* (London: Peinguin, 2005), 5.3.262–263, p. 125.
182   Eileen Battersby, 'A Double Take of Savage Realism' in *The Irish Times*, 7 February 2009.

'A dream of Lear and Cordelia. Immediately you delete the woman.'[183] In the spirit of the dream-like supremacy enshrined in Renaissance, patriarchal and sovereign rule, Man conspicuously omits the alternative authority of the female, styling the self-sacrifice of Woman necessary for his salvation. 'Cordelia wanted to be hung,' Man dismissively tells Woman.[184] His omission of the female is the metaphor for abjection, which can recur at any stage of life and results in the creative renegotiation of the terms of the subject/other complex.

The play charts the demise of the father/daughter relationship, underscored by their music careers. Sadly the music aspect of the play was largely missing in Cartmell's production, as some theatre reviews noted. Michael Coveney in *The Independent* observed, 'The musicians aren't sufficiently integrated. In fact, I didn't even know they were there until they came on for a bow with their fiddles.'[185] Similarly, Fiona Mountford commented in the *Evening Standard* that the actors 'trek stoically through the reams of lines while never once convincing us they'd know a concerto from a concertina.'[186] Coveney's view was that in this production, Man's work was heard as 'a sort of plangent, hysterical modernist mish-mash composed by Conor Linehan, played spiritedly at the side of Wilton's on a string trio against a piano recording,' and that this contributed to the gap in the production which should have been the central catalyst for the failure of the father/daughter relationship.[187]

Man tells Woman that her music is very mediocre but that 'the gods have favoured [her].'[188] Her music gift outstrips him, although Man con-

183   Carr, *The Cordelia Dream* (Oldcastle, Co. Meath: Gallery Press, 2008), p. 19.
184   Carr, *The Cordelia Dream*, p. 19.
185   Michael Coveney, *The Independent*, 1 January 2009, http://www.independent.co.uk/arts-entertainment/theatre-dance/reviews/the-cordelia-dream, accessed 4 April 2009.
186   Fiona Mountford, *Evening Standard*, 17 December 2008, http://www.thisislondon.co.uk/theatre/show-23586428-details/The+Cordelia+Dream/showReview, accessed 4 April 2009.
187   Coveney, *The Independent*, 1 January 2009
188   Carr, *The Cordelia Dream*, p. 17.

siders that she holds only a quarter of his gift. His competitive musical jealousies betray his desire for Woman to be silenced. Woman replies: 'You want me alive and silent? What is that but a sentimental form of murder?'[189] Her words echo Hélène Cixous's observations on the feminine in 'Aller á la Mer':

> And if like Cordelia, she finds the strength to assert a femininity which refuses to be the mirror of her father's raving, she will die. For in every man there is a dethroned King Lear who requires his daughter to idealise him by her loving words and build him up, however flat he may have fallen, into the man he wishes to appear: 'Tell me I am the me-est, the most like a king, or I'll kill you.'[190]

Once again, as seen in *Ariel*, the parent works towards some kind of salvation in the protracted demise of the offspring for its own sake. In a version of the denouement of *King Lear*, *The Cordelia Dream* explores the dark consequences of Woman's death necessary for Man's musical redemption. Woman is deprived of her place in her family, and socially, her identity as a composer is resisted. The play demonstrates how she must be eliminated by Man. Her self sacrifice, necessary for his musical progress, is the result of their fall out of the Symbolic order, the world of language, of expression, of codified behaviour and of rules and regulation. Subsequently, both Man and Woman pursue a self-directed abjection or subject/object dismissal that explores the outcomes of boundary failure, or the failure of the individual to conceive himself/herself as a subject within a Symbolic economy. Supporting a music-centred conception of the world, Man and Woman learn to see and to contribute to that aspect of familial identity which figures subject-hood as effacement of the self/other binary.

Kristeva's notion of sacrifice, in her theory of abjection, sees human existence as a practice of absence. At the early stages of development, infants experience the world through rhythmic movements and without prescribed sense. They then pass through the 'mirror stage', at which point persons

---

189   Carr, *The Cordelia Dream*, p. 20.
190   Hélène Cixous, 'Aller á la Mer' in Richard Drain (ed.), *Twentieth Century Theatre: A Source Book* (London: Routledge, 1995), pp. 133–135, p. 133.

or objects are reflected back through representation, images or figures, thereby establishing subjectivity. The infant is thus beginning to experience the world as signified in language, governed by rules that points to meaning, where the subject abides by this Law if it is to secure its fragile position in the world. Kristeva, like Lacan, imagines that to take objects, enter language, separate from the maternal and abide by the Law of the Father is necessary in order to gain subjecthood.

Unlike Lacan, however, Kristeva produces a category of non-being, in which individuals experience themselves as 'neither subject, nor object'.[191] Instead of being 'nothing', like the object, the individual who experiences the abject experiences a 'something' that cannot be defined.[192] In the state of abjection, the individual undergoes boundary failure, a realm of existence Kristeva calls the maternal matrix, the pre-linguistic site of disunity. The entry into language rescues the subject from this stance, but if experienced again, later in life, can result in 'matricide' and/or sacrifice of women's bodies. This chapter explores the theory of sacrifice applied to the body of the Other, and demonstrates how the state of abjection can reconfigure the terms of the subject/other relations in the process of destruction.

Man's struggle for musical greatness, and his ability to compose, shore up his sense of self and, by extension, his sense of power, privilege and justified destruction. He recognises that his musical scores are dependent on Woman's silence, demonstrating his understanding that playing to his daughter and for the public is an act bound to the desire to find subjecthood in the absence or annihilation of the other. Man describes, with delightful viciousness, Woman's 'two dreadful symphonies' which she composed last spring. He denounces her music at every turn, exposing what he sees as her musical ignorance and telling her: 'I am a genius. A genius! And you are a charlatan! A charlatan who stole my gift when I wasn't looking. You are a charlatan who has plagiarised from everyone.'[193] Man acts as aggressor, projecting his self-hatred and destructiveness onto Woman. Their

---

191 Kristeva, *Powers of Horror*, p. 20.
192 Kristeva, p. 2.
193 Carr, *The Cordelia Dream*, p. 24.

altercation grows more and more ferocious, emphasising how ingrained is his sense of the subject/object binary, specifically demonstrated by his detailed disinterest in paternity from the outset:

> You'd scream for hours and one night I went down and stared at this screaming thing, blue with an untraceable rage, sweating and stinking. I tried to calm you. Nothing doing, I remember thinking I can do one of two things. I can pick her up or I can kill her.[194]

He makes his choice not to kill her, because he believed she was weak and pathetic. He reminds her that all her siblings are 'unlovable children' from 'a loveless bed'.[195] Woman cries out to her father at the end of Act 1, 'We can't part like this,'[196] because she is subject to the consequences of dying for his redemption, in the face of external signs/the facade of otherness. On the other hand, Man tells her that he will come to her funeral with his speech prepared.

As with all Carr's plays, *The Cordelia Dream* stages rituals of deference to authority, signified by the marginalised, the peripheral figure, or the outsider, enacted for the health and well being of the individual. Cartmell's production, designed by Giles Cadle, presented Man's elected isolation in his one-roomed home, sparsely populated with a piano, stool, coat hanger and monitors, ironically similar to the back of a stage set, where beyond the flats, a fully fledged performance might be happening. The stage set blended in well with the decaying and crumbling walls of Wilton's Music Hall, showing how what has been performed beyond the stage set points to a deeply engrained damaged past that continues to impinge on the present world of the wrathful characters on stage.

The Cordelia Dream also has the mythic resonance of the fairytale, specifically *Cinderella*, *Meat and Salt* and *Cap O' Rushes*.[197] This tale, told

---

194   Carr, *The Cordelia Dream*, p. 25.
195   Carr, *The Cordelia Dream*, p. 25.
196   Carr, *The Cordelia Dream*, p. 25.
197   Bernadette Sweeney observes the similarity between *Meat and Salt* and the English fairytale *Cap O' Rushes*, See Sweeney's *Performing the Irish Body* (Basingstoke, UK: Palgrave Macmillan, 2008), p. 191.

in many cultures, of a daughter who falls into disfavour by telling her father that she loves him as much as salt, admonishes the father/daughter relationship in terms of the faith that is put into such a bond. Carr invokes a paternal sovereignty, only to chronicle its destruction in scenes of annihilation and power, as Lear does with Cordelia.

> LEAR: Here I disclaim paternal care,
> Propinquity and property of blood,
> And as a stranger to my heart and me,
> Hold thee from this for ever [...]198

The Cordelia Dream points to a familial disinheritance where parent or offspring demand or seek to be left to the natural order of things. 'Just put them in a field. Leave them alone' is Man's advice to his daughter about her children, which is reminiscent of Hester being left alone, chained to the caravan or put in the swan's lair by her mother in *By the Bog of Cats*.199 Offspring, the play suggests, have a greater chance of unified subjectivity without the emotional nurturance of parents, which are a threat to a secure sense of being.

For Man, the external signs tell the truth. There is no gap between the sign and the signified: the 'gift' that hides Woman's true self, in fact, will allow Man to fulfil his true wish – to sacrifice his daughter and thereby flourish musically (echoing Ariel's sacrifice for Fermoy to flourish politically). Man's greatest wish is to have words match empirical truth, because if language fails to signify in a one-to-one relationship, then his subjectivity, vested in the Symbolic order, will inevitably falter. Thus, when Woman, who 'ghosts' Act 2, tells Man that she is dead, he questions this; 'What are you saying?'200 Woman takes the opportunity to show him the proof of the sign made or uttered: 'You want to see the weals on my neck?'201 He replies, 'You always went too far, always had to go further than the next

---

198 George Hunter (ed.), William Shakespeare, *King Lear* (London: Penguin, 2005), 1.1.113–116, p. 9.
199 Carr, *The Cordelia Dream*, p. 17.
200 Carr, *The Cordelia Dream*, p. 41.
201 Carr, *The Cordelia Dream*, p. 42.

even if it meant taking yourself out.'[202] Man both desires and is threatened
by his need to see his desire, the violence of language and by association
the violence of the body, inscribed on Woman. He revels in the idea that
Woman will deny the arbitrariness of this violence, 'I was wondering why.
You're too much my dear. You're too much.'[203] He works from the assump-
tion that those who have mastered language (the language of music) are
those who hold the power of interpretation and meaning and will abide
by this Law. He tells her, 'Most come with half a gift, or a longing for a
gift, or a smidgeen of a longing. I came with the gold. All I had to do was
scatter it.'[204]

However, Man experiences boundary failure because his daughter
threatens the symbolic order in which he invests. Despite his attempts to
maintain a distance from her by employing the violence of language, he
recognises that she is musically literate after all and he does acknowledge
early in the play that she has achieved public recognition for her music
even if it doesn't live up to his standards. He undermines Woman's sense of
subject-hood by investing in the body or the abject, rather than language, in
a manner that favours himself: 'I am a great composer, yes, I am complex,
erudite, difficult. I set trends. I am a winged horse to your braying mule'[205]
As with Fermoy in *Ariel*, his fear of the female emerges and he calls out for
help in Act 2 once he realises it is his daughter returning from her grave to
take him, 'Someone come and save me from this dog-hearted, snake-eyed
vicious ingrate.'[206]

Correspondingly, the well-being of Man is complicated by the ghost
of Woman, an apparition in Act 1 that releases his hold on the reality of
his world. The hat, a Beckettian signifier used by Bender in *Low in the
Dark*, here becomes the Shakespearian device used by The Fool in *Lear*.
The Fool, who offers Lear his cap to wear as a symbol of foolishness, sees
Man demanding it for protection from the dead Woman. Man sanity is

202 Carr, *The Cordelia Dream*, p. 42.
203 Carr, *The Cordelia Dream*, p. 42.
204 Carr, *The Cordelia Dream*, p. 39.
205 Carr, *The Cordelia Dream*, p. 37.
206 Carr, *The Cordelia Dream*, p. 31.

submerged in Act 2. Reminiscent of Shalome in *On Raftery's Hill*, who first '*enters across the landing and down the stairs. She wears a nightdress, a straw hat and struggles with a suitcase and an armful of flowers.*'[207] Like Man, she wavers in and out of lucidity. Man wets his trousers, fears his mother's rebuke and blesses himself, to ward Woman off. The elements of nineteenth-century music-hall clowning, suggested by props such as piano, pyjamas, toothbrush and hat ('*a woman's straw bonnet with flowers*')[208] and seen in Carr's early plays, turn poignantly childlike and pathetic in *The Cordelia Dream*, echoing Cordelia's observations of the Lear.

> CORDELIA: O you kind gods,
> Cure this great breach in his abused nature!
> Th'untuned and jarring senses, O! wind up
> Of this child-changed father.[209]

Whether Cordelia's statement means that her father has been driven to madness by the cruelties of his children or has changed into second child-ishness, spurred on by old age, are all relevant in Man's behaviours in Act 2 where he appears to wander in and out of lucidity. Woman tries to make Man realise that she has come back from the dead to take him, that nei-ther of them will survive one another. Man's stubborn and defiant attitude towards Woman throughout the play echoes Regan's observation of Lear after he has banished Cordelia and divided the land between herself and Gonerill:

> REGAN: Tis the infirmary of his age; Yet he hath ever but slenderly known himself.[210]

207 Carr, *On Raftery's Hill*, p. 10.
208 Carr, *The Cordelia Dream*, p. 30.
209 *Lear*, 4.7.15–18, p. 106.
210 *Lear*, 1.1.292–293, p. 15.

Man's self-ignorance and fallen status, which looms from the outset in *The Cordelia Dream* are all consuming and stem, as Woman proclaims, from 'some ancient battle between us. Eternal.'[211]

Man reads his diary from nine days before when Woman hanged herself, as a way to show Woman that his music career has not prospered, therefore she cannot be dead, but instead he misunderstands the significant entry and reads his insert about *Lear* and about how sublime Act three is, 'Or the great four howls at the end of act five or the five nevers.'[212] He reads the next day's entry for the eighteenth, 'Spent the whole day sketching out "Lear's Lullaby". Had a bit of a breakthrough towards dusk. What can Lear say about Cordelia? He can follow her. Something momentous is about to happen.'[213] As the symbolic order crumbles around Man, his labour, which uses absence to create presence or subjectivity, becomes attuned to a sacrificial economy. Under threat of loss of place, subjects, as Kristeva outlines, 'transfer the [dissolved] object to the refulgent point of dazzlement in which I stray in order to be. As soon as I perceive it, as soon as I name it, the sublime triggers a spree of perceptions and words that expand memory boundlessly'[214]

As neither subject nor object, Man perceives himself as abject, a position from which he is prepared to sacrifice his daughter in order to re-assert his subject-hood. As Kristeva suggests, the only method of re-asserting difference, once one has already emerged from the maternal matrix is by laying bare its abject marks: 'With material, visceral gestures, subjects return to the bar of the signifier, "killing substance to make it signify."'[215] Man declares, 'What women don't know is all a man gets from the moment he is born is rejection.'[216] When Man allows violence on Woman's body in exchange for his music to flourish, he does so because he directly perceives her to pose the same threat as a face-to-face encounter with the maternal

211   Carr, *The Cordelia Dream*, p. 37.
212   Carr, *The Cordelia Dream*, p. 43.
213   Carr, *The Cordelia Dream*, p. 43.
214   Kristeva, p. 12.
215   Kristeva, p. 30.
216   Carr, *The Cordelia Dream*, p. 33.

matrix. Kristeva believes that violence is acted out, in such moments, primarily on the bodies of women, revealing the human investment in signs and making it desirable to equate disunity and pre-lingual arenas with the womb. Woman is both 'other,' as a female whom Man berates because of her fascination with childbirth and the maternal, and as an alternative representative of the subject in a symbolic economy, as she effortlessly composes music which is regularly aired on radio.

As a body that struggles to signify in the symbolic order, Man matches the description of the Imaginary or maternal matrix, the space in which the subject is not yet a subject nor an object, where the self is expressed as fragmentary. He refrains from recognising Woman's death by hanging, her sign of the abject and an echo of Cordelia's death in *Lear*. He continues the denial in his description: 'Cordelia is blue when he carries her on. Blue from the neck up. Her tongue is four times the normal size. Her eyes bulge. I remembered all this when I wrote my Cordelia suite. Not a pretty sight.'[217] Once Man decides to make the connection between Woman and Cordelia and acknowledge that Woman looks 'a little woebegone' as a result of hanging, he finally enters the symbolic realm.[218] Kristeva explains such boundary failure: 'My body extricates itself, as being alive, from that border. Such wastes drop so that I might live, until from loss to loss, nothing remains in me and my entire body falls beyond the limit – *cadere*, cadaver.'[219] For Man, sacrificing Woman means owning a place in the symbolic order.

Lear's four bleak howls and his pentameter of 'nevers' at the death of Cordelia and prior to his own death voice the climactic poetics of despair that now interpenetrate *The Cordelia Dream*.

LEAR: Thou'lt come no more never, never, never, never, never.[220]

---

217 Carr, *The Cordelia Dream*, p. 36.
218 Carr, *The Cordelia Dream*, p. 41.
219 Kristeva, p. 3.
220 *Lear*, 5.3.255–258, p. 124.

In the second act of Cartmell's production, Woman changes into Man's soiled coat and tails, used to conduct his imaginary orchestra, she paints her face blue, and Man strips to his underpants. His near nakedness is resonant of Lear at one of his lowest moments:

> LEAR: Why thou wert better in thy grave Than to answer with thy uncovered body this extremities of the skies. Is man no more than this? [...] Unaccommodated man is no more than such a poor, bare, forked animal as thou art. Off, off you lendings! Come, unbutton here.[221]

The scene portrays the increasingly fallen status of Man in exchange for the silence of Woman. As *The Cordelia Dream* comes to its final conclusion, Man learns that he too will be subject to the violence of language. 'Did you enjoy your death?', he asks Woman, to which she responds, 'It was so-so. A bit quick.'[222] She describes the place beyond the grave in a surreal fashion, and tells Man to be afraid of this place because they are 'savage here'.[223] They are savage to her in the afterworld because the way she lived was unforgivable, and she expects they will tell Man the same. Woman and Man are victims of each other, their bodies only able to signify when one is sacrificed at the expense of the other. Yet both persist in beating one another down, as was their destined fate and declared by Woman to Man as their blood bond: 'I'm talking about something different, older, something ancient, something civilisation is founded upon.'[224]

In line with Kristeva's notion of sacrifice, subjecthood in *The Cordelia Dream* is formed against the Symbolic order. Both Woman and Man demonstrate an initial commitment to the Law of language and its ability to guarantee subjectivity. Their sacrifice, coupled with the pressure from one another and the illusion of pressure from the public, illuminates the problem of language, its relation to the body and the violence of inscription. Recognising the self-deception inherent in the practice of absence,

---

221   *Lear*, 3.4.103–112, p. 70.
222   Carr, *The Cordelia Dream*, p. 44.
223   Carr, *The Cordelia Dream*, p. 45.
224   Carr, *The Cordelia Dream*, p. 23.

both Woman and Man finally choose to accept boundary failure as a state of creative potential, demonstrated by their deaths and accompanied by Man's haunting sonata that closes the play. Yet the sense of abjection remains very much the context of the play. Man's comment to Woman, 'Lear is impossible',[225] aptly endorses the critic Charles Lamb, who commented that 'Lear is essentially impossible to be represented on stage.'[226] The kind of sacrifice offered up in *The Cordelia Dream* is revealed as specific to the Lear/Cordelia relationship, where the impossibility of boundary representation is dramatised as all-consuming.

225 Carr, *The Cordelia Dream*, p. 18.
226 Stephen Greenblatt (general editor), *The Norton Shakespeare: based on the Oxford Edition*, 2nd Edition (Oxford University Press, 2008), p. 575.

CHAPTER 5

New Blood

As in *Woman and Scarecrow* and *The Cordelia Dream*, in *Marble*, boundaries help to move to action. Such was not the case in *On Raftery's Hill*, where boundaries preserved abuse and hindered action. Subjectivity, as an effort of boundary setting, guards against unwanted subjects, repressed desires or repulsive entities, that might otherwise request attention from the past and from the protagonist. *Marble* explores these boundary settings differently. Unlike in *The Cordelia Dream*, where the dream operates as the dramatic reunion device, or in *The Mai*, where the dream punctuates the narrative as a site of guilt and as a realm of escape for the characters, in *Marble* the dramatic narrative is haunted by a dream that grows and becomes more frequent: a dream of a lover figure, silhouettes of here and now, thought not only to be real, but to be *the* reality itself, obscuring other 'objects' in the world of the play and rejecting them. This dream world, itself another boundary, is beyond the everyday boundary wall presented in the play, and is crossed over in *Marble*.

The play engages with traditional dramatic conventions of heterogeneous notions of gender and stereotypical aspects of domesticity, albeit through the urban landscape of a 'post Celtic Tiger'. Peadar Kirby has drawn attention to the conditions of the economic successes of the Celtic Tiger in what Karl Polanyi believes are the dangers of 'reducing the economy to a market system and making the welfare of society dependent on this system.'[1] While 'after the Celtic Tiger' suggests dealing with the cultural and social issues and concerns brought on as a result of the economic boom, the term

---

1   Peadar Kirby, *The Social Sciences in Post-Celtic Tiger Ireland*, Inaugural Lecture, University of Limerick, 25 February 2008 (Department of Politics and Administration: University of Limerick, 2008), p. 4.

'post Celtic Tiger' removes the historical connection between the Celtic Tiger and the thriving economy. The Celtic Tiger period saw 'tradition', 'spirituality' and the connection to the land compromised in exchange for a 'post Celtic Tiger' fractured society, whose belief system pulls away from rather than unites people. With *Marble*, the audience meets a 'post Celtic Tiger type world', a society at the stage where economic improvement has come at the price of social dislocation. The play is not formed in the narrative of the past but by the predicament of the here and now and its consequences for the future. Thus, individual action taken by Carr's characters in this context is of and for itself, still working with concerns of absence and loss. Carr is now without the demands of sacrifice, and the realm of the mythic is tentatively drawn upon as the impending sense of doom, which pervades the work. Thus *Marble* does not carry intimations of the inevitable set down in classical proportions. The play contends that subjectivity in post Celtic Tiger Ireland, shaped by an individual and social malaise, can recover or at least be acted upon, whatever the consequences of that recovery or action may be.

As is familiar across the spectrum of Carr's plays, *Marble* is deeply concerned with the inadequacy of day-to-day living and the inability to articulate experience. As it uses for the most part the expression of 'living' to point to experiences that lie beyond its scope, so it uses constituents of character that alter what he or she has become, as in Catherine who takes, 'a dive into the blue, blue dark'[2] or Art who, 'instead of dying he had a dream,'[3] who at the end of the play answer their dream-calls to point to the complexities of their being.

But these matters that come through are more clearly in the study of the play than onstage. The most powerful single dimension of the play's world for its spectators is its continual reference to the nature and significance of human society. 'A simple police state,' Anne tells Catherine, and the play wins through to efforts to flee it. When Catherine and Art, two of the four characters in the play and spouses to Ben and Anne, leave their

2   Carr, *Marble*, p. 59.
3   Carr, *Marble*, p. 65.

families, homes and lives to confront their dreams, abandonment and the individual is also a kind of victory, in refusing to submit to the demands and interdicts set down by society.

Carr's imagination is oriented towards presenting human connection as a fragile web of ties that influence characterisation, action, language and theme. The play's imagined spaces and behaviours, 'of steel and concrete [needed] to survive this place'[4] of 'children, gardens, afternoons looking out on the bay,'[5] of 'cappuccinos and emptying dishwashers'[6] and of tickets to art galleries and theatres, only exist in characters' speeches and are always emphatically social. Even the stage setting outlined by Carr ('One space, One couch, One table. Two chairs. One drinks cabinet. One lamp. All use this space as if it was their own'[7]) prevents characters from having a presence of their own, which ironically works to demonstrate their lack of a shared experience. Issues of overcrowding and of personal privacy which emerged during the explosion of the homogeneous, tight living spaces that populated Ireland's urban landscape during the 'Celtic boom' arise. Lisa Fitzpatrick notes:

> The re-imagining of Ireland and of Irish identity in recent years, linked to both the globalisation of the economy and the country's embrace of European integration, is being expressed in theatrical performance and in dramaturgy in a number of ways. [Declan Hughes'] *Shiver* [2003] is one of a number of plays that represents the shift from a homeland of mammies and tweed and potatoes and bogs to a curiously featureless, sterilized, suburban nowhere.[8]

Reminiscent of *Portia Coughlan* and *On Raftery's Hill*, the way that living spaces organise people's existence and the proximity between people within these spaces, is called into question in *Marble*. Boundary dynamics within,

4   Carr, *Marble*, p. 27.
5   Carr, *Marble*, p. 34.
6   Carr, *Marble*, p. 51.
7   Carr, *Marble*, p. 8.
8   Lisa Fitzpatrick, 'Nations and Myth in the Age of the Celtic Tiger: Muide Éire' in Patrick Lonergan and Riana O'Dwyer, *Echoes Down the Corridor* (Dublin: Carysfort Press, 2007), pp. 169–179, p. 169.

between and among people unfold. Subjectivity is affected by physical space and its relationship to the psychological development of Carr's characters. Just as the protagonists in Carr's other plays find themselves isolated amidst their family in the rural landscape, so too, characters in the city make for a desolate place every bit as lonely as the bogs, lakesides and hilltops of her earlier works. In an interview with Eileen Battersby, Carr describes the characters of *Marble*: 'They have everything materially, yet have nothing; they want more yet are terrified.'[9]

Marble, produced at The Abbey Theatre, Dublin, spanned 17 February to 14 March 2009 and was directed by Jeremy Herrin, with Stuart McQuarrie playing Art, a long-term friend and business partner to Ben, played by Peter Hanly, who declares his dream of sleeping with Ben's wife, Catherine, played by Aisling O'Sullivan, in a marble room. Catherine's confession that she too is having a similar dream about Art as lovers in a marble room sets the drama in motion, and issues of melancholy, suspicion and desire emerge. Art's wife Anne, played by Derbhle Crotty, refuses to participate in the dream ordeal or indeed in life itself, existing instead according to her strict schedule of daily routines that keep her functioning. Carr sets up from the beginning, the Freudian postulate of a two tiered world, one in which people get on with their living practices under the pressures of daily existence, and the other an inner psychic world which refers back to the repressions and frustrated desires of their past. Typically, the latter does not supersede or replace the demands of the former but in *Marble*, Carr dramatises this possibility.

Freud's *Interpretations of Dreams* refers to the ingredients of dreams as 'the residues of the day', asserting that psychological residues of the preceding day are essential in the formation of dreams, because they offer points of attachment to the unconscious through which its impulses manifest.[10] For Freud, dreams express a wish fulfilment of some kind or other and are

---

9   Eileen Battersby, 'A Double Take of Savage Realism' in *The Irish Times*, 7 February 2009.

10   See Sigmund Freud's 'The Interpretation of Dreams' Vols 4–5 in *The Standard Edition of the Complete Psychological Works of Sigmund Freud*, trans. James Strachey (London: Hogarth Press, 1959), pp. 562–564.

closely tied to issues of loss. *Marble* dramatises wishes concerning nurturance, life and death, in connection with loss.

The production encompassed loss, by keeping the audience appropriately detached, embodied in Robert Innes Hopkins' design, reflecting Giorgio de Chirico's *Melancholy and Mystery of a Street* (1914). As Carr suggests, 'there should be an emptiness to the set.'[11] Fintan Walsh's review of *Marble* underlines how 'the contributions of Freud and de Chirico heavily inflect Marina Carr's latest offering.'[12] Renowned for his dreamscapes of estranged urban life, de Chirico's *Melancholy and Mystery of a Street* is referenced as the kind of setting Carr seeks the theatre designers to achieve with *Marble*. De Chirico's empty city is skewed by angular renderings of a desolate space surrounded by sharp foreshadowed arcades. Invariably, the lone figure in the picture, a girl wheeling a wheel, reflects Catherine's central longing to be alone, in line with Freud's observation of a child at play 'creat[ing] a world of his own, or, rather, re-arrang[ing] the things of his world in a new way.'[13] De Chirico's acclaimed chiaroscuro creates the light and hard shadows that appears in sunlight, again echoing Catherine's desire for an empty space: 'all this clutter is too much for me,' she laments.[14] The melancholic silence is captured in the barrenness of the space. In the Abbey, Hopkins' stretched marble column beyond the audience's view and the marble walls of the stage, encased the home of Ben, Catherine, Art and Anne, populated with sofas that electronically moved between and across the space, a coffee table, chairs and drinks cabinet.

Somewhere just beyond the stage space, and suitably framing the cold contemporary residence (but unfortunately not pointed enough in the production), Carr evokes, through speeches of displacement and anomie,

11 Marina Carr, *Marble*, p. 8.
12 See Fintan Walsh's review of 'Marble' in *Irish Theatre Magazine*, Spring Vol. ix issue 37, or http://www.irishtheatremagazine.ie/Reviews/reviewsMarble.htm, accessed 13 April 2009.
13 Sigmund Freud, 'Creative Writers and Day-Dreaming' in *The Standard Edition of the Complete Psychological Works of Sigmund Freud*, Vol. 14, trans. James Strachey (London: Hogarth Press, 1959), pp. 143–144.
14 Carr, *Marble*, p. 30.

a concrete community of 'scaffolding, building, building, building, an avalanche of warrens and rat holes to stuff us in'[15] where people 'wander through this hostile landscape,'[16] and 'at the appointed hour I do this or that and so time does not encroach on me or weigh me down or disturb me in any way.'[17] This 'community', if given emphasis either in the stage design or through the medium of acting, might have confronted one of the ways in which the tensions between the character's private world and the 'post Celtic Tiger' public world could be shown. Lisa Fitzpatrick's questions too might have been addressed: 'How is it possible to represent the absence of community in an art form that is inherently communal, both in its creation and reception? How can the artist represent the absence of a shared mythology, without a shared mythology to ground the work?'[18] Therefore, through Art and Ben, the one philosophical, the other cynical, the audience could take a look at a corporate society, equally adapted to the movement of the plot, educated and wealthy, a society of 'decimals and fractions, the square root of nothing,' where business deals are argued about and rejected 'in a boardroom looking up some fella's hairy nostril,' as Ben tells Art.[19]

It is the movement between these 'real' and hyper-real backgrounds and conflations that Carr dilates this family story into a story of society in all times and places. Battersby notes how Carr's plays, 'which are set in the present, could take place anywhere and yet in the present possess a chilling contemporary relevance.'[20] The 'chilling contemporary relevance' hints at the surreal, but like *On Raftery's Hill*, it largely lacks the mythic framework, such as the world of ghosts and mystical landscapes, and it contains less of Carr's poetic language, which have become regular signifiers of her plays

15   Carr, *Marble*, p. 59.
16   Carr, *Marble*, p. 43.
17   Carr, *Marble*, p. 52.
18   Lisa Fitzpatrick, 'Nations and Myth in the Age of the Celtic Tiger: Muide Éire' in Patrick Lonergan and Riana O'Dwyer (eds), *Echoes Down the Corridor* (Dublin: Carysfort Press, 2007), pp. 169–179, p. 178.
19   Carr, *Marble*, p. 28.
20   Battersby, *The Irish Times*, 7 February 2009.

since 1994. Instead, characters move in an identifiable metropolitan space, sharing somewhat more the non-aligned tones of day-to-day speech.

As individuals, the characters show the diversification of struggles within themselves, to exhibit a range of human potentiality that tends towards destruction. Anne resists living, as do the characters in *Ullaloo*, *Low in the Dark* and *Woman and Scarecrow*, by strategic measurements of daily ritual and repetition. Anne's conditions of drudgery are carefully observed, to counteract her suicidal tendencies, 'As long as it keeps me off window ledges' she tells Catherine.[21] Ben suppresses living, telling Catherine, 'We are surrounded by mystery, glutted in it, so much so, we must deny it all to go on,'[22] and Catherine and Art flee and escape living by retreating into their dreams, refusing, as Catherine states, 'this grey nightmare with its ridiculous rules and its lack of primary colours.'[23]

The dream world in *Marble*, in terms of boundary crossing, is representative of the forbidden, and is related to identity, exile and displacement. Kristeva notes, 'Dreams and fantasises continue to remind us of the presence of the semiotic in our mental life, as do artistic and poetic productions.'[24] For Kristeva, and as portrayed in *The Cordelia Dream*, creativity and the silencing of the body are stifled by the symbolic order. Retrieving the semiotic energy through poetic language, or as in *Marble*, through dreams and the framing device of de Chirico's *Melancholy and Mystery of a Street*, makes possible the freedom from the law-governed constraints of the symbolic order. For Kristeva, to articulate and thereby name the forbidden allows the imagination to unlock it and ultimately accept it.[25] Catherine's comment 'I've crossed some line or other without realising it. And it's fantastic,

21 Carr, *Marble*, p. 52.
22 Carr, *Marble*, p. 59.
23 Carr, *Marble*, p. 60.
24 Julia Kristeva, *Revolution in Poetic Language* (New York: Columbia University Press, 1984), p. 24.
25 See Julia Kristeva, *New Maladies of the Soul* (New York: Columbia University Press, 1995), pp. 84–220.

Ben, something is happening to me'[26] is the 'sublime yearning'[27] made real in the revival of the semiotic, through the naming process.

Marble's portrayal of melancholy manifests through dreams, and interior spaces which disrupt subjectivity. Dreams, symptomatic of melancholy, portray mechanisms such as identification, loss and incorporation. The content of the dreams displays the tensions between the characters' governing self-image and their performance in the world. Kristeva, interpreting Freud's notion of melancholy, associates it with the maternal body, in the process of abjection. The subject, who comes into being during the subject/object division, carries the sense of melancholy which is a necessary part of the process.

Freud's *Mourning and Melancholia* (1917) distinguishes between them in contending that mourning is all that has been lost from consciousness, with a necessary withdrawal from what has been lost, while with melancholia it is not clear what has been lost, because the identification has involved unconscious components. The successful work of mourning then represents the triumph of the reality principle, whereas with melancholia that which is lost is not abandoned. The subject entombs the object within, neither relinquishing nor separating from it, becoming according to Freud 'the ego itself', which only then can claim the 'proper' work of mourning.[28] Therefore, for Freud, what is encrypted in melancholy is the absence of a lost object, and not absence itself; the ego has become empty.

By the turn of the twentieth century, melancholia had come to encompass a wide spectrum of subjectivities exceeding gendered distinctions while in the 1960s it had lost its associated pathological quality. In Freud's *The Ego and the Id* of 1923, the revised theory of melancholy saw it accepted as a constitutive psychic mechanism which could encompass subjectivity itself. He concluded that the melancholic process was more common than he had originally thought and that identification with lost objects has 'a great share

26 Carr, *Marble*, p. 40.
27 Carr, *Marble*, p. 60.
28 Sigmund Freud, 'Mourning and Melancholia' in *The Standard Edition of the Complete Psychological Works of Sigmund Freud*, Vol. 14, trans. James Strachey (London: Hogarth Press, 1959), pp. 124–140, 127.

in determining the form taken by the ego and that it makes an essential contribution towards building up what is called its "character".[29]

The characters in *Marble* display a composite sense of emptiness, depicted by the dissolution of subjectivity, and the play dramatises how this emptiness becomes more manageable. The drama played out within the melancholic ego sees itself critically judging the lost object (the object may not have actually died but has been lost as an object of love), reinvesting that loss back into the self. Kristeva confirms this view of melancholia as a form of abandonment in the development process, which the subject has not mourned: 'The disappearance of that essential being continues to deprive me of what is most worthwhile in me.'[30] Through the language of incorporation and ambivalence, the Freudian concept of melancholy names a failure, a disruption of self-identification. In *Marble*, the characters' loss is unsubstantiated and is 'rattled by drives and desires that no longer make sense to themselves.'[31] Carr, once again, portrays resistant subjects created out of loss, a process of subjectivity in which the ego becomes aware of itself through its consuming desire for the lost object, place or ideal.

The pattern of the melancholic sensibility, repeated throughout the play, traces the characters' attempts to deal with their individual lack of fulfilment and also suggests a dislocated community at large. Carr's depiction of wealth as 'success' in the play in the conversations surrounding work, and in the details of the contemporary home, works to contradict the myth of success associated with money and its relationship to the individual. In this context, the characters' constant and repetitive drinking, smoking cigars, entering and exiting in suits, carrying briefcases, and the ways in which the dream world is elaborated upon, reveal their attempts to negotiate subjectivity within the boundaries of a society defined by the prior loss of a preferred past, a society with a minority 'who believe in the

---

29   Sigmund Freud, *The Ego and the Id*, trans. Joan Riviere (New York: Norton (1923) 1960), p. 23.

30   Jon Millis (ed.), *Rereading Freud: Psychoanalysis Through Philosophy* (Albany: State University of New York, 2004), p. 93.

31   Walsh, *Irish Theatre Magazine*, Spring Vol. ix issue 37.

individual and the individual's rights and choices and responsibilities.'[32]
Judith Butler has observed that the movement of the 'object to ego' is
what enables the self to recognise itself: 'the desire of the ego for the lost
object is also an acknowledgement that one exists as an independent and
separate entity.'[33]

   Marble in this context, in terms of the relationship between subject and
object, between the melancholic and the idealised object of loss, explores
the possibility of agency for the subject who comes into being through
the melancholic sensibility. For most of the play, characters engage in self-
abnegating ways, their actions and articulations framed as their attempts to
deal with the limitations set upon them by themselves, their family and their
society. The characters' unstable subjectivity is shaped by the material effects
of social commitment and is reflexively related to the psychic ambivalence
that marks their melancholic outlook. Anne responds to Catherine's virtual
relationship with her husband in a practical way: 'Art belongs here. You
can't have him. He is necessary for my life and for my children's lives to run
smoothly, without event or upset.'[34] Her consumption of 'three generous
measures' of wine every night accompanied by a cigarette with each glass,
is a form of solace in her 'battle against the dark.'[35] In a similar vein, Ben
tells Catherine that her life 'is not yours. It's mine, too. It's the children's.'[36]
The material conditions that shape Ben, Catherine, Art and Anne's consciousness as subjects point up an internalised loss; they lack any reliable
external arrangement which might alleviate the sense of loss.

   The drama of *Marble* from the beginning is brought into being by Art's
dream of making love to Catherine in a beautiful room at the end of a long
panelled corridor, 'where the light and the smell and the sound from it is
intoxicating. I walk into the room holding my breath, afraid I will sully
this beautiful space, that it's not for me, but someone far more deserving.

32   Carr, *Marble*, p. 53.
33   Judith Butler, *The Psychic Life of Power: Theories in Subjection* (Stanford, CA: Stanford
     University Press, 1997), p. 170.
34   Carr, *Marble*, p. 55.
35   Carr, *Marble*, p. 51.
36   Carr, *Marble*, p. 60.

And the marble glistens all round her as she lies there on the bed.'[37] The dream symbolises Art's longing to escape. The light, smell and sound are forces which draw him on towards his freedom, but he is not without feelings of fear, inadequacy and reservations for the beauty and pleasure that is presented before him. Art's dreams of infidelity continue, with Catherine and himself shipwrecked on a beach. Art tells Ben that while they were making love, he kept thinking, 'I'm the one whose going to have to find water, build a hut, fight off native, lions, scorpions, and night was coming on.'[38] In this version of his dream, he is away from society, from the tie of service that is his marriage and work, having what his society would forbid (his friend and colleague's wife) and playing the traditional gender stereotype of man as hunter/gatherer, to nourish his idealised self-image. His early dreams of Catherine move to getting beyond his loyalty towards his wife, children and friend, in asserting his individual self-fulfilment at the expense of what might be deemed socially inappropriate.

Ben's response to Art's dreams marks his character as hesitant and defensive: 'I'm not sure about anything'[39] and 'I am a good husband and father.'[40] There is a link made between dreams, the non-dream world, the sense of loss and what comes to develop as processes of death and dying in the play. While Art struggles to convince Ben that dreams are harmless and don't hold any sense, 'We're dealing with elusive things, without rhyme or reason,' the play says otherwise.[41] Ben reacts to the content of Art's dream by immediately going home to check on Catherine to 'make sure she's still there' and to ensure her hair is still dark and not blond as it was in Art's dream.[42]

Dream images of virtual infidelity are maintained, as Catherine tells Ben of her dream of making love to Art 'on a white, white bed, marble windows, was it? Or was it a marble door? Anyway lots of marble.'[43] Catherine's dream

---

37   Carr, *Marble*, p. 13.
38   Carr, *Marble*, p. 27.
39   Carr, *Marble*, p. 13.
40   Carr, *Marble*, p. 14.
41   Carr, *Marble*, p. 47.
42   Carr, *Marble*, p. 14.
43   Carr, *Marble*, p. 16.

is more about the highly polished texture that is marble, which draws reference to the prized medium for sculptors and architects of classical times and
the subject of de Chirico's painting, bringing together the melancholic sensibility and her sense of estrangement and escape. While Art and Catherine's
dreams share similarities, what is significant is what determines them, to
whom they are being determined and how they are responded to.

As Catherine's and Art's dreams persist, so too does their 'relationship'
and the development of their feelings towards death and dying. Catherine
enquires about Art, and Ben tells her, 'Talks about dying a lot.'[44] She tells
Ben, 'Only recently have I started noticing graveyards, hearses, churches.
I always thought they were some kind of decoration that had nothing to
do with me, but now they follow me everywhere.'[45] Indeed Hopkins' long
marble-like column at the end of the Abbey production was raised up, leaving a black hole, like an open grave, with Catherine and Art staring down.
The closing moments of the performance resonated with some of Ben's
final conversation with Catherine, 'Is that what you want? A marble bed?
And to be under it, not over, because you won't in this world and probably
won't in the next. A marble bed, all its weight fastening you down, glinting
dimly under star and moon but mostly dull, weed-strangled, forgotten.'[46]

The dislocation felt by Ben, Catherine, Art and Anne from any sense
of place, is, as Ben tells Catherine, the 'premonition of an impending sense
of catastrophe' and resonates with the fated sense of doom later referenced
by Catherine, as the mythic cities of Troy or Babylon.[47] But the characters
know that existence can be modified by a deliberate or unconscious act. As
a result, Ben and Anne resign themselves to the 'codes, rules and contracts
we must live by', while Catherine and Art develop fantasies of subjectivity
based on their 'extramarital affair'.[48] As in *The Mai*, *Portia Coughlan*, *By the
Bog of Cats*, *Ariel*, *Woman and Scarecrow* and *The Cordelia Dream*, loyalty
between couples in *Marble* is not possible and the roles and responsibilities

44   Carr, *Marble*, p. 16.
45   Carr, *Marble*, p. 16.
46   Carr, *Marble*, p. 59.
47   Carr, *Marble*, p. 31.
48   Carr, *Marble*, p. 40.

that comes with parenthood are once again abandoned. The boundaries between the world of the play, the symbolic, and the dream world, the semiotic, are struggled against, embraced or are blurred by the characters. Catherine tells Ben, 'It's as if my real life is happening when I go to sleep and you and I are a dream, a fragment, difficult to remember on waking. Being awake is no longer important.'[49] Ben tells Art, 'I've been thinking that all this dreaming is just a front, hiding the real thing that's going on.'[50] Existence is inseparable from our relation to one another, be it between fathers, mothers, husbands, wives, children or businessmen, and portrayed in the waking world or sleeping world. Loss, abandonment and estrangement are affected by human action. Melancholia too, as a psychic paradigm in which the lost object is central, is, as Adam Phillips notes, a reminder of our enduring attachment to others.[51]

In the play's own terms, the fated doom in the work is summarised in the concept of regret, the theme centrally explored in Carr's *Ullaloo* or in the trilogy, where the protagonist's sense of loss is exacerbated and tormented by the incapacity to bear up what they didn't act upon, so they fully depart from the world. In *Marble*, Catherine tells Ben 'the life not lived is what kills' yet where regret in Carr's earlier work is a personal suffering, in *Marble*, regret is rooted in the fact of being human, even if founded on loss.[52] However, rather than accept it as unalterable, Carr confronts it, in Catherine's and Art's act of deserting their home and family. Catherine tells Ben:

> A dream was given to me, inside me from birth, a dream of marble, a woman in a marble room with her lover. And all the waking world can do is thwart it and deny it, and say, no, it cannot be, childish, impossible, you must walk the grey paths with the rest of us, go down into the wet muck at the close.[53]

49 Carr, *Marble*, p. 32.
50 Carr, *Marble*, p. 33.
51 See Adam Phillips, 'Keep It Moving: Commentary on Judith Butler's Melancholy Gender/Refused Identification' in Judith Butler, *The Psychic Life of Power: Theories in Subjection* (Stanford, CA: Stanford University Press, 1997), pp. 151–159.
52 Carr, *Marble*, p. 17.
53 Carr, *Marble*, p. 60.

Before Art leaves Anne, he tells her:

> Then the man got up and left the room, left his sleeping wife, his children, his sofas, his brandy, his expensive cigars, and he went and found the marble woman who lived not far. [...] They vowed to one another that they would stay in the marble room together forever.[54]

If the melancholic sensibility is the infinite insistence on an attachment to someone or something, then Carr brings that someone or something into the realm where the conscious and the unconscious are brought together on the same plane. The boundaries between the conscious and unconscious are crossed and the cracks in doing so are bridged. The semiotic forces that made their way into Art's and Catherine's dreams were interpreted as innovative imaginative spaces that could nourish their relation with one another. Psychic spaces are essential for transformation. Unlike the invasion of the abject in *On Raftery's Hill*, where no action is taken in respect to the sexual offence, or the playful and harmless crossing of gendered and sexual boundaries depicted in Carr's early plays, or the destructive patriarchal setting of rigid social boundaries in *Meat and Salt*, the dynamic of limits that surround objects either with the glare of the sacred or with the flavour of the profane, comes with images of boundary fluctuations in *Marble*. This is an enabling configuration, where one constitutes itself in the fantasy image of another, and the quality of this relationship, between the conscious and unconscious, crucially affects the way the world is experienced and believed by the individual. Thus Catherine, Ben, Art and Anne have found their identities and power from the commonality of individual, human emptiness, and they will go on to confront, as Carr has in *Marble*, the deepest conundrums of human existence, especially the problem of living and dying and its attendant melancholic sensibility in a post Celtic Tiger Ireland. And they will do so from a marble place.

---

54   Carr, *Marble*, p. 65.

Conclusion

My aim in this book is to explore processes of identity and the loss of selfhood read predominantly through the lens of abjection in Carr's plays from 1988 to 2009. The discussion considers the nature, condition and consequences of forms of different abject subjectivities, responding in various ways to boundary construction, deconstruction and failure. The book demonstrates how the form and content of Carr's dramas offer a complex and imaginative conduit between past and present, in both individual and cultural contexts. Specifically, 'home', 'gender' and 'family' are sites where borders and boundaries of abjection are interrogated and explored.

The problematic concept of gender, elaborated through Kristeva's notion of abjection, underlines the fragility of individual and cultural boundaries throughout Carr's work. Kristeva observes: 'The abject from which he does not cease separating is for him, *a land of oblivion* that is constantly remembered.'[1] For the abject individual, such a remembered time is also the moment of disclosure, a dual process of self-recognition and self-repression, whose powers lay bare the course of self-destruction. From Tilly to Curtains to Portia to The Mai, to Hester to Dinah, to Sorrel and to Woman, all the female protagonists respond in various ways to cultural interpretations of gender, highlighting how the exclusion of the (female) 'other' always returns to haunt the self. Carr's theatre both perpetuates and challenges stable conventional notions of identity in Irish society, revealing subjectivity as ambivalent and harmful. Applying Kristevan theory to Carr's plays points up constructions of abject selfhoods, where destruction is presented as a form of entrapment, and the extent to which processing these destructive identities might serve to negotiate a productive renewal.

Chapter 1: 'Unnatural Blood' explored the struggle to communicate, the uncertainties of living and fluid forms of identity, in *Ullaloo, Low in the*

---

1   Kristeva, *Powers of Horror*, p. 9. [Emphasis in original]

Dark and *Woman and Scarecrow*, in terms of Kristeva's symbolic/semiotic modalities, in order to show that the manipulation of these boundaries can point to the instability of meaning or the collapse of meaning altogether. The rigid categories of sexuality and gender which, ironically, perpetuate these structures are also critiqued, as the lack of continuity between the symbolic and semiotic phases of development, and the destructive tendency that results. The discussion demonstrates that the threat to rigid 'masculine' and 'feminine' boundaries could transgress and/or fracture them in the context of social identity, portraying the fallibility, temporality and corporeality of human kind in the plays. Apparent is Carr's imaginative subversion of conventional cultural constructions of gendered and individual identity, in the context of 'normative' notions of behaviour. The plays challenge accepted forms of discourse in terms of the non-naturalistic theatrical form, specifically in relation to Martin Esslin's notion of the 'Theatre of the Absurd'. The meta-theatrical and performative nature of the plays not only resists traditions of Irish theatre, but also interrogates the ways in which theatre and performance reflect individual and social subjectivities.

Chapter 2: 'Coagulated Blood, Congealed Blood and Mixed Blood' considered the thematic concerns of 'the trilogy', such as female subjectivity, sexuality, discrimination, violence, bigotry and hypocrisy, viewed though the protagonists' journey towards suicide. Produced in the 1990s, the plays reflect a consciousness of the historical and cultural forces which have shaped them, specifically dramatising the response to the symbolic order which establishes its position by the abjection of 'woman' and 'the maternal'. Concerns of 'home', 'family', and related notions of 'femininity' are revealed as restrictive, in terms of the socio-historical position of women in Ireland in the plays, presenting an 'otherness' that confronts the mythologisation and idealisation of woman through various states of abjection. Yet ultimately, marginal states of subjectivity are read as painful, and Carr ends the pain by the suicide of the protagonists in all three plays.

The Mai focuses on the operation of memory as a mode of processing the ramifications of a painful past. Memory, in this sense, stages 'a return of the repressed' as a means to figure loss and rediscover that part of the self that is 'abjected'. Colonial theory, post-colonial theory and cultural theory usefully demonstrate the negotiations of individual and collective identities with regard to issues of power, authority and memory.

Portia Coughlan affirms Carr's representation of 'otherness' and processes of alterity in relation to the twin motif. The 'twins' and the 'twinning' of subjectivity to an 'otherness' are central to the problematising, politicising and negotiation of identity, sexuality and the body, exploring 'otherness' as a symbol of both confinement and escape. The displacement of identity lies at the borders between notions of 'home' and 'other', with the 'split self' device operating as disruptive to ideas of 'stable' or fixed identity, and soaring towards states of abjection.

By the Bog of Cats politicises the notion of cultural borders and boundaries regarding individual and social subjectivities and considers the politics of inferiority, dominance and hegemony in relation to cultural aspects of Ireland. The call on the dissolution of the Travellers as a cultural minority, in exchange for a homogeneous settled community, reveals their rigid distinctions: one is a Traveller because s/he is not a Settled person and one is a Settled person because s/he is not a Traveller. However, dramatising the ambivalent position of the half-traveller-half-settled-person underscores the ambivalence of the marginalized figure and also positions it as a threat to the homogeneity of the 'settled' identity, with the 'unity' of the settled community fissured by the liminal figure.

On Raftery's Hill and *Meat and Salt* (Chapter 3) demonstrate how constructed boundaries promote destruction. These boundaries, representative of the symbolic order, show subjecthood formed within and outside of the symbolic order. *On Raftery's Hill* focuses exclusively on abjection within the symbolic, as a system of abusive familial relationships, and paints a devastating critique of the intra-subjective tensions of self-destruction, in ways that surrender the ability to understand that self-destruction in inter-subjective ways. Yet demonstrating the power of abjection within systems of abuse reveals its construction. In the context of Carr's other plays, this depicts possibilities of deconstructing the power of abjection, as was shown in *Meat and Salt*, where the figurative portrayal of the symbolic/semiotic modalities, particularly in dramatising female subjectivity outside of the symbolic realm, reveals a more independent and stable female subjectivity.

Carr's representation of the abject in *Ariel* and *The Cordelia Dream* (Chapter 4) is dramatised in terms of the subjective fear and anxiety of confronting the internal sense of estrangement. The sacrifice of the female, as a means of confrontation, demonstrates the fragility of what is signified as a result. The plays' deference to authority, presented once again in the 'family', is the site through which to interrogate the abject self in both public and private realms. In *Ariel*, forms of extreme fail to make meaning in a wider context individualism and highlight the vacuum situated at the centre of the contemporary world of the play. Murder, revenge and betrayal, together with related issues of power and corruption in contemporary rural Ireland, end in repetitious argument, before culminating in pointless murders. *The Cordelia Dream* dramatises the experience of the 'other' and of oneself, as the journey into an irreconcilable destruction that, like *Ariel*, ends in death.

Marble (Chapter 5) announces a different direction to the work, diluting the abject sensibility and moving towards a melancholic world of loss. This chapter demonstrated a different kind of boundary fluctuation, which enables the characters to use melancholy as their motivation for action, whatever the consequences. The play demonstrates the ability to imagine (in the form of dreams) as essential to opening up psychic spaces of possibility, where whatever was excluded or repressed returns to a form of representation and interpretation. Articulating repressed experiences, providing access to the self, to the body and to others, gives meaning to living.

In response to Carr's distinctive voice in her complex work and extraordinary vision, other readings and viewpoints will continue to emerge.

Appendix

Carr was born in 1964 in Dublin but raised in the Midlands, in the townland of Gortnamona (which translates from Irish as 'Turf Field'), near Tullamore, Co Offaly. As the second eldest of six children, she grew up in a creative household and could not have escaped such influence. Her mother played music and read and wrote poetry, her sister Deirdre is a poet and artist and her father Hugh has written stage and radio plays as well as novels. Carr tells Mike Murphy in an interview of her earliest experiences of the 'theatre':

> We had a theatre in the shed. We had boards on top of the turf, an old sheet for a curtain, and we had a bicycle lamp. We had the whole works. We had the spot and we even had it focused at an angle so you could walk into it. We used to write little plays and put them on.[1]

The lifestyle of the Midlands that Carr describes is quaint, carefree and picturesque, with little disturbances from the outside world, a world radically different to the worlds depicted in her plays. She tells Murphy:

> My first seven or eight summers were spent running around the fields, eating grass, chasing tractors, picking mushrooms, blackberries, all that stuff. It was quite idyllic for a child.[2]

Carr graduated from University College Dublin with a BA degree in English and Philosophy in 1987 and, after working in New York for one year teaching and writing, she returned to embark upon a Master's programme, also at University College Dublin. However, her Master's degree, which was to examine the works of Samuel Beckett, was abandoned because of

[1]   Mike Murphy, *Reading the Future: Irish Writers in Conversation with Mike Murphy*, p. 46.

[2]   Murphy, *Reading the Future*, p. 45.

her playwriting commitments. Carr then lived in Dublin until Christmas 2005. In early 2006, her family moved to Co. Kerry where she currently resides with her husband and four children.

Carr's literary achievements are wide and prestigious and to date they include: The Irish American Literary Award in 2003 and The E.M. Forster Award for literary achievement from the American Academy of Arts and Letters in 2001. Faber and Faber published her first collection of plays in 1999. She was Writer in Residence at Dublin City University in 1999, Writer in Residence at Trinity College Dublin from 1998 to 1999 and held the Heimbold Professorship at Villanova University in 2003. She became a member of Aosdana in 1996. From 1995 to 1996 she was Writer in Residence at the Abbey theatre. She was the Hennessy Short Story Winner for *Grow Mermaid* in 1994.

Bibliography

Books

Abbott, Pamela, and Wallace, Clare (eds), *Gender, Power and Sexuality* (Basingstoke: Macmillan, 1991)

Adams, Bert N., *Kinship in an Urban Setting* (Chicago: Markham, 1968)

Ardrigh, [pseudonym], *The Hills of Holy Ireland* (Dublin: Catholic Truth Society of Ireland, Not dated.)

Arensberg, C.M. and Kimball, S.T., *Family and Community in Ireland* (Cambridge, MA: Harvard University Press, 1968)

Armitt, Lucie, *Theorising The Fantastic* (London: Arnold Hodder Headline Group, 1996)

Aston, Elaine, *An Introduction to Feminism and Theatre* (London: Routledge, 1995)

Axelrod, Steven Gould, *Sylvia Plath: The Wound and the Cure of Words* (Baltimore: Johns Hopkins Press, 1990)

Bablet, Denis, *The Theatre of Edward Gordon Craig*, Daphne Woodward Translator (London: Methuen, 1981)

Barker, Chris, *Cultural Studies: Theory and Practice* (London: Sage, 2000)

Barnes, Ben, Artistic Director, Abbey Theatre Programme, *Ariel* (Dublin: Abbey, 2002)

Barrett, Michèle, *The Anti-Social Family* (London: Verso, 1991)

Barry, Sebastian, *Plays: Sebastian Barry* (London: Methuen, 1997)

Beckett, Samuel, *Proust* (London: Chatto and Windus, 1931)

Beckett, Samuel, *The Complete Dramatic Works* (London: Faber, 1986)

Beckett, Samuel, *Waiting for Godot* (London: Faber, 1965)

Bentley, Eric (ed.), *The Theory of the Modern Stage: An Introduction to Modern Theatre and Drama* (London: Penguin, 1992)

Ben-Zvi, Linda (ed.), *Women in Beckett: Performance and Critical Perspective* (Urbana: University of Illinois Press, 1990)

Berlin, Lisa J. (ed.), *Enhancing Early Attachments: Theory, Research, Intervention and Policy* (London: Guilford, 2005)

Bhabha, Homi K., *The Location of Culture* (London: Routledge, 1994)

Boland, Eavan, *Object Lessons: The Life of the Woman and the Poet in Our Time* (Manchester: Carcanet, 1995)

Boland, Eavan, *Outside History* (Manchester: Carcanet, 1990)

Bolger, Dermot (ed.), *Druids, Dudes And Beauty Queens: The Changing Face of Irish Theatre* (Dublin: Arts Council, 2001)

Bolger, Dermot, *Dermot Bolger: Plays* (London: Methuen, 2000)

Bottigheimer, Ruth B. (ed.), *Fairy Tales and Society: Illusion, Allusion and Paradigm* (Philadelphia: University of Pennnisylvania Press, 1986)

Boss, Pauline G., et al. (eds), *Sourcebook of Family Theories and Methods: A Contextual Approach* (New York: Plenum, 1993)

Bourke, Angela (ed.), *The Field Day Anthology of Irish Writing*, Vol. IV (Cork University Press, 2002)

Bowie, Malcolm, *Psychoanalysis and the Future Of Theory* (Oxford: Blackwell, 1993)

Bowlby, John, *Attachment and Loss* (London: Hogarth, 1974)

Boylan, Thomas A., *Irish Political Economy* (London: Routledge, 2003)

Bradby, David, *Beckett: Waiting for Godot* (Cambridge University Press, 2001)

Bradley, Anthony and Valiulis, Maryann Gialanella (eds), *Gender and Sexuality in Modern Ireland* (Amherst: University of Massachusetts Press, 1997)

Bradshaw, Jonathan et al. (eds), *Absent Fathers?* (London: Routledge, 1999)

Breathnach, Proinnsias, *Exploring the 'Celtic Tiger' Phenomenon: Causes and Consequences of Ireland's Economic Miracle* (Maynooth, Co. Kildare: Geographical Society of Ireland, 1998)

Brecht, Bertolt, *Brecht on Theatre: The Development of an Aesthetic* (London: Methuen, 1978)

Briere, John N., *Child Abuse Trauma: Theory and Treatment of the Lasting Effects* (Thousand Oaks, CA: Sage Publications, 1992)

Bronfen, Elisabeth, and Kavka, Misha (eds), *Feminist Consequences: Theory for the New Century* (New York: Columbia University, 2001)

Brown, John Russell (ed.), *The Oxford Illustrated History of Theatre* (Oxford University Press, 1995)

Brown, Lesley (ed.), *The New Shorter Oxford English on Historical Principles Dictionary* (Oxford: Clarendon Press, 1993), Vol. 2, N–Z

Brown, Terence, *Ireland: A Social and Cultural History 1922–1985* (London: Fontana Press, 1985)

Bunch, Charlotte and Carrillo, Roxanna, *Gender Violence: A Development and Human Rights Issue* (Dublin: Attic Press, 1992)

Butler, Judith P., *Gender Trouble: Feminism and the Subversion of Identity* (London: Routledge, 1999)

Butler, Judith, *The Psychic Life of Power: Theories in Subjection* (Stanford, CA: Stanford University Press 1997)

Buzawa, Eve S. and Schlesinger, Eve, *Domestic Violence: The Criminal Justice Response* (London: Sage, 2003)

Cairns, David and Richards, Shaun, *Writing Ireland: Colonialism, Nationalism and Culture* (Manchester University Press, 1988)

Calvo, Clara, *The Literature Workbook* (London: Routledge, 1998)

Carlson, Marvin, *Performance: A Critical Introduction* (London: Routledge, 1996)

Carr, Marina, *Ariel* (Oldcastle, Co. Meath: Gallery Press, 2002)

Carr, Marina, *By the Bog of Cats* (Oldcastle, Co. Meath: Gallery Press, 1998)

Carr, Marina, *Marble* (Oldcastle, Co. Meath: Gallery Press, 2009)

Carr, Marina, *On Raftery's Hill* (Oldcastle, Co. Meath: Gallery Press, 2000)

Carr, Marina, *Plays One* (London: Faber and Faber, 1999)

Carr, Marina, *Portia Coughlan* (Oldcastle, Co. Meath: Gallery Press, 1996)

Carr, Marina, *The Cordelia Dream* (Oldcastle, Co. Meath: Gallery Press, 2008)

Carr, Marina, *The Mai* (Oldcastle, Co. Meath: Gallery Press, 1994)

Carr, Marina, *Woman and Scarecrow* (Oldcastle, Co. Meath: Gallery Press, 2006)

Case, Sue Ellen (ed.), *Performing Feminisms: Feminist Critical Theory and the Theatre* (Baltimore: Johns Hopkins University Press, 1990)

Cashford, Jules, *The Moon: Myth and Image* (London: Cassell Illustrated, 2003)

Castells, Manuel, *The Power of Identity* (Oxford: Blackwell, 1997)

Chambers, Lillian, Fitzgibbon, Ger and Jordan, Eamonn (eds), *Theatre Talk: Voices of Irish Theatre Practitioners* (Dublin: Carysfort Press, 2001)

Cheal, David, *Sociology of Family Life* (Basingstoke: Palgrave, 2002)

Cixous, Hélène, *Coming to Writing and Other Essays* (London: Harvard University Press, 1991)

Cleaver, Hedy, *Parental Perspectives in the Cases of Suspected Child Abuse* (London: HMSO, 1995)

Cohn, Ruby (ed.), *Samuel Beckett: A Collection of Criticism* (London: McGraw-Hill, 1975)

Coll, Cynthia García, Bearer, Elaine L. and Lerner, Richard M. (eds), *Nature and Nurture, The Complex Interplay of Genetic and Environmental Influences on Human Behavior and Development* (Mahwah, NJ: Lawrence Erlbaum Associates, 2004)

Collins, Neil and O'Shea, Mary, *Understanding Corruption in Irish Politics* (Cork University Press, 2000)

Conacher, D. J., *Aeschylus' Oresteia: A Literary Commentary* (University of Toronto, 1987)

Corry, Percy, *Planning the Stage* (New York: Pitman Publishing, 1961)

Coulter, Colin and Coleman, Steve (eds), *The End of History?: Critical Reflections on the Celtic Tiger* (Manchester University Press, 2003)

Counsell, Colin and Wolf, Laurie (eds), *Performance Analysis: An Introductory Coursebook* (London: Routledge, 2001)

Cultures of Ireland Group Conference: *Culture in Ireland: Regions: Identity and Power*, 1992: Ballyconnell, Ireland (Belfast: Institute of Irish Studies, 1993)

Cunliffe, Barry, *The Celtic World* (London: Constable, 1992)

Curtin, Chris, Jackson, Pauline and O'Connor, Barbara (eds), *Gender in Irish Society* (Galway University Press, 1987)

Daniel, E. Valentine and Peck, Jeffrey M. (eds), *Culture/Contexture: Explorations in Anthropology and Literary Studies* (Berkeley: University of California Press, 1996)

D'Art, Daryl and Turner, Thomas (eds), *Irish Employment Relations in the New Economy* (Dublin: Blackhall, 2002)

De Valera, Eamon, *Speeches and Statements by Eamon de Valera, 1917–73* (Dublin: Gill and Macmillan, 1980)

Deacon, Lynda, *Understanding Perpetrators, Protecting Children: A Practical Approach* (London: Whiting & Birch, 1999)

Dearlove, J. E., *Accommodating the Chaos: Samuel Beckett's Non-relational Art* (Durham, NC: Duke University Press, 1982)

Deevy, Teresa, *Three Plays: Katie Roche: The King of Spain's Daughter: The Wild Goose* (London: Macmillan, 1939)

Dept of the Environment, *Report of the Commission on Itinerancy* (Dublin: Stationery Office, 1963)

Dept of the Taoiseach, *Census of Population of Ireland* (Dublin: Irish Central Statistics Office, 1996)

Dept of the Taoiseach, *Census of Population of Ireland* (Dublin: Irish Central Statistics Office, 2002)

Devlin, Anne, *After Easter: Anne Devlin* (London: Faber, 1994)

Dillon, John and Wilmer, S. E., *Rebel Women* (London: Methuen, 2005)

Drain, Richard (ed.), *Twentieth Century Theatre: A Source Book* (London: Routledge, 1995)

Dublin Travellers, Racism and Development, *Anti-Racist Law and the Travellers* (Dublin: Irish Traveller Movement, 1993)

Easthope, Antony and McGowan, Kate (eds), *A Critical and Cultural Theory Reader* (Buckingham: Open University Press, 1992)

Edwards, R. Dudley, *Irish Families: The Archival Aspect* (Dublin: National University of Ireland, 1974)

Eldridge, J. E. T. (John Eric Thomas) *Raymond Williams: Making Connections* (London: Routledge, 1994)

Epstein, Debbie and Sears, James T. (eds), *A Dangerous Knowing: Sexual Pedagogies and the 'Master' Narrative* (London: Cassell, 1999)

Esslin, Martin (ed.), *Samuel Beckett: A Collection of Critical Essays* (Englewood Cliffs, NJ: Prentice-Hal, 1965)

Esslin, Martin, *The Theatre of the Absurd* (Harmondsworth: Pelican Books, 1980)

Etherton, Michael, *Contemporary Irish Dramatists* (Basingstoke: Macmillan Education, 1989)

Felman, Shoshana, *Jacques Lacan and the Adventure of Insight: Psychoanalysis in Contemporary Culture* (London: Cambridge University Press, 1987)

Finch, Janet, *Family Obligations and Social Change* (Cambridge: Polity Press, 1989)

Fletcher, John, *Beckett: A Study of His Plays* (London: Methuen, 1972)

Frazier, Adrian, *Behind the Scenes: Yeats, Horniman and the Struggle for the Abbey Theatre* (Berkeley: California University Press, 1990)

French, Mikela, *Resurrecting the Live Body: Medbh McGuckian, Marina Carr and Felim Egan* (Belfast: The Author, 2001)

Freud, Sigmund, *The Ego and the Id*, trans. Joan Riviere (New York: Norton, 1923, 1960)

Freud, Sigmund, 1856–1939 *The Standard Edition of the Complete Psychological Works of Sigmund Freud* (London: Hogarth Press for the Institute of Psycho-Analysis, 1966)

Freud, Sigmund, *The Standard Edition of the Complete Psychological Works of Sigmund Freud*, James Strachey (ed.), Vol. 17 (London: Hogarth Press, 1955)

Friel, Brian, *The Freedom of the City* (London: Faber, 1974)

Friel, Brian, *Selected Plays* (London: Faber, 1984)

Friel, Brian, *Dancing at Lughnasa* (London: Faber, 1990)

Friel, Brian, *Wonderful Tennessee* (Oldcastle, Co. Meath: Gallery Books, 1993)

Furay, Julia and O'Hanlon, Redmond (eds), *Critical Moments: Fintan O'Toole on Modern Irish Theatre* (Dublin: Carysfort Press, 2003)

Furstenberg, Frank F., *Divided Families: What Happens To Children When Parents Part* (Cambridge, MA: Harvard University Press, 1991)

Gamme, Irene (ed.), *Confessional Politics: Women's Sexual Self-representations in Life Writing and Popular Media* (Carbondale: Southern Illinois University Press, 1999)

Gilbert, Helen and Tompkins, Joanne, *Post Colonial Drama Theory Practice, Politics* (London: Routledge, 1996)

Gmelch, George, *The Irish Tinkers: The Urbanisation of an Itinerant People* (Menlo Park, CA: Cummings, 1977)

Goffman, Erving, *The Presentation of Self in Everyday Life* (New York: Penguin, 1959)

Gogarty, Oliver St John, *William Butler Yeats: A Memoir* (Dublin: Dolmen Press, 1963)

Goldhill, Simon, *Aeschylus: The Oresteia* (Cambridge University Press, 1992)

Golding, Sue, *The Eight Technologies of Otherness* (London: Routledge, 1997)

Gontarski, S. E., *Beckett's Happy Days: A Manuscript Study* (Columbus, OH: Publications Committee, 1977)

Good News Bible: Todays English Version (London: Collins, 1976)

Goodman, Lizbeth and deGay, Jane (eds), *The Routledge Reader in Politics and Performance* (London: Routledge, 2000)

Goodman, Lizbeth, and de Gay, Jane (eds), *The Routledge Reader in Gender and Performance* (London: Routledge, 1998)

Graham, Colin, *Deconstructing Ireland: Identity, Theory, Culture* (Edinburgh: Edinburgh University Press, 2001)

Gramsci, Antonio, *Selections from the Prison Notebooks* (London: Lawrence and Wishart, 1971)

Grant, David (ed.), *The Crack in the Emerald: New Irish Plays* (London: Nick Hern Books, 1994)

Gregory, Lady Augusta, *Our Irish Theatre: A Chapter of Autobiography* (Gerrards Cross: Smythe, 1972)

Gregory, Lady Augusta, *Selected Writings* (London: Penguin, 1995)

Grene, Nicholas, *The Politics of Irish Drama: Plays in Context from Boucicault to Friel* (Cambridge University Press, 1999)

Griffin, Victor Gilbert Benjamin, *Enough Religion to Make Us Hate: Reflections on Religion and Politics* (Dublin: Columba Press, 2002)

Griffiths, Trevor and Llewellyn-Jones, Margaret (eds), *British and Irish Women Dramatists Since 1958: A Critical Handbook* (Buckingham: Open University Press, 1993)

Gwynn, Denis, *Edward Martyn And The Irish Revival* (London: J. Cape, 1930)

Hantrais, Linda, *Families and Family Policies in Europe* (London: Longman, 1996)

Harp, Richard and Evans, Robert C. (eds), *Companion to Brian Friel* (West Cornwall, CT: Locust Hill Press, 2002)

Harries, Elizabeth Wanning, *Twice Upon a Time: Women Writers and the History of the Fairy Tale* (Princeton, NJ: Princeton University Press, 2001)

Harrington, John P. (ed.), *Modern Irish Drama* (New York: W. W. Norton & Company, 1991)

Hartnoll, Phyllis, *The Theatre: A Concise History* (New York: Hudson, 1998)

Hawkins-Dady, Mark (ed.), *International Dictionary of Theatre – 1 Plays* (London: St James Press, 1992)

Hayes, Alan and Urquhart, Diane (eds), *The Irish Women's History Reader* (London: Routledge, 2001)

Helleiner, Jane, *Irish Travellers: Racism and the Politics of Culture* (University of Toronto, 2000)

Hogan, Robert and Kilroy, James (eds), *Lost Plays of the Irish Renaissance* (Dublin: Proscenium Press, 1970)

Howarth, David, Norval, Aletta J. and Stavrakakis, Yannis (eds), *Discourse Theory and Political Analysis: Identities, Hegemonies and Social Change* (Manchester University Press, 2000)

Howe, David (ed.), *Attachment Theory, Child Maltreatment and Family Support* (Basingstoke: Macmillan, 1999)

Humphreys, Alexander J., *New Dubliners: Urbanisation and the Irish Family* (London: Routledge, 1966)

Hunter, George (ed.), William Shakespeare, *King Lear* (London: Penguin, 2005)

Irigaray, Luce, *An Ethics of Sexual Difference*, trans. Carolyn Burke and Gillian C. Gill (Ithaca, NY: Cornell University Press, 1993)

Irigaray, Luce, *Je, Tu, Nous: Toward a Culture of Difference*, trans. Alison Martin (New York: Routledge, 1993)

Jackson, Rosemary, *Fantasy: The Literature of Subversion* (London: Routledge, 1998)

Jones, David P. H., *Child Sexual Abuse: Informing Practice* (Abingdon: Radcliffe Medical Press, 1999)

Jones, David P. H. and Ramchandani, Paul, *Child Sexual Abuse: Informing Practice from Research* (Abingdon: Radcliffe Medical Press Ltd, 1999)

Jones, Helen and Millar, Jane (eds), *The Politics of the Family* (Aldershot: Avebury, 1996)

Jones, Steven Swann, *The Fairy Tale: The Magic Mirror of Imagination* (New York: Twayne Publishers, 1995)

Jordan, Eamonn (ed.), *Theatre Stuff: Critical Essays on Contemporary Irish Theatre* (Dublin: Carysfort Press, 2000)

Joyce, Patrick Weston, *Irish Local Names Explained* (Dublin: F. Hanna, 1979)

Kalb, Jonathan, *Beckett in Performance* (Cambridge: Cambridge University Press, 1989)

Keane, John B., *The Field: A Play in Three Acts* (Cork: The Mercier Press, 1966)

Keane, John B., *Big Maggie: A Play in Three Acts* (Cork: The Mercier Press, 1969)

Keaney, Siobhan, *A Giant Soap Opera: The Role of the Family and Place* (Belfast: The Author, 1999)

Keith, Michael, and Pile, Steve (eds), *Place and the Politics of Identity* (London: Routledge, 1993)

Kelly, J. M., *The Irish Constitution* (Dublin: Jurist Publishing Company, 1980)

Kennedy, Andrew K., *Samuel Beckett* (Cambridge University Press, 1989)

Kennedy, Finola, *Family, Economy and Government in Ireland* (Dublin: Economic and Social Research Institute, 1989)

Kennedy, Liam, *Colonialism, Religion and Nationalism in Ireland* (Queen's University Belfast, 1996)

Kennedy, Liam (ed.), *Ireland in Transition* (Cork and Dublin: Mercier Press, 1986)

Kennedy, Valerie, *Edward Said: A Critical Introduction* (Oxford: Polity Press, 2000)

Kennelly, Brendan, *Euripides' Medea: A New Version* (Newcastle upon Tyne: Bloodaxe, 1991)

Kiberd, Declan, *Inventing Ireland* (Cambridge, MA: Harvard University Press, 1995)

Kilroy, Thomas, *Double Cross* (Oldcastle, Co. Meath: Gallery Books, 1994)

Kirkpatrick, Kathryn (ed.), *Border Crossings: Irish Women Writers and National Identities* (Tuscaloosa: University of Alabama Press, 2000)

Knights, Ben, *Writing Masculinities: Male Narratives in Twentieth-Century Fiction* (Basingstoke: Macmillan, 1999)

Kristeva, Julia, *Powers of Horror: An Essay on Abjection*, trans. Leon S. Roudiez (New York: Columbia University Press, 1982)

Kristeva, Julia, *Revolution in Poetic Language*, trans. Leon S. Roudiez (New York: Columbia University Press, 1984)

Kristeva, Julia, *Black Sun: Depression and Melancholia*, trans. Leon S. Roudiez (New York: Columbia University Press, 1989)

Kristeva, Julia, *New Maladies of the Soul* (New York: Columbia University Press, 1995)

Kuspit, Donald, *The End of Art* (Cambridge University Press, 2004)

Lacan, Jacques, *Écrits: A Selection* (London: Routledge, 1977)

Lacan, Jacques *Écrits*, trans. Bruce Fink (New York: W. W. Norton & Company, 2002)

Laing, R. D., *Self and Others* (London: Tavistock Publications, 1969)

Laing, R. D., *Sanity, Madness and the Family* (London: Tavistock Publications, 1970)

Landman, Isaac (ed.), *The Universal Jewish Encyclopedia* (New York: 1939)

Larner, Christina, *Witchcraft and Religion: The Politics of Popular Belief* (Oxford: Blackwell, 1984)

Lash, Scott, *Sociology of Postmodernism* (London: Routledge, 1990)

Leeney, Cathy and McMullan, Anna (eds), *The Theatre of Marina Carr: "before rules was made"* (Dublin: Carysfort Press, 2003)

Leidholdt, Dorchen and Raymond, Janice G. (eds), *The Sexual Liberals and the Attack on Feminism* (Oxford: Pergamon, 1990)

Lennon, Joseph, *Irish Orientalism: A Literary and Intellectual History* (Syracuse, NY: Syracuse University, 2004)

Levin, Thomas Y., Frohne, Ursula and Weibel, Peter (eds), *CTRL [Space]: Rhetorics of Surveillance from Bentham to Big Brother* (Karlsruhe, Germany: ZKM, 2002)

Lewellyn-Jones, Margaret, *Contemporary Irish Drama & Cultural Identity* (Bristol: Intellect, 2002)

Leyton, Elliott, *The One Blood: Kinship and Class in an Irish Village* (St John's, Newfoundland: Institute of Social and Economic Research, 1975)

Littleton, Michael (ed.), *From Famine to Feast: Economic and Social Change in Ireland 1847–1997* (Dublin: Institute of Public Administration, 1998)

Locke, Courtenay, trans., *Witchcraft Magic and Alchemy* (Boston: Houghton, 1931)

Lonergan, Patrick, *Theatre and Globalisation: Irish Drama in the Celtic Tiger Era* (Basingstoke: Palgrave Macmillan, 2009)

Lonergan, Patrick and O'Dwyer, Riana (eds), *Echoes Down the Corridor* (Dublin: Carysfort Press, 2007)

Lorraine, Tamsin E., *Gender, Identity, and the Production of Meaning* (Oxford: Westview Press, 1990)

Lupton, Deborah, *Constructing Fatherhood: Discourses and Experiences* (London: Sage, 1997)

Lyons, F.S.L., *Culture and Anarchy in Ireland 1880–1939* (Oxford: Clarendon Press, 1980)

Marler, Joan (ed.), *The Civilization of the Goddess: The World of Old Europe* (San Francisco: Harper San Francisco, 1991)

Martin, J.P. (ed.), *Violence and the Family* (Chichester: Wiley, 1978)

Martyn, Edward, *The Heather Field: Play in Three Acts* (London: Brenta, 1917)

Matthews, J. H., *The Surrealist Mind* (Selinsgrove, PA: Susquehanna University, 1991)

McCann, May, Ó Síocháin, Séamas and Ruane, Joseph (eds), *Irish Travellers: Culture and Ethnicity* (Belfast: Queen's University, 1994)

McDonagh, Martin, *Plays* (London: Methuen Drama, 1999)

McDonald, Marianne and Walton, J. Michael (eds), *Amid Our Troubles: Irish Versions of Greek Tragedy* (London: Methuen, 2002)

McDonald, Ronan, *Tragedy and Irish Literature: Synge, O'Casey, Beckett* (Basingstoke: Palgrave, 2002)

McDowell, Mark David, *Nationality: Politics, Family and Religion, and the Individual* (Belfast: The Author, 2003)

McGlathery, James M., *Fairy Tale Romance: The Grimms, Basile, and Perrault* (Urbana: University of Illinois Press, 1991)

McGuinness, Frank (ed.), *The Dazzling Dark: New Irish Plays* (London: Faber and Faber, 1996)

McKee, Lorna and O'Brien, Margaret (eds), *The Father Figure* (London: Tavistock, 1982)

McKeown, Kieran, Ferguson, Harry and Rooney, Dermot (eds), *Changing Fathers?* (Cork: Collins Press, 1997)

McLean, Stuart, *The Event and Its Terrors: Ireland, Famine, Modernity* (Stanford, CA: Stanford University, 2004)

McNeill, T. E., *Castles in Ireland: Feudal Power in a Gaelic World* (London: Routledge, 1997)

Meaney, Gerardine, *(Un)Like Subjects: Women, Theory, Fiction* (London: Routledge, 1993)

Millis, Jon (ed.), *Rereading Freud: Psychoanalysis Through Philosophy* (Albany: State University of New York, 2004)

Miller, Nancy K. (ed.), *The Poetics of Gender* (New York: Columbia University Press, 1986)

Moi, Toril, *The Kristeva Reader* (Oxford: Basil Blackwell, 1986)

Moi, Toril, *What is a Woman? and Other Essays* (Oxford University Press, 1999)

Mongia, Padmini (ed.), *Contemporary Postcolonial Theory: A Reader* (London: Arnold, 1996)

Moran, D. P., *The Philosophy of Irish Ireland* (Dublin: James Duffy & Co. Ltd, 1905)

Morrison, Kristin, *Canters and Chronicles: The Use of Narrative in the Plays of Samuel Beckett and Harold Pinter* (Chicago University Press, 1983)

Morse, Donald E. and Bertha, Csilla (eds), *More Real than Reality: The Fantastic in Irish Literature and the Arts* (New York: Greenwood Press, 1991)

Moynihan, Maurice (ed.), *Speeches and Statements by Eamonn De Valera 1917–1973* (Dublin: Gill and Macmillan, 1980)

Murphy, Paul, *Hegemony and Fantasy in Irish Drama 1899–1949* (London: Palgrave Macmillan, 2008)

Murphy, Thomas, *Plays* (London: Methuen, 1989)

Murray, Christopher, *Twentieth Century Irish Drama: Mirror to a Nation* (Manchester University Press, 1997)

Ni Anluain, Cliodhna (ed.), *Reading the Future: Irish Writers in Conversation with Mike Murphy* (Dublin: Lilliput Press, 2000)

Nicholson, Linda J., *The Play of Reason: From the Modern to the Postmodern* (Buckingham: Open University Press, 1999)

Nicholson, Linda (ed.), *The Second Wave: A Reader in Feminist Theory* (New York: Routledge, 1997)

O'Brien Johnson, Toni and Cairns, David (eds), *Gender in Irish Writing* (Buckingham: Open University Press, 1991)

O'Casey, Sean, *Plays Two* (London: Faber, 1998)

O'Connell, James, *The Meaning of Irish Place Names* (Belfast: Blackstaff Press, 1979)

O'Neill, Eugene, *Plays* (New York: Random House, 1954)

O'Reilly, Anne F., *Sacred Play: Soul Journeys in Contemporary Irish Theatre* (Dublin: Carysfort Press, 2004)

Ó Ríordáin, Seán P., *Tara: The Monuments on the Hill* (Dundalk: Dundalgan Press, 1964)

Parker, Andrew (ed.), *Nationalisms & Sexualities* (London: Routledge, 1992)

Parker, Andrew, Russo, Mary, Sommer, Doris and Yaeger, Patricia (eds), *Nationalism and Sexualities* (New York: Routledge, 1992)

Payne, Michael, *Reading Theory: An Introduction to Lacan, Derrida and Kristeva* (Oxford: Blackwell, 1993)

Pearsall, Judy (ed.), *The New Oxford Dictionary of English* (Oxford University Press, 1998)

Philo, Chris and Wilbert, Chris (eds), *Animal Spaces, Beastly Places: New Geographies of Human–Animal Relations* (London: Routledge, 2000)

Pierce, David (ed.), *Irish Writing in the Twentieth Century* (Cork: Cork University Press, 2000)

Pilkington, Lionel, *Theatre and The State in Twentieth Century Ireland* (London: Routledge, 2001)

Pine, Richard, *Brian Friel and Ireland's Drama* (London: Routledge, 1990)

Plath, Sylvia, *Ariel* (London: Faber and Faber, 1976)

Policy Research Series, Paper no. 34, May 1999, *Tax and Welfare Changes, Poverty and Work, Incentives in Ireland 1987–1994* (Dublin: Economic and Social Research Institute, 1999)

Reinelt, Janelle G. and Roach, Joseph R. (eds), *Critical Theory and Performance* (Ann Arbor: University of Michigan Press, 1992)

Reineke, Martha J., *Sacrificed Lives: Kristeva on Women and Violence* (Bloomington: Indiana University Press, 1997)

Reynolds, James, *Ghosts in Irish Houses* (New York: Bonanza Books, 1947)

Richtarik, Marilynn J., *Acting between the Lines: The Field Day Theatre Company* (Oxford: Clarendon Press, 1994)

Richards, Shaun, ed., *The Cambridge Companion to Twentieth-Century Irish Drama* (Cambridge University Press, 2004)

Rutter, Michael, *Genes and Behavior: Nature Nurture Interplay Explained* (Oxford: Blackwell Publishing, 2006)

Said, Edward W., *Orientalism* (Harmondsworth: Penguin, 1985)

Salisbury, Joyce E., *Church Fathers, Independent Virgins* (London: Verso, 1991)

Saunders, Kate, *Catholics and Sex: From Purity to Perdition* (London: Heinemann, 1992)

Schechner, Richard, *Performance Theory* (London: Routledge, 1988)

Schechner, Richard, *The Future of Ritual: Writings on Culture and Performance* (London: Routledge, 1993)

Schechner, Richard, *Performance Studies: An Introduction* (London: Routledge, 2002)

Sekine, Masaru (ed.), *Irish Writers and the Theatre* (Gerrards Cross: Smythe, 1986)

Sellers, Susan (ed.), *The Hélène Cixous Reader* (London: Routledge, 1994)

Shakespeare, William, *The Complete Works* (London: Michael O'Mara Ltd, 1988)

Sidnell, Michael J. and Chapman, Wayne K. (eds), *Yeats, W. B.: The Countess Cathleen: Manuscript Materials* (Ithaca, NY: Cornell University Press, 1999)

Sihra, Melissa (ed.), *Women in Irish Drama: A Century of Authorship and Representation* (London: Palgrave Macmillan, 2007)

Silva, Elizabeth B. and Smart, Carol (eds), *The New Family?* (London: Sage, 1999)

Smart, Carol, *Family fragments?* (Cambridge: Polity Press, 1999)

Smart, Carol and Sevenhuijsen, Selma (eds), *Child Custody and the Politics of Gender* (London: Routledge, 1989)

Smyth, Carolyn, *Cultivating Suicide? Destruction of Self in Changing Ireland* (Dublin: Liffey Press, 2003)

Somerville, Jennifer, *Feminism and the Family: Politics and Society* (Basingstoke: Macmillan, 2000)

States, Bert O., *Great Reckonings in Little Rooms, On the Phenomenology of Theater* (Stanford: University of California, 1987)

States, Bert O., *The Shape of Paradox: An Essay on 'Waiting for Godot'* (Berkeley: University of California Press, 1978)

Stephenson, Heidi and Landridge, Natasha (eds), *Rage and Reason: Women Playwrights on Playwriting* (London: Methuen, 1997)

Storey, John (ed.), *What is Cultural Studies?: A Reader* (London: Arnold, 1996)

Sweeney, Bernadette, *Performing the Body in Irish Theatre* (Basingstoke, Palgrave Macmillan, 2008)

Synge, J.M., *The Shadow of the Glen and Riders to the Sea* (London: E. Mathews, 1905)

Teevan, Colin, *Iph* (London: Nick Hern Books, 1999)

Townshend, Charles, *Ireland: The 20th Century* (London: Arnold, 1999)

Turner, Victor, *The Forest of Symbols. Aspects of Ndemba Ritual* (Ithaca and London: Cornell University Press, 1967)

Uberoi, Patricia (ed.), *Family, Kinship and Marriage In India* (Oxford University Press, 1993)

Vice, Sue (ed.), *Psychoanalytic Criticism: A Reader* (Cambridge: Polity Press, 1996)

Wagner, Erica, *Ariel's Gift: A Commentary on 'Birthday letters' by Ted Hughes* (London: Faber, 2000)

Walby, Sylvia, *Theorizing Patriarchy* (Oxford: Basil Blackwell, 1990)

Warhol, Robyn R. and Price Hernell, Diane (eds), *Feminisms – An Anthology of Literary Theory and Criticism* (Basingstoke: Macmillan Press, 1997)

Watt, Stephen, Morgan, Eileen and Mustafa, Shakir (eds), *A Century of Irish Theatre* (Bloomington: Indiana University Press, 2000)

Weekes, Ann Owens, *Irish Women Writers: An Uncharted Tradition* (Lexington: University Press of Kentucky, 1990)

Weeks, Jeffrey, *Invented Moralities: Sexual Values in an Age of Uncertainty* (Cambridge: Blackwell Publishers, 1995)

Weitz, Eric (ed.), *The Power of Laughter: Comedy and Contemporary Irish Theatre* (Dublin; Carysfort Press, 2004)

Weitz, Eric, *The Cambridge Introduction to Comedy* (Cambridge University Press, 2009)

Whitford, Margaret, *Luce Irigaray: Philosophy in the Feminine* (London: Routledge, 1991)

Wiehe, Vernon R., *Understanding Family Violence: Treating and Preventing Partner, Child, Sibling and Elder Abuse* (London: Sage, 1998)

Williams, Raymond, *Marxism and Literature* (Oxford University Press, 1977)

Williams, Robert (ed.), *The Politics of Corruption 1: Explaining Corruption* (Cheltenham: Edward Elgar, 2000)

Yeats, W. B., *Plays, Selections The Hour Glass; Cathleen Ni Houlihan; The Pot of Broth* (Dublin: Maunsel, 1905)

Yeats, W. B., *Collected Plays* (London: Macmillan, 1982)

Zipes, Jack David, *Fairytales and the Art of Subversion: The Classical Genre For Children and the Process of Civilization* (London: Heinemann, 1983)

Journal Articles

Bullan – An Irish Studies Journal, Summer/Fall, 2001 VI 1
Irish University Review, Spring/Summer, 31.2.2001
Irish University Review, Spring/Summer, 28.1.1998
Irish Theatre International, 1.1.2008
Irish Theatre Magazine, 1.1. 1998
Modern Drama Vol. XLIII 2/2000
(Per)forming Ireland; Australasian Journal of Drama Studies, 43/2003
Princeton University Library Chronicle, 68:1–2:2006

Manuscript

Carr, Marina, *Ullaloo*, ms 36,099/3/8 (Dublin: National Library of Ireland)

Video/Dvd

Ullaloo, Dir. David Byrne, Perf., Peacock Theatre 1991 (Dublin: Abbey Archive, 23 August 2004)
Meat and Salt, Dir. Andrew Ainsworth, Perf., Peacock Theatre 2003 (Dublin: Abbey Archive, 27 August 2008)

Newspapers

Irish Press 11–17 February 1992
Irish Independent 11–17 February 1992
Irish Times 11–17 February 1992
Irish Times 2 November 1994

Readings and Public Lectures

Sihra, Melissa, '*"For She A Jolly Good Fella"*: *Transformative Moments of Being and Becoming in the Theatre of Marina Carr*,' Lecture, Synge Summer School, Co. Wicklow, Ireland, 1 July 2005

Programme Notes

Hederman, Mark Patrick, *Abbey Theatre Programme Note of Ariel* (Dublin: Abbey, 2002)

Internet

http//www.deir.ie/onrafteryshill

http//www.newadvent.org/cathen [Catholic Encyclopedia Dictionary]

http://www.independent.co.uk/arts-entertainment/theatre-dance/reviews/the-cordelia-dream

http//www.thisislondon.co.uk/theatre/show-23586428-details/The Cordelia+Dream/show/Review

http://www.irishtheatremagazine.ie/Reviews/reviewsMarble.htm

Index

Reimagining Ireland

Series Editor: Dr Eamon Maher, Institute of Technology, Tallaght

The concepts of Ireland and 'Irishness' are in constant flux in the wake of an ever-increasing reappraisal of the notion of cultural and national specificity in a world assailed from all angles by the forces of globalisation and uniformity. Reimagining Ireland interrogates Ireland's past and present and suggests possibilities for the future by looking at Ireland's literature, culture and history and subjecting them to the most up-to-date critical appraisals associated with sociology, literary theory, historiography, political science and theology.

Some of the pertinent issues include, but are not confined to, Irish writing in English and Irish, Nationalism, Unionism, the Northern 'Troubles', the Peace Process, economic development in Ireland, the impact and decline of the Celtic Tiger, Irish spirituality, the rise and fall of organised religion, the visual arts, popular cultures, sport, Irish music and dance, emigration and the Irish diaspora, immigration and multiculturalism, marginalisation, globalisation, modernity/post-modernity and postcolonialism. The series publishes monographs, comparative studies, interdisciplinary projects, conference procee-dings and edited books.

Proposals should be sent either to Dr Eamon Maher at eamon.maher@ittdublin.ie or to Joe Armstrong, Commissioning Editor for Ireland, Peter Lang Ltd, P.O. Box 38, Kells, County Meath, +353 (0) 46 924 9285, joearmstrong@eircom.net.

Vol. 14   Edwina Keown and Carol Taaffe (eds): Irish Modernism:
           Origins, Contexts, Publics
           ISBN 978-3-03911-894-6. 256 pages. 2010.

Vol. 15   John Walsh: The Irish Language and Ireland's Development
           ISBN 978-3-03911-914-1. Forthcoming.

Vol. 16   Michelle Woods: Ernest Gébler: The Unlikely Irishman
           ISBN 978-3-03911-926-4. Forthcoming.

Vol. 17   Susan Cahill and Eóin Flannery (eds): This Side of Brightness:
           Essays on the Fiction of Colum McCann
           ISBN 978-3-03911-935-6. Forthcoming.

Vol. 18   Brian Arkins: The Thought of W.B. Yeats
           ISBN 978-3-03911-939-4. Forthcoming.

Vol. 19   Forthcoming.

Vol. 20   Rhona Trench: Bloody Living: The Loss of Selfhood in the
           Plays of Marina Carr
           ISBN 978-3-03911-964-6. 327 pages. 2010.

Vol. 21–29 Forthcoming.

Vol. 30   Maureen O'Connor (ed.): Back to the Future of Irish Studies:
           Festschrift for Tadhg Foley
           ISBN 978-3-0343-0141-1. 359 pages. 2010.